# Children's Thinking

# Children's Thinking

*second edition*

## Robert S. Siegler

*Carnegie-Mellon University*

PRENTICE HALL, Englewood Cliffs, New Jersey 07632

**Library of Congress Cataloging-in-Publication Data**

Siegler, Robert S.
  Children's thinking / Robert S. Siegler.—2nd ed.
    p.  cm.
  Includes bibliographical references and index.
  ISBN 0-13-131210-3
  1. Cognition in children.  I. Title.
BF723.C5S54  1991
155.4'13—dc20                                    90-46234
                                                 CIP

Editorial/production supervision: Colby Stong
Interior design: Douglas Gordon
Cover design: Lundgren Graphics, Ltd.
Prepress buyer: Mary Ann Gloriande
Manufacturing buyer: Debra Kesar

Printed in the United States of America
10  9  8  7  6  5  4  3  2  1


ISBN   0-13-131210-3


Prentice-Hall International (UK) Limited, *London*
Prentice-Hall of Australia Pty. Limited, *Sydney*
Prentice-Hall Canada Inc., *Toronto*
Prentice-Hall Hispanoamericana, S.A., *Mexico*
Prentice-Hall of India Private Limited, *New Delhi*
Prentice-Hall of Japan, Inc., *Tokyo*
Simon & Schuster Asia Pte. Ltd., *Singapore*
Editora Prentice-Hall do Brasil, Ltda., *Rio de Janeiro*

*To Alice*

# Contents

# *Preface*

Children's thinking is inherently fascinating. All of us were children once; most of us either have or expect to have our own children some day. The ways in which children think are both familiar and foreign. We remember some of the ways in which we thought at younger ages and have impressions of the thinking of many other children as well. As adults, we observe that children's thinking seems generally reasonable, and at times surprisingly insightful. At other times, though, we see children reasoning in ways that are difficult to comprehend. Why, for example, would an otherwise reasonable 5-year-old insist that pouring water into a differently shaped container changes the amount of water, even after an adult has just told the child that the amount of water is the same as before?

Until recently, many of the most intriguing aspects of children's thinking were inaccessible to our understanding. For example, philosophers argued for hundreds of years whether infants see the world as a "blooming, buzzing confusion" or in much the same way that older children and adults do. Only in the past few years, with the development of revealing experimental methods, has the answer become clear. Even newborns see certain aspects of the world quite clearly, and by four months of age, infants' perception resembles that of adults. This and other discoveries about children's thinking are the subject matter of this book.

Who would be interested in such a book? Anyone who is curious about children should find interesting observations and ideas in it. Anyone sufficiently motivated to take an undergraduate or graduate course in this area should find a great deal to intrigue the imagination and stimulate further interest in children's thinking.

One reason why writing about this area is so enjoyable is that understanding of many fundamental issues is rapidly increasing. This rapid growth has necessitated extensive updating of the book from its earlier edition. The largest change involves adding a new chapter on problem solving. Advances in understanding of such fundamental processes as planning, analogy, tool use, and deductive reasoning make it essential to include such a chapter. Major additions also have been made to many other chapters. These additions include research on infants' attention and perception in the first days of life; on the contribution of brain maturation to memory and conceptual development; on how understanding of principles and naive theories guide young children's language and conceptual development; on the relation between language and thought; on the development of such fundamental concepts as time, space, and mind; on the role of the social environment in shaping cognitive development; and on the very nature of intelligence and the process of cognitive development.

While writing this book, I found that Carnegie Mellon University was a unique, exciting place to be. One reflection of the intellectual atmosphere is the amount of high-quality suggestions and comments I received while writing the book. Janet Davidson, David Klahr, Carl Granrud, and Brian MacWhinney all read and offered useful comments on one or more chapters of this edition. Of course, good colleagues are not limited to any one university. Rob Guttentag, Frank Keil, Stan Kuczaj, Bill Merriman, Kevin Miller, Wolfgang Schneider, Tom Shultz, and Harriet Waters also provided useful comments, as did several anonymous reviewers. I am confident that their suggestions moved the book in the right direction; only readers can judge just how far in the right direction it evolved.

I would like to single out my secretaries, Darlene Scalese and Barbara Dorney, for special thanks. They worked with me throughout the writing process and were models of calm, efficiency, and dedication at all times. A different kind of thanks is due to my children, Aaron, Beth, and Todd, for greatly enriching my understanding of children's thinking, as well as providing a number of colorful comments that I quoted at various places in the book. I also want to thank my wife, Alice, for keeping things going on the home front during the many times that I was preoccupied with the book. I hope that the text is worthy of all the confidence that she and the children have shown in me.

Robert S. Siegler

# Acknowledgments

I would like to thank a number of individuals and publishing companies for permission to reproduce material in this book.

**Figure 3–2**   Case, R. (1978). Intellectual development from birth to adulthood: A neo-Piagetian approach. In R. S. Siegler (Ed.) *Children's thinking: What develops?* Hillsdale, NJ: Erlbaum.

**Figures 3–3 and 3–4**   Siegler, R. S., & Jenkins, E. (1989). *How children discover new strategies.* Hillsdale, NJ: Erlbaum.

**Figure 4–6**   Ginsburg, A. (1983). *Contrast perception in the human infant.* Unpublished manuscript.

**Figure 4–7**   Dannemiller, J. L., & Stephens, B. R. (1988). A critical test of infant pattern preference models. *Child Development, 59,* 210–216.

**Figure 4–8**   Shimojo, S., Bauer, J., O'Connell, K. M., & Held, R. (1986). Pre-stereoptic binocular vision in infants. *Visual Research, 26,* 501–510.

**Figure 4–10**   Granrud, C. E., Haake, R. J., & Yonas, A. (1985). Infants' sensitivity to familiar size: The effect of memory on spatial perception. *Perception and Psychophysics, 37,* 459–466.

**Figure 5–1**   Newport, E. L. (1982). Task specificity in language learning? Evidence from speech. In E. Wanner & L. R. Gleitman (Eds.), *Language acquisition. The state of the art.* Cambridge, MA: Cambridge University Press.

**Figure 6–3**    Vurpillot, E. (1968). The development of scanning strategies and their relation to visual differentiation. *Journal of Experimental Child Psychology, 6,* 632–650.

**Figure 6–5**    Chi, M. T. H., & Koeske, R. D. (1983). Network representation of a child's dinosaur knowledge, *Developmental Psychology, 19,* 29–39.

**Figure 7–2**    Younger, B. A., & Cohen, L. B. (1983). Infant perception of correlations among attributes. *Child Development, 54,* 858–867.

**Figure 7–3**    Bomba, P. C., & Siqueland, E. R. (1983). The nature and structure of infant form strategies. *Journal of Experimental Child Psychology, 35,* 294–328.

**Figure 10–1**    MacWhinney, B., Leinbach, J., Taraban, R., & McDonald, J. (1989). Language learning: Cues or rules: *Journal of Memory and Language, 28,* 255–277.

**Figure 10–4**    Stigler, J. W. (1984). "Mental Abacus": The effect of abacus training on Chinese children's mental calculation. *Cognitive Psychology, 16,* 145–176.

# 1

# *An Introduction to Children's Thinking*

When did the sun begin? *When people began living.* Who made it? *God.* How did God do this? *He put a real lot of light bulbs in it.* Are these light bulbs still in the sun? *No.* What happened to them? *They burnt out. No, they stay good a long time.* So are the light bulbs still in it? *No. I think he made it out of gold. And he lit it with fire.* (Conversation with my son, 1985)

What do these answers, advanced by my younger son one week before his fifth birthday, tell us about the way in which he viewed the world? Can we attribute his explanations to a simple lack of knowledge about astronomy and physics? Or do they indicate a fundamental difference between young children's reasoning and that of older children and adults? An adult who did not know the origins of the sun would not ascribe its origins to God putting light bulbs in it. Nor would an adult link the origins of the sun to the fact that people began to be alive. Do these differences mean that children generally reason in more literal and self-centered ways than adults? Or do they just reflect a child grasping at straws when he did not even know the kind of explanation that would be acceptable?

For hundreds of years, people who have interacted with children have wondered about these and related questions. Where do children's ideas come from? Do infants see the world in the same way as adults? Why do

**TABLE 1–1   Chapter Outline**

I.   What Is Children's Thinking?
II.  Key Issues About Children's Thinking
     A.   What Capabilities Are Innate?
     B.   Does Development Progress Through Stages?
     C.   How Does Change Occur?
     D.   How Do Individuals Differ?
III. The Book's Organization
     A.   The Chapter-by-Chapter Organization
     B.   The Central Themes
IV.  Summary

societies throughout the world first send children to school between ages 5 and 7? A century ago, people could speculate about these issues, but now we have concepts and methods that magnify our ability to observe, describe, and explain the process of development. As a result, our understanding of children's thinking is growing rapidly.

The goal of this chapter is to introduce some central issues and ideas about children's thinking. The discussion initially focuses on what "children's thinking" involves. The next section places current ideas about children's thinking in historical perspective. Finally, the overall organization of the book is considered, both the content of each chapter and the central themes that recur in many chapters. The organization is outlined in Table 1–1.

## WHAT IS CHILDREN'S THINKING?

Defining children's thinking sounds like a trivial task. We all know what children are, we all know what thinking is, and combining the terms poses no special problems. Providing a concrete definition of children's thinking turns out to be far from a trivial task, however. No sharp boundary divides activities that involve thinking from those that do not. Similarly, no particular age marks the end of childhood.

Listing examples of thinking turns out to be easier and more fruitful than formally defining the term. The first activities that come to mind when we think about thinking refer to higher mental processes: problem solving, reasoning, creativity, conceptualizing, remembering, classifying, symbolizing, planning, reading, writing, and so on. Other examples of thinking involve more basic processes, processes at which even young children are skilled: using language and perceiving objects and events in the internal environment, to name two. Still other activities might or might not be viewed as types of thinking. These include being socially skillful, having a keen moral sense, feeling appropriate emotions, and so on. The qualities in this last group involve thought processes, but they also involve many other, nonintellectual features. In this book we give these boundary areas some attention, but the spotlight is on problem solving, memorizing, using language, understanding concepts, and the other more purely intellectual activities.

All types of thinking involve both products and processes. The products of thinking are the observable end states—what children know at different points in development. The processes of thinking are the initial and intermediate steps, often accomplished entirely inside people's heads, that produce the products. In studying children's understanding of causality, for example, we might ask them what causes rain. An older and a younger child both might answer that clouds do. However, the older child's answer might be based on observing that dark clouds usually appear in the sky before and during a storm, whereas the younger child might simply be parroting what his parents told him. The product of the two children's thinking—their statement that clouds cause rain—would be identical, but the processes that led to the answer would differ. Both processes and products must be part of any reasonable definition of thinking. However, this book emphasizes *processes*, because focusing on them usually yields deeper understandings of development.

Some of the most interesting parts of children's thinking are the parts where children differ most markedly from adults. DeVries (1969) provided a particularly compelling example of such a difference. She was interested in 3-to-6-year-olds' understanding of the difference between appearance and reality. The children were presented an unusually sweet-tempered cat named Maynard and were allowed to pet him. When the experimenter asked what Maynard was, all of them knew that he was a cat. Then the experimenter put a mask on Maynard's head, in plain sight of the children. The mask was that of a fierce-looking dog. The experimenter asked, "Look, it has a face like a dog. What is this animal now?"

DeVries found that many of the 3-year-olds thought that Maynard had become a dog. They refused to pet him and said that under his skin he had a dog's bones and a dog's stomach. In contrast, most 6-year-olds argued that a cat could not turn into a dog, and that the mask did not change the animal's identity.

The reasons such thinking is interesting are easy to see. How can a human being, even a very young one, think that a cat can turn into a dog? Overemphasizing such differences, however, can create an imbalanced view of *cognitive development* (another term for children's thinking). Even young children demonstrate surprisingly adultlike reasoning in many situations. Considering such developmental similarities, as well as developmental differences, is essential for a comprehensive understanding of children's thinking. Both are given substantial attention throughout the book.

Defining *children* should be and is considerably easier than defining *thinking*. The only issue is where to draw the boundary between childhood and other periods of life. We consider infants and adolescents, as well as preschoolers and elementary school students, as falling within the category of children. This allows a broader depiction of cognitive development than would otherwise be possible.

A final, crucial characteristic of children's thinking may not be apparent from the name: Children's thinking inherently involves change. How children think at particular points in development is interesting in and of itself, but the most interesting part of development is the changes that occur. Comparing infants with adolescents, it is easy to appreciate the huge magnitude of these changes. More subtle, but just as intriguing, is the question of how the changes occur. What processes could imaginably transform the mind of a newborn baby into the mind of an adolescent? This is the central mystery of cognitive development.

## KEY ISSUES ABOUT CHILDREN'S THINKING

What are the most important issues about children's thinking? Many different answers are possible, but there is widespread agreement that the following four issues are among the most important. What capabilities are innate? Does children's thinking progress through qualitatively different stages? What processes cause developmental changes? How do individual children differ? Each of these issues is introduced in the following sections.

### What Capabilities Are Innate?

When infants are born, how do they experience the world? What capabilities do they possess, and what capabilities remain to be developed through the interaction of experience and maturation? If we assume that infants come into the world poorly endowed, the question becomes how they are able to develop as rapidly as they do. But if we assume that infants come into the world richly endowed, the question becomes why development takes so long.

The nature of infants' initial capabilities has elicited many speculations. Three of the most prominent are the associationist perspective, the constructivist perspective, and the competent infant perspective.

The associationist perspective was developed by English philosophers of the 18th and 19th centuries, such as John Locke, David Hume, and John Stuart Mill. They suggested that infants come to the world with only minimal capabilities, primarily the ability to associate experiences with each other. Therefore, the infants must acquire virtually all capabilities and concepts through learning.

The constructivist perspective, associated with Piaget (e.g., 1954), suggests that infants are born possessing a small but important set of perceptual and motoric capabilities. Although few in number and limited in range, these capabilities provide a basis for interacting with the environment and constructing progressively more sophisticated skills and representations.

The competent infant perspective, based on more recent research, suggests that both of the other approaches seriously underestimated infants' capabilities. Within this view, even young infants have a much wider range of perceptual skills and conceptual understandings than had previously been suspected. These capacities allow infants to perceive the world quite clearly and to classify their experiences along many of the same dimensions that older children and adults use.

The impressive capabilities that recent investigations have uncovered can be illustrated in the context of distance perception. Philosophers have long speculated about how people are able to perceive an object's distance from themselves. Some, such as George Berkeley, an associationist philosopher of the 18th century, concluded that the only way in which infants could come to accurately perceive distance was through moving around the world and associating how objects looked with how much movement was required to reach them. Yet, Granrud (1989) demonstrated that the day after infants are born, they can already perceive which objects are closer and which are farther away. Clearly, distance perception does not require experience crawling or walking around the environment.

Other capabilities of infants are more conceptual. For example, even infants less than one week old possess a primitive concept of number. They treat groups of three dots as being similar, even when the groups differ in how the dots are arranged (Antell & Keating, 1983). When the infants are repeatedly shown groups of three dots, their interest in looking at the dots declines. However, they show renewed interest when the experimenter switches to showing two rather than three dots. The finding suggests that infants possess concepts of "twoness" and "threeness" and understand that sets of two and three differ from each other.

In addition to primitive versions of important concepts, infants also possess general learning mechanisms that help them acquire a wide range of new knowledge. One such learning mechanism is imitation. When 2-week-olds see an adult stick out his tongue, they subsequently do the same thing more often than they otherwise would (Meltzoff & Moore, 1977; 1983). This is especially evident if they watch the adult repeating the behavior for a minute or more (Anisfeld, 1990). Such repetitions provide a way for infants to learn new behaviors and also to strengthen their bond with those they imitate, particularly their parents.

Findings like these have given rise to a view of infants as being quite cognitively competent. But like the earlier views that they have largely supplanted, the new view raises as many questions as it answers. If infants possess basic understandings of concepts such as number, why do considerably older children experience such difficulty with the very same concepts? For example, why does spreading out a row of 7 checkers lead 3- and 4-year-olds to say that the row has more objects than it did when the checkers were closer together (Piaget, 1952)? Reconciling the strengths that are present in infancy and early childhood with the weaknesses that are also present is one of the greatest challenges in understanding children's thinking.

### Does Development Progress Through Stages?

When a girl misbehaves, her parents might console each other by saying, "It's just a stage she's going through." When a boy fails utterly to learn something, his parents might lament, "I guess he just hasn't reached the stage where he can understand this." It is interesting to think about how the stage idea came to be applied to child development, what exactly it means to say that a child is in a stage, and whether children in fact progress through qualitatively distinct stages of thinking.

Charles Darwin usually is not thought of as a developmental psychologist. In many ways he was one, though. In his book *The Descent of Man,* Darwin discussed the development of reason, curiosity, imitation, attention, imagination, language, and self-consciousness. He was most interested in these topics in a comparative context, that is, in the development of such qualities from other animals to man. However, many of his ideas could be and were translated into concepts about the development that occurs in an individual human lifetime.

Perhaps Darwin's most influential observation was his most basic one: that over vast time periods, life progresses through a series of qualitatively distinct forms. This observation suggested to some (among them G. Stanley Hall, widely viewed as the father of developmental psychology) that in any given lifetime, development would progress through distinct forms or stages. Hall and many other developmental theorists of his day further hypothesized that children would make the transition from one stage to the next quite suddenly. This stage approach directly contradicted speculations by associationist philosophers such as John Locke that children's thinking developed through the gradual influence of thousands of particular experiences. Associationists compared the developmental process to a building being constructed brick by brick. Stage theorists compared it to the metamorphosis from caterpillar to butterfly.

In the early part of the 20th century, James Mark Baldwin hypothesized a set of plausible stages of intellectual development. He suggested that children progressed from a sensorimotor stage, in which interactions with the physical environment were the dominant form of thought, to a quasilogical, a logical, and a hyperlogical stage. The idea that children progress through these stages receives a certain amount of support in everyday observations of children. Infants' interactions with the world do seem, at least at first, to emphasize perceptual impressions and motoric actions. At the other end of the developmental period, not until adolescence do people spend much time thinking about purely logical issues, such as whether the laws that apply to adolescents (laws about draft ages, driving ages, drinking ages, etc.) are logically consistent with each other. Baldwin's stage theory was ignored by most of his contemporaries, but exerted a strong influence on at least one later thinker: Jean Piaget.

Piaget, without question, added more than any other individual to our understanding of cognitive development. He made a huge number of fascinating observations about children's thinking. For example, the conversation with my son that I quoted at the beginning of this chapter was based on my wondering whether modern children still respond to questions about the origin of the sun like the children Piaget questioned in the 1920s. (They do.) Piaget also developed the stage notion to a much greater extent than Baldwin had and popularized the general idea of viewing human intellectual development in terms of stages.

Stages are a sufficiently complex idea that it is important to specify exactly what we mean when we say that children's thinking progresses through certain stages. Flavell (1971) noted four implications of the stage concept. First, stages imply qualitative changes. We do not say that a boy is in a new stage of understanding of arithmetic when he progresses from knowing 50 percent to knowing 100 percent of the multiplication facts. Instead, we reserve the term for situations where the child's thinking seems not only considerably better but different in kind. For example, when a girl makes up her first genuinely amusing joke, after several years of making up stories that are intended to be humorous but do not even make sense to adults, it seems like a qualitative change. Note the ambiguity of the term *seems like*, however. Perhaps the efforts had been improving slowly for a long time, but had not quite reached the threshold for what an adult recognizes as a joke.

A second implication of stages is that children make the transition from one stage to another on many concepts at the same time. When they are in Stage 1, they show Stage 1 reasoning on all of these concepts; when they are in Stage 2, they show Stage 2 reasoning on all of them. Flavell labeled this the *concurrence assumption,* because changes are believed to occur at the same time across a wide range of understandings, resulting in children thinking similarly across many different domains. When the parent in the above example said, "He's just not in a stage where he can understand this," the implication was that a general deficiency would keep the child from understanding other concepts of comparable complexity.

Viewing children's thinking as progressing through a series of stages also has two other implications. One is that changes occur abruptly. Children are in Stage 1 for a prolonged period of time, enter briefly into a transition period, and then are in Stage 2 for a prolonged period. The other is that children's thinking is structured into a coherent organization, rather than being composed of a large number of independent, unrelated ideas. Neither of these positions is controversial today, though for entirely different reasons. The view that important transitions in children's thinking are limited to certain transitional periods is no longer controversial because it almost certainly is wrong. Children's thinking is continually changing, and most changes seem to be gradual rather than sudden. The issue of whether children's thinking is structured is no longer controversial for the opposite reason; it is clear that children's thinking is coherently structured. The issues of whether children's thinking shows qualitative changes and whether their thinking shows similar patterns across many tasks remain controversial, however; these issues are discussed in greater depth in the next chapter.

### How Does Change Occur?

Above all, development involves change. Figure 1–1 illustrates some of the types of changes that occur. The illustration was developed by Aslin and Dumais (1980) to illustrate changes in perceptual development, but the classification applies to all changes in children's thinking. The left side of the figure illustrates three types of changes that can occur in the prenatal

**FIGURE 1–1**   Illustration of several paths of developmental change (after Aslin & Dumais, 1980).

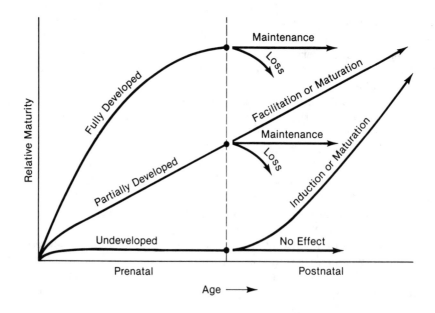

period (before birth): a particular capability can develop fully, partially, or not at all during this time. The right-hand side depicts changes occurring after birth. An already developed ability either can be maintained or can decline; an undeveloped ability can grow or stay undeveloped; and a partially developed ability can grow, stay the same, or decline.

The diversity of these patterns multiplies even further when we realize that any given ability involves many components that may follow quite different developmental courses. For example, as is discussed in Chapter 4, infants can produce sounds that are not part of their native language and that they later lose the capability of making. On the other hand, their facility in producing at will the sounds that are part of their native language increases tremendously after infancy. Thus, ability to produce sounds both declines and grows during childhood.

How can changes in children's thinking be explained? One type of explanation involves the concept of readiness. Just as people often say that a child is in a particular stage of development, they also say that the child is (or is not) ready to move ahead. In school, for example, 5- and 6-year-olds are often tested to see if they are ready to learn to read. The idea of readiness corresponds to a deep insight into the nature of cognitive development: that when and what children learn depends on the fit between their general level of thinking, what they already know about the particular topic, and the complexity of the material they encounter. Hunt (1961) labeled this whole issue "the problem of the match."

Piaget described a plausible and appealing means by which changes in children's thinking might occur. He suggested that the basic mechanisms were *assimilation* and *accommodation*. Assimilation is the idea that people represent their experience in terms of their existing understandings. A 1-year-old girl given a round candle by her mother might think of it as a ball if she knew about balls and not about candles. Accommodation is the opposite tendency. Just as previous understandings influence acquisition of new information, the new information alters the previous understandings. The 1-year-old who was given the candle might notice that this "ball" was different from others in having a thin object protruding from it and in having an indentation around the thin object. This discovery might lay the groundwork for eventually learning that this round object was a candle, not a ball.

A group of contemporary theorists known as information-processing theorists have been particularly interested in the process of change. They have focused on four change mechanisms that seem to play large roles in cognitive development: *automatization, encoding, generalization,* and *strategy construction.*

Automatization involves executing mental processes increasingly efficiently so that they require less and less attention. With age and experience, processing becomes increasingly automatic on a great many tasks. The more efficient processing allows children to see connections among ideas and events that they otherwise would miss. For example, in the first few months of walking home from school, a 5-year-old girl might need to attend carefully to go in the right direction and cross the street at the right time. Later, her going home would become automatized, and she could pay greater attention to what other people were saying and learn more from them.

Encoding involves identifying the most informative features of objects and events and using the features to form internal representations. The importance of improved encoding in children's increasingly good understanding of the world is evident in the context of their learning to solve story problems in arithmetic and algebra. Often such stories include irrelevant as well as relevant information. The trick to solving the problems is to encode the relevant information and to ignore the irrelevant parts.

The third and the fourth change mechanisms, generalization and strategy construction, can be illustrated through a single example. After repeated experience with nonfunctioning televisions, lamps, toasters, and radios, a child might reach the generalization that when machines do not work, it often is due to their not being plugged in. On drawing this generalization, the child might form a strategy of always first checking the plug whenever any machine did not work.

The child's construction of this strategy illustrates that change processes work together to produce cognitive growth, rather than working in isolation. Construction of the strategy depends on reaching the generalization that plugs are often involved in machines' not working, of encoding the plug as a distinct feature of the machine, and of automatizing processing sufficiently to note the relations among the seemingly different balky machines. As will be evident throughout the book, improvements in children's thinking in areas ranging from 2-year-olds' language learning to adolescents' computer programming depend heavily on these four change processes: automatization, improved encoding, generalization, and strategy formation.

### How Do Individuals Differ?

Just as children of different ages vary, so do children of any given age. Such individual differences have received especially intense examination in the study of intelligence. The attention began in earnest in the 1890s, when France initiated a program of universal public education. Recognizing that not all children would benefit from the same instruction, the French minister of education commissioned Alfred Binet and Theophile Simon to develop a test to identify children who would not benefit from standard classroom procedures and therefore who would need special education.

The first Binet–Simon test was released in 1905. It included questions that were intuitively related to many aspects of intelligence: language, memory, reasoning, and problem solving. In 1916, Lewis Terman, a professor at

Stanford, revised the test for use in the United States and relabeled it the Stanford–Binet. Updated versions of the test remain in wide use today.

The Stanford–Binet and other intelligence tests are based on the assumption that not all children of a given age think and reason at the same level. Some 7-year-olds reason as well as the average 9-year-old; others reason no better than the average 5-year-old. To capture these individual differences among children, Binet and Simon distinguished between a child's *chronological age (CA)* and the child's *mental age (MA)*. Chronological age reflects the time since the child was born; if a girl was born 60 months ago, her chronological age is 5 years. Mental age is a more complex idea, in that it reflects the child's performance on an intelligence test relative to that of other children. Specifically, a child's mental age is defined as the age at which 50 percent of all children answer correctly as many items on the test as the particular child did. For example, if the average 5-year-old correctly answers 20 questions on a test, then a child who answered 20 items correctly would be said to have a mental age of 5 years, regardless of whether the child is a 4-year-old, a 5-year-old, or a 6-year-old.

Terman combined the concepts of mental and chronological age to form the concept of the *intelligence quotient,* or *IQ.* He reasoned that the implications of a 4-year-old, a 5-year-old, and a 6-year-old all having a mental age of 5 are quite different. For a 4-year-old, this level of performance is somewhat precocious; for a 5-year-old, it is average; for a 6-year-old, it is below average.

To provide an index of performance relative to age norms, Terman defined IQ as a ratio between the child's mental and chronological ages. This ratio was multiplied by 100, so that the IQ could be expressed as an integer, as shown below.

$$IQ = \text{Mental Age} \div \text{Chronological Age} \times 100$$

Thus, a child whose mental age was 4 and whose chronological age was 5 would have an IQ of 80 (⅘ × 100). The average IQ score is 100, since the average mental age for any given age group is by definition that group's chronological age. Whether the IQ score is above or below 100 (whether the child's mental age exceeds his or her chronological age) indicates whether the child scored above or below average for the age group; the distance of the score from 100 indicates how far above or below average the score was.

One reason that IQ scores have been used so widely is that they predict performance in school quite well. Another reason is their stability over long periods of time. For example, a 6-year-old's IQ quite accurately predicts the child's IQ at age 16. The relation is not perfect; some children show large increases over time, and others show large decreases. There is also considerable controversy about what intelligence is and how well these or other tests can measure it. There is substantial agreement though, that on average, scores on the tests are quite stable from first grade through adolescence, and that they do correlate quite well with school achievement.

Until recently, no comparable predictive relation between early and later performance had been established for very young children. Scores on intelligence tests developed for 1- and 2-year-olds were essentially unrelated to IQ scores of the same children a few years later. This suggested that individual differences in infant intelligence might be unrelated to individual differences in later intelligence.

Recently, however, a measure of infants' information processing has been found that suggests considerable continuity between infants' and older children's intelligence. The measure is surprisingly simple. As noted above, when a picture is shown repeatedly, infants lose interest in it and look at it less and less. That is, they *habituate* to it. The rates at which different infants habituate vary considerably; some infants stop looking quite quickly, whereas others take much longer to do so. The key finding is that the more rapidly that infants in the first six months of life stop looking, and the more they resume looking when a different picture is shown, the higher their IQ scores tend to be four to six years later (Fagan & Singer, 1983; Rose & Wallace, 1985; Sigman, Cohen, Beckwith, & Parmalee, 1986).

Why should rate of habituation in the first six months predict IQ test scores years later? One explanation is that both the early and the later performance reflect the effectiveness of the child's encoding (Bornstein & Sigman, 1986). Within this view, more intelligent infants are quicker to encode everything of interest about the picture. This leads those infants to be the first to lose interest in it. They perk up more when the new picture is shown, because they more clearly encode the differences between it and the old one. Superior encoding has also been found to be related to the ability of gifted older children and adolescents to solve problems and learn quickly (Davidson, 1986). Thus, quality of encoding may link very early and later intelligence.

This example illustrates the way in which views of intelligence are influenced by whether we focus on processes or products. Initial approaches to intelligence, such as those of Binet and Terman, focused primarily on products of intelligence. The IQ score is the product of a large variety of cognitive and social processes that together contribute to performance on the test. The score says nothing about how the IQ score was obtained or what particular processes contributed to its being high or low. In contrast, Piagetian and information-processing theories focus more on specific processes, such as encoding, that contribute to problem solving, reasoning, learning, and performance on intelligence tests. This emphasis on processes allows a more precise understanding of what it means to be intelligent, and often suggests ways in which people can be helped to solve problems and learn more intelligently. In the next two chapters, we examine Piagetian and information-processing theories in greater detail.

## THE BOOK'S ORGANIZATION

The organization of this book can be viewed either on a chapter-by-chapter basis or in terms of the central themes that recur in many chapters. In the sections that follow, the book is described from each perspective.

### The Chapter-by-Chapter Organization

The book is divided into three sections. The first section, which includes Chapters 1–3, explores broad perspectives on children's thinking, such as Piaget's theory of development. The second section, which includes Chapters 4–9, focuses on more specific aspects of children's thinking, such as how they perceive the world, how they use language to communicate, and how they learn reading, writing, and arithmetic. The third section includes only a single chapter, Chapter 10. It is a summing up of what has gone before and a look forward toward the questions and issues that promise to be most important in the future.

The first chapter, which you are just finishing, is an attempt to define the field that is considered in this book and to introduce ideas that are important within it. Chapter 2 is devoted to a set of observations and ideas about children's thinking that can fairly be said to have created the modern field of cognitive development. These are the ideas and investigations of Jean Piaget. Piaget's observations, and his theoretical interpretations of what he saw, were what created initial interest in the field among whole generations of students and researchers. On topics ranging from how children infer the origins of the sun to how they order the weights of different objects, he saw much that other people had missed. In addition, Piaget observed children of an extremely wide age range, stretching from the first days of infancy into late adolescence. Thus, his observations provide a feel for many aspects of development in many parts of childhood.

Chapter 3 examines the other dominant theory of children's thinking, the information-processing approach. In some ways, this approach represents a modern extension of Piaget's theory; in other ways, it represents an alternative. The basic assumptions of the information-processing approach are that children's mental activities can be characterized in terms of processes that manipulate symbols; that the information-processing system imposes a variety of constraints on the processing that is possible at different ages; and that the interaction between the processing system and the environment leads to self-modification of the system and thus to cognitive growth (Klahr, 1989). The information-processing approach has proved especially useful for studying development, because it provides precise ideas about the mechanisms that produce cognitive change.

The second main section of the book examines six specific aspects of children's thinking: the development of perception, language, memory, conceptual understanding, problem solving, and academic skills. Chapter 4 explores perceptual development. The emphasis is on the surprising number of visual and auditory skills children possess from early in infancy. By age 6 months, their visual and auditory worlds seem to be largely similar to those of adults.

Chapter 5 examines language development. Here the discussion centers on what types of words children use first, when and how they learn grammar, how they acquire word meanings, and how they use their knowledge to communicate with others.

Chapter 6 is about the development of memory. Are developmental differences in memory due to differences in older and younger children's basic capacities, strategies, prior knowledge, or all of the above? The chapter also focuses on whether some of these sources of memory development are particularly influential in particular periods of development.

Chapter 7 concerns conceptual development. The early part of the chapter examines whether children represent concepts primarily in terms of dictionary-like definitions, in terms of loosely-related characteristic features, in terms of specific examples, or in terms of causally connected theories. The latter part examines the development of several specific concepts of especially great importance: time, space, number, and mind.

Chapter 8 focuses on problem solving. All of us need to solve problems daily, but the process plays an especially large role in the lives of young children. The reason is that many tasks that older individuals find routine pose novel challenges for younger ones. Among the problem solving processes examined in the chapter are planning, causal inference, analogy, tool use, and logical deduction.

Chapter 9 concerns the development of the three R's: reading, writing, and arithmetic. In the past, these areas often have been thought of as "educational" rather than "developmental." As we learn more about how children acquire cognitive skills, however, educational and developmental changes seem more closely related.

The third main section of the book is Chapter 10. It attempts the impossible tasks of summarizing what we know about children's thinking at present and predicting what we may find out in the not-too-distant future. Among the topics receiving greatest emphasis in this chapter is how social factors influence children's thinking: the influence of the culture into which the child is born, the influence of parents and teachers, and the role of available technologies from abacuses to computers. These are among the least well understood topics relevant to children's thinking; they also are among the most important.

### The Central Themes

This chapter-by-chapter organization provides one way of thinking about the material the book covers. Another way is to consider the themes that arise in many chapters. The following are eight of the most frequently recurring themes.

1. The most basic issues about children's thinking are "What develops?" and "How does development occur?"
2. Development is about change. Four change processes that seem to be particularly large contributors to cognitive development are automatization, encoding, generalization, and strategy construction.
3. Infants and very young children are far more cognitively competent than they appear. They possess a rich set of abilities that allow them to make rapid cognitive progress.
4. Differences between age groups tend to be ones of degree rather than kind. Not only are young children more cognitively competent than they appear, but older children and adults are less competent than we might think.
5. Changes in children's thinking do not occur in a vacuum. What children already know about material they encounter influences not only how much they learn but also what they learn.
6. The development of intelligence results in large part from increasingly effective deployment of limited processing resources.
7. Children's thinking develops within a social context. Parents, peers, teachers, and the overall society influence what children think about, as well as how and why they come to think in particular ways.
8. We have learned quite a bit about cognitive development, but there is far more remaining to learn.

A good strategy for reading the rest of this book is to think over these themes now, and try to notice how they apply to different aspects of children's thinking as you encounter them in later chapters.


## SUMMARY

For hundreds of years, people who have had contact with children have wondered about such questions as where the children's ideas came from and whether infants perceive the world in the same way as adults. Recent conceptual and methodological advances have greatly improved our ability to explore these and many other questions about children's thinking.

A number of the most important questions about children's thinking have long histories. What capacities are innate, and what capacities need to be developed? Do children proceed through qualitatively different stages of thinking, or is development continuous? How do changes in children's thinking occur? How do individuals differ in qualities such as intelligence, and how much continuity is there between early and later abilities? These continue to be among the most basic questions about cognitive development.

The book is organized into three sections. The first section discusses broad perspectives on children's thinking, such as those provided by Piaget's theory and by the information-processing approach. The second section examines six specific aspects of children's thinking: perception, language, memory, conceptual understanding, problem solving, and academic skills. The third section summarizes what is known about children's thinking and identifies questions and issues that seem critical for the future. The goal in all three sections is to identify general themes and ways of looking at development that apply across many areas of children's thinking, as well as describing particular aspects of how children think.

A number of themes also emerge as important throughout the book. Among these are the importance of the questions of what develops and how development occurs, the continuing challenge to children of coping with complex tasks while having only limited processing resources, the surprising cognitive competence of infants and young children, and the ways in which what children already know influences how they acquire new information.

## RECOMMENDED READINGS

Bornstein, M. H., & Sigman, M. D. (1986). **Continuity in mental development from infancy.** *Child Development, 57,* 251–274. This article provides a clear and comprehensive review of the exciting advances that are being made in establishing links between infancy and later intelligence.

Flavell, J. H. (1971). **Stage-related properties of cognitive development.** *Cognitive Psychology, 2,* 421–453. An excellent analysis of the nature of stage models of development and how they differ from other models.

Mehler, J., & Fox, R. (Eds.) (1985). *Neonate cognition: Beyond the blooming buzzing confusion.* Hillsdale, NJ.: Erlbaum. Presents many intriguing examples of capabilities possessed by infants in the first six months after birth.

Meltzoff, A. N., & Moore, M. K. (1983). **Newborn infants imitate adult facial features.** *Child Development, 54,* 702–709. An intriguing demonstration of newborns' ability to imitate.

# 2

## Piaget's Theory of Development

At age 7 months, 28 days, I offer him a little bell behind a cushion. So long as he sees the little bell, however small it may be, he tries to grasp it. But if the little bell disappears completely, he stops all searching.

I then resume the experiment, using my hand as a screen. Laurent's arm is outstretched and about to grasp the little bell at the moment I make it disappear behind my hand (which is open and at a distance of about 15 cm. from him). He immediately withdraws his arm, as though the little bell no longer existed. I then shake my hand. . . . Laurent watches attentively, greatly surprised to rediscover the sound of the little bell, but he does not try to grasp it. I turn my hand over and he sees the little bell; he then stretches out his hand toward it. I hide the little bell again by changing the position of my hand; Laurent withdraws his hand. (Piaget, 1954, p. 39)

What does this infant's odd behavior tell us? Piaget (1954) advanced one provocative interpretation: that Laurent did not search for the bell because he did not know that it still existed. In other words, his failure to search was due to his inability to mentally represent the bell's existence. It was as if the infant's thinking embodied the strongest possible version of the adage "Out of sight, out of mind."

This chapter is the only one in the book whose title includes a person's name. This is no accident. Jean Piaget's contribution to the study of cognitive development is a testimony to how much one person can do to shape an intellectual discipline. Before Piaget began his work, no recognizable field of cognitive development existed. Yet despite thousands of studies on children's thinking having been conducted in the interim, even Piaget's earliest research is still informative. What explains the longevity of Piaget's theory?

Perhaps the basic reason is that Piaget's theory communicates an almost tangible sense of what children's thinking is like. His descriptions feel right. Many of his individual observations are quite surprising, but the general trends that he detects appeal to our intuitions and to our memories of childhood.

A second important reason is that the theory addresses topics that have been of interest to parents, teachers, scientists, and philosophers for hundreds of years. At the most general level, the theory speaks to such questions as "What is intelligence?" and "Where does knowledge come from?" At a more specific level, the theory examines development of the concepts of time, space, number, and other ideas that are among the basic intellectual acquisitions of mankind. Placing the development of such fundamental concepts into a single coherent framework has made Piaget's theory one of the significant intellectual achievements of our century.

A third reason for the theory's longevity is its exceptional breadth. The theory covers an unusually broad age span—the entire range from infancy through adolescence. It is possible to see concepts such as cause and effect evolving from rudimentary forms in infancy to more complex forms in middle childhood to even more complex forms in adolescence. The theory also encompasses an unusually broad variety of children's achievements at any given age. For example, it brings together 5-year-olds' scientific and mathematical reasoning, their moral judgments, their drawings, their idea of cause and effect, their use of language, and their memory for past events. One of the purposes of scientific theories is to point out the meaning underlying seemingly unrelated facts. Piaget's theory is especially strong on this dimension.

A fourth reason for the theory's having endured is that Piaget had the equivalent of a gifted gardener's "green thumb" for making interesting observations. One of these observations was quoted at the outset of this chapter: the one concerning infants' failure to search for objects if they cannot see them. Many other intriguing observations are described throughout the chapter.

Because of the range and complexity of Piaget's theory, it seems worthwhile to approach it first in general terms and then in greater depth. The first section of this chapter provides an overview of Piaget's theory. The second describes children's thinking during each of his four stages of development. The third focuses on his description of the development of several especially important concepts from birth through adolescence. The fourth section is an evaluation of the theory. Table 2–1 depicts this organization.

**TABLE 2–1   Chapter Outline**

I.   An Overview of Piaget's Theory
  A.   The Theory as a Whole
  B.   The Stages of Development
  C.   Developmental Processes
  D.   Orienting Assumptions
II.  The Stage Model
  A.   The Sensorimotor Period (Birth to Roughly 2 Years)
  B.   The Preoperational Period (Roughly 2 Years to 6 or 7 Years)
  C.   The Concrete Operations Period (Roughly 6 or 7 Years to 11 or 12 Years)
  D.   The Formal Operations Period (Roughly 11 or 12 Years Onward)
III. The Development of Some Critical Concepts
  A.   Conservation
  B.   Classes and Relations
IV.  An Evaluation of Piaget's Theory
  A.   How Accurately Does the Theory Describe Particular Aspects of Children's Thinking
  B.   How Stagelike Is Children's Thinking?
  C.   How Well Do Piaget's General Characterizations Fit Children's Thinking?
  D.   The Current Status of Piaget's Theory
V.   Summary

## AN OVERVIEW OF PIAGET'S THEORY

Piaget's theory is sufficiently broad and complex that it is easy to lose the forest for the trees. This section provides an overview of the forest.

### The Theory as a Whole

To appreciate Piaget's theory, it is essential to understand the motivation behind it. This motivation grew out of Piaget's early interest in biology and philosophy. When he was 11 years old he published his first article, describing a rare albino sparrow he had observed. Between the ages of 15 and 18 he published several more articles, most of them about mollusks. The articles must have been impressive. When Piaget was 18, the head of a natural history museum, who had never met him but who had read his articles, wrote offering the position of curator of the mollusk collection at the museum. Piaget turned down the offer so that he could finish high school.

In addition to this early interest in biology, Piaget was keenly interested in philosophy. He was especially enthusiastic about *epistemology*, the branch of philosophy concerned with the origins of knowledge. Kant, an 18th-century philosopher who, like Piaget, was most interested in the origins of knowledge, received his closest attention.

The combination of philosophical and biological interests influenced Piaget's later theorizing in several ways. It led to the fundamental question underlying the theory: "Where does knowledge come from?" It also influenced the particular problems Piaget chose to study. He followed Kant in emphasizing space, time, classes, and relations as being central categories of knowledge. At the same time, he opposed Kant's position that these basic types of knowledge were innate to human beings; instead, he believed that children invented the concepts during their lifetimes. Perhaps most important, the joint interest in philosophy and biology suggested to Piaget that long-standing philosophical controversies could be resolved by the application of scientific methods. Just as Darwin attempted to answer the question "How did people evolve?" Piaget attempted to answer the question "How does knowledge evolve?"

With this background, we can consider the theory itself. At the most general level of analysis, Piaget was interested in intelligence. By this he meant a more general quality than what is measured on intelligence tests. He believed that intelligence influenced perception, language, morality—in fact, any act involving thinking. It produced both practical responses to particular situations and theoretical understandings of the nature of reality. It was basic to survival, as well as to the enjoyment of life. Piaget also believed that within a person's lifetime, intelligence evolves through a series of qualitatively distinct stages, with the evolution made possible by a set of developmental processes. In the sections that follow, these stages and developmental processes are discussed.

### The Stages of Development

Piaget's theory is a stage theory par excellence. As noted in Chapter 1, stage theorists make certain assumptions that distinguish their views from those of others. They assume that children's reasoning in earlier stages differs qualitatively from their reasoning in later ones. They also assume that at a given point in development, children reason similarly on many problems. Finally, they assume that after spending a prolonged period of time "in" a stage, children abruptly make the transition to the next stage. These assumptions have allowed stage theorists to paint a vivid picture of cognitive development.

Piaget's stage theory postulated that all children progress through four stages and that they do so in the same order: first the *sensorimotor period,* then the *preoperational period,* then the *concrete operational period,* and finally the *formal operational period.* The sensorimotor period typically spans the period from birth to roughly the second birthday, the preoperational period lasts roughly from age 2 to age 6 or 7, the concrete operational period extends from about age 6 or 7 to 11 or 12, and the formal operational period continues from approximately age 11 or 12 through adulthood and old age.

First consider the sensorimotor period, lasting from birth through age 2. At birth, a child's cognitive system is limited to motor reflexes. Within a few months, however, children build on these reflexes to develop more sophisticated procedures. They begin to systematically repeat initially inadvertent behaviors, generalize their activities to a wider range of situations, and coordinate them into increasingly lengthy chains of behavior. Children's physical interactions with objects provide the impetus for this development.

The preoperational period encompasses the age range from 2 to 6 or 7 years. The greatest achievement of this period is the acquisition of representational skills: language, mental imagery, and drawing. Perhaps the most dramatic growth takes place in the area of language. Vocabulary increases 100-fold between 18 and 60 months (McCarthy, 1954), and grammatical and sentence construction patterns become increasingly complex. In Piaget's view, however, preoperational children can use these representational skills only to view the world from their own perspective. They focus their attention too narrowly, often ignoring important information. They also cannot adequately represent transformations, instead being only able to represent static situations.

Concrete operational children (ages 6 or 7 to 11 or 12) can take other points of view, can simultaneously take into account more than one perspective, and can accurately represent transformations as well as static situations. This allows them to solve many problems involving concrete objects and physically possible situations. However, they do not consider all of the logically possible outcomes and do not understand highly abstract concepts.

Formal operations, attained at roughly age 11 or 12, is the crowning achievement of the stage progression. Children who achieve it are said to reason on the basis of theoretical possibilities as well as concrete realities.  This broad perspective brings with it the potential for solving many types of problems that children in earlier stages could not hope to conquer. Piaget likened formal operational reasoners to scientists who devise experiments on the basis of theoretical considerations and interpret them within a logical framework. Their particular beliefs and attitudes may need to be revised, but their basic mode of thinking is powerful enough to last a lifetime.

### Developmental Processes

How do children progress from one stage to another? Piaget viewed three processes as crucial: *assimilation, accommodation,* and *equilibration.*

*Assimilation.*   Assimilation refers to the way in which people transform incoming information so that it fits within their existing way of thinking. To illustrate, when my older son was 2, he encountered a man who was bald on the top of his head and had long frizzy hair growing out from each side. To my embarrassment, on seeing the man, he gleefully shouted, "Clown, clown." The man apparently possessed the features that my son believed separate clowns from other people. Therefore, the boy perceived him in that light.

An inability to assimilate new information to existing ways of thinking sometimes prevents people from forming any meaningful representation of the new material. The music critic Bernard Levin's description of his initial reaction to a Bartok piece provides one such case. Levin noted that when he heard the premiere performance of Bartok's *Concerto for Violin and Orchestra*, early in Bartok's career, neither he nor other critics could make sense of it or later remember it in any detail. When he next heard the piece, almost 20 years later, it seemed eminently musical. Levin's explanation was that in the ensuing period, "I had come to hear the world with different ears" (*London Daily Telegraph*, June 8, 1977). In Piaget's terms, he initially was unable to assimilate the Bartok piece. Twenty years later, he was able to do so.

One interesting type of assimilation that Piaget described is *functional assimilation*, the tendency to use any mental structure that is available. If children or adults have a capacity, they seek to use it, especially when they first acquire it. Illustratively, when my older son was first learning to talk, he spent endless hours talking in his crib, even though no one else was present. He also would turn somersaults over and over again, despite considerable encouragement from his parents to stop. Piaget contrasted this source of motivation with behaviorists' emphases on external reinforcers as motivators of behavior. In reinforcement, the reason for engaging in an activity is the external reward that is obtained. In functional assimilation, the reason for engaging in the activity is the sheer delight children obtain from mastering new skills.

*Accommodation.*   Accommodation refers to the ways in which people adapt their ways of thinking to new experiences. Returning to the clown anecdote, after biting my lip to suppress a smile, I told my son that the man we had seen was not a clown; that even though his hair was like a clown's, he wasn't wearing a funny costume and wasn't trying to make people laugh. I hope that the experience helped his concept of clowns to accommodate to the concept's generally accepted meaning.

Assimilation and accommodation mutually influence each other; assimilation is never present without accommodation and vice versa. On seeing a new object, an infant might try to grasp it as he has other objects (thus assimilating the new object to an existing approach). However, he also would have to adjust his grasp to conform to the shape of the object (thus accommodating his approach as well). The extreme case of assimilation is *fantasy play*, in which children gloss over the physical characteristics of objects and treat them as if they were what the children are momentarily interpreting them to be. The extreme case of accommodation is *imitation*, in which children minimize their interpretations and simply mimic what they see. Even at the extremes, elements of each process are present. A child at play still must recognize physical properties. (Chairs almost never are assimilated as teacups, even in fantasy play.) Conversely, when we do not understand what we are doing, imitation often is imperfect. (Try to repeat verbatim a 10-word Arabic sentence.)

*Equilibration.* Equilibration encompasses both assimilation and accommodation. It refers to the overall interaction between existing ways of thinking and new experience. It also is the keystone of developmental change within Piaget's system. Piaget saw development as the formation of ever more stable equilibria between the child's cognitive system and the external world. That is, the child's model of the world would increasingly resemble reality.

Piaget also suggested that equilibration takes place in three phases. First, children are satisfied with their mode of thought and therefore are in a state of equilibrium. Then they become aware of shortcomings in their existing thinking and are dissatisfied. This constitutes a state of disequilibrium. Finally, they adopt a more sophisticated mode of thought that eliminates the shortcomings of the old one. That is, they reach a more stable equilibrium.

To illustrate the equilibration process, suppose a girl thought that animals were the only living things. (In fact, Richards and Siegler [1984] found that most 4-to-7-year-olds do think this.) At some point she would hear plants referred to as being alive. This new information might create a state of disequilibrium, in which the girl was unsure what it meant to be alive. After all, plants share few obvious features with animals. Eventually she would discover commonalities between plants and animals that are critical to the meaning of being alive: the ability to grow and to reproduce, in particular. These discoveries would pave the way for a new understanding, in which the girl identified life with the ability to grow and to reproduce. The new understanding would constitute a more stable equilibrium, since further observations would not call it into question (unless the girl later became unusually interested in certain viruses and bacteria whose status as living things continues to be debated by biologists.)

This overview of assimilation, accommodation, and equilibration might create an impression that these change processes apply solely to specific, short-term cognitive changes. In fact, Piaget was especially interested in their capacity to produce far-reaching, longer-term changes, such as the change from one developmental stage to the next. Illustratively, the particular realizations that frizzy hair that looks like a clown's does not make its bearer a clown, that things that do not move can still be alive, and that the sun's looking like gold does not mean it is made of gold are part of a more general trend from preoperational to concrete operational reasoning. Children generalize the assimilations, accommodations, and equilibrations involved in these particular changes into a general shift from emphasizing external appearances to emphasizing deeper, enduring qualities.

### Orienting Assumptions

*The child as scientific problem solver.*    The basic metaphor underlying Piaget's work was a likening of children's thinking to that of scientists solving problems. This metaphor emerges most clearly in the account of formal operations reasoning, in which preadolescents and adolescents are asked to solve classic physics problems. Even in infancy, however, the comparison is clear. When infants systematically vary the height at which they drop food from their highchair to the floor to see what will happen, Piaget detects the beginnings of scientific experimentation.

At least three considerations led Piaget to concentrate on problem solving. One was his views concerning what development was. Piaget viewed development as a form of adaptation to reality. A problem can be viewed as a miniature reality. The way children solved problems thus could lead to insights about how they adapted to all kinds of challenges that life posed.

A second reason why Piaget emphasized problem solving relates to his views about how and why development occurs. Equilibration only happens when some problem arises that disturbs a child's existing equilibrium. Thus, problems, which by their very nature challenge existing understandings, have the potential for stimulating cognitive growth. If encountering problems stimulates cognitive growth, then an interest in cognitive growth would naturally lead to an interest in problem solving.

A third reason for Piaget's focus on problem solving concerns the insights that can be gained by observing children's reactions to unfamiliar situations. Piaget noted that everyday activities may be performed by rote and thus reveal little about children's reasoning. By contrast, to the extent that children are unfamiliar with problems, their solution strategies may reveal their own logic.

*The role of activity.*    Piaget emphasized cognitive activity as the means through which development occurs. Assimilation, accommodation, and equilibration all are active processes by which the mind transforms, and is transformed by, incoming information. As Gruber and Voneche (1977) noted, it was significant that Piaget titled one of his most famous books *The Construction of Reality in the Child.* Within Piaget's approach, reality is not waiting to be found; children must construct it from their own mental and physical actions.

This distinction between a found reality and a constructed reality is analogous to the distinction between a picture of a bridge and an engineer's model of the forces operating on the bridge. The picture would simply reflect the superficial appearance of the bridge. The engineer's model would emphasize the relations among components and how they combined to distribute stresses. Piaget believed that children's mental representations, like the engineer's model, emphasize active functions and mechanisms.

*Methodological assumptions.*    Early in his career, Piaget perceived the trade-off between the precision and replicability that accompany standardized experimental procedures and the rich descriptions and theoretical insights that can emerge from flexible interview procedures. He also recognized the trade-off between the developmental continuities that can be demonstrated by observing individual children over many years and the greater generality that may emerge from observing large groups of children at one point in time. Yet a third trade-off involved the unexpected information that can emerge from talking with children and having them explain their reasoning, and the possibility of underestimating young children's reasoning because of their inarticulateness.

Recognizing these trade-offs, Piaget used different methods to study different topics. His studies of infants, conducted early in his career, were based on intense and repeated observations of his own children, Jacqueline, Laurent, and Lucienne. His early studies of moral reasoning, causation, play, and dreams relied almost entirely on children's explanations of their reasoning. His later studies of numbers, time, velocity, separation of variables, and proportionality relied on a combination of children's interactions with physically present materials and their explanations of their reasoning.

Generally, when the choice was between richness and standardization, Piaget opted for richness. This choice may have led him astray at times. Some of his conclusions seem today to be due to his methods' underestimating children's knowledge. However, his choice of methods also resulted in many discoveries that no one else had made using more standardized procedures.

Possessing this overview of Piaget's theory, we now can examine the major trends that characterize his four hypothesized periods of development. The goal is to communicate the basic nature of children's thinking at different times in life. To present as clean a description as possible, I avoid phrases such as "Piaget said," "Piaget believed," and "Piaget argued." These qualifying phrases should be understood, since many of the claims are controversial. Before getting into the controversies, though, we need to know how Piaget saw children's thinking.

## THE STAGE MODEL

### The Sensorimotor Period (Birth to Roughly 2 Years)

Several years ago, at the first class meeting of a developmental psychology course I was teaching, I asked each student to name the five most important aspects of intelligence in infancy, early childhood, later childhood, and adolescence. A number of students commented that they found it odd to describe infants as having intelligence at all. By far the most frequently named characteristics of infants' intelligence were physical coordination, alertness, and ability to recognize people and objects. It was evidence of Piaget's genius that he perceived much more than this. He saw the beginnings of some of humankind's most sophisticated thought processes in infants' early flailings and graspings.

Piaget's account of the development of sensorimotor intelligence constitutes a theory within a theory. Infants are said to progress through six stages of intellectual development within a two-year period. This might seem like too large a number of stages for such a brief time span, but when we consider the immense cognitive differences between a newborn baby and a 2-year-old, the number does not seem unreasonable. With this introduction, we can consider the six stages of infant development.

*Stage 1: Modification of reflexes (birth to roughly 1 month).* Newborn infants enter the world possessing many reflexes. They suck when objects are placed in their mouths, close their fingers around objects that come into contact with their hands, focus on the edges of objects with their eyes, turn their heads toward noises, and so on. These seemingly primitive responses constitute the building blocks of intelligence within Piaget's system.

Even within the first month after birth, infants begin to modify the responses to make them more adaptive. In the first days, they suck quite similarly regardless of the type of object that is in their mouth. Later in the first month, however, they suck differently on a milk-bearing nipple than on a harder, drier finger, and differently on both of them than on the side of their hand. Thus, even in the first month out of the womb, infants begin to accommodate to new situations.

*Stage 2: Primary circular reactions (roughly 1 to 4 months).* By the second month, infants exhibit *primary circular reactions*. The term *circular* is used here in the sense of a repetitive cycle of events. The circles involve infants' actions, the effects those actions produce in the environment, and the impacts on the infants' subsequent actions of the effects of the earlier actions on the environment.

In primary circular reactions, if infants inadvertently produce some interesting effect, they attempt to duplicate it by repeating the action. If they are successful, the new instance of the interesting outcome triggers another similar cycle, which in turn can trigger another cycle, and so on.

These primary circular reactions are possible because infants have begun to coordinate actions that they originally performed only as separate reflexes. In Stage 1, infants grasp objects that come into contact with their palms. They also suck on objects that come into their mouths. During Stage 2, infants put these actions together. They bring to their mouths objects that their hands grasp, and grasp objects with their hands that they are sucking on. Thus, the reflexes have already begun to serve as building blocks for more complex activities.

Primary circular reactions are more versatile than the earlier reflexes and allow infants to learn a great deal about the world. However, they also are limited in at least three ways. First, the 1-to-4-month-olds only try to reproduce the exact behavior that produced the original interesting event. Second, their actions are poorly integrated and have a large trial-and-error component. Third, they only try to repeat actions where the outcome of the action involves their own bodies, as in sucking a finger.

*Stage 3: Secondary circular reactions (roughly 4 to 8 months).* In this stage, infants become increasingly interested in outcomes occurring beyond the limits of their own bodies. For example, they become interested in batting balls with their hands and watching them roll away. Piaget labeled the activities *secondary circular reactions.* Like all circular reactions, these activities are repeated over and over. Unlike the primary circular reactions, though, the interesting outcome (such as the ball rolling away) occurs beyond the child's body.

Between the ages of 4 and 8 months, infants also make considerable progress toward more efficiently organizing the components of their circular reactions. Piaget described instances in which, after he started a mobile swinging, his children kicked their legs to continue the movement. As in the primary circular reactions, infants seemed only to be trying to reinstate the original amusing occurrences. However, they now could do so more efficiently. They reacted more quickly to the original event and wasted less motion in trying to repeat it.

At this point it is tempting to conclude that infants understand the causal connection between their actions and the effects of their actions. Piaget was reluctant to credit them with this understanding, though. Rather, he thought that infants' activities were not sufficiently voluntary to say that they had independent goals. In the first month, infants' behavior simply involved reacting reflexively; between 1 and 8 months they would form goals directly suggested to them by immediate events in the environment; only after 8 months would they form true, mentally generated goals, independent of immediate events in the environment.

*Stage 4: Coordination of secondary reactions (roughly 8 to 12 months).*  Infants approaching 1 year of age become able to coordinate two or more secondary circular reactions into an efficient routine. Piaget (1952) observed his son Laurent combine the two activities of knocking a barrier out of his way and grasping an object. When Piaget put a pillow in front of a matchbox that Laurent liked, the boy pushed the pillow aside and grabbed the box. In earlier stages, placing the pillow in front of the matchbox might have led the boy to forget entirely about the box.

This example also illustrates another major development that occurs as children approach their first birthday. They clearly understand that if they produce certain causes, particular effects will follow. Thus, the child knows that pushing the pillow aside will provide a clear path to the matchbox.

*Stage 5: Tertiary circular reactions (roughly 12 to 18 months).*  With the onset of *tertiary circular reactions,* shortly before 1 year of age, infants transcend the remaining limits on their circular reactions. They actively search for new ways to interact with objects, and actively explore the potential uses to which objects can be put. As implied by the "circular reaction" label, they still repeat their actions again and again. Unlike previously, though, they now deliberately vary both their own actions in producing the event and the objects on which they act. Thus, the activities involve similar rather than identical behaviors. The following description of Piaget's son Laurent gives a flavor for the developments in this period.

> He grasps in succession a celluloid swan, a box, etc., stretches out his arm, and lets them fall. He distinctly varies the positions of the fall. Sometimes he stretches out his arm vertically, sometimes he holds it obliquely, in front of or behind his eyes, etc. When the object falls in a new position (for example on his pillow), he lets it fall two or three times more on the same place, as though to study the spatial relation; then he modifies the situation. (Piaget, 1951, p. 269)

These changes from primary to secondary to tertiary circular reactions show just how far infants come in the first year and a half. As shown in Figure 2–1, primary circular reactions, first seen between 1 and 4 months, involve repetitions of events whose outcomes center on the infants' own bodies, such as putting their fingers into their mouths. Secondary circular reactions, first seen between 4 and 8 months, again involve repetition of an event that by chance produced an interesting outcome, but the interesting outcome is at least slightly removed from the infants' bodies (e.g., the ball rolling away from them). Tertiary circular reactions, first seen between 12 and 18 months, involve deliberate variations on the behavior whose outcome was originally interesting, and thus reflect clear goals.

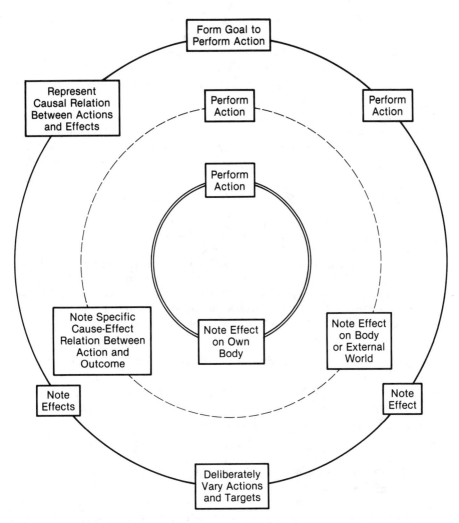

**FIGURE 2–1**   The child's expanding universe: primary (═══), secondary (– – – –), and tertiary (──────) circular reactions.

These developments are useful for thinking about a broad range of developments in infancy. At first, infants' activities center on their own bodies; later, they increasingly center on the external world. Goals begin at a concrete level (dropping an object) and become increasingly abstract (varying the heights from which objects are dropped). Correspondence between intentions and behaviors becomes increasingly precise, and exploration of the world becomes increasingly venturesome.

*Stage 6: Beginnings of representational thought (roughly 18 to 24 months).*
The developments in this age range could as easily be placed in the preoperational period as in the sensorimotor period. In the sensorimotor
period, children can only act; they cannot form internal mental representations of objects and events. In the preoperational period, children can
form such internal mental operations. The following description communicates almost literally the way in which representations are internalized
during the last half of the second year. Piaget has been playing with his
daughter Lucienne. The game involves hiding a watch chain inside an
otherwise empty matchbox. Previously, he had left the matchbox open far
enough that Lucienne could get the chain out, but now he has closed it far
enough that the chain stays inside even when the matchbox is turned over.

> She looks at the slit with great attention; then, several times in succession, she
> opens and shuts her mouth, at first slightly, then wider and wider! Appar-
> ently, Lucienne understands the existence of a cavity subjacent to the slit and
> wishes to enlarge the cavity. The attempt at representation which she thus
> furnishes is expressed plastically, that is to say, due to inability to think out the
> situation in words or clear visual images, she uses a simple motor indication as
> "signifier" or symbol. (Piaget, 1951, p. 338)

As Lucienne opens her mouth, symbolizing her desire for the opening
in the matchbox to become wider, we can almost see her representation of
the situation becoming internalized. That is, the representation is moving
from her external actions to her mind. Such internalized representations
are the hallmark of the preoperational period.

### The Preoperational Period (Roughly 2 Years to 6 or 7 Years)

Miller (1983) nicely captured children's position as they complete the
sensorimotor period and enter the preoperational period. She likened
them to mountain climbers who, after a hard climb, discover that what they
have climbed is merely a foothill to Mt. Everest. By the end of the sensorimotor stage, infants have become toddlers. They interact smoothly with
objects and people in their immediate environment. These achievements
may not be paralleled by the development of true internal representations,
however. Sensorimotor-period children may be able to throw a ball, catch a
ball, and even name it "ball," but they cannot think about the ball unless it is
present. The development of internal mental representations that allow
children to think about objects in their absence is the key development of
the preoperational period.

*Early symbolic representations.*   Piaget suggested that the earliest sign of internal representations is *deferred imitation*, the imitation of an activity hours or days after the activity occurred. It is an interesting phenomenon, because for children to imitate an activity long after it occurred, they must have formed a durable representation of the original activity. How else could they imitate it?

Children do not exhibit deferred imitation until late in the sensorimotor period. One of the best-known illustrations of the phenomenon involves a description of Piaget's daughter Jacqueline kicking and screaming in her playpen.

> At 1;4(3) [Piaget's notation for 1 year, 4 months, and 3 days] Jacqueline had a visit from a little boy of 1;6 whom she used to see from time to time, and who, in the course of the afternoon, got into a terrible temper. He screamed as he tried to get out of a playpen and pushed it backward, stamping his feet. Jacqueline stood watching him in amazement, never having witnessed such a scene before. The next day, she herself screamed in her playpen and tried to move it, stamping her foot lightly several times in succession. (Piaget, 1951, p. 63)

Jacqueline had never, to her father's knowledge, engaged in these behaviors before. Thus, an internal representation of the playmate's tantrum must have helped her reproduce the scene.

Piaget distinguished between two types of internal representations: *symbols* and *signs*. The distinction is not identical to the standard English distinction between the two. Rather, it is the difference between idiosyncratic representations intended only for one's personal use (symbols) and conventional representations intended for communication (signs).

Early in the preoperational period, children make extensive use of idiosyncratic (symbolic) representations. They may choose a particular piece of cloth to represent their pillow or a popsicle stick to represent a gun. Typically, these personal symbols physically resemble the object they represent. The cloth's texture is similar to that of the pillow, and both are comforting; the popsicle's shape and texture are something like those of a gun barrel. Signs, by contrast, often do not resemble the objects or events they signify. The word *cow* does not look like a cow, nor does the numeral 6 have any inherent similarity to six objects.

As children develop, they make less use of the idiosyncratic symbols and more of the conventional signs. This shift is an important achievement, as it greatly expands their ability to communicate. The transition from personal to publicly accepted representations is not an easy one, however.

The difficulty is illustrated in Piaget's description of *egocentric communication*. Piaget applied the term *egocentric* to preschool-age children not to castigate them for being inconsiderate, but rather in a more literal sense.

**FIGURE 2–2**   Two young children more or less having a conversation—an example of egocentric communication.

Their thinking about the external world is always in terms of their own perspective, their own position within it. Their use of language reflects this perspective, particularly their frequent use of idiosyncratic symbols that are meaningless to other people.

Although even very young children use signs as well as symbols, they at first do not use them consistently in a social manner. Figure 2–2 portrays an instance of this frequently observed aspect of young children's conversations. Preschoolers sometimes speak right past each other, without appearing to pay any attention to what others are saying. Even sympathetic adults often cannot figure out what the children mean.

Between the ages of 4 and 7, speech becomes less egocentric. One of the earliest signs of progress can be seen in children's verbal quarrels. The fact that a child's verbal statements elicit a playmate's disagreement indicates that the playmate is at least paying attention to a perspective other than his own.

Piaget suggested that mental imagery is like language in being a way of representing objects and events. He also suggested that the development of mental imagery resembles that of language. As children become able to describe situations verbally, they also become able to represent them as images. Further, he believed that the initial representations in both domains are limited to the child's own perspective. That is, they are egocentric.

Although language, mental imagery, and many other skills grow greatly during the preoperational period, Piaget's heaviest emphasis was on what preoperational children cannot do. He viewed them as unable to solve many problems that were critical indicators of logical reasoning. Even the name, "*pre*operational," suggests deficiencies rather than strengths.

One of the limits on preschoolers' thinking has already been mentioned: their egocentrism. This trait is evident in their conversations and also in their ability to take different spatial perspectives. Piaget sat 4-year-olds down at a square table in front of a model of three mountains of different sizes. The task was to choose which of several photographs corresponded to what children sitting at chairs at different points around the table would see. To solve the problem, children needed to recognize that their own perspective was not the only one possible and to mentally rotate the arrangement they saw to correspond to what the view would be elsewhere. This was impossible for most of the 4-year-olds; they could not identify what the view would be from the other positions.

A second, related limit on preschoolers' thinking is that it centers on individual, perceptually striking features of objects, to the exclusion of other, less striking features. One good example of this *centration* is found in Piaget's research on children's understanding of the concept of time.

Piaget's interest in this concept has an interesting history. In 1928, Albert Einstein posed a question to Piaget: In what order do children acquire the concepts of time and velocity? The question was prompted by an issue within physics. Within Newtonian theory, time is a basic quality and velocity is defined in terms of it (velocity = distance/time). Within relativity theory, in contrast, time and velocity are defined in terms of each other, with neither concept being more basic. Einstein wanted to know whether understanding of either or both concepts was present from birth; whether children understood one before the other, and if so, how initial understanding of one influenced subsequent understanding of the other.

Almost 20 years later, Piaget (1946a, 1946b) published a two-volume, 500-page reply to Einstein's query. Piaget concluded that children did not understand time, distance, or velocity in infancy or early childhood. Only in the concrete operations period would they finally grasp the three concepts.

To test this view, Piaget presented a task involving two toy trains running along parallel tracks in the same direction. After the cars stopped moving, Piaget asked the question, "Which train traveled for the longer time (or the faster speed, or the farther distance)?"

Most 4- and 5-year-olds focused entirely on a single dimension, usually the stopping point. They chose the train that stopped farther down the track as having traveled faster, for the longer time, and for the greater distance. Stated differently, they ignored when the trains started, when they stopped, and the total time for which they traveled.

The example illustrates another of the basic qualities of children's thinking in the preoperational period. They tend to focus on static states rather than transformations. The point where each train ended constitutes a static position, readily perceivable and available for repeated inspection.

The dimensions of time, speed, and distance are more fleeting and, in the case of time and distance at least, not as easy to perceive. The single dimensions on which preoperational-period children focus most often are static states; the dimensions they ignore often involve transformations.

Thus, 2-to-6-year-olds are viewed as having difficulty taking perspectives other than their own, as paying too much attention to individual, perceptually salient dimensions and ignoring other dimensions, and as focusing on static states rather than on transformations. All these descriptions suggest that such young children think about the world clearly, but too simply and rigidly. They largely surmount these limitations in the next period of development.

### The Concrete Operations Period (Roughly 6 or 7 Years to 11 or 12 Years)

The central development in the concrete operations period is the acquisition of *operations*. This is the achievement for which all development up to this time has been prelude. In the sensorimotor period, children learned to operate physically on the environment. In the preoperational period, they learned to internally represent static states. Finally, in the concrete operations period, they become able to manipulate mentally their internal representations, much as they earlier became able to manipulate physical objects. These operations, or internalized actions as they are sometimes called, make children's thinking much more powerful.

Two crucial features of operations are that they are reversible and that they are organized with other operations into larger systems. Saying that an operation is reversible means that its steps can be executed in reverse order and the original situation recreated. Saying that operations are organized into larger systems means that the child integrates a number of different ways of looking at a problem and realizes their mutual implications.

Understanding what operations are helps clarify the close relation between the pre*operational* and the concrete *operational* periods. Piaget sometimes indicated that these two periods are best viewed as two parts of a larger stage, spanning the ages from 2 to 11 years. The preoperational period laid the groundwork for operations by enabling children to represent events internally. In the concrete operations period, children become able to manipulate the internal representations and thus realize the potential for flexible and powerful thinking that they make possible.

The importance of operations can most easily be illustrated in the context of conservation problems. Consider children's understanding of three interesting types of conservation: conservation of number, liquid quantity, and solid quantity. Although these three conservation problems differ among themselves in certain respects, all share a basic three-phase procedure (Figure 2–3). In the first phase, children see two or more identi-

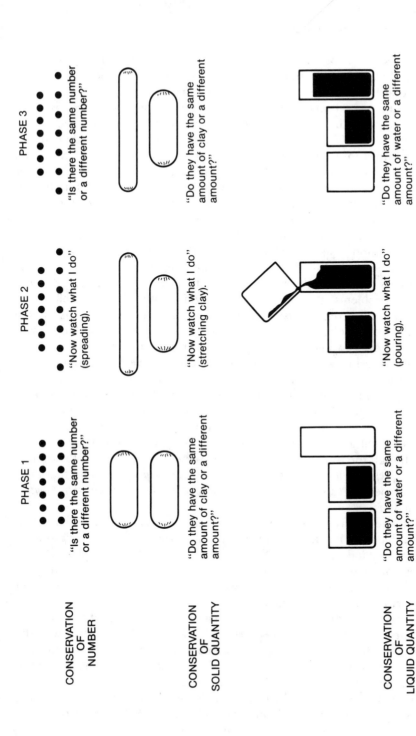

**FIGURE 2–3** Procedures used to test children's understanding of conservation of number, solid quantity, and liquid quantity.

cal objects or sets of objects—two identical rows of checkers, two identical glasses of water, two identical clay cylinders, and so on. Once the children agree that the two are equal on some dimension, such as the number of objects, the second phase begins. Here, one object or set of objects is transformed in a way that changes its appearance but does not affect the dimension of interest. Children might see the row of checkers lengthened, the water poured into a differently shaped glass, the clay cylinder remolded into a ball, and so on. Finally, in the third phase, children are asked whether the dimension of interest, which they earlier said was equal for the two choices, remains equal following the transformation of one of them. The correct answer invariably is "yes."

These problems seem trivially easy to adults and older children. However, almost all 5-year-olds answer them incorrectly. On number-conservation problems, they claim that the longer row has more checkers (regardless of the actual numbers in each row). On conservation-of-liquid-quantity problems, they claim that the glass with the taller column of liquid has more (regardless of the cross-sectional areas of the glasses). On conservation-of-solid-quantity problems, they believe that the longer sausage has more clay (again regardless of the cross-sectional areas).

Considering what children need to do to solve conservation problems makes understandable the 5-year-olds' difficulty. They must mentally represent the spreading, pouring, or remolding transformation involved in the problem. They also must not focus all their attention on the perceptually salient dimension of height or length; they need to consider cross-sectional area and density as well. Finally, they need to realize that even though the transformed object may seem to have more of the dimension in question, it might not. That is, they need to understand that their own perspective can be misleading. Each of these is difficult for 5-year-olds to do.

In the concrete operations stage, children master all three conservation problems. They also master the train problem that was used to measure understanding of time, distance, and velocity. Piaget explained their mastery of these and many other concepts in terms of the children's now possessing mental operations. These operations allowed them to represent transformations as well as static states.

Children's explanations of their reasoning on conservation problems are especially revealing. When 5-year-olds are asked to explain why the amount of water has changed, they regularly say that the water in the new glass is higher. When 8-year-olds are asked to explain why the amount of water remains the same, they point to the nature of the transformation ("You just poured it"), to changes in the less-striking dimension offsetting the changes in the more-striking one ("The water in this one is taller, but the water in that one is wider), to the water looking different but really being the same, and to the reversible nature of the operation ("You could pour it back and it would be the same"). Interestingly, 5-year-olds will grant many of these same points. Unlike older children, though, they do not see these facts as necessarily implying that the two glasses must have the same amount of water.

Although children in the concrete operations period become capable of solving many problems, certain types of abstract reasoning remain beyond them. Some of these problems involve reasoning in sophisticated ways about contrary-to-fact propositions ("If people could know the future, would they be happier than they are now?"). Others involve treating their own thinking as something to be thought about. To quote one adolescent, "I was thinking about my future, and then I began to wonder why I was thinking about my future, and then I began to think about why I was thinking about why I was thinking about my future" (Mussen, Conger, Kagan, & Geiwitz, 1979). Still others involve thinking about abstract scientific concepts such as force, inertia, torque, and acceleration. These types of ideas become possible in the formal operations period.

### The Formal Operations Period (Roughly 11 or 12 Years Onward)

Formal operations resemble concrete operations in two important senses: Both involve mental operations, and both are reversible. However, in formal operations, the particular reversible operations are organized into more elaborate systems, with the original reversible operations functioning as the basic unit within the more elaborate system. For this reason, formal operations often are described as being operations on operations. The story of the boy thinking about why he was thinking about why he was thinking about his thinking illustrates the aptness of this description.

Perhaps the most striking development during the formal operations period is that adolescents begin to see the particular reality in which they live as only one of several imaginable realities. This leads at least some of them to think about alternative organizations of the world and about deep questions concerning the nature of existence, truth, justice, and morality. As Inhelder and Piaget (1958) put it, "Each one has his own ideas (and usually he believes they are his own) which liberate him from childhood and allow him to place himself as the equal of adults" (pp. 340–341). From this perspective, it is no coincidence that many people first acquire a taste for science fiction during adolescence.

Where possible, formal operational reasoners consider all possibilities. This allows them to achieve a broad overview, to plan in considerable detail what they are going to do, and to interpret whatever they do within the total context. In contrast, concrete operational children tend to reason on a case-by-case basis and to plan less thoroughly. This sometimes leads them to misinterpret what they see and to leap to conclusions too quickly.

All these differences between formal and concrete operational reasoners are evident in Inhelder and Piaget's (1958) descriptions of children's and adolescents' approaches to a chemistry problem. The task was to generate all possible combinations of the contents of four chemical beakers and then to infer what caused the mixtures sometimes to turn yellow. Concrete operational children typically generated a number of the possible pairs of the chemicals, then tried all four together, and then generated a few of the possible sets of three. They often repeated combinations they already had tried and left out other combinations altogether. In contrast, formal operational children first devised a systematic plan for generating all possible combinations of the chemicals. Then they used their plan to generate the combinations without redundancies or omissions.

The formal operational reasoners' more planned approach also helped them draw a more appropriate conclusion about when and why the yellow color appeared. Concrete operations children often stopped trying combinations after they found a single combination that turned the solution yellow. They were content to say that that combination of chemicals was the cause. Formal operations children, who tried all 16 possible combinations, eventually learned that 2 different combinations produced the yellow color. What these combinations had in common was the presence of two of the chemicals and the absence of a third. Therefore, these adolescents reached the correct conclusion that two of the chemicals were necessary to produce the change in color, that a third would prevent it from happening even if the first two were present, and that the fourth had no effect. Their focusing on the system of possible combinations allowed them to obtain the relevant data. Their identification of the relation between the events that actually produced the outcome of interest and the total set of events and outcomes allowed them to solve the problem.


## THE DEVELOPMENT OF SOME CRITICAL CONCEPTS

The broad sweep of Piaget's descriptions of children's thinking emerges most clearly in his accounts of the development of particular concepts. Some concepts where his descriptions are especially interesting are conservation, classes, and relations. He traced the development of each of these from the earliest origins in the sensorimotor period, through more and more sophisticated refinements in the preoperational and concrete operational periods, to the highest level of mastery in the formal operations period. People do not usually think of infants' and young children's early understandings as having anything to do with their later thinking. Part of Piaget's genius was that he saw the connection.

## Conservation

*Conservation in the sensorimotor period.*      During the sensorimotor period, children acquire a simple but important part of the conservation concept. This might be labeled the conservation of existence, though Piaget chose to call it *object permanence.* For adults, it is the most trivial of matters that objects do not just disappear from the world (although they sometimes seem to). When objects move away from our gaze, we move our eyes to follow them. When they are hidden, we remove objects that might be shielding them and look from different angles. Piaget observed that infants do not show such searching. He did not attribute their failure to do so to poor coordination or to loss of interest, but rather to their not understanding that the objects still existed. This understanding needed to be constructed gradually over the six stages of the sensorimotor period.

In the first stage, from birth to 1 month, infants look at objects in their visual fields. However, if an object moves away, they do not follow it with their eyes. Thus, an infant will look at her mother's face if the face is directly above, but will stop looking if the mother moves aside. Next, between 1 and 4 months, infants prolong their looking at the place where an object disappeared, but do not actively attempt to find out where it went. If they are playing with a toy and drop it, they continue looking at their hand rather than at the floor. Between about 4 and 8 months, they anticipate where moving objects will go, and look for them there. However, if the object is completely covered, they do not attempt to retrieve it (as illustrated in the quotation at the beginning of this chapter).

In Stage 4 of the sensorimotor period, between 8 and 12 months, infants begin to search for objects that have disappeared. This indicates that they realize objects do have a permanent existence. Under certain circumstances, however, 8-to-12-month-olds make an interesting mistake, known as the *Stage 4 error.* If they see an object hidden twice in succession under the same container, they retrieve the object from there each time. If they then see the same object hidden under a different container, however, they look under the original container where they found it before. It is as if this original container had assumed an independent status as a hiding place.

In Stage 5, roughly between 12 and 18 months, infants stop making the Stage 4 error and search wherever they last saw the object hidden. However, they remain unable to deal efficiently with invisible displacements. When a toy is first hidden under a cover, and then the toy and cover together are hidden under a pillow, and then the cover is removed so that the toy remains under the pillow, the 12-to-18-month-old does not look under the pillow. By 18 to 24 months, however, babies understand even this type of complex displacement and immediately search in the right place.

I remember that when I first read about Piaget's research on object permanence, I found his account fantastic. I mean the term *fantastic* both in the sense of extremely interesting and in the sense of extremely improbable. It seemed to me much more likely that the infants below 8 months failed to search for objects either because they were not well enough coordinated to do so or because they had lost interest.

An experiment by Bower and Wishart (1972), however, rendered unlikely both of my initial suspicions. Five-month-olds saw a toy hidden under a transparent cup. The large majority of infants retrieved it. Then the infants saw the same toy hidden under a cup they could not see through. Only 2 of 16 retrieved it. This experiment, in addition to ruling out motoric immaturity as an explanation for the lack of searching, also ruled out lack of motivation. If infants lacked sufficient interest in the toy to retrieve it, why would they retrieve it when it was hidden under the transparent cup? Thus, at least the most obvious alternative explanations to Piaget's account of the development of the object-permanence concept can be ruled out.

*Conservation in the preoperational and concrete operational periods.*    In the sensorimotor period, babies come to realize that the existence of objects is conserved over certain types of transformations, specifically, ones where the object is hidden. In the preoperational and concrete operational periods, children come to realize that certain qualities of objects also are conserved under transformations that may change their appearance. We discussed several of these earlier. Spreading out objects increases the length of the row but leaves unchanged the number of objects. Pouring water from one glass to a taller, thinner glass changes the height of the liquid but leaves unchanged the amount of water. By the end of the concrete operational period, children realize that a great many tangible dimensions are conserved over transformations that alter their appearances: number, amount, length, weight, perimeter, area, and so on.

*Conservation in the formal operational period.*    During the formal operations period, adolescents become able to conserve dimensions that themselves involve transformations. (They understand transformations of transformations.) One such problem, presented by Inhelder and Piaget (1958), involves conservation of motion. A spring-powered plunger shoots balls of various sizes. Children need to predict where the balls will stop, to explain why some balls stop earlier than others, and to explain why balls stop at all.

Children's performance on this problem at different ages illustrates the types of reasoning that Piaget thought to be fundamental at those ages. Preoperational children often focus on only one dimension. They might consistently predict that a big ball will go farther because it is stronger. Concrete operational children begin to rethink the problem. Rather than just focusing on what factors inside the ball cause it to go farther, they begin to consider factors both inside and outside the ball that might cause it to stop. Thus, they consider two perspectives.

By the formal operations stage, children think of the problem in terms of conservation of motion. That is, they conceptualize the problem in idealized terms ("If there were no air resistance or friction . . ."). This way of thinking is a distinctive formal operations achievement, because it involves conservation of a dimension—motion—that itself involves a transformation. In addition, it illustrates how adolescents proceed from the actual to the possible, since no one has experienced an environment without air resistance or friction.

### Classes and Relations

Another of Piaget's insights was seeing the connection between children's understanding of classes and relations. This connection can be illustrated with regard to numbers. What does it mean when we say that a girl understands the concept "three"? She should be able to see what three balls, three cars, and three spoons have in common. That is, she should understand that they are all members of a certain class—the class of three-member sets. At the same time, she also should understand the relation of this class to other classes—larger than sets with two members and smaller than sets with four. As will be evident in the following account, Piaget viewed children as originally thinking of classes and relations as separate ideas, but eventually organizing them into a single, powerful system of operations.

*Understanding of classes and relations in the sensorimotor period.*    Piaget contended that infants classify objects according to the objects' functions. He illustrated this point by describing his daughter Lucienne's reaction to a plastic parrot that sat atop her bassinet. Lucienne liked to make the parrot move by kicking her feet while lying in the bassinet. At 6 months of age she made similar kicking motions when she saw the parrot some distance away. By 7 months she abbreviated her motion, moving her feet in short distinct arcs when she was out of the bassinet. Piaget interpreted this as Lucienne thinking, "That's the parrot. It swings when I kick my feet." Far more sophisticated categories are seen as evolving from this initial functional classification.

Understanding of relations, like understanding of classes, is seen as developing out of sensorimotor actions. Piaget described his children at 3 and 4 months as being greatly amused by the relation between their actions and the consequences of those actions. The more vigorously they acted, the greater reaction they produced. More vigorous kicking produced more vigorous swinging of objects on the bassinet, more vigorous shaking of a rattle produced louder noises, and so on.

*Understanding of classes and relations in the preoperational period.*    Children progress considerably in classificatory ability during the preoperational period. This progress is evident when children are asked to put together the objects that go together from among a group of blocks including large blue squares and triangles, small blue squares and triangles, large red squares and triangles, and small red squares and triangles. Thus, children could arrange the objects on the basis of size, color, or shape.

Early in the preoperational period, children might put together a small red square and a small blue square and then add a small red triangle, a large blue triangle, and a large red triangle. Apparently, they start out thinking about one quality (small size, in our example), but midway through the task lose their focus and shift to a different dimension (triangular shape, in the example). Later in the preoperational period, children classify on a consistent basis, so that all objects in a group are there for the same reason.

Although children learn to solve this type of problem during the preoperational period, other classification problems remain difficult. The limitations of their reasoning are most evident when they simultaneously need to consider competing bases of classification, as in the *class inclusion* problem. On such problems, children might be presented eight toy animals, six of them cats and two dogs. They then would be asked, "Are there more cats or more animals?" Most children below age 7 or 8 answer that there are more cats, despite the number of cats inherently being less than or equal to the number of animals.

Piaget saw this behavior as stemming from preoperational children's tendency to focus on a single dimension to the exclusion of others. To solve the problem, children need to keep in mind that an object (Garfield) may simultaneously belong both to a subset (cats) and to a superset (animals). They find this difficult. Therefore, to simplify, they reinterpret the question in a way that allows them to compare the number of cats to the number of dogs and conclude that there are more cats.

Children's understanding of relations also grows considerably during the preoperational stage. However, their ability to ignore irrelevant relations and to concentrate on relevant ones remains limited. To illustrate both the growth and the remaining deficiencies, Piaget (1952) presented preoperational children the type of *seriation problem* shown in Figure 2–4. He asked them to arrange the sticks from shortest to longest in a single row. If they succeeded at this task, he presented them with a second problem. Here they needed to insert a new stick of medium length at the appropriate point in the row they had made.

Early in the preoperational stage, between ages 2 and 4, children

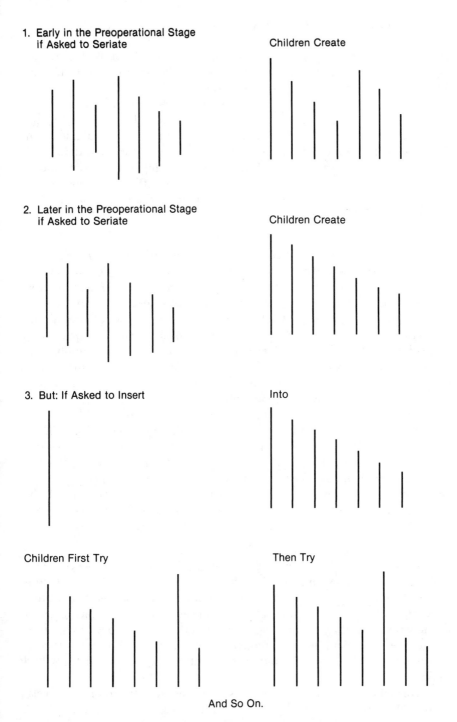

**FIGURE 2–4** Typical responses to seriation problems of children early and late in the preoperational stage.

encounter great difficulty creating correct orderings. As in the first row of Figure 2–4, they might arrange two subsets of the sticks correctly, but not integrate the two into a single overall ordering.

Later in the preoperational stage, children can correctly order the lengths of the original set of sticks. However, they often fail to find the correct place to insert the additional stick without extensive trial and error. Again, Piaget attributed such remaining difficulties to preoperational children's tendency to pay too much attention to a single dimension and to ignore other dimensions. In particular, they find it difficult to view the new stick as being both smaller than the one just larger than it and larger than the one just smaller than it.

*Understanding of classes and relations in the concrete operations period.*    Piaget contended that in the concrete operations period, children come to treat classes and relations as part of a single, unified system. Their attempts to solve *multiple classification problems* illustrate this development. Consider the problem in Figure 2–5. Children see intersecting rows of stimuli that vary along two dimensions, in this case shape (square, circular, or oblong) and color (black, white, or striped). They are asked to choose an object to put in the blank space so that all nine objects are ordered along the two dimensions. This requires that they attend to two different dimensions (shape and color) in classifying each object.

Inhelder and Piaget (1964) reported that 4-to-6-year-olds selected objects that included at least one of the desired dimensions on 85 percent of problems. However, they chose the single object that included both desired dimensions on only 15 percent. In other words, given the Figure 2–5 problem, they would choose a nonstriped oblong or a striped square or circle far more often than the correct answer. By 9 or 10 years of age, the large majority of children correctly chose the striped oblong object, revealing an ability to consider classes and relations together.

*Understanding of classes and relations in the formal operational period.*    Formal operational reasoning enables adolescents to think about relations among relations and about classes of classes. For example, they might first generate a class of the most successful political leaders from each country in the world and then form a higher-order class of the types of countries where the successful leaders tended to be moral visionaries, efficient economic administrators, sly and ruthless infighters, wheeler-dealers, and so on.

Formal operational reasoning also leads adolescents to view the relations and classes that actually are relevant in a given situation as only a subset of the ones that could possibly be relevant. This type of reasoning was illustrated in the description of the chemical combinations problem

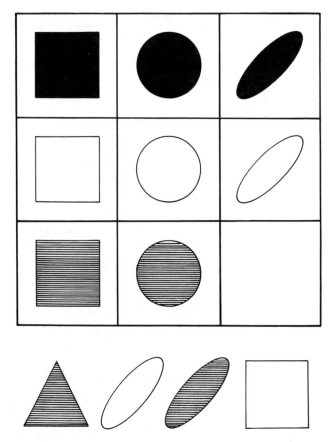

**FIGURE 2–5** Type of matrix used to test children's understanding of multiple classification. The task was to decide which of the four objects at the bottom belonged in the empty square in the matrix (after Inhelder & Piaget, 1964).

earlier in the chapter. Formal operational adolescents not only planned a way to generate all possible combinations of the chemicals, but also interpreted the two combinations that produced the yellow color in the context of all possible combinations. In particular, only by comparing the 2 combinations that did produce the yellow color to the 14 that did not could they realize that one of the chemicals actively prevented the color from changing.

*A chronological summary.* It is easy to become confused among the numerous developmental changes Piaget described. Table 2–2 places some of the most important changes in relation to each other and may create a better feel for which types of changes occur when in development.

**TABLE 2–2   Children's Thinking at Different Ages: The Piagetian Model**

| STAGE OF DEVELOPMENT | RELEVANT AGE RANGE | TYPICAL ACHIEVEMENTS AND LIMITATIONS |
|---|---|---|
| *Sensorimotor Period* (Birth to 2 years) | Birth to 1 month | Modification of reflexes to make them more adaptive. |
| | 1 to 4 months | Primary circular reactions and coordination of actions. |
| | 4 to 8 months | Secondary circular reactions. No searching for hidden objects. |
| | 8 to 12 months | Coordination of secondary circular reactions. Baby retrieves hidden objects but continues searching where objects were previously found rather than where they were last hidden. |
| | 12 to 18 months | Tertiary circular reactions. Baby systematically varies heights from which it drops things. |
| | 18 to 24 months | Beginning of true mental representations. Deferred imitation. |
| *Preoperational Period* (2 to 7 years) | 2 to 4 years | Development of symbolic capacities. Growth of language and mental imagery. Egocentric communication. |
| | 4 to 7 years | Good language and mental imagery skills. Inability to represent transformations. Child focuses on single perceptual dimensions in conservation, class inclusion, time, seriation, and other problems. |
| *Concrete Operational Period* (7 to 12 years) | Whole period | Child can perform true mental operations, represent transformations as well as static states, and solve conservation, class inclusion, time, and many other problems. Child still has difficulty thinking of all possible combinations, as in the chemical problem, and of transformations of transformations. |
| *Formal Operational Period* (12 years through the rest of life) | Whole period | Adolescent can think about all possible outcomes, interpret particular events in terms of their relation to hypothetical events, and understand abstract concepts such as conservation of motion and chemical interactions. |

## AN EVALUATION OF PIAGET'S THEORY

How can we evaluate this rich and diverse theory of cognitive development? Some of the strengths of the theory were mentioned at the outset of the chapter. It provides us with a good feel for what children's thinking is like at different points in development. It addresses issues that parents, teachers, philosophers, and scientists have been interested in for hundreds of years. It covers a remarkably broad spectrum of developments in children's thinking. It covers the entire age span from infancy through adolescence. It includes uncountable interesting observations and discoveries.

With these clear virtues in mind, we can consider three crucial questions. How accurately does the theory describe the specifics of children's reasoning at different ages? How useful are its stages as descriptions and explanations of children's thinking? How valid are its general trait characterizations of children's thinking, such as that preoperational children are egocentric?

### How Accurately Does the Theory Describe Particular Aspects of Children's Thinking?

Piaget's theory makes many specific claims about how children think and reason at different ages. How have these claims held up in the face of contemporary research?

The first issue to consider is whether other people can replicate Piaget's findings when they use similar methods. Piaget's claims about children's thinking were so surprising that many early experiments were conducted simply to replicate them. These replication experiments used larger, more representative samples of children and more standardized versions of Piaget's clinical method, but otherwise closely resembled his approach.

In general, the attempts to replicate were successful. Larger samples of American, British, Canadian, Australian aboriginal, and Chinese children tested in the 1960s and 1970s showed the same type of reasoning that Piaget's small samples of Swiss children had almost half a century earlier (Corman & Escalona, 1969; Dasen, 1973; Dodwell, 1960; Elkind, 1961a, 1961b; Goodnow, 1962; Lovell, 1961; Uzgiris, 1964). Children in less-advanced societies reached the stages of reasoning later, but they eventually did show the expected type of reasoning. This was especially true for the sensorimotor, preoperational, and concrete operational periods. Formal operational reasoning seems to be exhibited by some adolescents, but only by a minority of them, even in advanced societies, at least on the scientific-reasoning problem typically used to assess formal operations (Byrnes, 1988).

Can we accept these replications at face value? Perhaps the immature reasoning that children display in many situations is due not to their reasoning actually being immature, but rather to the verbal methods used by both

Piaget and the replication studies underestimating their knowledge. Critics of such methods argue that young children's inarticulateness often creates a falsely pessimistic impression of their cognitive capabilities (e.g., Brainerd, 1978). Just because children cannot explain their reasoning very well does not mean that the reasoning itself is deficient.

It now is apparent, however, that use of verbal methods per se is not the cause of the young children's immature reasoning. When tested with nonverbal versions of Piaget's methods, they typically exhibit similar reasoning to that described by Piaget. I have been involved in one such series of experiments in which I employed a nonverbal method to examine a number of Piaget's tasks: among them the balance scale; conservation of liquid quantity; conservation of solid quantity; conservation of number; speed; time; and distance problems (Siegler, 1976, 1978, 1981; Siegler & Richards, 1979; Siegler & Vago, 1978). On each of these tasks, children reasoned much as would have been expected from Piaget's descriptions.

A third question is whether children possess conceptual understanding not revealed by Piaget's experiments. Here the situation is quite different. Throughout development, children seem to have basic understandings not evident in their performance on Piaget's problems. Many of the demonstrations of children's early understandings have been extremely clever.

Consider Baillargeon's (1987) experiment on object permanence. Piaget claimed that infants younger than 9 months do not realize that objects continue to exist when they are hidden from view. Baillargeon developed a more sensitive measure that showed that even with infants as young as 4 months, out of sight does not mean totally out of mind. Her experiment involved placing a box behind a wooden board. An axle went horizontally through the middle of the board so that the board could swing if pushed. At first, the board was in a position where the box was clearly visible. Then, the experimenter set the board swinging, which hid the box from the child's line of sight. In the physically possible condition, the swinging board reached the box, which was near the apex of its swing anyway, and then swung the other way. In the physically impossible condition, however, the board appeared to swing right through the place where the box had been. (This effect was accomplished with trick lighting and mirrors.) Despite the box's not being visible anymore, the 4-month-olds appeared surprised when they saw the seemingly impossible event. They looked much longer than they did when the physically possible event occurred. They apparently thought the box should continue to exist, and to impede the board's swinging, even when they could not see it. Thus, children as young as 4 months possess some understanding of object permanence.

The demonstrations of earlier-than-predicted cognitive competence are not limited to infants. Consider Levin's (1977) experiment on 5-year-olds' understanding of the concept of time. When children were presented with two cars running along parallel tracks, they behaved much like the children described by Piaget; they chose whichever train stopped farther down the track as having traveled for the greater time. However, when they observed two cars traveling in circular paths, the children judged which traveled for more time very accurately. Thus, when the perceptually appealing stopping points were no longer such a large distraction, 5-year-olds displayed understanding that was not apparent in the situation previously used to measure their grasp of the concept of time.

Discoveries of unsuspected cognitive strengths in infants and young children have been one of *the* leading stories in the recent study of cognitive development. It is interesting to consider why these competencies are being discovered now. One reason is the development of new methods for finding out what children understand. These new methods will emerge as particularly important in Chapter 4, where we consider infants' perceptual capabilities.

Another reason for the discoveries is that a broader range of children's thinking is being considered. The research of Gelman and her colleagues illustrates this trend (Gelman, 1972, 1978; Gelman & Gallistel, 1978; Miller & Gelman, 1983). Piaget focused on preschoolers' frequent failures on number conservation tasks and concluded that they do not grasp the concept of number. Gelman's research indicated that whether or not preschoolers grasp the concept of number, they know a great deal about numbers. They count accurately, and in a way that suggests understanding of the principles underlying counting; they know the effects that addition and subtraction have on small collections of objects; they know which numbers are bigger and which smaller; and so on. The number of insightful demonstrations of early competence is too large to review in any detail here. Examples include work on children's understanding of causality (Bullock, Gelman, & Baillargeon, 1982; Shultz, 1982), class inclusion (Markman & Seibert, 1976; Smith, 1979), conservation (McGarrigle & Donaldson, 1974; Markman, 1979), time (Levin, 1977, 1979; Wilkening, 1981), and object permanence (Baillargeon, 1984; Kelman & Spelke, 1983). In short, although Piaget's observations about children's thinking reveal a great deal about how they think, and although they can be replicated using both verbal and nonverbal methods, they tend to underestimate children's understanding.

### How Stagelike Is Children's Thinking?

What does it mean to say that children's thinking progresses through a series of stages? Among the implications are that children's thinking changes qualitatively from one stage to another; that within any one stage, their reasoning is similar across diverse problems; and that they are unable to learn to think in ways associated with the next higher stage until they are near that stage or in it (Brainerd, 1978; Flavell, 1971).

*Qualitative changes.*    Stage theories such as Piaget's imply that development is discontinuous and that transitions from one type of reasoning to another are qualitatively distinct. As noted in Chapter 1, the analogy is to development from caterpillar to butterfly rather than to the brick-by-brick construction of a house. How well does this analogy fit children's thinking?

In large part, the answer depends on what is meant by continuous and discontinuous development. When viewed from afar, many changes in children's thinking appear discontinuous; when viewed from closeup, the same changes often appear as part of a continuous, gradual progression. Consider the way in which infants and young children search for hidden objects. As noted in the discussion of the object concept, Piaget and a number of other researchers have found that infants younger than 7 or 8 months often do not search at all for objects hidden from their view. Older children almost always search for objects they see hidden. These results were interpreted as meaning that the younger and older infants' understanding of object permanence differed qualitatively.

Harris (1983) suggested an alternative interpretation, however, that was more consistent with an assumption of continuity. Infants might be quite sure that the missing object still exists, but fail to search because they simply do not know where the object might be. In this view, development involves becoming able to infer the location of hidden objects under a gradually increasing number of conditions rather than suddenly realizing that hidden objects continue to exist. This interpretation, unlike Piaget's, seems consistent with the Baillergeon (1987) swinging board experiment described earlier.

Even if we believe that infants do experience some type of insight that elevates their understanding of the continued existence of hidden objects, it is still clear that, following this insight, they gradually expand their ability to locate such objects. That is, realizing that objects do not disappear forever when they are placed under containers is part of a more general cognitive trend—improved skill in searching the physical environment for lost or hidden objects. These searching skills develop over a long period; even 4-year-olds err on some hidden-object problems. Further, when older children err, their mistakes parallel those of younger children. When presented with three, rather than two, potential hiding places, infants, 1-year-olds, and 4-year-olds most often make the same type of errors. They look at locations where they have found the object previously, rather than locations where they never have found it. The frequency of errors declines, but the type of errors remains the same. (For interesting articles on young children's abilities to search physical environments and find missing objects, see DeLoache, 1980, 1984; DeLoache & Brown, 1983; Perlmutter, 1980; Sophian, 1984; Wellman, Ritter, & Flavell, 1975; and Wellman & Somerville, 1980, 1984).

A branch of mathematics known as *catastrophe theory* provides justification for viewing development as both continuous and discontinuous. Catastrophe theory examines situations such as the collapse of bridges. The forces that lead to bridges collapsing often build up slowly over a period of years. The visible collapse, however, can be breathtakingly sudden. Analogously, despite the seeming abruptness of cognitive progress when a boy solves a problem one day that he could not solve the day before, the progress may be based on years of gradually accumulating experiences. In the boy, as in the bridge, the change can be viewed as either continuous or discontinuous.

*Similar reasoning on different problems.*    A central feature that differentiates stage theories such as Piaget's from other approaches is the stage theories' assumption of unities in reasoning. Saying that children are in a certain stage of reasoning implies that their reasoning across many tasks shares that stage's characteristics. Within Piaget's theory, an 8-year-old ideally would grasp all concrete-operations-level concepts—conservation of liquid quantity, class inclusion, seriation, and so on—and would fail to grasp all formal-operations-level concepts—thinking in terms of all possible combinations, conserving motion, and so on.

It has become increasingly apparent that this view does not accurately characterize children's thinking. Consider three concrete-operations-level conservation concepts: conservation of number, conservation of solid quantity, and conservation of weight. ("If I remold this clay ball into a sausage, will it weigh the same as it did before?") Theoretically, all of these should be mastered simultaneously; a child should understand either all or none of them. Actually, however, most children seem to master the number conservation task at around age 6, the solid quantity conservation task at around age 8, and the weight conservation task at around age 10 (Elkind, 1961a; Katz & Beilin, 1976; Miller, 1976). These data do not support the idea of concurrent development, even within the concept of conservation. Piaget named this phenomenon of children's differing understanding of related concepts—he called it *horizontal decalage*—but did not explain it.

Despite the evidence against the view that children generally reason similarly across many problems, potential consistencies of reasoning across different tasks continue to be of great interest. The motivation is rooted deeply in everyday observations of children's reasoning. There is something characteristic in 2-year-olds' reasoning that distinguishes it from 5-year-olds'; there is something about 5-year-olds' reasoning that distinguishes it from 10-year-olds'; and so on. That is, children of a given age do seem to reason in a characteristic way in different contexts.

In one attempt to address the issue, Flavell (1982) hypothesized that the amount of consistency of reasoning across tasks may depend on whom, what, and when we observe. *Whom* we examine may be important in that some children may exhibit more consistent reasoning across tasks than others. This possibility is suggested by findings that some people exhibit more consistency in personality traits than others (Bem & Allen, 1974; Carver & Scheier, 1981). *What* we investigate also may influence how much similarity we find. Children may show more similar reasoning within certain relatively self-contained areas, such as mathematics and music, than in other, more open domains.

*When* we observe may exert an especially large influence. Children seem to reason more consistently when they are just beginning to understand various concepts than when they understand them better. For example, 5-year-olds solve a large variety of problems by focusing exclusively on a single dimension. On conservation of liquid quantity, they predict that whichever glass has the taller liquid column also has more water, regardless of the cross-sectional areas. On conservation of solid quantity, they predict that whichever clay sausage is longer also has more clay, again regardless of the cross-sectional areas. In judging amount of time, they focus entirely on spatial end points, ignoring the amount of time that has actually passed. In judging which side of a balance scale will tip, they rely entirely on relative amounts of weight, ignoring distance of the weights from the fulcrum. They exhibit similar reasoning with concepts as diverse as temperature, happiness, and morality (Case, 1981; Ferretti, Butterfield, Cahn, & Kerkman, 1985; Levin, Wilkening, & Dembo, 1984; Siegler, 1981; Strauss, 1982).

In contrast, children master these same concepts at very different ages. Even 9-year-olds generally can solve conservation of liquid and solid quantity problems; even college students often cannot solve balance scale problems. Differing amounts of experience with the problems, differences in the ease of drawing analogies to other, better-understood problems, and differences in the complexity of the most advanced solution formulas contribute to these differences in conceptual mastery.

Another potential source of consistency in children's reasoning is the level of their most advanced reasoning (Fischer, 1980; Halford, 1985). This possibility might sound directly opposed to the one just discussed, but it actually is not. Children might not in general reason similarly across problems where they have specific knowledge, but all of their most advanced reasoning might be at the same level. For example, the most advanced thinking of 9-year-olds might involve single operations. This would mean that none of their thinking would involve operations on operations (as in the formal operations period). However, it would not mean that they would solve correctly all problems that could be solved using single operations. Whether they could do so would depend on how much experience they had had with the type of problem, whether it occurred in a familiar context, and so on. In sum, unities in children's reasoning may be most apparent in their early reasoning, when they have little knowledge of the concepts involved, and in the level of the most advanced reasoning of which they are capable.

*Can development be accelerated?*   Piaget's views concerning the possibility of accelerating cognitive development through training are among his most controversial. Some of his comments appear to rule out the possibility of any training being successful. Others suggest that training might at times be effective, but only if the child already possesses some understanding of the concept and if the training procedure involves active interaction with materials. Both types of statements indicate that many young children will not be able to benefit from any training technique, and that many types of training techniques will not benefit any children.

In fact, young children can learn more than Piaget thought they could, and they can benefit from a greater variety of instructional techniques. Among the most convincing demonstrations are those of Brainerd (1974), Field (1977), Gelman (1969), Murray (1972), and Zimmerman and Rosenthal (1974). The findings dovetail with the unsuspected early competence that children have been found to have even without direct training. Not only do children understand more than previously thought, they also can learn more.

It is important not to throw out the baby with the bathwater, however. Although young children can learn to solve these problems, they often find doing so exceptionally difficult. Older children who cannot yet solve the same problems typically learn them much more easily. Similarly, although young children show beginning understanding of many important concepts even without training, they demonstrate the understanding in far fewer situations. The nature of their understanding also seems to differ in important ways from older children's understanding of the same concepts. Just how young children's existing understanding and learning abilities resemble and differ from older children's represents a much more intriguing and controversial issue than whether it is possible for young children to learn concepts under any conditions.

### How Well Do Piaget's General Characterizations Fit Children's Thinking?

In addition to describing children's thinking in terms of particular examples of their reasoning (5-year-olds think that the taller liquid column always has more water) and in terms of stages (type $x$ thinking is typical of the preoperational period), Piaget characterized children's thinking in terms of intellectual traits. For example, he described preoperational-period children as being egocentric, precausal, semilogical, and perceptually oriented. These terms fit in some ways, but not in all. The characterization of preoperational children as egocentric illustrates many of the issues.

Recall from the discussion of egocentric communication that 2-to-4-year-olds often omit critical information. They also often seem to ignore what other people say to them, and have trouble taking other people's point of view. These types of observations led Piaget to label their thinking egocentric.

But consider other situations in which young children communicate nonegocentrically. If you ask 3-year-olds to show you their drawings, they hold the side with the artwork toward you. If they were completely egocentric, they would do the opposite, because they would assume that what they see is what you see. Similarly, preschoolers who have an experience with one adult later allude to the experience in conversations with that adult, but not in conversations with others. Again, if they assumed everyone knew what they did, they would have no reason to differentiate in this way (Menig-Peterson, 1975).

Conversely, people well beyond the preoperational period continue to be "at risk" for egocentrism (Flavell, 1985). A classic demonstration of this involved a situation analogous to a phone conversation. Two children were seated opposite each other at a table with a board between them preventing them from seeing each other. Each child could see the same set of pictures on the table, each picture containing an irregular design. The speaker had to describe the particular design he was thinking of in a way that would allow the listener to figure out which one was being described (Krauss & Glucksberg, 1969).

Not surprisingly, older children communicate which picture they have in mind more effectively than younger ones. More surprisingly, even 8- and 9-year-olds often have difficulty overcoming their knowledge of what they are referring to sufficiently to generate a description that will allow the other child to understand. Further, children well beyond the preoperational period experience difficulty knowing who is to blame for the missed communication—whether the message is inadequate or whether the listener simply failed to respond properly to it. (See Ford, 1985; Patterson & Kister, 1981; Robinson & Robinson, 1981; Waters & Tinsley, 1985; and Whitehurst & Sonnenschein, 1981 for detailed discussions of egocentric communication.) There seems little doubt that young children are egocentric in some important ways that older children are not. Attaching the label to any one group is too strong, though. It leads us to ignore both the ways that younger children's thinking is not egocentric and the ways that older children's thinking is.

### The Current Status of Piaget's Theory

If Piaget's theory underestimates young children's reasoning abilities, overestimates adolescents' reasoning abilities, and describes children's thinking in terms such as egocentrism that are misleading as well as revealing, why pay so much attention to it? The simple reason is that with all of its shortcomings, the theory gives us a good feel for how children think. It also points us in the right direction for learning more about children's thinking. Piaget recognized previously unsuspected intelligence in infants' early activities. In making these discoveries, he raised the question of what other unsuspected capabilities infants might have, a question that underlies the many remarkable recent discoveries about infants' perception and cognition. Piaget also recognized that children do not see the world as adults do. In this recognition, he raised the questions of what mental processes lead them to see the world differently and how exactly they represent what they do see. His estimate of the degree of unity in children's thinking may have been too high, but he discovered some important unities and pointed to the importance of searching for more of them. Finally, Piaget's basic questions are the right ones: What capabilities do infants possess at birth, what capabilities do they possess at later points in development, and what developmental processes allow them to make the transitions? The remainder of the book is an attempt to answer these questions.

## SUMMARY

Piaget's theory remains a dominant force in developmental psychology despite the fact that much of it was formulated half a century ago. Some of the reasons for the approach's lasting appeal are the interesting topics it addresses, the large span of childhood it encompasses, and the reliability and charm of many of its observations.

At the most general level, Piaget's theory focused on the development of intelligence. Intelligence included four stages of development and several developmental processes. The purpose of all these was to organize experience in ways that allowed successful adaptation to the cognitive environment. This adaptation was achieved not simply through learning new responses, but rather through reorganizing existing systems of understandings.

The four main stages of development were the *sensorimotor, preoperational, concrete operational,* and *formal operational* periods. The sensorimotor period occupies the age range between 0 and 2 years, the preoperational period between 2 and 6 or 7, the concrete operational period between 6 or 7 and 11 or 12, and the formal operational period from early adolescence to the end of life. Each of the periods includes large changes in understanding of such important concepts as conservation, classification, and relations.

The three major developmental processes are *assimilation, accommodation,* and *equilibration.* Assimilation refers to the means by which children interpret incoming information to make it understandable within their existing mental structures. Accommodation refers to the ways in which children's current means for understanding the world change in response to new experience. Equilibration is a three-stage process that includes assimilation and accommodation. First, children are in a state of equilibrium.

Then, failure to assimilate new information leads to their becoming aware of shortcomings in their current understanding. Finally, their mental structure accommodates to the new information in a way that creates a more advanced equilibrium.

The sensorimotor period witnesses large improvements in many types of conceptual understanding. Infants acquire primary, secondary, and tertiary circular reactions in which their actions become more deliberate and more systematic, and extend farther beyond their bodies. They also acquire a simple form of conservation—the object permanence concept—in which they realize that objects continue to exist even if they move out of sight and come to understand increasingly complex displacements. They also form simple understandings of classes and relations.

In the preoperational period, children become able to represent their ideas in language and mental imagery. Despite this development, Piaget emphasized what preoperational children cannot do more than what they can. He noted that 5- and 6-year-olds usually fail conservation, class inclusion, and seriation problems. He attributed such failures to the children's focusing on perceptual appearances rather than transformations, to their being egocentric, and to their centering on a single dimension rather than considering multiple variables simultaneously.

In the concrete operations period, children master many of the concepts they did not possess in the preoperational period. Their acquisition of true *operations* is what allows this cognitive progress. These operations allow them to represent transformations and to understand many concepts they could not previously grasp. The operations are reversible and are organized with other operations into larger systems. Among the concepts that children first grasp in this period are conservation of liquid and solid quantity, time, seriation, and class inclusion.

The formal operations period, according to Piaget, brings ability to think in terms of all possible outcomes, to relate actual outcomes to these logically possible outcomes, and to plan ahead. Children in this stage can perform systematic experiments, a skill made possible by sophisticated understanding of classes and relations. In sum, they think much like scientists.

Piaget made a number of controversial statements about what children know at different points in development, about stages of development they pass through, and about general traits that characterize their thinking. When given either the original or nonverbal versions of Piaget's problems, children typically reason much as he described them as doing. However, they appear to have important cognitive capabilities that he did not detect. His stage descriptions predict that children think in qualitatively different ways in different periods of development, that they reason similarly on many problems, and that they cannot learn modes of thought much more advanced than those that characterize their current stage.

Each of these views contains a certain amount of truth, but also has certain problems. When viewed at a general level, many developments appear to represent qualitative changes. However, when examined closely, the same changes often appear to be part of a gradual progression. In general, the consistency of reasoning that Piaget predicted children would show across many tasks has not been found. However, considerable consistency has been apparent in children's early conceptual understanding. Young children do not learn as rapidly as older children, but it is possible for them to learn a great many concepts that are well beyond their current understanding.

Piaget also described children in terms of general intellectual traits, such as egocentrism. These trait descriptions fit young children's thinking in many ways, but not in all. For example, although 5-year-olds are egocentric in some situations, they and even younger children behave nonegocentrically in other situations. Moreover, even older children and adults sometimes behave egocentrically. The trait descriptions thus seem to be in the right ballpark, but to gloss over important exceptions. More generally, however, Piaget's theory continues to be of contemporary interest because it communicates a good feel for children's thinking and raises the right questions.

## RECOMMENDED READINGS

Brainerd, C. J. (1978). The stage question in cognitive developmental theory. *Behavioral and Brain Sciences. 1*, 173–213. A fair but critical discussion of Piaget's theory in light of subsequent research.

Flavell, J. H. (1963). *The developmental psychology of Jean Piaget.* New York: Van Nostrand. *The* classic summary of Piaget's work from 1925–1960.

Gelman, R. A. (1978). Cognitive development. *Annual Review of Psychology, 29,* 297–332. A compelling description of the impressive understanding that preschoolers possess of such complex concepts as number, cause-and-effect, classification, and ordering.

Inhelder, B., & Piaget, J. (1958). *The growth of logical thinking from childhood to adolescence.* New York: Basic Books. One of the clearest presentations of Piaget's theoretical ideas, and some of the most interesting of Piaget's reasoning tasks. Emphasizes the development of formal operations, but also shows how understanding of the tasks develops during the preoperational and concrete operational periods.

Piaget, J. (1952). *The child's concept of number.* New York: W. W. Norton. In this book, Piaget describes a number of his classic experiments: experiments on the conservation of liquid quantity, conservation of number, and seriation among them.

# 3

# Information-Processing
# Theories of Development

As a final point, we concentrated on "what develops" in keeping with the title
of the volume. However, we would like to point out that an equally important
question is how development occurs. . . . The problems of growth and change
are quintessential developmental questions, and are of fundamental importance no less to the instructional psychologist who wishes to accelerate growth
than to the theorist who seeks to understand development. (Brown &
DeLoache, 1978, p. 31)

Brown and DeLoache are not discussing trivial issues. "What develops?" and "How does development occur?" are probably the two most
fundamental questions about children's thinking. Piaget's theory offers one
potential set of answers to the questions: that what develops is qualitatively
distinct levels of intelligence, and that development occurs through the
operation of assimilation, accommodation, and equilibration. As discussed
in Chapter 2, these answers seem to be generally in the right direction. As
also was discussed, though, the answers offered by Piaget's theory need to
be built upon, refined, and changed in certain ways before children's thinking can be well understood. In this chapter, we discuss the major contemporary attempt to provide such revisions, refinements, and rethinkings—the
information-processing approach.

The information-processing approach to development is based on a flattering, almost heroic, depiction of children's thinking. It speaks directly to the essential tension within cognitive development, the tension produced by children being severely limited in the information they can process and remember, yet constantly striving to find ways of overcoming these limitations. To surmount these constraints, children use a variety of *strategies*. They use memory strategies such as *rehearsal* (repeating material over and over before recalling it, as when trying to remember a phone number) to overcome their limited memory capacity. They use external memory aids such as books to overcome their limited knowledge. They use problem-solving strategies, such as dividing problems into parts, to overcome their limited capacity to envision long sequences of future events. The conflicts involved in setting goals, the memory and processing limits that make it difficult to attain the goals, and the strategies that children devise to overcome the limitations highlight the drama inherent in children's efforts to understand the world.

Information-processing theories of development vary in a number of ways, but all share certain fundamental assumptions. The basic assumption is that thinking *is* information processing. Rather than focusing on stages of development, they focus on the information that children represent, the processes that they use to transform the information, and the memory limits that constrain the amount of information they can represent and process. The quality of children's thinking at any age depends on what information they represent in a particular situation, how they operate on the information to achieve their goal, and how much information they can keep in mind at one time.

A second defining characteristic of information-processing theories of development is an emphasis on precise *analysis of change mechanisms*. Two critical goals are to identify the change mechanisms that contribute most to development and to specify exactly how these change mechanisms work together to produce cognitive growth. The flip side of this emphasis on how development occurs is an emphasis on the cognitive limits that prevent development from occurring more rapidly than it does. Thus, information-processing theories attempt to explain both how children of given ages have come as far as they have and why they have not gone farther.

A third assumption of most information-processing approaches is that change is produced by a process of continuous *self-modification*. That is, the outcomes generated by the child's own activities change the way the child will think in the future. For example, in the Siegler and Shipley (in preparation) model of strategy choices, use of various strategies creates increasing knowledge concerning the effectiveness of each strategy, the difficulty of the problems that the strategies are used to solve, and which strategies work best on which problems. This knowledge, in turn, changes the strategies that are used and the answers that are generated. Such self-modifying processes eliminate the need to account for special age-defined transition periods, as in

Piaget's proposed transition from the concrete operations to the formal operations stage around age 12. Instead, children's thinking is viewed as continuously changing at all ages as a result of ongoing cognitive activity.

A fourth defining characteristic is that careful *task analyses* are viewed as crucial for understanding children's thinking. The reason is that people's representations and processing of information are in large part attributable to the task they are trying to perform. Consider the following description:

> We watch an ant make his laborious way across a wind-and-wave-molded beach. He moves ahead, angles to the right to ease his climb up a steep dunelet, detours around a pebble, stops for a moment to exchange information with a compatriot. Thus he makes his weaving, halting way back to his home. So as not to anthropomorphize about his purposes, I sketch the path on a piece of paper. . . .
>
> Viewed as a geometric figure, the ant's path is irregular, complex, hard to describe. But its complexity is really a complexity in the surface of the beach, not a complexity in the ant. On that same beach another small creature with a home at the same place as the ant might well follow a very similar path. (Simon, 1981, pp. 63–64)

As in the ant's journey across the beach, much of the complexity that we observe in people's thinking is really a reflection of the complexity of the environment. Only by analyzing in detail the demands of particular tasks can cognitive activity be understood, since so much of it is an effort to adapt to the task environment. In situations where people cannot solve problems effectively, analyses of the task environment play a different but equally important role. By indicating what processing is required, such task analyses provide a background against which to evaluate exactly where the processing difficulty lies. Thus, understanding the task environment can help distinguish those actions that people take because the actions are adaptive on the task from those actions that they take because of the inadequacy of their information-processing capabilities.

What is the relation of information-processing approaches to alternative views, such as the Piagetian approach? The two approaches have quite a bit in common. Both try to identify children's cognitive capabilities and limits at various points in development. Both try to describe the ways in which children do and do not understand important concepts at different points in life and try to explain how later, more-advanced understandings grow out of earlier, more-primitive ones. Both emphasize the impact that existing understandings can have on children's ability to acquire new understandings.

The two approaches also differ in important ways, though. Information-processing approaches place greater emphasis on the role of processing limitations, strategies for overcoming the limitations, and knowledge about specific content. There is also a greater emphasis on precise analyses of change and on the contribution of ongoing cognitive activity to that change. These differences have led to a greater use of formalisms, such as computer simulations and flow diagrams, that allow information-processing theorists to model in detail how thinking proceeds. A final difference is that information-processing theories assume that our understanding of how children think can be greatly enriched by knowledge of how adults think. The underlying belief is that just as we can more deeply understand our own adult thinking when we appreciate how it developed during childhood, we also can better understand the development of children's thinking when we know where the development is heading.

This chapter is divided into two main sections. In the first, we examine the basic information processing framework. This framework provides a way of thinking about the cognitive systems of both children and adults. In the second main section, we consider four information processing theories that focus specifically on development: Sternberg's, Case's, Klahr and Wallace's, and my own. No one of these theories covers the huge expanse of topics and ages encompassed by Piaget's theory. On the other hand, each provides more precise and complete characterizations of what develops and how development occurs in the area of its focus than Piaget did.

The four theories also have an interesting relation to each other. Each theory emphasizes one or more of the four critical change processes alluded to earlier: encoding, strategy construction, generalization, and automatization. These processes work together to produce substantial cognitive development. To solve problems effectively, children must encode the critical information within the problem. They must then use this encoded information and relevant previous knowledge to construct a strategy for dealing with the problem. To gain the full benefit from the newly-constructed strategy, they must generalize it to other problems where it is also applicable. Finally, new strategies are almost always slow and effortful; practice is needed to automatize the strategy's execution, and thus to maximize its effectiveness. Taken as a group, the four theories of cognitive development help us understand not only how these processes work, but also the capabilities with which children begin life, the types of changes they undergo, and the heights they eventually attain. The chapter's organization is outlined in Table 3.1.

**TABLE 3–1   Chapter Outline**

I.   An Overview of the Information-Processing System
    A.   Structural Characteristics
    B.   Processes

II.   Information-Processing Theories of Development
    A.   Sternberg's Theory
    B.   Case's Theory
    C.   Klahr and Wallace's Theory
    D.   Siegler's Theory

III.   Summary

## AN OVERVIEW OF THE INFORMATION-PROCESSING SYSTEM

Any cognitive theory must come to grips with two basic characteristics of human cognition. First, our thinking is limited, both in the amount of information that can be attended to simultaneously and in the speed with which the information can be processed. Second, our thinking is flexible, capable of adapting to constantly changing goals, circumstances, and task demands. Information processing theories have attempted to come to grips with this dual nature of cognition by focusing on both structural characteristics, that determine the limits within which information processing occurs, and processes, that provide the means for flexible adaptation to a constantly changing world.

### Structural Characteristics

Structural characteristics of the information processing system are often viewed within a three-part framework: sensory memory, short-term memory, and long-term memory (Atkinson & Shiffrin, 1968).

*Sensory memory.*    People seem to possess a special capacity for briefly retaining relatively large amounts of information that they have just encountered. This capacity is often labeled *sensory memory*. Sperling (1960) established several characteristics of sensory memory that influence processing of visual information. He presented college students a three-by-four matrix of letters for one-twentieth of a second. When asked immediately after the presentation to name the letters, the college students typically recalled four or five, about 40 percent of the list. Then Sperling changed the procedure in a small but important way. Rather than having the students recall all of the letters, he asked them to recall only the letters in one row. Since they could not anticipate the identity of the row, they needed to process all 12 letters, just as in the original format. However, requiring them to recite the contents of only one row eliminated the need to retain the information during the recitation period.

Sperling found that when the experimenter indicated which row to recall immediately after the display was shut off, the college students recalled 80 percent of the letters in the row. When the row's identity was indicated one-third of a second after the stimulus was turned off, their recall declined to 55 percent. When it was indicated one second after, performance declined to the original 40 percent. Sperling's interpretation was that a one-twentieth-second exposure was sufficient for letters to create a visual *icon* (a literal copy of the original stimulus), but that the icon faded within one-third of a second, and disappeared after one second. These estimates remain reasonable in light of subsequent research.

Sperling's clever method led to a surprising discovery about children's sensory memory. Simply put, the sensory memory of a 5-year-old seems to have as great a capacity as the sensory memory of an adult. In one study (Morrison, Holmes, & Haith, 1974), 5-year-olds and adults were presented with an array of seven geometric figures. The screen then went blank, and after a one-twentieth-second delay, a marker pointed to one of the seven positions. The child or adult needed to name the object that had been in that position. Under these conditions, 5-year-olds' recall was as good as adults'. Thus, the capacity of a 5-year-old's sensory memory appears to be equivalent to that of an adult.

*Short-term memory.*    Short-term memory is akin to a computer's central processing units. It is here that information from the immediate environment and information from long-term memory are combined to perform whatever calculations are necessary. The active nature of short-term memory has led some investigators to refer to it as *working memory*. It also is often thought of as the conscious part of memory, or the part that is receiving attention. People are not aware of the contents of either sensory or long-term memory, but they often are aware of the contents of short-term memory.

The operation of short-term memory is limited in several ways. The first is its capacity, the number of symbols it can include at one time. This number is not large; it is usually estimated to be between three and seven units, though determining the exact number is extremely difficult. The limit on short-term memory capacity is a limit on the number of meaningful units (chunks) rather than the number of physical units. A letter, a number, a word, or a familiar phrase can function as a single chunk, because each is a single unit of meaning. Thus, it is as easy to remember a set of three unrelated words with nine letters (e.g., *hit, red, foot*) as to remember three unrelated letters (e.g., *q, f, r*) (Miller, 1956).

The rate at which information is lost from short-term memory also limits cognitive functioning. Material ordinarily is lost within 15 to 30 seconds. However, rehearsing or otherwise attending to the information can preserve it for a longer time. The longer the item is kept active in short-term memory, the greater the probability that it will be transferred to long-term memory where its maintenance does not require active effort.

People can rapidly but not instantaneously retrieve information from short-term memory. The speed with which most children can gain such access increases considerably with age, but this may not be the case with all children. Keating and Bobbitt (1978) examined the speed with which high IQ and average IQ 9-, 13-, and 17-year-olds could retrieve information from short-term memory. They found that in general, older children could access this information more rapidly than younger ones, and that gifted (high IQ) children could do so more rapidly than average ones. However, gifted children already had reached adultlike rates by age 9, and showed no further improvement thereafter. The gifted children's early ability to retrieve information rapidly from short-term memory may help them see connections among a wide variety of events that other children do not connect until much later.

*Long-term memory.*    Even young children are able to remember a vast assortment of experiences and facts about the world. Some of their knowledge is about specific episodes, such as their feelings when they wandered around the playground on their first day of school. Other knowledge is about enduring qualities of the world, such as that a nickel is worth five pennies. Yet other knowledge concerns procedures, such as how to ride a bicycle. These varied types of knowledge are the contents of long-term memory.

Unlike sensory and short-term memory, there are no limits on either how much information can reside in long-term memory or how long the information can remain there. Consider an experiment on recognition of faces in high school yearbooks (Bahrick, Bahrick, & Wittlinger, 1975). People were asked 35 years after they had graduated to recognize which yearbook pictures were of people in their high school class and which were of people from a nearby high school. In spite of all of the time that had passed, people correctly recognized 90 percent of the pictures. Thus, the name *long-term memory* is truly a fitting one.

An interesting property of the way people store information in long-term memory is that the storage is not in all-or-none form. Rather, people store information in separable units and can retrieve some units without retrieving others. This quality has been demonstrated in adults in experiments on the tip-of-the-tongue phenomenon. When adults can almost but not quite remember a word, they can often recall several of its characteristics: its first letter, its number of syllables, a word it sounds like, and so on (e.g., Brown & McNeil, 1966). I do not know of any formal research on the topic, but everyday observations of my own children lead me to suspect that the description applies to children's storage of information in long-term memory as well. For example, in trying to remember a friend who had moved away, my then 6-year-old daughter said, "She was from South America, she had black hair, she was just as silly as I am, why can't I remember her name?" A few minutes later, she succeeded in recalling the friend's name, Gabriella.

### Processes

Processes are used to actively manipulate information in sensory, short-term, and long-term memory. Some processes, such as retrieval of information from long-term memory, are quite simple; other processes, such as plans, procedures, rules, and strategies, are much more complex. In the sections that follow, we examine two heavily used processes that play important roles in cognitive development: automatization and encoding.

*The role of automatization.*   Processes vary considerably in how much attention they require. Those that require a great deal of attention are often labeled *controlled,* whereas those that require little if any attention are labeled *automatic.* The amount of attention required is influenced both by the type of information being processed and by the amount of experience the child has had processing that type of material. Some types of information inherently require less attention than others. However, even with processes that at first require a great deal of attention, practice reduces the amount of attention that is needed.

Automatic processing is important in development, because it provides an initial basis for learning about the world. One example involves processing of frequency information, that is, data on how often various objects and events have been encountered. People seem to retain this information even when they are not trying to do so. For example, we have a good sense of the relative frequency with which letters of the alphabet appear, although no one tries to remember such trivia. Further, efforts to remember frequency information more effectively seem to have little effect. Recall of such information is influenced neither by instructions to remember it nor by practice in trying to remember it. Recall of frequency information also is equivalent over a wide age range. Children as young as 5-year-olds are as proficient as college students in retaining this type of information (Hasher & Zacks, 1984).

Children's automatic retention of information about frequencies seems to contribute to cognitive development in many ways. When children form concepts, they must learn which features go together most frequently. (Learning the concept "bird" requires learning that the same animals tend to fly, have feathers, have beaks, and live in trees.) More subtle learning, such as learning of sex roles, also may depend on automatic processing of frequency information. Only when children see a large difference in the frequency with which men and women engage in an activity do they imitate the same-sex models more than the different-sex ones (Perry & Bussey, 1979). Children are almost never conscious of gathering information about how often men engage in an activity and how often women do. Rather, they seem to acquire the information automatically and then base their behavior on what they have observed.

Thus, processing of frequency information appears to be automatic from early in development, perhaps from birth. Other processes, however, may change from controlled to automatic as people gain experience with them. For example, when people learn to drive a car with a stick shift, they need to concentrate to change gears at the right time. Later, they shift effortlessly, often without even being aware that they are doing so. The process is known as *automatization.*

Spelke, Hirst, and Neisser (1976) demonstrated that sufficient practice can lead to automatization of even those processes that we think of as being inherently controlled. To make this point, they trained two people to simultaneously read passages and write down words that they heard dictated. Ordinarily, when people try to do these two tasks at the same time, performance on one or both suffers. This was the case for the two experimental subjects when they began the experiment. After six weeks of daily practice, however, they could read a book and write words simultaneously as efficiently as they could do either one alone. Apparently, joint execution of the two tasks had become automatized.

*The role of encoding.*   People cannot represent all features of the environment; the world is simply too complex. Children seem to be especially prone to fail to encode important features of tasks, sometimes because they do not know what the important features are and sometimes because they do not know how to encode them efficiently. This failure to encode critical elements can prevent children from learning from potentially useful experiences. If they are not taking in the relevant information, they cannot benefit from it.

Kaiser, McCloskey, and Proffitt (1986) provided one demonstration of how inadequate encoding can keep people from learning from their experiences. They presented 4- to 11-year-olds and college students with a moving electric train carrying a ball on a flatcar. At a predesignated point, the ball dropped through a hole in the moving flatcar and fell several feet to the floor. The task was to predict the trajectory of the ball as it fell.

More than 70 percent of the children and a sizable minority of the college students predicted that the ball would fall straight down. After they advanced this hypothesis, the experimenter demonstrated what actually happened. (The ball fell in a parabolic trajectory.) The children and the college students were faced with reconciling their predictions with the outcome they had seen. Their explanations revealed how their encoding of the event was influenced by their expectations. Some said that the ball actually had fallen straight down but that it was released from the train later than the experimenter said it was. Others said that the train gave the ball a push forward just before it was released. Interestingly, a number of the college students who encoded the ball as having gone straight down had previously taken and passed college physics courses. Apparently this experience was insufficient to change either their expectations or their encoding of what they saw.

## INFORMATION-PROCESSING THEORIES OF DEVELOPMENT

In the remainder of this chapter we consider four theories of how information-processing capabilities develop: Sternberg's, Case's, Klahr and Wallace's, and my own. These theories are of particular interest when considered as a group, because they provide distinct but related perspectives on how automatization, encoding, generalization, and strategy construction contribute to cognitive development. Sternberg's theory is especially useful in describing the role of encoding and strategy construction. Case's theory illustrates how automatization contributes to children's increasing ability to circumvent memory capacity limits. Klahr and Wallace's theory emphasizes children's ability to generalize, that is, to detect consistent relations and to extend them to new situations. My own theory emphasizes how children construct new strategies and generalize them to situations beyond the ones in which they made the discoveries.

Before discussing each theory in detail, it seems worthwhile to consider each one briefly so as to provide an overview. Sternberg's theory focuses on how specific information-processing components contribute to children's general intelligence. For example, he has analyzed the types of components that distinguish gifted from average children, and those that distinguish average from retarded children.

Case adopts a general stage framework much like Piaget's. However, he suggests that cognitive growth stems from changes in the amount of information that can be retained in short-term memory and to acquisition of central conceptual structures. He attributes these changes to automatization of processing and to biological maturation.

Klahr and Wallace's theory focuses on the contribution of three processes to children's ability to draw general conclusions about the world: retention of experiences in a time line, detection of regular relations within the time line, and elimination of unnecessary processing. Their research also illustrates the use of computer simulation as a tool for analyzing cognitive development.

My own theory is based on an analogy between cognitive development and biological evolution. It focuses on two processes: strategy choice and strategy construction. The research illustrates how children's information-processing abilities can generate the variation and selection that seem essential for cognitive change to be adaptive.

All of these theories reflect the contributions of both Piagetian and adult information-processing approaches, as well as a number of other influences. Table 3–2 lists some of these. It also summarizes the goals of the theories and the mechanisms of development that they emphasize.

### Sternberg's Theory

Since the beginning of the twentieth century, intelligence has been characterized by a single number, the IQ score. This practice has several drawbacks: Intelligence tests may be culturally biased; they do not directly measure such critical capacities as the ability to learn and to create; and a single number is inherently inadequate to capture a quality as rich and complex as intelligence. IQ tests also have certain unique virtues, however. Scores

**TABLE 3–2  Overview of Information-Processing Theories of Development**

| THEORIST | GOAL OF THEORY | MAIN DEVELOPMENTAL MECHANISMS | FORMATIVE INFLUENCES |
|---|---|---|---|
| Sternberg | To provide an information-processing analysis of the development of intelligence | Strategy construction, based on the use of knowledge acquisition components, metacomponents, and performance components. Also encoding and automatization. | Information-processing theories' emphasis on encoding, time course of processing, and dividing thinking into components. Intelligence testing emphasis on individual differences in intellectual ability. |
| Case | To unite Piagetian and information-processing theories of development. | Automatization and biologically based increases in working memory, both of which increase processing capacity. Also strategy construction. | Piaget's emphasis on stages of reasoning and on between-concept unities in reasoning. Information-processing theories' emphasis on short-term memory limits, automatization, and problem-solving strategies. |
| Klahr & Wallace | To formulate a computer simulation model of cognitive development. | Generalization, based on the workings of regularity detection, redundancy elimination, and the time line. Also encoding and strategy construction. | Piaget's emphasis on self-modification and on assimilation. Information-processing theories' emphasis on encoding and on computer simulation as a means for characterizing thinking. |
| Siegler | To understand the adaptive character of cognitive development. | Choices among existing strategies and construction of new strategies. Also generalization. | Piaget's emphasis on self-modification and equilibration. Information-processing theories' emphasis on adaption to the task environment and on computer simulation. |

on them are closely related to school performance at the time they are given; they predict later school performance quite well; and they provide a solid base from which to examine individual differences in cognitive functioning.

To preserve these virtues while reducing or eliminating the negative qualities, Sternberg has attempted to develop an information-processing analysis of intelligence. He has applied the analysis to diverse tasks and diverse groups of children and has related his results to those yielded by traditional intelligence tests.

As shown in Figure 3–1, Sternberg's (1985) theory divides intelligence into three types of information-processing components: performance components, knowledge acquisition components, and metacomponents. Essentially, the metacomponents serve as a strategy construction mechanism, orchestrating the other two types of components into goal-oriented procedures. When the child already possesses sufficient understanding to solve a problem, only the metacomponents and the performance components are needed to construct a problem-solving strategy. The metacomponents select which performance components to use and the order in which to use them, and the performance components do the work of actually solving the problem. When the child does not yet possess sufficient understanding to solve the problem, the knowledge acquisition components also come into play. That is, the knowledge acquisition components obtain new information relevant to solving the problem and communicate this information to the metacomponents. Then the metacomponents combine the new and previous understanding to construct a problem-solving strategy from among the performance components.

**FIGURE 3–1** A schematic diagram of Sternberg's theory of intelligence.

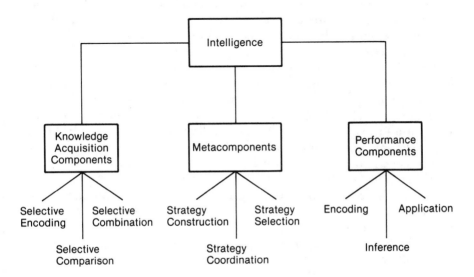

Now we can analyze each of these types of components in greater detail. First consider *performance components*. These are processes that a problem solver uses to implement a decision to solve a problem in a particular way. Sternberg has identified four performance components that people use to solve a great many problems: encoding, inference, mapping, and application.

The way in which these performance components work can be illustrated by thinking about analogy problems. Consider the problem

Turkey : Cranberry sauce :: Eggs: (1) Corn (2) Ham

The task is to decide whether corn or ham has the same relation to eggs that cranberry sauce has to turkey.

Sternberg suggested that the first step in solving this problem is to encode each term. This step involves identifying each term's attributes—for example, noting that turkey is a kind of food, that it is a meat, that it is a bird, that it is eaten on Thanksgiving, and so on. Next, inference is used to specify the relation between the first and second term, in this case that turkey is often eaten with cranberry sauce. Then, mapping is used to establish the relation between the first and third terms, that turkey and eggs are both foods. Finally, application involves inducing a relation between the third term and one of the possible answers that parallels the relation between the first and second terms. Here, eggs go with ham in much the same way that cranberry sauce goes with turkey.

Sternberg and Rifkin (1979) found that 7-year-olds use the same components as adults to solve analogy problems. However, they differ in the amount of cognitive resources they devote to each component. In particular, adults spend more time encoding the terms but then move much more quickly through the remaining steps. The children's strategy of encoding only one or a few features of each term reduces the initial memory load, but ultimately lengthens the time needed to solve the problem.

Sternberg and Rifkin found that encoding time correlated positively with children's IQ and with success on the task. Although high IQ children generally tend to be fast on intellectual tasks, they, like adults, spent an especially long time encoding. Marr and Sternberg (1986) added the finding that higher IQ children spent more of their encoding time on the most-relevant information. Lower IQ children did not focus as strongly on the most-relevant information. Thus, complete encoding of the critical information is associated both with high IQs and with success in solving analogy problems. This type of linking of the information-processing construct of encoding with the psychometric construct of IQ is representative of the kinds of bridges between psychometric theory and information processing that Sternberg is trying to build.

The second part of Sternberg's theory involves *knowledge acquisition components*. Sternberg has focused on three of these: selective encoding, selective combination, and selective comparison. Selective encoding involves sifting out relevant from irrelevant information. Selective combination involves integrating information in a meaningful way. Selective comparison involves relating newly encoded or combined information to previously stored information.

These constructs have proved especially useful for analyzing what makes a child intellectually gifted. Sternberg and Davidson (1983) tested use of each of the three types of knowledge acquisition components on insight problems—problems much like the brain teasers in puzzle books. Their reason for using these problems was that knowledge acquisition processes would be especially important on them, since such problems are new to everyone. The following is an example of the insight problems Sternberg and Davidson used: "If you have black socks and brown socks in your drawer, mixed in the ratio of 4 to 5, how many socks will you have to take out to be sure of having a pair of socks of the same color?"

The basic assumption underlying the experiment was that intellectually gifted children can execute knowledge acquisition components more effectively than other children. They therefore would be expected not only to perform better on all problems but also to benefit less than intellectually average children from conditions that lessened the need for effective execution of knowledge acquisition processes. The reason was that they would execute the process effectively even without help.

The experimental procedures generated by this logic can be illustrated with regard to the selective encoding component. Its role in the socks problem just cited was tested by either including or omitting the irrelevant information about the 4:5 ratio of the two colors. If this information was present, children would need to ignore it and selectively encode only the essentials of the problem. (If you had socks of two colors, how many socks would you need to look at to be sure that two would match?) If the irrelevant information were absent, skill in selective encoding would be less important because there would be less distracting information.

Sternberg and Davidson's predictions were confirmed. Gifted children correctly solved the insight problems more often than nongifted children, and the hints were less essential for their success. This was the case for all three knowledge acquisition components.

Then the investigators went a step further. They offered a Saturday morning course designed to train gifted and nongifted children in executing the three processes. The course included 14 hours of instruction, distributed over a 7-week period. At the end, children were given a posttest. The posttest included mathematical insight problems, hypothesized to require use of the knowledge acquisition processes the children had been taught. It also included logical deduction problems, hypothesized to require different processes.

The nongifted children showed greater gains on the mathematical insight problems than the gifted children, which was consistent with the view that they were more in need of the instruction. Neither group showed gains on the logical deduction task, in accord with the view that this task required skills that were not part of the Saturday morning training program. In sum, gifted children's superior knowledge acquisition components seemed to account for their superior performance on the insight problems.

The third part of Sternberg's theory involves *metacomponents,* components used to construct strategies. Metacomponents govern the use of the other components. They also are responsible for most aspects of developmental change. As Sternberg (1984) commented, "There can be no doubt that in the present conceptual scheme, the metacomponents form the major basis for the development of intelligence" (p. 172).

Just as Sternberg argued that superiority in the use of knowledge acquisition components is especially important in intellectual giftedness, he argued that inferiority in the use of metacomponents is especially important in retardation. He focused on three ways in which inferior functioning of metacomponents might lead to intellectual retardation. One source would be inadequate choices of performance and knowledge acquisition components for inclusion within strategies. Retarded people might possess sufficient capabilities to solve certain problems, but fail to use the capabilities because their metacomponents did not construct strategies with the right components.

Another potential problem was poor coordination between controlled and automatized problem-solving routines. For example, in reading, people need to move back and forth between the automatized programs used to recognize individual words and the controlled processes that often are used to integrate meanings in texts. Failure to move smoothly back and forth between these two modes can disrupt processing.

Finally, metacomponents are responsible for reacting to experience and making midcourse corrections in processing. Again, retarded individuals seem to be deficient in these skills. In particular, retarded children differ from nonretarded ones especially greatly in their ability to transfer, to draw on all their knowledge to solve problems, and to be sufficiently flexible to construct new strategies to adapt to changing task demands (Butterfield, Siladi, & Belmont, 1980).

How should Sternberg's theory be evaluated? Two weaknesses can be noted. One is that the theory summarizes more than it predicts. It is not clear what types of evidence would be inconsistent with the approach. Another involves the role of metacomponents in the organization of the system. These are crucial parts of the overall theory, but their workings remain somewhat mysterious. On the other hand, the theory is exceptional in the breadth of phenomena and of populations to which it has proven applicable. It encompasses a large number of intuitively important aspects of development and organizes them in an easy-to-grasp way. It provides a plausible outline of how a strategy construction mechanism would operate. In short, it constitutes a useful framework within which to view development.

### Case's Theory

Case's theory is an attempt to unite Piagetian and information-processing theories. It incorporates stages much like Piaget's with the emphasis on goals, short-term memory limitations, and problem-solving strategies typical of information-processing approaches. Its greatest emphasis is on how the biologically based growth of working memory capacity, together with automatization of processing, allows children to progressively overcome processing limits. The theory can be divided into two main parts: the developmental stages themselves and the transition processes that produce progress between stages.

Like Piaget, Case (1985) hypothesized that children progress through four developmental stages. Case characterized these stages in terms of the types of mental representations children can form while they are in them and the types of mental operations they can use. The first stage involved *sensorimotor operations*. Children's representations in this stage are composed of sensory input. The actions they produce in response to these representations are physical movements. In the *representational operations stage*, children's representations include durable concrete internal images, and their actions can produce additional internal representations. In the stage of *logical operations*, children represent stimuli abstractly; they can act on these representations with simple transformations. In the *formal operations stage*, children also represent stimuli abstractly, but they are capable of performing complex transformations of the information. (Note: In all stages, children also produce representations and actions like those that were possible earlier.)

Examples may clarify the differences in the representations that become possible in different stages. A sensorimotor operation might involve a child's seeing a frightening face (the sensory representation) and then hastily leaving the room (the motor action). A representational operation might involve the child's producing a mental image of the same frightening face (the internal representation) and using the image to draw a picture of the face the next day (the representational action). A logical operation might involve a child's realizing that two of his friends did not like each other (the abstract representation) and telling them that they all could have more fun if they all were friends (the simple transformation). A formal operation might involve the child's realizing that such direct attempts at producing friendships rarely succeed (the abstract representation) and therefore leading all three into a situation in which they would need to overcome some common danger, thus producing friendly feelings (the complex transformation). The resemblance to Piaget's stages of development seems clear.

Case's view of the developmental sequence by which children acquire understanding of particular concepts also resembled Piaget's views. These views are exemplified by Case's description of children's reasoning on the orange juice problem. This task involved two sets of small drinking glasses, each glass containing either orange juice or water. Children needed to predict which pitcher would taste more strongly of orange juice if the contents of the glasses in one set were poured into one pitcher and those in the other set into another. In other words, they needed to choose which pitcher would have the higher proportion of juice.

Case identified four strategies that children use on this task. Three- and 4-year-olds judged on the basis of the presence of orange juice. If only the glasses in one set contained orange juice, they predicted that that set's liquid would taste more strongly of orange juice. If both sets included orange juice, the children predicted that both would taste more strongly of it. Five- and 6-year-olds predicted on grounds that seem more plausible to adults. They compared the number of glasses in each set that contained orange juice, and said that whichever set had more would have the stronger taste (regardless of the number of glasses in each set that had water). Seven- and 8-year-olds considered both the number of glasses containing orange juice and the number containing water. If one set had more orange juice than water, they said that that set would taste more like orange juice. If both or neither set had more orange juice than water, they said the two would taste the same. Finally, 9- and 10-year-olds subtracted the number of glasses containing water from the number containing orange juice, and chose whichever set had the greater remainder.

Where Case differs most clearly from Piaget, and shows the strongest influence of the information-processing approach, is in his account of transition mechanisms. Case hypothesized that children begin life with an innate kernel of processing capabilities. Among these capabilities are the potential for setting goals, for formulating problem-solving strategies to meet the goals, and for integrating different problem-solving strategies into more-elaborate and effective strategies. These innate capabilities allow children to make a considerable amount of cognitive progress.

However, the innate capabilities do not allow children to make all kinds of cognitive progress. Whether they can make a given kind of progress depends, according to Case, on the fit between the child's short-term memory capacity and the capacity needed to make such progress. If the new acquisition demands no more memory capacity than the child possesses, then the acquisition will be possible; otherwise, it will not.

How do children ever surmount their short-term memory limits to acquire capabilities that require greater capacity? The simplest explanation would be that with age, the capacity of short-term memory grows larger. However, there is little evidence to support this proposition.

If the absolute capacity of short-term memory does not increase, how do children become able to hold more information in short-term memory? Case (1985) proposed two transition mechanisms by which this progress might occur. One was automatization. With practice, a cognitive operation that previously required all the capacity of the short-term store could be accomplished more efficiently. This would free up part of the short-term memory capacity for other processing. It may be useful to think of this view of short-term memory in terms of an analogy to a car's trunk. The capacity of a car's trunk does not change as the owner acquires experience in packing luggage into it. Nonetheless, the amount of luggage that can be packed into the trunk does change. Whereas the trunk at first might hold three suitcases, it might eventually come to hold four or five. With more-efficient packing, trunk space is freed for additional materials.

The second major transition process was biological maturation. Case (1985) hypothesized that degree of myelinization of the neurons in the brain that was required for executing the operations characteristic of a given stage might determine the efficiency that was possible. Case noted that different systems within the brain are myelinated at different times during development. He perceived a correspondence between the timing of the myelinization and the timing of changes in efficiency of operations controlled by those parts of the brain. Thus, myelinization might account for transitions between stages, whereas automatization might account for transitions within stages.

More recently, Case and Griffin (1990) noted a third way in which children transcend short-term memory limitations: through acquiring *central conceptual structures*. As they defined it, a central conceptual structure is "an internal network of concepts and conceptual relations which plays a central role in permitting children to think about a wide range (but not all) situations at a new epistemic level" (p. 224). In one of their examples, they proposed that 4-, 6-, 8-, and 10-year-olds each have a different conceptual structure for thinking about quantitative relations, and that differences in these structures lead to differences in thinking about the many topics where quantitative relations come into play (e. g., conservation, class inclusion, seriation, etc). They also demonstrated that teaching new conceptual structures helped children think about many concepts in more advanced ways. The importance of such structures was attributed in large part to their providing efficient ways of organizing goals and procedures for accomplishing the goals, and thus allowing children to circumvent short-term memory limits.

Case and his colleagues have applied this theory to an exceptional variety of tasks. They range from balance scales (Case, 1978) to musical sight reading (Capodilupo, in press), telling time (Case, Sandieson, & Dennis, 1987), handling money (Marini, 1984), and understanding a variety of social phenomena such as moods and interpersonal conflict (Case & Griffin, 1990; McKeough, 1986). In all instances, the findings have been generally consistent with theoretical predictions.

Case's theory appears to have significance for practical as well as theoretical issues. Consider his analysis of missing addend problems, those of the form 4 + ? = 7. Although the task appears simple and is part of most first-grade curricula, children find it a major obstacle. Many first-grade teachers find it so frustrating that they do not even try to teach it, despite its presence in their teaching manuals and in the children's textbooks (O'Hara, 1975).

After analyzing several correct and several commonly used incorrect strategies for solving missing addend problems, Case noted that most correct strategies required more short-term memory capacity than 6- and 7-year-olds usually possess. However, he also noted that the simplest correct strategy and the most-demanding incorrect strategy made the same memory demands. The least-demanding correct strategy, according to his analysis, was to count on from the one addend given in the problem and to note the number of counts required to reach the sum. On the problem 4 + ? = 7, this simplest correct strategy would involve counting from 4 to 7 and keeping track of the number of counts needed to get from one to the other. The most-demanding (and the most-common) incorrect strategy was to count up first to the addend that was given and then to count on from there the number of times indicated by the sum. Illustratively, on the problem 4 + ? = 7, children would first count to 4, then count up 7 more times to 11, and finally answer that the missing addend was 11. Case reasoned that if 6-year-olds could learn the incorrect strategy, they also could learn the correct one.

The instructional strategy that Case used was straightforward. As shown in Figure 3–2, the first step was to illustrate that the equal sign (=) meant that entities on each side of the sign were equivalent. The next step (third pair of faces) was to illustrate that the plus sign ( + ) meant to sum the entities adjacent to the sign. After the child finished working with the faces, the focus of the instruction shifted to direct consideration of problems involving numbers. In one part of this instruction, the experimenter demonstrated the incorrectness of children's existing strategy for solving missing addend problems involving numbers by having them compare the numbers on the two sides of the equal sign that their strategy yielded. This would allow them to see that on 4 + ? = 7, the 11 that their strategy yielded was not equivalent to the 7 on the other side of the equal sign. Following this, the simplest correct procedure for solving missing addend problems (the counting-on strategy described in the previous paragraph) was introduced, one step at a time.

Case (1978) reported that his teaching strategy allowed 80 percent of kindergarten children to learn missing addend problems. This percentage

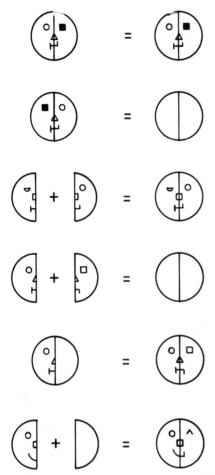

**FIGURE 3–2** Faces used by Case (1978) to teach missing addend problem. First pair of faces was used to demonstrate meaning of equal sign. Second pair was used to test whether child could make right-hand face equal to left-hand face. Third pair was used to demonstrate that whole on right could be created from parts on left. Fourth pair was used to test whether child could create whole out of parts. Fifth pair, like missing addend problem, showed one part of whole on left and whole on right; task was to fill in other part of whole on left. Sixth pair introduced plus sign, to make problem even more like standard missing addend problems with numbers.

represented a considerable improvement over the 10 percent of children who were able to learn such problems from the standard State of California arithmetic workbook. The procedure also enabled retarded children of mental age 6 to learn missing addend problems. Thus, Case's approach seems useful for applied as well as theoretical purposes.

Several criticisms of Case's theory have been voiced. Flavell (1984) noted that Case has not explicated the principles by which he determines how much short-term memory capacity a procedure requires. As a result, it is often difficult to evaluate whether the estimates are comparable from one task to the next. Further, his ideas about the role of myelinization in between-stage transitions are quite speculative at present. On the other hand, Case's theory is exceptional among information-processing approaches to development in its attempt to relate basic capacities, strategies, and learning. It has yielded compelling analyses of development on many tasks and has proved practically useful, as well. Also, there is a strong intuition among many researchers that improved ability to surmount memory limits does underlie much of cognitive development, though it is difficult to provide evidence that unambiguously supports the position. Thus, it seems that Case has taken a difficult but potentially rewarding path. To the extent that the effort succeeds, it will be a grand achievement.

### Klahr and Wallace's Theory

Klahr and Wallace have been in the forefront of those urging more explicit specification of how change mechanisms operate. Klahr's (1982) critique of Piaget's hypothesized change mechanisms—assimilation, accommodation, and equilibration—reflects this view.

> For 40 years now we have had assimilation and accommodation, the mysterious and shadowy forces of equilibration, the Batman and Robin of the developmental processes. What are they? How do they do their thing? Why is it after all this time, we know no more about them than when they first sprang on the scene? What we need is a way to get beyond vague verbal statements of the nature of the developmental process. (p. 80)

As an alternative, Klahr and Wallace advocated the writing of *self-modifying production systems*. These are computer simulations equipped with mechanisms that allow them to develop in response to their experience. The key developmental mechanism in Klahr and Wallace's theory was generalization. They divided generalization into three more-particular representation and processing units: the time line, regularity detection, and redundancy elimination.

The *time line* contains the data on which generalizations are based. It is a record of all the situations the system has ever encountered, the responses produced in those situations, the outcomes of the actions, and the new situations that arose. Its workings, as well as those of the other two mechanisms, can be explained in the context of Klahr and Wallace's theory of number conservation. (Recall from the chapter on Piaget's theory that number conservation is the task on which children are presented two rows of objects and then, after seeing one row spread out or compressed, are asked if the rows still have the same number of objects.)

Table 3–3 illustrates the type of information that might be included in the time line's record of a single event. A child saw a group of cookies and discovered that there were three. The discovery was made by *subitizing* (simply looking at a group and perceiving the number of objects; people can subitize sets of one to four objects, but not larger sets). Next, the child transformed the spatial position of the cookies by picking them up in his

**TABLE 3–3  A Portion of a
Child's Time Line**

| *(PREVIOUS PROCESSING EPISODES)* | |
|---|---|
| — | — |
| — | — |
| — | — |
| 87456. | Cookies on table |
| 87457. | I subitized |
| 87458. | There were three |
| 87459. | I heard a bird |
| 87460. | I picked up the cookies |
| 87461. | I subitized the cookies |
| 87462. | There were three again |
| — | — |
| — | — |
| — | — |

hand. Finally, the child again subitized the collection of cookies and found that there still were three.

Such detailed records of situations, responses, and outcomes might at first seem unnecessary. Why would it be useful to remember so much about each experience? In fact, the information could be invaluable for cognitive development. In many situations, children cannot know beforehand what will turn out to be relevant. If they retain detailed information that may or may not be relevant, they later may be able to draw unanticipated generalizations. If they retain only what they know to be relevant, however, they may miss much relevant information.

Is it realistic to think that children have a memory record similar to a time line? Observing the level of detail with which they remember certain information suggests that it is. Almost all parents have anecdotes to this effect. One of mine concerns a vacation on which my wife, our almost-2-year-old son, and I were staying in a motel. We wanted to go to dinner but could not find our room key. After 10 minutes of searching, I finally listened to my son long enough to understand what he was saying: "Under phone." As soon as I understood, I knew he was right. I had put it there (for reasons that I no longer remember). It seems likely that if he remembered this relatively inconsequential detail, he probably was remembering a great many other details as well. Hasher and Zacks's (1984) ideas about automatic processing of frequency information and of several other aspects of experience, such as spatial locations and time of occurrence, suggest the types of content that might be entered into the time line. Thus, at least to me, Klahr and Wallace's contention that children retain a detailed ledger of their experiences seems quite plausible.

The second key process, *regularity detection,* operates on the contents of the time line to produce generalizations about experience. This is accomplished by the system's noting places in the time line where many features are similar and where variation in a single feature does not affect an outcome. In number conservation, regularity detection could produce at least three types of generalizations. One would involve generalizing over different objects. Regardless of whether two checkers, two coins, two dolls, or two cookies were spread, there still would be two objects. Children also could generalize over equivalent transformations. Spreading, compressing, piling up, and putting in a circle all preserve the initial number of objects. They also could generalize over different numbers of objects. The results of compressing a row are the same regardless of the number of objects in the initial arrangement.

The third crucial process in Klahr and Wallace's model, *redundancy elimination,* accomplishes a different type of generalization. It improves efficiency by identifying processing steps that are unnecessary, thus reaching the generalization that a less-complex sequence can achieve the same goal. In the number conservation example, children eventually would note that it is unnecessary to subitize after picking up the cookies. Since there were three cookies before, and since picking up objects never affects how many there are, the number still must be the same. Klahr and Wallace hypothesized that the information-processing system eliminates redundancy by examining procedures within the time line and checking if the same outcome always occurs even if one or more steps are deleted. If so, the simpler procedure is substituted for the more-complex one.

When does the information-processing system have time to detect regularities and to eliminate redundancies? Klahr and Wallace (1976) advanced one intriguing possibility: Perhaps children do it in their sleep. Other possibilities are that moments of quiet play, relaxation, or daydreaming are when children accomplish these functions.

Klahr and Wallace's approach, unlike stage theories, implies that different children develop skills in different orders. In the cognitive system's attempts at self-modification, there is no obvious reason why one type of regularity always should be detected before another type. Children learning about number conservation either could first detect that it does not matter if the rows of objects contain cookies or checkers or could first detect that it does not matter if the cookies are pushed together or stretched apart. Thus, there is less of a lock-step feel to the model than there is to stage approaches.

Another implication of Klahr and Wallace's theory relates to the idea of encoding. The way in which information is encoded in the time line shapes the learning that can later occur. Suppose, for example, that in a liquid quantity conservation experiment, a child encodes only the heights of the water in the glasses. Such a child would not be able to detect the regular relation between increments in the height of water and decrements in its cross-sectional area. The information about cross-sectional area simply would not be available in the time line.

Klahr and Wallace have been in the forefront of investigators arguing for greater use of computer simulation as a tool for modeling development. They have noted that such simulations allow more explicit and precise models of how development occurs than would otherwise be possible.

Not everyone shares their enthusiasm for such models, though. The critics note that people are not computers and that unlike computers, people develop. This leads them to the conclusion that development cannot be modeled appropriately on a computer (Beilin, 1983; Liben, 1987a).

As Klahr (1989) pointed out, however, ideas about development are embodied in the computer *program*, not the computer on which the program runs. The computer is simply the device used to test whether these ideas account for the known phenomena. To illustrate the point, Klahr noted that computer simulations of cognitive development do not imply that children are computers any more than computer simulations of hurricanes imply that the atmosphere is a computer.

Klahr also addressed a second criticism: that using computer simulations to model findings about children's thinking is circular, because "given that the particular computer program was written expressly to simulate children's observed behaviors, it is not remarkable that there is a good match between them" (Liben, 1987a, p. 114). Klahr countered this argument by noting that it was akin to saying, "Given that Newton's inverse-square law of gravitation was formulated expressly to account for empirical observations of planetary motion, it is not remarkable that there is a good match between his theory and the actual motion of the planets" (p. 155). His point was that what matters is how well a model can account for diverse phenomena, not whether the model was intended to account for the phenomena.

Several limitations of Klahr and Wallace's theory should be mentioned. Although they proclaim the virtues of self-modifying computer simulations, neither they nor other investigators interested in children's thinking have yet written many of these. (For one interesting example of such a model, see Wallace, Klahr, & Bluff, 1987). In addition, Klahr and Wallace's computer simulations thus far has been more useful for explaining other researchers' results than for generating new findings. On the other hand, these shortcomings do not detract from the potential of self-modifying computer simulations as models of development. In addition, Klahr and Wallace's explanation of generalization in terms of the time line, regularity detection, and redundancy elimination is more precise and explicit than almost all other mechanisms of cognitive development that have been proposed. These are important virtues and may well foreshadow additional breakthroughs.

### Siegler's Theory

One of the most-profound intellectual contributions of all time is Darwin's theory of evolution. Within evolutionary theory, competition among species is a basic aspect of existence. Species originate and change through two main processes: variation and selection. Genetic combination and mutation produce *variation;* survival of offspring is the basis of *selection.* Together, these processes have produced our planet's ever-changing mosaic of living things.

My own recent work has been aimed at developing an evolutionary theory of cognitive development. As in the biological context, competition seems to be a basic feature of cognition. Rather than species competing, however, the competitions are among concepts, rules, and strategies. The main challenges for this theory are to describe the competing entities within the human cognitive system, to describe how the competition among these entities leads to adaptative outcomes, and to identify the mechanisms that produce cognitive variation and selection.

My colleagues and I have pursued this evolutionary model within a variety of areas: arithmetic, time telling, reading, spelling, problem solving, and memory tasks, among them (McGilly & Siegler, 1989; Siegler, 1986, 1988a; Siegler & Jenkins, 1989; Siegler & McGilly, 1989; Siegler & Shrager, 1984; Siegler & Taraban, 1986). In each of these areas, we have found that competition leads to adaptive consequences, and that basic strategy choice and discovery mechanisms produce the adaptation. The findings can be illustrated in a context as simple as addition of small numbers.

First consider the competing entities. Even 5-year-olds use a variety of strategies to solve basic addition problems such as 3 + 5. Sometimes they *count from one;* when they do this, they typically put up fingers on one hand to represent the first addend, put up fingers on the other hand to represent the second addend, and then count all of the fingers on both hands. Other times, they put up fingers but recognize the number of fingers that are up without counting. Yet other times, they retrieve an answer from memory. Some children also know another strategy, the *count-on strategy.* Children using this strategy choose the larger of the two addends and count-on from that point the number of times indicated by the smaller addend. For example, on 3 + 9, children might think to themselves, "9, 10, 11, 12."

It is not the case that some children use one of these strategies and some use another. Rather, almost all children use several different strategies. In addition, subtraction, multiplication, spelling, time telling, and memory for lists of numbers, the majority of children have been found to use at least three strategies. Even on individual problems, the outcomes of the competition vary, so that one strategy is chosen one day and a different one the next (Siegler, 1987a).

Children's choices among these strategies are adaptive in several different ways. One sense in which their choices are adaptive is that they use retrieval, the fastest strategy, predominantly on simple problems where it can yield accurate performance, and use other, more time-consuming and effortful strategies on more-difficult problems, where such strategies are necessary for accurate performance (Siegler, 1986).

Children also choose adaptively among strategies other than retrieval. In particular, they tend to use each strategy most often on problems where it works especially well compared to alternative approaches. In evolutionary terms, strategies find their niches. For example, the counting-on strategy is used most often on problems such as 2 + 9, where the smaller addend is quite small and the difference between addends is large. On such problems, counting-on is both easy to do and very effective relative to alternative procedures such as counting-from-one (Siegler, 1987b).

Changes over time in strategy use also are adaptive. For example, in simple addition, children move toward increasingly frequent use of the most-efficient strategies, such as retrieval and counting-on, and toward decreasing use of the least-efficient strategies, such as guessing and counting-from-one. They also acquire new strategies, such as counting-on, which depend on more-sophisticated knowledge of numbers than was available earlier.

What type of selection mechanisms could produce such adaptive strategy choices? The model that I have formulated divides the information-processing system into representations and processes. The representations include factual information and data; the processes operate on the representations to produce behavior. For example, in the context of arithmetic, the representation includes associations between problems and various possible answers to the problems. The processes are strategies such as counting-from-one, counting-on, and retrieval that can operate on the representation so as to solve problems.

Figure 3–3 illustrates how this type of organization could yield effective choices among strategies at any one time and adaptive changes in strategy use over time. Within the model, the use of strategies to solve

**FIGURE 3–3** Overview of Siegler & Shipley strategy choice model (from Siegler & Jenkins, 1989).

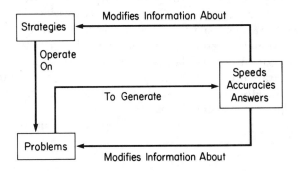

problems generates answers to the problems and also generates information about the speed and accuracy with which the problem was solved. This information feeds back to provide increasingly detailed knowledge about both the strategies and the problems. Subsequent choices among strategies are made on the basis of their past effectiveness in solving problems in general, in solving particular kinds of problems, and in solving specific problems. The more effective a strategy has been in solving problems in the past, the more often it will be chosen in the future. Further, the choices among strategies become increasingly refined as children learn that a strategy that in general is the most effective is not necessarily the most effective for a particular type of problem.

This view of development has provided the basis for computer simulations of the development of arithmetic and memory strategies (Siegler & Shipley, in preparation). To illustrate how the general theoretical assumptions are realized within a specific simulation, I will describe the simulation of the development of single-digit addition. This simulation modeled how children learn to choose among three approaches: counting-from-one, counting-on from the larger addend, and retrieval. Its working can be illustrated by considering its strategy choices on 9 + 1. The simulation gradually learns that it is easier to solve this problem by counting-on from the larger addend than by counting-from-one. It requires far fewer counts to say "9, 10" than "1, 2, 3, 4, 5, 6, 7, 8, 9, 10." This lesser amount of counting results in fewer errors and shorter solution times, which in turn leads to more-frequent future choices of the counting-on strategy. The simulation uses this experience and similar experience with other problems to draw the generalization that counting-on works better than counting-from-one on related problems, such as 9 + 2 and 8 + 1. This ability to generalize allows the simulation to make adaptive strategy choices on unfamiliar problems when they are introduced.

As children increasingly choose strategies that correctly solve problems, they also increasingly associate the correct answers with the problems. For example, they come to associate 9 + 1 with 10. This association allows them to retrieve 10 as the answer to the problem. Retrieving an answer is even faster than counting "9,10" and is just as accurate once the answer is strongly associated with the problem. Thus, the very success of the counting-on strategy in producing correct answers leads to its own obsolescence, because it makes accurate retrieval possible.

An evolutionary perspective raises the further issue of the source of strategic variation. In particular, how are new strategies acquired? Two relatively easy ways involve being taught the strategy and imitating another person using it. However, of special interest is *strategy discovery*, in which children invent strategies for themselves.

How do children discover new strategies? To find out, Siegler and

Jenkins (1989) examined 4- and 5-year-olds' discovery of the counting-on strategy. Recall that this strategy involves solving problems such as 2 + 9 by thinking, "9, 10, 11." Children in the Siegler and Jenkins experiment knew how to add by counting-from-one, but did not yet know how to do so by counting-on from the larger addend. The children practiced solving addition problems three times per week for 11 weeks. Because even young children can accurately report immediately after an addition problem how they solved the problem (Siegler, 1987b), it was possible to identify the exact trial on which each child first used the new strategy. This made it possible to examine what led up to the discovery, the quality of the discovery itself, and how children generalized the new strategy to other problems once they discovered it.

Almost all (seven of eight) of the children discovered the new strategy during the course of the experiment. The time that they took to make the discovery varied widely; the first discovery came in the second session of the study, whereas the last one did not come until the thirtieth session. The quality of the discoveries also varied widely. Some discoveries showed a great deal of insight, as exemplified by "Lauren's" protocol:

E: How much is 6 + 3?
L: (Long pause) Nine.
E: OK, how did you know that?
L: I think I said . . . I think I said . . . oops, un . . . I think he said . . . 8 was 1 and . . . um . . . I mean 7 was 1, 8 was 2, 9 was 3.
E: How did you know to do that? Why didn't you count "1, 2, 3, 4, 5, 6, 7, 8, 9"?
L: Cause then you have to count all those numbers.
E: OK, well how did you know you didn't have to count all of those numbers?
L: Why didn't . . . well I don't have to if I don't want to.

Other children did not show nearly as much understanding. In fact, some of them claimed not to have counted at all, despite audible and visible evidence on videotapes of their performance that they had used the new strategy.

What led up to discovery of the new strategy? Our expectation had been that difficult problems, or situations in which children had failed to solve previous problems, would lead to discoveries. This proved not to be the case, however. The problems on which discoveries were made, and the accuracy of performance just prior to discovery, did not differ from performance in the rest of the experiment. The only distinguishing characteristic of performance immediately before the discovery was solution times that greatly exceeded the usual amount. For example, Lauren, the child quoted above, took 67 seconds on the trial just before her discovery and 35 seconds on the trial where she first used the new strategy. Both trials were much longer than her average solution time of 11 seconds. These long times were accompanied by numerous false starts, pauses, odd statements (as in Lauren's comment referring to her own counting "I think *he* said"), and other indicators of cognitive ferment.

Another striking characteristic of the children's performance was how slowly they generalized the new strategy to other problems. For example, one girl used the new strategy on only 7 of the first 84 problems after her discovery; another girl did so on only 2 of the first 49. Temporarily, the children continued to rely heavily on the familiar counting-from-one approach, even though they knew the potentially more effective count-on strategy.

The amount of generalization increased dramatically, however, when *challenge problems* were presented. These were problems such as 24 + 2, that were easy to solve via counting-on but almost impossible by counting from 1 or retrieval. Encountering such problems seemed to increase children's awareness both of the new strategy as constituting a different approach and of the goals that the new strategy could meet. In a sense, they *re*discovered the strategy in a way that increased their understanding of how it served the goals of addition. After encountering the challenge problems, they generalized the count-on strategy much more widely than they had before, on small as well as large number problems (Figure 3–4).

What are the main limitations of this theory? One problem is that the mechanisms that produce variation have not been spelled out in the same detail as the mechanisms that produce selection. Whereas the computer simulations of strategy choice indicate in detail how choices are made

**FIGURE 3–4**  Percent use of min (counting from larger addend) strategy before and after challenge problems in Siegler & Jenkins (1989). The challenge problems, such as 24 + 2, were presented in trial block 0. Thus, percent use of the min strategy increased from roughly 20% before the challenge problems to more than 70% after them.

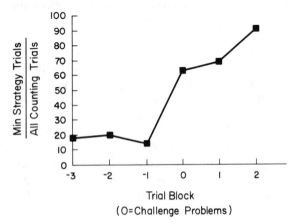

among existing strategies and how choices among the strategies change over time, no similarly detailed model exists for how new strategies are discovered. Also, the theory seems most applicable to domains in which children use clearly defined strategies; its applicability to areas in which strategies are less well defined remains to be demonstrated. Still, it would be disingenuous of me to appear pessimistic about it. The basic observation that cognitive development resembles in important ways biological evolution is beginning to emerge in many areas: perceptual development (Greenough, Black, & Wallace, 1987), language development (MacWhinney, Leinbach, Taraban, & McDonald, 1989), conceptual development (Diamond & Goldman-Rakic, 1989), analogical reasoning (Gentner, 1989), and problem solving (Holland, Holyoak, Nisbett, & Thagard, 1986), among them. If the approach proves half as useful in understanding cognitive development as it has in understanding biological evolution, the effort to apply the idea will be well worthwhile.

*Developmental mechanisms work together.* In this chapter, the contributions to cognitive development of automatization, encoding, generalization, and strategy construction have been discussed in the contexts of different theories. The separate discussions may have created an impression that the mechanisms operate in isolation, despite previous assurances to the contrary. In fact, all the mechanisms work together to contribute to the growth of children's thinking. A single development can reflect each of their contributions.

Consider a hypothetical process through which a girl might learn to attach an "ed" sound to verbs to indicate that the action occurred in the past. Early in the process of language development, all her mental resources would be needed just to perceive clearly words and phrases she heard. (Think of hearing conversation in a foreign language that you don't known or are just starting to learn.) With greater experience listening to language, her processing of the words and phrases would become automatized, freeing up cognitive capacity for other types of processing. This free capacity would allow her to notice that similar meanings were expressed by words that sometimes ended with an "ed" sound and sometimes did not (e.g., like and liked; jump and jumped). This realization, in turn, would lead her to encode the "ed" sound as a separate unit, to find out just what it meant. She then could note the regular connection between the "ed" sound being present and the action's having occurred in the past. Finally, she could construct a new strategy based on the generalization: Whenever you want to indicate that an action occurred in the past, attach an "ed" to the end of the word describing the action. By working together in this way, automatization, encoding, generalization, and strategy construction may account for many improvements in children's thinking.

## SUMMARY

Information-processing theories of development have several distinguishing characteristics. Their basic assumption is that thinking *is* information processing. They emphasize precise analysis of change mechanisms. They view development as a process of self-modification. They focus on which processes are performed, in what order, and for how much time.

Within information-processing approaches, cognition is viewed as reflecting both structure and process. Structure refers to relatively fixed aspects of the information-processing system, process to relatively variable and changeable ones. Among the most critical structural features are sensory, short-term, and long-term memory. Sensory memory is devoted to taking in a relatively large amount of unanalyzed information in the first second after the information is encountered. Short-term memory involves the information in the current situation and in long-term memory that is receiving attention at any given time. The amount of information that can receive such attention is quite limited, which makes critical appropriate deployment of the limited attentional resources. Without continual attention, information is lost from short-term memory within 15 to 30 seconds. Long-term memory involves our enduring knowledge of procedures, facts, and specific events. It appears to be of unlimited capacity, and information remains in it indefinitely.

In contrast to this relatively small number of structures, each of which influences thinking in huge numbers of situations, a much larger group of processes contributes in more delimited situations. These processes vary greatly with the particular circumstances, thus giving human cognition much of its flexibility. The same situation also elicits different processes in different people, depending on their past experience and abilities. Rules, concepts, and strategies are among the types of processes that people most often use.

Several information-processing theories of development have been formulated to make understandable how creatures as helpless and unknowledgeable as infants eventually attain the power and flexibility of the adult information-processing system. These theories have emphasized the roles of four mechanisms that seem especially important in producing cognitive development: strategy construction, automatization, generalization, and encoding.

Sternberg's theory has attempted to link information-processing ideas with earlier ideas developed in studying intelligence. He divided intelligence into three types of components: metacomponents, performance components, and knowledge acquisition components. Metacomponents function as a strategy construction mechanism, arranging the other two types of components into goal-oriented procedures. Knowledge acquisition components are used to obtain new information when no solution to a problem is immediately possible. The theory has been applied to diverse cognitive skills and to many populations, including gifted and retarded children.

Case's theory is aimed at uniting Piagetian and information-processing theories. It suggests that one major obstacle to cognitive growth is limited short-term memory capacity. By automatizing their processing, and through biological maturation and acquisition of central conceptual structures, children become able to perform increasingly difficult cognitive feats. Case's approach has proved to be of practical value as well as theoretical interest—for example, in teaching young children how to solve missing addend problems.

Klahr and Wallace's theory focuses on the developing system's capacity for drawing generalizations. In their analysis, generalization includes three more-particular processes: the time line, regularity detection, and redundancy elimination. The time line is a record of all the situations the system has encountered, the responses to the situations, and the outcomes. Regularity detection operates on the data in the time line to generalize about experience. Redundancy elimination looks for parts of procedures that could be eliminated without changing the outcome of processing. Together, these mechanisms allow children to identify regular relations and to extend the realizations to new situations.

My theory is based on an analogy between biological and cognitive evolution. In both cases, the critical contributors to change seem to be sources of variation and sources of selection. In children's thinking, strategy discovery provides one source of variation; strategy choice procedures provide a means of selection. The two types of processes work together to change not only how often children use different strategies, but also when they use each approach. Thus they provide a model of how self-modification occurs. The theory has stimulated observations of how children construct new strategies and of how use of existing strategies changes over time.

## RECOMMENDED READINGS

Case, R. (1985). *Intellectual development: A systematic reinterpretation.* New York: Academic Press. The most up-to-date presentation of Case's theory; an appealing synthesis of ideas from Piaget's and Newell and Simon's theories together with an emphasis on the role of short-term-memory limitations and automatization.

Klahr, D. (1989). *Information-processing approaches.* In R. Vasta (Ed.), *Annals of Child Development, Vol. 6.* Greenwich, CT: JAI Press. A witty and insightful description of current information-processing approaches to development. In the article, the author characterizes Piaget as "a charter member of the soft-core information processing club." Klahr also describes his own work as a founder of the club's hard-core faction.

Siegler, R. S., & Jenkins, E. (1989). *How children discover new strategies.* Hillsdale, NJ: Erlbaum. An in-depth look at the process of cognitive change, including the changes leading up to a discovery, the discovery itself, and the subsequent generalization of the strategy to new contexts.

Simon, H. A. (1981). *The sciences of the artificial.* Cambridge, MA: MIT Press. A lucid presentation of the surprising similarities that unite cognitive psychology, architecture, computer science, and other fields. Page for page, one of the most worthwhile books I have ever read.

Sternberg, R. J. (1985). *Beyond IQ: A triarchic theory of human intelligence.* New York: Cambridge University Press. The most up-to-date presentation of Sternberg's deservedly influential theory of human intelligence.

# 4

# Perceptual Development

A 4-month-old girl is shown two movies, with their screens side by side. In one movie, a woman is playing peekaboo. She repeatedly hides her face with her hands, uncovers it, and says "Hello baby, peekaboo." In the other film, a hand holds a stick and rhythmically strikes a wood block. The experimenter plays either the one sound track, with the woman saying peekaboo, or the other, with the drum beat, but not both at the same time.

Somehow, the infant knows which sound track goes with which visual sequence. She demonstrates this knowledge by looking at the screen showing the pictures that go with the sound track more than at the screen showing the other movie.

Spelke (1976) found that almost all 4-month-olds do this. Of the 24 infants she tested, 23 looked for more time at the screen with the appropriate video accompaniment than at the alternative. Their performance was not simply due to their preferring one movie; they looked at the appropriate screen regardless of which sound track was playing.

This example is representative of current findings about perceptual development in a number of ways. The children in the study were less than 6 months old. The investigator used a simple experimental procedure yet asked a fundamental question about human nature: Do people innately know how to integrate sights with sounds? The results of the study showed greater perceptual abilities in young infants than might have been expected.

The central theme of this chapter is the remarkable rapidity with which perceptual functioning reaches adultlike or near-adultlike levels. In many aspects of perception, infants reach adultlike levels of functioning by age 6 months. To put this in perspective, consider other facts about 6-month-olds. They ordinarily cannot say even one word. They do not appear to understand anything that is said to them. They can solve few problems. They do not search for playthings that suddenly disappear from view. The advanced status of 6-month-olds' perception stands in marked contrast. Indeed, given the obvious value of skilled perception for remembering, solving problems, and learning language, perceptual development may function as a launching pad from which other aspects of cognitive development take off.

*Perception and human nature.*    One reason that perceptual development is such a fascinating topic is the questions it raises about human nature. Many of these center around the nature/nurture issue: How does people's biological inheritance contribute to the way in which they perceive the world? How does their experience contribute? Above all, how do the two interact? Empiricist philosophers such as John Locke, David Hume, and Bishop Berkeley suggested that perception might be a learned skill. Infants might at first experience the world in terms of isolated lines and angles. Gradually, they would learn that these lines and angles constitute objects. Later still, they would learn to infer properties of the objects, such as how far away they were. The type of impoverished initial endowment that these philosophers envisioned led the great early psychologist William James (1890) to hypothesize that infants experienced the world as "one great blooming, buzzing, confusion."

Other theorists, such as J. J. and Eleanor Gibson, envisioned a much richer initial endowment. They noted that humans, like all animals, evolved in an environment of objects and events. To survive, younger as well as older animals needed to perceive in terms of these basic units. The Gibsons also emphasized that to be effective, perceptions need to be tied to actions. For example, animals need to perceive whether this is terrain they can walk on (solid ground) or terrain they cannot (water or a cliff). Thus, within this theory, perceptual capabilities essential for survival are built into the infant.

Subsequent research has revealed a picture much more like that posited by the Gibsons than like that of the empiricists. Even in the first months of life, infants seem to experience a world of objects and events that is in important ways similar to that experienced by adults (Granrud, 1989; Kellman, 1988). All current theories recognize that people are biologically prepared to perceive the world in certain ways, that many important perceptual capabilities are present at birth, and that others emerge in the first few months of infancy given all but the most abnormal experience.

*The task of perception.* We perceive the world through a number of sensory systems: vision, audition (hearing), gustation (taste), olfaction (smell), and a few others. Regardless of the particular sense being considered, however, the task that we face can be thought of in terms of the need to accomplish three functions: attending, identifying, and locating.

*Attending* involves determining what in a situation is worthy of detailed processing. *Identifying* involves establishing what a perceptual pattern is by relating the pattern to entries already in memory. *Locating* involves determining how far away an object is and in what direction relative to the observer. In addition to being conceptually distinct, these functions seem to trigger the most-intense activity in different parts of the brain (Squire, 1987; Ungerleider & Mishkin, 1982).

An example may make more meaningful the distinctions among the three functions. If you are in an Asian jungle and a tiger is charging, you need to orient your attention toward the tiger, to identify it as a tiger, and to locate how far away it is so that you can decide whether to climb a tree, shoot a gun, or pray. The example illustrates how attending, identifying, and locating are conceptually distinct, but also interrelated. A blur of motion in the periphery of the eye might stimulate the initial attention to the tiger. More-careful and focused attending would presumably follow identifying the moving object as a tiger. Yet-more-careful attention would follow locating the tiger as nearby and rapidly approaching.

Humans experience the world through a number of senses: seeing, hearing, smelling, tasting, touching, and so on. However, our perceptions rely most heavily on sights and sounds. Therefore, this chapter focuses on the development of vision and audition (hearing), as well as on the way in which information from these and the other senses is integrated. The chapter's organization is outlined in Table 4–1.

**TABLE 4–1   Chapter Outline**

I.  Vision
   A.  Attending to Visual Patterns
   B.  Identifying Objects and Events
   C.  Locating Objects

II.  Hearing
   A.  Attending to Sounds
   B.  Identifying Sounds
   C.  Auditory Localization

III.  Intersensory Integration
   A.  Attending
   B.  Identifying
   C.  Locating

IV.  Summary

## VISION

As recently as 1960, many psychologists, pediatricians, and nurses believed that newborn infants were functionally blind (Lamb & Campos, 1982). A very different picture has emerged recently, however. The visual capabilities of newborns are not so great as they will be even six months later, but the newborns definitely can see enough to start to learn about the world.

In order to understand visual development, it is essential to understand at least a little about the mature visual system. Visual perception ordinarily originates with light being reflected from or emitted by an object in the environment. The light impinges on the eye and progresses through the *cornea* and *pupil* to the *lens* (Figure 4–1). The lens bends the light rays to project a focused image on the light-sensitive *retina* behind it; change in the shape of the lens that brings the object into focus is known as *accommodation*.

The retina includes two kinds of *photoreceptors* (receivers of light): *rods* and *cones*. The cones are concentrated in the *fovea*, which is a small, approximately circular area near the center of the retina. In contrast, the rods are absent from the fovea; they are in the *periphery* of the eye. In normal lighting, vision is most acute in the foveal region, in large part because cones are very densely packed into it.

From the retina, information is relayed to the brain by way of the optic nerve. The *visual cortex* of the brain registers the information and integrates it with previous information to form a representation of the visual scene.

This description provides the framework within which visual development occurs. But it also leaves many questions open. For example, is the development of visual perception primarily due to changes in the eye or to changes in the brain? Does the early immaturity of the brain mean that *subcortical mechanisms* (the retina, optic nerve, etc.) initially play a larger role in perception than they will later? Is perception direct, in the sense of depending only on currently perceivable stimuli, or do previously formed memories also influence it?

Although people have long wondered about these questions, only recently has substantial progress been made in answering them. Development of experimental methods that allow infants to demonstrate their visual competence has contributed crucially to this progress. Infants cannot verbally describe how they see the world. They also cannot follow instructions, thus ruling out almost all conventional methods for studying perception.

The key to learning about infants' capacities, then, was identifying some behavior that reflected the capacities. An incredibly mundane-seeming behavior—head turning—proved to provide such a key to unlocking the previously closed perceptual world of the infant. Infants turn their heads to look at what interests them. Such behavior reflects perception, because for an object to be of interest, it must be perceived.

Recognizing that infants possess this ability led researchers to devise

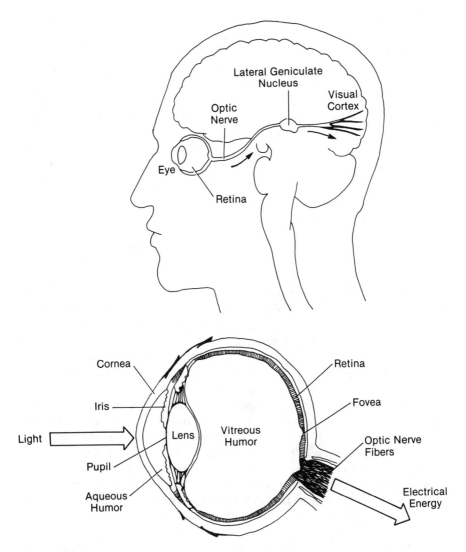

**FIGURE 4–1** Flow of information within human visual system (top), and more detailed depiction of the eye (below).

the two main methods for studying infant perception: the *preferential looking paradigm* and the *habituation paradigm.* Typically, the preferential looking paradigm involves showing infants objects or events that differ in only one way and seeing whether the infants consistently look more at one of them. If they do, they must be perceiving the difference. For example, if infants consistently look at a red ball rather than at an otherwise identical gray one, they must perceive the difference between the two colors.

The habituation paradigm is based both on infants' ability to look more at objects that interest them and on the fact that they, like older individuals, grow increasingly bored with objects as the objects are presented repeatedly. The approach includes two phases. First is the familiarization phase, in which an object is presented repeatedly. When infants no longer look at it much, a new object or sound that differs in some specific way is introduced. If infants show renewed interest in the new object or sound, they must be able to perceive the difference between the old and the new stimuli. As will be evident throughout this chapter, these simple methods have allowed researchers to make great progress in answering some of parents' and philosophers' fundamental questions concerning how infants perceive the world.

### Attending to Visual Patterns

From the day of birth, infants look at some objects and events more than others. These preferences may be crucial to development. Cognitive growth will presumably be more rapid if infants orient to informative parts of the environment rather than to uninformative ones. But how informative should informative be? Objects and events that are too far beyond infants' current knowledge of the world may be impossible for them to understand.

Cohen (1972) made an important distinction between *attention-drawing* and *attention-holding* properties of stimuli. The idea is that gross physical characteristics of objects attract initial attention, but the objects' meaningfulness determines whether the initial attention persists. Cohen suggested that the same attention-drawing properties continue to influence perception throughout life, but that attention-holding properties change greatly with age and experience. Movement grabs the attention of adults as well as infants, but infants and adults differ considerably in what they find interesting enough to continue looking at. Next we consider two influences on what commands infants' initial attention (the orienting reflex and scanning rules), and then two other factors that affect whether the interest continues (stimulus complexity and the infant's expectations).

*The orienting reflex.*   When people see a bright flash of light or hear a sudden loud noise, they orient their attention to it even before they can identify what it is. The Russian physiologist Pavlov explicitly noted that this phenomenon includes intense stimuli such as bright lights and loud noises, but is not unique to them. Rather, people orient toward any novel stimulus. The *orienting reflex*, as it has been labeled, seems to be present from the time of birth. It seems adaptive in two ways. It helps people react quickly to events that call for immediate action. It also helps us direct attention away from other objects that have been attended to for some time and that are now "old news."

Sokolov (1963) asked whether the orienting reflex was due to subcortical activities (activities in the brain below the level of the visual cortex) or to activities within the cortex itself. He hypothesized that sensory stimulation (sights or sounds) leads to signals being sent to the cortex. There, the representation formed from these signals is compared to representations of other recently-encountered stimuli. If the new representation does not match previous ones, then an orienting reflex occurs and attention is drawn to the source of the stimulation.

Subsequent research aimed at testing Sokolov's hypothesis has shown that orienting can involve cortical activity, but that it does not have to do so. This conclusion emerged from a study of an *anencephalic* infant (an infant born without a cortex) (Graham, Leavitt, Strock, & Brown, 1978). The anencephalic infant showed an orienting response when novel stimuli were presented. The infant also habituated to familiar stimuli. That is, as shown in Figure 4–2, the infant's heart rate, which initially showed a large decrement five to seven seconds after a speech sound (a typical orienting response), stopped showing this response after six exposures to the sound. Since this infant did not have a cortex, its abilities to orient and habituate demonstrate that cortical activity is not needed for these processes to occur. Subcortical mechanisms must be sufficient for both.

Especially intriguing, the pattern of orienting and habituating in Graham et al.'s 1-month-old anencephalic infant actually was precocious. It was typical of a 2-month-old intact infant. Graham et al. concluded that very early in development, cortical activity may hinder rather than facilitate orienting. Similar hypotheses of early cortical activity interfering with relatively more mature subcortical functioning appear in several contexts in this chapter.

*Rules for scanning the environment.*   Even in their first days of life, infants do not just orient to attention-grabbing objects that appear in their visual fields; they actively seek out interesting stimulation. Haith (1980) suggested that newborns possess rules for finding the interesting parts of their environments. In particular, he suggested that they use the following five rules to guide their looking:

1. If you are awake and alert, and the light is not too bright, then open your eyes.
2. If opening your eyes reveals darkness, then scan the environment intensively.
3. If opening your eyes reveals light, then scan the environment broadly.
4. If you find an edge, stop scanning broadly and continue scanning around the edge. Cross the edge and look at the other side if you can.
5. When you are scanning near an edge, reduce the range of fixations perpendicular to the edge if there are a lot of contours in the area.

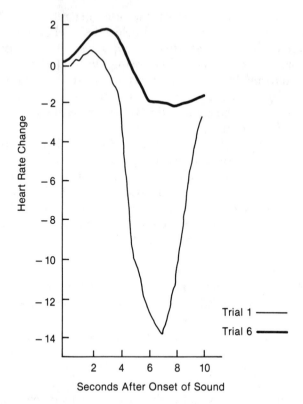

**FIGURE 4-2** Orienting response of an infant born without a cortex. The curves indicate changes in the infant's heartbeat rate after he heard someone talk. On the first trial, there was a large decrease in the infant's heartbeat rate 5 to 7 seconds after the word was pronounced. This is a typical orienting-response pattern. By the sixth trial, there was little change in heartbeat rate. Thus, the infant habituated to the sound despite not having a cortex. (Adapted from Graham, Leavitt, Strock, & Brown, 1978).

These rules help infants find certain interesting aspects of their environments, but may result in their missing others. In particular, they may give rise to infants' scanning the edges of objects to the exclusion of their interiors. Salapatek (1975) presented infants with a display in which one shape was inside another. For example, a circle might be inside a triangle. Almost all of the newborns' eye fixations fell on the outer edges of the external figure. Not until 2 months of age did infants scan the interior as well as the exterior shape. As shown in Figure 4-3, the same pattern holds for the scanning of faces. One-month-olds scan the external contours of faces, but not until 2 months do they focus on the internal details (Haith, Bergman, & Moore, 1977; Salapetek, 1975).

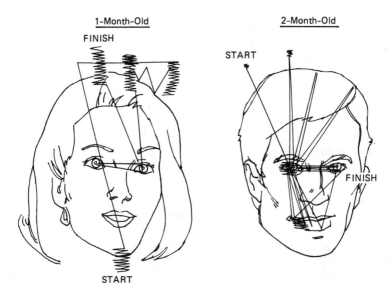

**1-Month-Old**

FINISH

START

**2-Month-Old**

START

FINISH

**FIGURE 4–3**   Visual scanning of a person's face by 1- and 2-month-olds (after Salapatek, 1975). The concentration of horizontal lines on the chin and hairline of the face on the left indicates that the 1-month-old focused on the external contours. The concentration of horizontal lines on the mouth and eye of the face on the right indicates that the 2-month-old focused on internal features.

Bronson (1974) suggested that these age-related changes in scanning patterns, as well as other changes in infants' attention, are due to the relative rate of maturation of the visual cortex of the brain and of subcortical visual structures. He noted that scanning can be controlled either by the visual cortex or by subcortical structures involved in vision, such as the retina and the lateral geniculate (page 95). He further argued that the subcortical structures are relatively more mature at birth than the visual cortex is and that they play a larger role in directing attention in the first months after birth than they do later. One effect of this early subcortical dominance is that attention-drawing properties of objects, which are especially salient subcortically, dominate the deployment of attention early on. With greater influence of the visual cortex, attention-holding properties become increasingly important later.

One source of evidence supporting this analysis is the anatomical immaturity of the visual cortex at birth. It is unclear that this part of a newborn's brain is sufficiently developed to direct choices of where to look. Another reason to think that subcortical functioning is largely responsible for directing infants' earliest looking is that infants in the first month of life behave in many ways like animals with known lesions (damaged tissues) on the visual cortex that render the cortex inoperative. A third source of evidence is that infants' scanning in the second and third months focuses increasingly on internal detail, which has greater salience for the cortical than for the subcortical mechanisms.

Bronson's theory has not gone unchallenged. The most-significant criticism is that the visual cortex may be more functional at birth than he recognized. Detailed physiological analyses have revealed that certain cells and synapses in the visual cortex are functional even before birth (Maurer & Lewis, 1979). Nonetheless, Bronson's views are consistent with a wide range of physiological and behavioral data. The trend toward increasing cortical involvement in the deployment of attention seems likely to exert a major influence on where infants look.

*Stimulus complexity.*    What qualities of objects and events hold an infant's attention beyond the initial attention-drawing occurrence? One attention-holding property appears to be a preference for situations that are neither too stimulating nor too unstimulating. Given a choice between a moderately bright object, a very dim object, and a very bright object, even 1- and 2-*day*-olds preferred the moderately bright one (Lewkowicz & Turkewitz, 1981). Even more striking, when the infants were stimulated by a loud noise just before such objects were presented, their preference shifted to the dim object. Maurer (in press) suggested that this was due to the infants' trying to modulate the total amount of incoming stimulation; the loud noise and the dim light together constituted a moderate level of incoming stimulation. In keeping with this interpretation, Maurer found that simultaneously increasing by a small amount the amount of stimulation in each of three sensory modalities (sight, sound, and touch) had the same effect on infant's attention as increasing one of them (sound) by a large amount.

Infants cannot regulate the amount of incoming information by leaving a noisy room or telling other people to be quiet. However, they do have one powerful means for coping with overstimulation; they can go to sleep. Maurer and Maurer (1988) documented a seemingly paradoxical phenomenon noted by many parents. In the first weeks of life, infants respond to increases in the amount of light and noise by sleeping *more.* Given less stimulation, they sleep less. The Maurers speculated that infants may use sleep as a primitive strategy for regulating the amount of incoming stimulation. When stimulation becomes too intense, they reduce it by falling asleep.

The preference for moderate stimulation seems related to infants' preference for looking at moderately complex objects, rather than at ones that are extremely simple or extremely complicated. Of course, the meaning of moderate complexity changes as the infant develops. Situations that seem moderately complex to a 2-month-old may seem simple to a 6-month-old. These observations have led to the formulation of the *moderate-discrepancy hypothesis:* that infants are most interested in looking at objects that are moderately discrepant from their existing capabilities and knowledge (Greenberg & O'Donnell, 1972; McCall, Kennedy, & Applebaum, 1977). Several findings seem consistent with the moderate-discrepancy hypothesis. As infants grow older, they increasingly look at more-complex stimuli. For example, in studies in which infants are shown checkerboards, 3-week-olds spend more time looking at 2-by-2 than at 8-by-8 boards; in contrast, 14-week-olds prefer the more-complex 8-by-8 checkerboards (Brennan, Ames, & Moore, 1966). The familiarity of the specific pattern also influences preferences. When initially shown 2-by-2 and 24-by-24 checkerboards, 4-month-olds initially preferred the simple 2-by-2 boards. After repeated exposure to both boards, however, the infants preferred the more-complex 24-by-24 patterns (DeLoache, Rissman, & Cohen, 1978). Again, as the children's ability to deal with complexity increased, they preferred more complexity.

Part of the appeal of the moderate-discrepancy hypothesis is that it suggests a mechanism of great potential importance for all aspects of cognitive development. If people are programmed to orient toward material that is just beyond their current understanding, they continually will be pulled toward more-sophisticated attainments. If there were 10 possible levels of understanding in an area, they would first attend to the material that could be grasped with the simplest level of understanding, then to the material that could be grasped with the next more complex understanding, and so on. They spontaneously would choose the optimal sequence of experiences for learning, and thus would effectively regulate their own development. Because it is difficult to measure infants' knowledge, however, it also is difficult to know what is moderately discrepant from it. Thus, at present, the moderate-discrepancy hypothesis has more the status of an intriguing possibility than of a scientifically validated phenomenon.

*Expectations.* At least by the time they are three months, infants form expectations about where interesting events will occur. They use these expectations to guide their looking. This was learned in a series of studies in which the location at which an interesting picture would appear varied either in a regular alternating sequence (Left-right-left-right . . .) or in an unpredictable sequence (Haith, in press; Haith, Hazan, & Goodman, 1988). Within less than one minute, 3-months-olds detected the alternating pattern and used it to anticipate where the pictures would appear next. That is, they were more likely than infants who saw the irregular sequence of locations to look left after the picture appeared on the right, and vice versa.

Three-month-olds also proved able to form expectations about more-complex patterns of events. For example, they were shown sequences in which the slide's location varied in a 2/1 pattern (LLRLLR . . .) or in a 3/1 pattern (LLLRLLLR . . .). The 3-month-olds detected these patterns and used them to guide their looking, just as they had with the alternating sequence. Interestingly, 2-month-olds gave no evidence of forming expectancies about these patterns. Thus, the expectations that infants can form seem to depend on their age and cognitive level.

What, then, can we conclude about development of visual attention during infancy? Certain events, such as loud noises, bright lights, and changes in the environment, attract the attention of newborns, just as they do with adults. Even in the absence of such events, newborns scan the environment in ways that lead them to attend to the most-important information. For example, their eyes focus on the contours of objects rather than on internal details. Infants' attention also is guided from early in life by a preference for moderate degrees of stimulation and by the expectations they form. However, what constitutes moderate stimulation, and what expectations are formed changes considerably with age and experience.

Next we turn from considering the determinants of infants' visual attention to considering how they identify the objects and actions that they see.

### Identifying Objects and Events

General ability to see objects clearly is one major determinant of infants' ability to identify objects and events. However, it is not the only one. Movement and color also contribute to the identification process. Further, people seem to be equipped to identify especially well certain important classes of objects and events, such as faces and the type of motion typical of animals (biological motion). This section focuses on how each of these factors contributes to our identification of objects and events.

*Visual acuity.* The single capability that is most crucial for identifying objects and events is the ability to discriminate them from the ongoing flux of the visual field. This ability to discriminate stimuli—to see clearly their similarities and differences—is known as *visual acuity*. Typically, the Snellen chart, which for years has hung in virtually every optometrist's office, is used to measure visual acuity. The letters you can read from 20 feet away are used as the reference point. If you can just read at 20 feet the letters that a person with "normal" vision can read at 150 feet, your vision is said to be 20/150.

Infants' visual acuity cannot be measured by asking them to read the letters on an eye chart. However, their preferences for looking at one object rather than another can yield very similar information. Almost all infants would rather look at alternating black and white stripes than at undifferentiated gray fields. By showing infants a gray field on one side and a set of stripes on the other, and examining whether the infants look more toward the stripes, researchers have been able to determine how much space between stripes (*spatial frequency*) infants need to see the difference.

Figure 4–4 illustrates the finest level of stripes that most 1-week-old infants can discriminate from a gray field at a distance of one foot (Maurer & Maurer, 1988). This is approximately 1/30 as fine a discrimination as an adult with normal vision can make. By 2 months of age, discriminations of 1/15 adult levels are possible; by 4 months, 1/8; and by 8 months, 1/4. The level of visual acuity at 8 months is about as good as that of an adult who

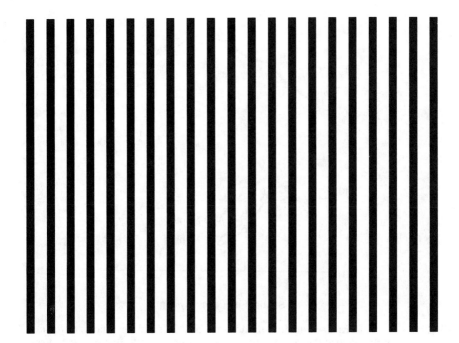

**FIGURE 4–4**  Finest stripes that 1-week-olds can discriminate from gray field (after Maurer & Maurer, 1988).

could see better if she wore glasses but would not usually bother to do so. Subsequent improvements proceed slowly, not reaching adult levels until about age 5.

Visual acuity is influenced by the amount of contrast in the pattern as well as by its spatial frequency. *Contrast* refers to the difference between the brightest part of the white space and the darkest part of the dark space. To illustrate the notion, it is easier to read a book in a brightly lit room than in a dimly lit one, because the contrast between black print and white background is greater under the brighter illumination.

Newborns require far more contrast to identify a given pattern than do older individuals. About the finest difference that they can see is that between white bond paper and a standard black and white newspaper (Maurer & Maurer, 1988).

Spatial frequency and contrast inherently work together; whenever we see a pattern, the pattern incorporates both spatial frequencies and levels of contrast. The two influences on visual acuity can be integrated into a single measure, the *contrast sensitivity function* (Banks & Salapatek, 1981). This function provides an especially revealing depiction of the development of visual acuity.

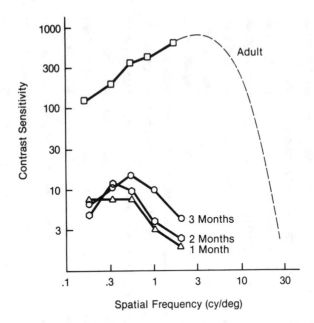

**FIGURE 4–5** Contrast sensitivity functions for an adult and for infants tested at 1, 2, and 3 months of age. (Data from Banks & Salapatek, 1978; Banks, 1982). From *Sensation and Perception,* Third Edition by E. Bruce Goldstein, Copyright © 1980, 1984, 1989 by Wadsworth, Inc. Reprinted by permission of the publisher.

Figure 4–5 shows typical contrast sensitivity functions for adults and infants. The curves indicate the sensitivity of vision at varying spatial frequencies; the less contrast that is necessary for the person to see a given spatial frequency, the higher the curve will be at that point. As can be seen in the figure, differences between infants' and adults' visual acuity are present not just in the absolute level of contrast sensitivity, but in where the greatest sensitivity is. One-month-olds' sensitivity is greatest at very low spatial frequencies. Over the first six months, development occurs not only in the absolute sensitivity in vision, but also in the shapes of the curves. With age, visual acuity becomes best at progressively higher spatial frequencies. This means that 1-month-olds are maximally sensitive to very coarse outlines; after this, optimal vision is found with increasingly detailed patterns. The 1- and 2-month-olds' relatively good acuity at low spatial frequencies allows them to see most clearly the borders of objects. As noted above, such borders provide critical information about what the infants are seeing. Older infants' and adults' increasingly good acuity at higher spatial frequencies allows them to see detail as well as borders increasingly well. What these changes mean for infants' ability to see a woman's face is illustrated in Figure 4.6.

Banks (in press; Banks & Bennett, 1988) elegantly analyzed the causes

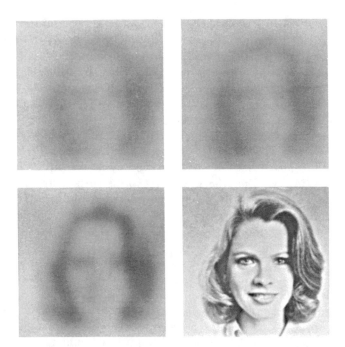

**FIGURE 4–6**   A woman's face, as it would appear from a distance of 5 feet to 1-, 2-, and 3-month-olds and adults (from Ginsburg, 1983).

of these early improvements in infants' visual acuity. His *ideal observer approach* involved determining the best vision that is possible at different points in life, given the optics and anatomy of the eye at that time. The difference between infants' actual vision and the best vision possible given the characteristics of their eyes would indicate what limitations on vision are imposed by visual mechanisms, above and beyond those imposed by the eye.

Banks' analyses indicate that for the most part, improvement in visual acuity from infancy to adulthood is due to changes in the eye rather than in the brain. Some of the changes stem from the increasing size of the pupil, which allows a larger and clearer image to appear on the retina. Additional changes are due to the efficiency with which the outer segments of the individual cones in the retina pick up light energy. A third source of change involves the density of cones in the fovea; at birth, cones are spaced fairly evenly throughout the retina, but over the next few months, the cones seem to migrate toward the fovea, resulting in a 30 times denser concentration of cones in that area, and much better vision. The overall impact of these changes is profound; adults' foveal areas absorb 350 times as much light energy as the foveal areas of newborns (Banks & Bennett, 1988). These changes in the eye seem to be responsible for many aspects of visual development.

*A clinical application of visual acuity research.* Above and beyond what they have revealed about normal development, methods developed to study visual acuity are proving useful for diagnosing infants suspected of having abnormal vision. One technique, described by Dobson (1983), involves showing infants cards divided into two halves. One half is an undifferentiated gray field; the other is a striped area with alternating black and white columns like that in Figure 4–4. When shown such cards, infants strongly prefer looking at the striped area *if their visual acuity is sufficiently good so that they do not see the striped area as just another gray field.* Presenting such cards to infants with known or suspected visual difficulties provides a means of assessing whether the infants' vision is sufficiently impaired to warrant corrective surgery. Because it does not demand any verbal skills, the procedure has proved useful with both normal and retarded infants ranging in age from 2 months upward (Teller, McDonald, Preston, Sebris, & Dobson, 1986).

Dobson (1983) described several case histories in which ophthalmologists referred to her infants with suspected visual problems. In one case, a 2-month-old boy, born four weeks prematurely, was suspected of being blind. In pediatric examinations, he seemed neither to fixate on stable objects nor to follow moving ones. Dobson's preferential looking procedure revealed that the boy's vision was well within normal limits; he consistently looked toward the striped area rather than the gray field even when this required quite good acuity. By 4 months of age, the boy also was showing everyday evidence of appropriate looking. In this case, the technique saved the boy's parents several months of unnecessary worrying, and saved the boy from being treated as a blind child.

The preferential looking technique also has proved valuable for diagnosing whether children with a variety of problems need surgery. Among these problems are cataracts, muscular weakness in the eyelids, and cross-eyedness. Even when infants have these problems, their visual acuity may still be sufficiently good that there is no need for surgery; in other cases, surgery is required. Given the inherently conflicting needs to correct many visual impairments as early as possible, while at the same time avoiding surgery that is not absolutely necessary, any technique that allows early accurate diagnosis of what an infant actually can see is welcome news to both physicians and parents.

*Motion.* From day one out of the womb, infants' attention is strongly drawn to moving objects (Kremitzer, Vaughan, Kurtzberg, & Dowling, 1979). Their ability to follow the movement, however, is limited by their imperfect control of their eyes. Typically, they fixate at the location where an object used to be for a second or two after it has moved away. Then, they jerk their eyes forward to a position roughly, but often not precisely, in line with the object's new location. Not until infants are 2 or 3 months old do their eyes follow moving objects smoothly, and then only when the movements are slow (Aslin, in press).

The attractiveness of motion exemplifies the subtle and varied ways in which our perceptual system has evolved to help us adapt to our environment. In the world in which people evolved, moving objects could represent threatening predators, enticing prey, or any number of critical events. Attending to moving objects was, and continues to be, useful for our survival.

The fact that motion attracts our attention also is useful in another way: It helps us identify objects. Intuitively, it might seem that identifying moving objects would be more difficult than identifying stationary ones. After analyzing the information available in the physical environment, however, Gibson (1966) noted that movement provides critical data about properties of objects that persist throughout the movement, such as that all parts of a single rigid object move together. Thus, infants might find it easier to perceive the unity of different parts of a single object (though not its fine details) if the object were moving.

Subsequent research has indicated that this analysis is correct. Infants' perception of objects as single entities often does appear to be based in large part on information provided by movement (Kellman & Short, 1987; Kellman & Spelke, 1983). Thus, motion not only attracts infants' attention, it also helps them know what they are seeing.

*Color vision.* Why have so many animals evolved to see the world in color? Bornstein (1978) suggested that one reason is that color vision enhances ability to identify objects and events. It does this by heightening contrasts and by increasing visibility.

Adults can perceive wavelengths of light ranging from roughly 400 to 700 nanometers (nm). They see particular wavelengths as particular colors. For example, they perceive wavelengths of 450–480 nm as clearly blue, 510–540 as clearly green, 570–590 as yellow, and 615–650 as red. Although adults see some wavelengths as mixtures (for example, 500 nm is perceived as bluish-green), they see most as unambiguously one color or another.

Anthropologists often have speculated that division of the wavelengths into colors is culturally relative; that is, people in different cultures would classify different wavelengths as different colors. For example, Ray (1953) claimed that "each culture has taken the spectral continuum and divided it upon a basis which is quite arbitrary" (p. 102). Subsequent research in infant perception and other areas has indicated that this view is false, however. Bornstein repeatedly presented 4-month-olds with a particular wavelength until they lost interest and stopped looking at it. Then he presented one of two alternative wavelengths. These alternatives were equally far from the original, now "uninteresting" wavelength in physical terms. However, at least to adults, one of the new wavelengths looked like a different color than the original wavelength, whereas the other looked like a slightly different shade of the same color. Infants looked more at the alternative that adults saw as the different color than at the one adults saw as the slightly different shade of the original, suggesting that they too saw the one wavelength as a different color. It has since been found that even 1-week-olds show such discriminations for some colors (Adams, Maurer, & Cashin, 1985). Thus, long before they learn color names, infants place the boundaries between colors at the same places that adults do. These results, together with identification of cells that respond differently to different colors (DeValois & DeValois, 1975) and observations that people all over the world classify the same wavelengths as being the best examples of particular colors (Berlin & Kaye, 1969), indicate that our biological makeup plays a critical role in the way we perceive colors.

Despite infants' clearly perceiving colors, considerably older children continue to have difficulty learning the names of the colors. This can be quite disconcerting for parents. When my oldest child remained poor at naming colors at age 3 years, I seriously entertained the possibility that he might have some strange defect that interfered with his learning of this material. Later, I learned that his difficulty was far from abnormal. Bornstein (1985) noted that children generally are remarkably slow in learning color names. Not until between 3½ and 5 years do most children know them. Before this, they often know which words can be used to label colors, but not which word goes with which color. Thus, they typically either assign color words arbitrarily to colors or use the same color word to label all colors. Nobody knows the reason for the difficulty, but the difficulty itself is both striking and venerable; Charles Darwin (1877) wondered about it in his own children (Bornstein, 1985).

*Social perception.* Attention to the faces of mothers, fathers, and other people has been hypothesized to play a unique role in early infant development. Having an infant son or daughter concentrate on your face is a gratifying experience for a parent, and having the child show that he or she recognizes you is even better. From an evolutionary perspective, these responses seem adaptive in increasing the likelihood that the parent will care for the infant.

Some researchers have argued that infants are born with a predisposition to look at faces. Others have argued that infants learn to associate faces with food and comfort and that these associations account for infants' interest in faces. Yet others have argued that infants find faces no more appealing than many other objects.

Fantz (1958, 1961) conducted some of the earliest and most important studies on face perception. In one study, he presented 6-month-olds with three patterns: a standard face, the same face but with features in scrambled positions, and a bull's-eye pattern. Fantz reported a small but consistent preference for looking at the real face rather than the scrambled one, and a strong preference for both faces over the bull's-eye pattern.

Well before this age, infants prefer looking at faces over most other objects. Until recently, however, it was unclear whether this preference was due to the infants' seeing the faces as faces or whether it was due to other properties of the faces that infants like. Faces contain many characteristics that attract infants' attention. Faces move, have curves, have high contrast, are roughly symmetrical, and make sounds. Liking for these individual features, rather than the perception that the faces are faces, could have explained infants' preferences.

A particularly clever study by Dannemiller and Stephens (1988), however, established that at least by 3 months, faces as such are special for infants. Groups of 6- and 12-week-olds saw the computer-generated stimuli depicted in Figure 4–7. Although stimuli A and B differ only in having

**FIGURE 4–7**   Stimuli presented to infants by Dannemiller and Stephens (1988). Despite *A* and *B* being identical except for the reversals of the black and white shading, *A* looks more facelike to adults and attracts more attention from 12-week-olds. The same infants had no preference between *C* and *D*, indicating that their preference for *A* was due to their perceiving its facelike quality, rather than generally preferring stimuli with dark borders and light interiors.

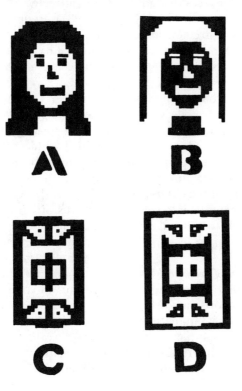

their contrast reversed, adults see Figure A as much more facelike. At 6 weeks, infants looked at the two figures equally often; by 12 weeks, however, they strongly preferred the more facelike Figure A. Thus, 12-week-olds seem to identify faces as faces and to look at them at least in part for that reason. Younger infants also like looking at faces, but their attraction may be based on details such as motion and symmetry rather than faceness as such.

*Distinctions among faces.*    In addition to liking to look at faces generally, infants have clear preferences concerning which faces they like to look at. One preference is that by age 3 months, they prefer to look at photographs of their mother's face over photographs of a female stranger (Maurer & Barrera, 1981). They recognized the differences even when the photos were matched for general characteristics, such as brightness and hair color. In addition to illustrating infants' recognition of and preference for their mothers at an early age, this result also indicates that infants have no trouble relating the two-dimensional depiction in a photograph to the three-dimensional object (the mother) being depicted.

Infants also have aesthetic preferences among faces. Quite remarkably, infants as young as 2 and 3 months prefer looking at faces that adults rate attractive over faces that adults rate unattractive (Langlois, Ruggman, Casey, Ritter, Reiser-Danner, & Jenkins, 1987). Roughly two-thirds of infants looked for a greater amount of time at photographs of attractive women than at photos of unattractive ones. The preference was present regardless of raters' judgments of the attractiveness of the infants' own mothers.

Why might infants show this preference? One possibility discussed by Langlois and her colleagues was that it might be part of a general preference for symmetry. In general, the more-attractive faces were also more symmetrical. Studies of stimuli other than faces have shown that 4-month-olds quickly recognize patterns that are vertically, horizontally, and diagonally symmetrical and prefer looking at them (Humphrey & Humphrey, 1989; Humphrey, Humphrey, Muir, & Dodwell, 1986). As with division of wavelengths into colors, judgments of attractiveness cannot be attributed entirely to cultural conventions. Innate predispositions also play a role.

*Identification of biological motion.*    Faces are not the only biologically-important stimuli that interest infants. Infants as young as 4 months also can identify the coordinated rhythmic patterns of movement characteristic of people and other animals. They look at them longer than at similar stimuli that move in other ways (Bertenthal, Proffitt, Spetner, & Thomas, 1985; Fox & McDaniel, 1982). As with the attractive faces, part of the appeal of these movements seems to be their symmetry. Infants encode symmetrical movements quickly and seem to like looking at them (Bertenthal, Proffitt, Kramer, & Spetner, 1987).

To summarize, in the first 6 months, we see both extensive initial ability to identify objects visually and extensive further development. Infants enter the world with some degree of visual acuity. They are far from blind, though their acuity also increases considerably in the first six months and beyond. Even in the first month, infants see the outlines of objects quite clearly, as well as some high-contrast interior detail. They also seem to see the same qualitatively distinct colors as adults do. Both faces and biological motion attract and hold infants' attention. This is probably due in part to their symmetry. Consistent with this view, 2- and 3-month-olds look more at faces that adults consider attractive, and that seem to be especially symmetric, than at other faces. Thus, preferences that were once thought of as purely cultural turn out to emerge so early in infancy that they very probably reflect biological predispositions as well.

In the next section we examine how infants determine where objects are relative to themselves.

### Locating Objects

Perceiving an object's location requires perceiving both its direction and its distance from oneself. When the object can be seen, perceiving its direction presents no special problem; however, determining its distance is more problematic. At any one time, the display of light on the retina only specifies height and breadth, not depth; how can a three-dimensional world be represented in a two-dimensional retinal image? Yet, as noted in Chapter 1, even 1- and 2-day-olds can solve the problem so that they perceive an object's distance from themselves (Granrud, 1989). In this section, we consider some of the *monocular cues* (cues available separately to each eye) and some of the *binocular cues* (cues available only when both eyes focus on an object) that make depth perception possible. Then, the focus turns to how infants use depth information to avoid falling from objects that are high above the adjoining surface and to how their prior memories influence their depth perception.

*Monocular cues to depth.* The cues to depth that can be perceived through one eye working alone fall into two groups: those that rely on motion, and those that are present even in stationary scenes such as pictures. First consider some cues that involve motion. As objects approach us, or we approach them, they fill an increasing portion of our visual field; this is known as *visual expansion.* Similarly, when a person moves his or her head, the retinal images of closer objects move faster than those of more distant objects; this is known as *motion parallax.* A third monocular cue based on motion is *occlusion;* when one object moves in front of another, the closer object occludes the overlapping parts of the more-distant one. Infants seem to use all of these monocular cues based on motion in the first months of life (e.g., Banks, 1980).

In contrast, not until 6 or 7 months do infants seem to infer depth on the basis of monocular depth cues that do not involve motion. These are frequently referred to as *pictorial* depth cues, since they were originally described by Leonardo da Vinci as ways of conveying distance within pictures. One such cue is *interposition,* which is like occlusion except that the objects are stationary. Another is *relative size,* in which other things being equal, objects that look larger are usually closer. A third is *texture,* in which closer objects seem to have more differentiated surfaces. A fourth is *familiar size,* in which objects that are larger relative to other objects than they usually would be (e.g., a chair bigger than a person) are interpreted as being closer. Five-month-olds do not appear to perceive depth from any of these cues, whereas each of them is effective in conveying information about depth to 7-month-olds. The reason all of these pictorial depth cues would become effective at this age, and not before, is not understood at present.

*Binocular cues to depth.*    Because people's eyes are several centimeters apart, the pattern of stimulation that impinges on the two retinas almost always differs. This retinal disparity is valuable for estimating the distance of objects from oneself. The value can be illustrated by going to an unfamiliar location, closing one eye, and trying to estimate how far away objects are. Most people estimate considerably more accurately with two eyes open than with only one.

To perceive depth on the basis of binocular cues requires (1) focusing the foveas of both eyes on the same target point, (2) fusing the two retinal images into a perception of a single object, and (3) perceiving depth based on the disparity between the two retinal images. Even 1-month-olds often focus both eyes on the same point, but not until 4 months do most infants possess *stereopsis,* the ability to perceive depth solely on the basis of binocular cues (Aslin & Dumais, 1980).

The emergence of stereopsis is quite dramatic. Individual infants consistently move within a week or two from clearly not having such binocular depth perception to clearly having it (Figure 4–8). This change seems to reflect maturation of the route by which information is carried from eye to brain. More formally, stereopsis appears to arise because of segregation of neural pathways from each eye to the brain, so that information from the two eyes arrives at different cells in the visual cortex rather than converging at the same ones. This makes it possible for the brain to detect disparities in the input from the two eyes and to infer depth based on the degree of the disparity (Held, 1985; Shimojo, Bauer, O'Connell, & Held, 1986).

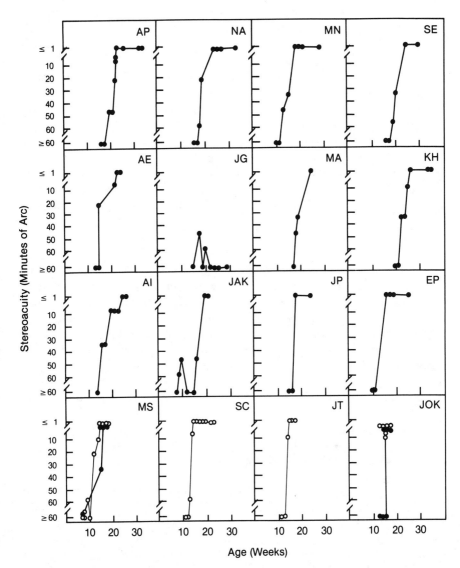

**FIGURE 4–8**  Changes in 16 infants' steroacuity between 10 and 30 weeks. Note the dramatic increases that occurred for most infants between the 15th and 20th weeks (after Shimojo, Bauer, O'Connell, & Held, 1986).

In addition to this apparently maturational effect, visual experience also plays an important role in the development of binocularly based depth perception. Banks, Aslin, and Letson (1975) tested binocular functioning in children and adults who, due to being cross-eyed, did not focus bifoveally until the condition was corrected by surgery. After surgery, all the children and adults focused both eyes on the same point in space. However, only those whose vision was corrected before age 3 years had normal binocular depth perception. The two eyes not focusing on the same point did not seem to have any detrimental effects until roughly age 4 months, the time at which bifoveal fixation ordinarily becomes the rule. The degree of harm resulting from continued binocular deprivation was found to grow until about 3 years, after which, unfortunately, surgery could not lessen the damage.

Thus, in addition to the normal developmental period for binocular depth perception, birth to 4 months, there seems to be a sensitive period within which the ability must be used if it is ever to function. This sensitive period seems to last for the first 3 years of life. The existence of such sensitive periods makes all the more valuable the development of techniques for diagnosing suspected visual abnormalities as early in infancy as possible.

*Using depth cues to avoid falling.*    Although studies of the visual cliff are among the best known of all psychology experiments, few people know what motivated their originators to conduct them in the first place. A psychologist, Richard Walk, was at Fort Benning, Georgia, watching paratrooper trainees practice jumping from a tower. The tower was 34 feet above the ground. The goal was for the trainees to learn to jump without becoming tangled in parachute strings and for them to relax before jumping. Strong straps would break their descent after 8 to 10 feet, and the device had an excellent safety record. As Walk (1979) described, however,

> The device is perfectly safe but perceptually it is like a jump off a 34-foot cliff. Strong individuals stride up the tower, walk to the open door with confidence, look down, blanch, tremble, and refuse to go farther. Others have the same physiological reactions, but they go forward; and in exiting, their knees collapse under them, and they fall out the door like limp sacks of wheat. (p. 84)

Walk and Gibson (e.g., 1961) conducted a large number of studies of a visual cliff apparatus like that shown in Figure 4–9. A chick or a kid (goat) would be placed on a board. It could move toward either of two glass surfaces. One surface had a pattern only a small distance below the glass. The other had the pattern considerably farther below. Thus, the one side looked like a small drop and the other like a cliff. Kids, chicks, and other animals consistently avoided the side that looked as if it would lead to a deep drop. Human newborns could not be tested, since they cannot move around independently. However, 6-month-olds, who can crawl, avoided the deep side just as the newborn animals had. The findings gave rise to speculation that depth perception was an inherent quality of newborn mammals.

Other observations have shed doubt on whether this interpretation

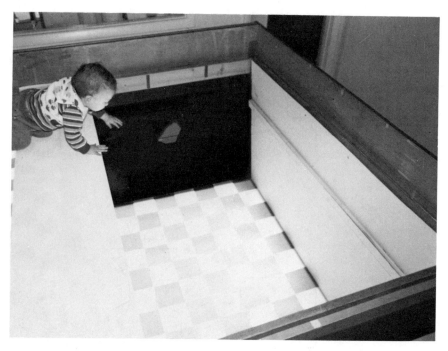

**FIGURE 4–9** An infant approaches the visual cliff (photo provided courtesy of Dr. Joseph Campos).

applies to human infants. In particular, human infants younger than 6 months, who cannot crawl but who have learned to use a walker, go to the deep side of a visual cliff without any apparent fear (Campos, Hiatt, Ramsay, Henderson, & Svejda, 1978). One possible explanation is that an innate visuomotor program that leads to the avoidance of cliffs among mammals that are born with the ability to walk does not take effect in humans until roughly 6 months of age (Rader, Bausano, & Richards, 1980). With animals that can locomote at birth, such as chicks and goats, ability to avoid sharp drop-offs is critical from day one. For human infants, the need is less urgent.

*Using memory to infer the distance of objects.* Is perception direct, in the sense that it is influenced only by currently visible stimuli? Or do memories of previous situations also contribute to it? This fundamental issue has been argued about for many years (e.g., Gibson, 1966, 1979; Hebb, 1949). Only recently, however, has definitive evidence emerged, in the form of an experiment by Granrud, Haake, and Yonas (1985).

Granrud et al. tested whether memories of the sizes of objects influ-

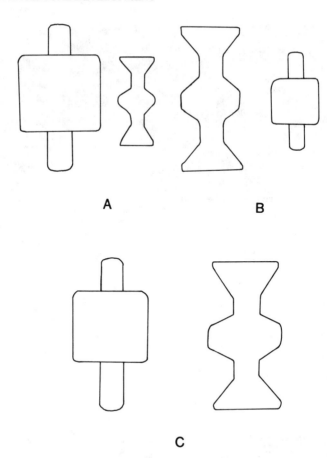

**FIGURE 4–10**    Stimuli used by Granrud, Haake, and Yonas (1985). In the habituation phase, some infants played with stimulus pair A, whereas others played with stimulus pair B. All were shown stimulus pair C in the dishabituation phase. The key prediction was that infants in both groups would usually reach for the object that previously was smaller if they used their memory of the objects' sizes to infer which one now was closer (figure provided courtesy of Dr. Carl Granrud).

enced 7-month-olds' perception of how far away the objects were. Their experiment was based on the simple observation that all else equal, infants reach for objects they perceive to be closer. The experiment included two phases. In the first, infants were given experience playing with two objects, one big and one small, so they could learn the objects' sizes (Figure 4–10). In the second, the experimenter placed two similar objects a moderate distance from the infants. The only difference between these objects and the original ones was that the smaller object had been replaced by a larger version of the same object (Figure 4–10C).

The experimental logic was that if infants' perception is influenced by memory, they should reach more often for the form that previously had been smaller. The infants' reasoning would be that if the object occupied as large an area on their retinas, it must be closer, because a smaller object would otherwise occupy a smaller area on the retina. On the other hand, if memory has no role in infants' perception, there would be no particular reason for them to reach for one object more often than the other.

In fact, the 7-month-olds more frequently reached for the object that originally had been smaller. This indicated that they used their memory of its previous smaller size to guide their perception that it must now be closer. Thus, infants can use their memories to guide their perceptions.

To summarize, infants use a variety of cues to locate how far away objects are. These include monocular cues, available to each eye working alone, and binocular cues, available only when both eyes work together. Monocular cues can be divided into motion-based and pictorial cues. Motion-based monocular cues include visual expansion, motion parallax, and occlusion. Pictorial monocular cues include interposition, relative size, texture, and familiar size. Even 1-month-olds seem to extract information about depth from the motion-based monocular cues, but not until 6 or 7 months are the pictorial cues effective.

The ability to perceive depth on the basis of binocular cues is called stereopsis. It arises quite suddenly at around 4 months of age, apparently based on maturation of the visual pathways connecting the eye and the brain. Humans, unlike many other mammals, do not shy away from cliffs from the time of birth. By the time they can locomote freely, however, they do avoid them. Infants' perception of depth seems to be influenced by inferences based on previous memories, as well as by stimuli in the immediate environment.

## HEARING

### Attending to Sounds

Even before birth, infants demonstrate surprising auditory abilities. When babies in the uterus are exposed to loud sounds, they move around more and their hearts beat faster. By 1 week of age, infants hear and respond to a wide range of sounds. When presented with loud noises, they look startled, blink their eyes rapidly if they are open or squeeze them tightly shut if they are already closed, and jerk their limbs erratically. Quieter sounds elicit less-dramatic reactions. Thus, the newborns' auditory system is functional from the first days.

One focus of research on infants' auditory perception has been on their intensity thresholds, the volume needed for them to hear that some sound is being made. Although newborns do not have as low intensity thresholds as adults, the differences are not huge. In addition, individual differences are quite marked in infant auditory perception. Some newborn infants show hearing approaching that of most adults, whereas others' hearing appears considerably less good (Acredolo & Hake, 1982).

Infants are more attentive to some sounds than to others. They appear especially attentive to speechlike sounds. Several general characteristics of their hearing predispose them in this direction. They react most noticeably to sounds in the frequency range (pitch) of 1,000 to 3,000 Hz, the range in which most speech occurs. They also react more to sounds that, like speech, include a range of frequencies, than to pure tones, in which all sound is at a single frequency.

The infants' heightened reactions to sounds in the frequency range of speech could be due either to greater ability to hear sounds of those frequencies or to greater interest in them. For many years researchers assumed that infants could hear sounds more clearly in that range. However, Schneider, Trehub, and Bull (1979) provided compelling evidence that the difference is in what sounds infants find interesting. Sounds at certain frequencies may be heard but may not elicit responses from the orienting system, just as Sokolov (1963) hypothesized that familiar visual stimuli might not.

To test this hypothesis, Schneider et al. first rewarded 6-, 12-, and 18-month-olds whenever they turned their heads in the direction of a tone. The purpose of doing this was to condition the infants to turn in the direction of any sound they could hear, even if they did not find it inherently interesting. When the infants learned to do this, the experimenter began to vary the intensity of the tones and their frequency. The goal was to determine the least-intense sound infants could hear at each frequency.

Infants of all ages proved to be at least as able to detect frequencies higher than those typical of speech as frequencies in the speech range. In addition, at the highest frequencies, the infants' auditory acuity approached that of adults. It was much poorer at lower frequencies. The results indicated that most auditory development beyond infancy occurs in the low-frequency ranges. It also indicated the need to distinguish between the sounds infants find sufficiently interesting to attend to and the sounds they can detect.

### Identifying Sounds

Infants show remarkable adultlike ability to identify and discriminate between sounds that differ only subtly. Many of the most impressive demonstrations of this ability concern speech perception. However, infants' ability to identify and discriminate among other sounds, such as musical tones, also is keen.

*Speech.*   First consider speech perception. Two-month-olds discriminate between such similar sounds as *ba* and *pa*, *ma* and *na*, and *s* and *z*. Their perception of the differences between these sounds seems to be categorical, just as their perception of the differences between colors is.

Eimas, Siqueland, Jusczyk, and Vigorito (1971) first demonstrated categorical speech perception. They noted that one of the dimensions along which speech sounds differ is voice onset time (VOT). To make some sounds, such as *ba*, people begin to vibrate their vocal cords almost as soon as they start making the sound. *Ba* thus has a short VOT, since the onset of voicing (vibration of the vocal cords) begins early in the sound. In making other sounds, such as *pa*, people do not begin vibrating their vocal cords until a longer time after the onset of the sound. *Pa* thus has a longer VOT. Despite the physical dimension underlying this difference (amount of time before vibration of the vocal cords begins) being continuous, adults hear sounds with VOTs less than a certain value as qualitatively distinct from sounds with VOTs greater than that level. A sound is either a *ba* or a *pa*, never something in between.

In the first experiment to demonstrate categorical perception in infants, Eimas et al. habituated infants as young as 1 month with a sound that adults perceive as being a *pa*. Then the infants were presented one of two sounds identical to the intial one except in their VOTs. The VOTs of the two new sounds were equally distant from that of the original sound to which the infants had habituated. However, one of these sounds was perceived by adults also to be a *pa*, whereas the other was perceived as a *ba*. If infants perceived the sounds categorically, they too would dishabituate more dramatically to the sound that adults heard as a *ba*. On the other hand, if they responded to the absolute difference in VOT between the old and new sounds, they would dishabituate equally to the two new sounds.

Apparently the infants heard the sounds as qualitatively distinct. They dishabituated to a greater extent to the *ba* than to the *pa*, despite the equal physical distance between the original and the two new stimuli. The finding is not unique to these two sounds. Infants have shown similar abilities to discriminate syllables on the basis of the role of the lips (*ba* versus *ga*), tongue height and placement (*a* versus *i*), and numerous other features of speech (Morse, 1972; Trehub, 1973). They also are sensitive to features that occur over a more extended chain of speech, such as rising or falling intonation and accenting of particular syllables (Aslin, Pisoni, & Jusczyk, 1983; Morse, 1972).

Might these discriminations be due to the particular language infants hear around them? A study with Guatemalan infants between 4 and 6 months suggests a negative answer. The Guatemalan infants were of interest because the Spanish they heard placed the VOT boundary between *ba* and *pa* at a different place than English and most other languages. In spite of this linguistic experience, the infants dishabituated in a way that indicated that they placed the VOT boundary between *ba* and *pa* where most languages do (Lasky, Syrdal-Lasky, & Klein, 1975). Thus, infants may enter the world with sensitivities attuned to particular boundaries.

These predispositions do not persist forever. Although infants are sensitive to many contrasts not used in the languages they hear, they later lose sensitivity to these features. Werker, Gilbert, Humphrey, and Tees (1981) demonstrated this phenomenon with English- and Hindi-speaking adults and 7-month-olds brought up in North America. The task was one in which two sounds differed only on a contrast that differentiates words in Hindi but not in English. After repeatedly presenting one sound, the experimenter abruptly switched to the other. To get a reward, subjects needed to turn their head to one side when the sound changed. Among the infants, 11 of 12 accurately perceived the change, as did all of the Hindi-speaking adults. However, only 1 of 10 English-speaking adults accurately perceived it. As the authors concluded, "There may be a decrease in speech perceptual abilities with either age or linguistic experience" (p. 354).

More recently, Werker (1986) linked the beginning of the decline to the beginning of speech. That is, as babies begin to speak in their native language, they begin to lose the ability to hear distinctions not used in the language. The decline continues for the next 8 to 10 years, at which time the perceptual ability has sunk to adult levels. Young children's greater ability to hear subtle distinctions that do not appear in their own native language seems likely to explain their greater facility in acquiring proper accents in new languages.

Speech perception involves more than the ability to discriminate among sounds. It also includes identifying the voices of different speakers. Infants as young as 3 days old not only seem able to identify their mothers' voices, but seem to prefer them. DeCasper and Fifer (1980) devised a situation in which an infant's sucking was followed either by presentation of the mother's voice or by the voice of a female stranger. They found that the 3-day-olds sucked at a higher rate when the reward was their own mother's voice.

In DeCasper and Fifer's experiment, none of the infants had spent more than 12 postnatal hours with its mother. Although this experience may explain the preference for the mother's voice, another possibility is that the preference was based on familiarity with the voice obtained before birth. Evidence supporting this possibility was found in a study in which expectant mothers were asked to recite a story a number of times over a several-week period prior to birth. After the babies were born, an experimenter played a tape recording of the mother reading that story or an unfamiliar one. The babies sucked at a higher rate in response to the familar story (Spence & DeCasper, 1982).

When adults talk to infants and young children, they often speak in a style known as *motherese*. This style is characterized by high pitch and exaggerated intonations. In a study of German mothers, Stern, Spieker, and MacKain (1982) found that 77 percent of the mothers' utterances to infants between birth and 6 months of age fell into the motherese category. Subsequent studies have shown that most men as well as women talk to infants in this way (Papousek, Papousek, & Bornstein, 1985).

Adults have good reason to use motherese in talking to infants. Infants as young as 4 months turn more toward statements in motherese than toward ones in standard intonations; thus, they seem to prefer the motherese (Fernald, 1985). Even younger infants have been shown to discriminate speech sounds in motherese more effectively (Korzan, 1985). The slower cadence and more-marked intonations of motherese thus both attract infants' attention and help them understand what they are hearing.

In sum, infants are able to discriminate speech sounds, voices, and intonation patterns from each other. They also have clear preferences concerning which voices, material, and intonations they wish to hear.

*Music.* Infants perceive the distinctions between some types of musical sounds categorically, just as they perceive colors and speech sounds. In listening to the types of sounds made on a violin, adults perceive some as plucks and others as bows. The differences between plucks and bows can be reduced to a single physical dimension known as *rise time.* Two-month-olds discriminate between plucks and bows, but not between stimuli equally discrepant in rise time that adults hear as two types of plucks or two types of bows (Jusczyk, Rosner, Cutting, Foard, & Smith, 1977).

Although both speech and musical sounds are processed categorically, it appears that different parts of the brain predominate in processing them. The left hemisphere of the brain predominates in speech perception, whereas the right hemisphere dominates in perception of complex nonspeech sounds such as music. This pattern of hemispheric dominance has been discovered by studying *auditory evoked responses.* The experimenter places electrodes at specific points on the left and right sides of the head, presents a stimulus simultaneously to the two ears, and records the amount of electrical activity on each side of the brain. When the stimulus involves speech, the left hemisphere shows greater brain activity—that is, a greater auditory evoked response. When the stimulus involves music, the pattern is reversed, with the right hemisphere showing greater activity.

Some *lateralization*—that is, specialization of different parts of the brain for processing different types of stimuli—may be present even before most babies are born. Newborns born four to six weeks prematurely show greater left-hemisphere responding to speech sounds, just as adults do (Molfese & Molfese, 1979). By age 2 months, infants show both differential hemispheric processing and some amount of memory for musical sounds. In one experiment (Best, Hoffman, & Glanville, 1982), infants heard a musical note or a speech sound presented to both ears until they had habituated to it. On the tenth trial, the alternative type of stimulus was presented to one of the ears. The 2-month-olds dishabituated to the musical sound to a greater extent when it was presented to the left ear, which transfers information to the right hemisphere of the brain. The finding demonstrated early specialization of the right hemisphere for processing complex nonspeech sounds such as musical tones and also sufficient memory for both the speech sounds and the tones so that infants could recognize new stimuli as different. Thus, the beginnings of lateralization may be among the reasons that very young infants can identify both speech and musical sounds.

### Auditory Localization

After his daughter was born, an unusually single-minded psychologist named Wertheimer entered the delivery room. Rather than simply admiring the child, Wertheimer brought a clicker and sounded it first on one side of the room and then on the other. From the first sounding of the clicker, the baby turned her head in the direction of the sound. Thus, at least a crude sense of *auditory localization* (the ability to locate sounds in space) seems to exist from birth (Wertheimer, 1961).

Surprisingly, newborns seem better able to localize sounds than 2- and 3-month-olds, though not better than 4-month-olds. This pattern of data, which appears in a number of contexts throughout the book, has been labeled a *U-shaped curve*. At first, performance is at a high level, then it drops, then it returns to a high level. The U-shaped pattern is of special interest because it often indicates that different mechanisms are responsible for the same behavior at different points in development. This seems to be the case in auditory localization.

Muir, Abraham, Forbes, and Harris (1979) conducted a longitudinal study in which they repeatedly examined four infants over the first four months of the infants' lives. They found that three of them showed a U-shaped pattern of auditory localization. As shown in Figure 4–11, the infants first showed high levels of head turning toward the side from which the sound came, then showed reduced levels, and then, by about 4 months, returned to the prior high levels. The decline in the middle was not due to lack of interest in the sounds. Even when an infant's mother or father called the child's name in the middle of a group of rattling sounds, the pattern of head turning did not change.

Muir et al. proposed an explanation much like what Bronson (1974) proposed for infants' visual behavior. They suggested that auditory localization in the first month after birth reflects subcortical functioning. In the second and third months, cortical activity increases and it replaces subcortical activity as the dominant influence on infant's auditory localization. However, at this point, the cortical activity is not sufficiently developed to

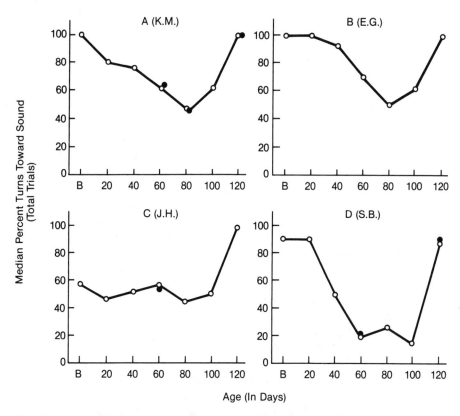

**FIGURE 4–11**  Percentage of trials on which four infants turned toward sounds. Infants were tested every 20 days from birth to 120 days (from Muir, Abraham, Forbes, & Harris, 1979).

produce accurate localization. Only in the fourth month does the cortical activity become sufficiently developed to reinstate accurate localization.

To summarize, infants enter the world with substantial auditory capabilities, and the capabilities develop further in the first few months. The capabilities are evident in which sounds attract infants' attention, in their ability to identify sounds, and in their ability to localize where sounds originate. Sounds with frequencies and other characteristics that resemble speech are especially likely to attract infants' attention. This seems to be due more to the sounds' interesting them than to the sounds' being especially easy for them to detect. When identifying either speech or musical tones, infants, like adults, appear to process the sounds categorically. Also like adults, the infants' left hemispheres seem to be most involved in processing speech sounds, and the right hemispheres in processing musical tones. The ability to localize sounds shows a U-shaped pattern between birth and 4 months. It is best at the two extremes, and is less good in between. A plausible explanation is that subcortical mechanisms produce the early high level of skill, whereas cortical mechanisms produce similarly good localization beyond age 4 months.

## INTERSENSORY INTEGRATION

How do infants integrate the information they receive from different sensory systems into a single coherent experience? One plausible developmental path would be that they first develop each system separately and then, when each has reached some level of competence, integrate the separate sources. Piaget (1971) proposed just such a theory. Recent investigations of infants' intersensory integration suggest a quite different picture, however. It now appears that sights and sounds are integrated from birth.

Demonstrations of intersensory integration have been presented under other headings throughout this chapter. These studies have shown that intersensory integration influences all three of the functions that have been examined: attending, identifying, and locating.

Sokolov's (1963) discussion of the orienting reflex exemplifies how intersensory integration influences infants' attention. One of Sokolov's observations was that a loud noise causes infants to attend to the source of the sound. The way Sokolov knew that the infants were attending to the source of the sound was that they looked at it. That is, they used auditory information to guide visual attention.

Both sights and sounds are also used to identify objects and events. Recall Spelke's (1976) study in which 4-month-olds looked more often at the movie whose visual images were in keeping with the sounds they were hearing (the mother playing peek-a-boo or the drum beat). If the infants were not trying to integrate visual and auditory information to understand the events, they would have had no reason to act in this way.

The Sokolov observation just cited also provides evidence for coordination of vision and audition in locating objects. In fact, all the studies of auditory localization that were discussed used head turns toward the source of the sound as the primary measure of localization. Head turning would not be a useful measure if infants did not look toward the sources of sounds.

Many additional findings about how infants use information from different senses to attend, identify, and locate have also been obtained.

### Attending

Newborns seem to follow rules concerning where to look when they hear sounds (Mendelson & Haith, 1976). One such rule is that when you hear a sound, and you are looking somewhere else, look toward the source of the sound. Another rule concerned what to do when you already are looking at the apparent source of a sound. Under this condition, you should center attention closely on that source and shorten the length of your eye movements. The rules seem likely to promote attention to animate objects, such as people and other animals, since most animals make noise. Consistent with this view, when 5- to 7-year-olds hear a voice, they increase their scanning of a face in front of them, particularly the eyes (Haith, Bergman, & Moore, 1977).

### Identifying

Spelke's earlier-described experiment demonstrated that 4-month-olds integrated auditory and visual information in identifying the events in the movie. More recently, she and a co-worker demonstrated that 4-month-olds also integrate tactile (touch) and visual information in identifying objects (Streri & Spelke, 1988). The infants first explored with their hands one of two objects: two rings connected by a rigid stick, or the same type of rings connected by a flexible band. A thick cloth was placed so as to prevent the infants from seeing the object that their hands were exploring. After the infants habituated to the object, they were shown either the rigidly or the loosely connected rings.

The 4-month-olds looked more at the object they had not seen previously. The demonstration was especially interesting because during the manual-exploration phase, most infants had not touched the connection; they only touched the rings. Thus, their visual identification of the object seemed to be based on an inference from the type of motion of the rings that their manual exploration had produced earlier.

### Locating

To get objects, infants must first locate them. Even newborns appear to use visual information about locations to guide their reaching. Von Hofsten (1982) presented newborns with appealing objects that slowly moved back and forth in front of them. The infants moved their hands toward the objects in all three dimensions. On their best-aimed movements, their hands slowed down as they approached the objects, just as older children's and adults' would. This coordination could not be a learned response, since the newborns would have had no experience with grasping and actively manipulating objects.

A surprising finding of von Hofsten's research is that infants reach skillfully for moving objects as soon as they are able to reach accurately for stationary ones. That is, they reached toward where the moving object would be by the time their hand intersected its path, rather than reaching toward its position at the moment when they started reaching. The degree of coordination between vision and reaching improves slowly over a pro-longed period of infancy and childhood, but the basic coordination seems to be present from early infancy.

*Sonar aids for blind children.*    Earlier we discussed how research on visual acuity had proved useful for diagnosing infants suspected of having defective vision. The recent development of sonar aids for blind children indicates that knowledge of perceptual development may be useful for devising innovative treatments as well as diagnostic procedures. These so-nar aids can be viewed as a kind of intersensory compensation, since they allow blind children to use their hearing to locate obstacles in their paths and thus allow them to move around freely in their environments.

A scientist from New Zealand, Leslie Kay, invented the sonar aid in the early 1960s. The device provides people with the same types of informa-tion used by dolphins and bats to locate objects in their environments. It sends out and receives back ultrasonic waves, and then transduces the reflected waves to frequencies that people can hear through earphones. The earphones are lightweight and comfortable. (Figure 4–12).

The sonar aid works by providing information about the distances, directions, and textures of objects. The frequency of the signal indicates the distance of the object. The closer the blind child comes to an object, the lower the tone that is reflected. The child can adjust the absolute frequen-cies depending on the type of distances of interest in a particular situation. If a girl wanted information about objects that were close by, as she might if playing indoors, the range could be set so that objects six feet away would make the highest sounds and closer objects proportionally lower sounds. If the girl were going to play with friends outside, she might set the sonar aid so that objects 20 feet away made the highest sounds.

**FIGURE 4–12**    A blind child wearing a sonic guide reaches for an object (photo provided courtesy of Dr. G. Keith Humphrey).

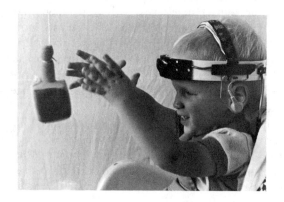

The direction of objects is indicated by relative volumes in the two ears. An object on the right side produces a louder signal to the right ear than to the left. The degree of the discrepancy indicates just how far from the forward position the object is.

Information about an object's texture is provided by the purity of the tone. The waves reflected from smooth surfaces such as glass and metal approach pure tones. Rougher surfaces, such as bushes and trees, reflect more-complex tones. In addition, a rough surface will give rise to characteristic patterns that can help in identifying the object.

If sonar aids can provide useful information to blind people, what is the optimal age for children to begin to wear them? To answer this question, some information about the typical development of blind individuals is essential. Much of the developmental course is like that of sighted children, including the ages at which children raise their heads and chests, sit, roll over, and stand. Walking, however, is considerably slower to develop in blind children. Fraiberg (1977) suggested that the sight of attractive objects provides a "lure" for walking, and that the absence of this lure among blind children was responsible for the delay. She also suggested that until blind children reach for objects that they hear making sounds, they do not learn to walk, and that the desire to make contact with objects that make sounds is a crucial motivator of walking in blind children. By this logic, the sonar aid's assignments of sounds to ordinarily silent objects might motivate blind children to begin walking earlier. The argument suggests that the sonar aid might best be introduced at the time when children begin walking or shortly before, that is, at about 9 to 15 months.

Aitken and Bower (1982) examined four blind children in an effort to determine the optimal age for starting them with the sonar aid. The children began to wear the aid at 6, 8, 13, and 14 months. The youngest infant developed at an unusually rapid rate for a blind person. She began reaching for objects with both hands at 7 months and began walking independently at 16 months. The infant who started using the device at age 8 months also developed fairly rapidly. At 8 months, he began reaching for objects with both hands; at 15 months, he used the aid to avoid objects when he was walking in a walker; and at 20 months, he walked independently. The two older infants, however, did not learn to use the aid effectively. This led the investigators to hypothesize that children must begin wearing the aid early for it be helpful.

However, Humphrey and Humphrey (1985) found that older children also can learn to use the sonar aid effectively. The two children they studied began using the device at 19 and 31 months respectively. The 31-month-old, Eddy, made especially impressive progress with the aid. When the aid was on, Eddy's exploration of a new environment was described as "smilingly confident." He both avoided obstacles and skillfully sought objects to climb on. When the aid was removed, Eddy's steps became "slower, smaller, and more hesitant." He became unwilling to explore further following repeated collisions with chairs and tables.

After several years of experience with the aid, Eddy most often wears it to explore new surroundings, such as a house he has not visited before. He rarely wears it in familiar locales (Humphrey, Dodwell, Muir, & Humphrey, 1988). Thus, he seems to use it to build an initial mental map of the new environment, but then discards it when he possesses such a map (presumably so he can hear other sounds from the surrounding world).

Perhaps the most eloquent testimony for the value of the sonar aid comes from an individual introduced to the device as an adult.

> In the first few months the Sonicguide functions primarily as an obstacle detector. Slowly but surely one starts putting things together and over a period of time begins using it as an environmental sensor. I can't tell you enough how gratifying it is to be able to recognize the sound of a tree, a person, a picket fence, etc. With the guide there is information which may help in not only mobility, but in providing a sense of what's "going on in the world around me."
>
> After using the Sonicguide 5–10 hours a week for the past three years, I am at the point that I react very naturally to its signals. I no longer have to think about what each signal could mean, rather I react instinctively. I go around someone on the sidewalk without even realizing I've done it: that's how much a part of you it becomes. (Lepofsky, 1980)

*A chronological summary.*   We have considered infants' perceptual development from the perspective of how each sensory system develops. Also considering what perceptual capacities infants possess at different ages in the first year may convey a larger picture of development in this period. Table 4–2 lists a number of the perceptual capabilities that we can be confident infants have developed by the ages listed. The estimates are deliberately conservative; infants may well possess some of these abilities earlier than is apparent in the table.

This table reveals an interesting pattern: Hearing seems to develop considerably more rapidly than vision or intersensory integration. All the basic developments in hearing that are listed are achieved by age 3 months. This is not the whole story, of course. Infants' hearing is still improving quantitatively. For example, they are becoming able to hear softer sounds, especially in the lower frequencies. They also will later lose the ability to perceive some speech contrasts as their hearing becomes increasingly attuned to their own language. And it also is possible that further research on infants' hearing will reveal some auditory abilities they do not possess at all until after they are 3 months old, or that further research will reveal that all the visual and intersensory capabilities also develop by equally young ages. For the present, though, it is striking just how advanced hearing is in early

**TABLE 4-2  Perceptual Abilities Infants Clearly Have at Different Ages**

| AGE | CAPABILITY | | |
| | VISION | HEARING | INTERSENSORY INTEGRATION |
|---|---|---|---|
| Birth | Orienting reflex. Looking rules. Color vision. Size constancy. Scan external contours of objects. | Orienting reflex. Almost adultlike volume thresholds in medium- and high-frequency ranges. Prefer mother's voice. | Look toward source of sounds. Looking rules for responding to sounds. Visually guided reaching. |
| 1 month | Motion-based monocular depth cues. | Categorical speech perception. | Sounds intensify visual scanning. |
| 2 months | Scan interiors of objects. | Categorical perception of musical sounds. | |
| 3 months | Form expectations. Eyes smoothly follow moving objects. Prefer mother's face. | | |
| 4 months | Prefer organized "biological" motion patterns. Binocular depth perception (stereopsis). | | Integrate sights and sounds with similar rhythms. Integrate visual and tactile information. |
| 5 months | Avoid visual cliffs. | | |
| 6 months | Pictorial depth cues are effective: interposition, relative size, etc. | | |
| 7 months | Use memory to infer distance. | | Blind infants benefit from sonar aids. |

infancy. The level of development seems even more impressive when we realize that we are viewing it against the backdrop of all these other extraordinarily early-developing capabilities.


## SUMMARY

Perceptual functioning reaches adultlike or near-adultlike levels remarkably rapidly. Even newborns see, hear, and integrate information from different sensory systems. These abilities develop considerably further in the next 6 months. This enables infants to attend to, identify, and locate objects and events quite effectively.

The properties that draw infants' visual attention differ from those that hold it. In general, the properties that draw attention remain the same throughout life. For example, the orienting reflex leads newborns as well as adults to attend to loud noises and bright lights, as well as to unfamiliar objects. Newborns as well as adults also respond to light, darkness, edges, and contours with characteristic scanning patterns that can be described as looking rules. Attention-holding properties, on the other hand, change greatly with age and experience. Although the visual attention of both infants and adults is held by moderate degrees of stimulation, what constitutes moderate stimulation changes greatly over the course of development. Similarly, although expectations seem to guide attention at all ages, the expectations that can be formed change greatly.

A number of abilities related to visual identification of objects and events show marked growth in the first six months. Visual acuity improves from roughly 20/500 to 20/100. The improvement is especially marked at moderate spatial frequencies. The anatomical immaturity of the eye during the first months after birth seems responsible for many properties of vision in this period, such as preferences for scanning contours rather than interiors and for looking at checkerboards with large checks. In addition to their general capabilities for identifying objects, infants also have clear preferences for looking at certain objects rather than others. Among these preferred objects are human faces, particularly attractive ones and especially one's own mother, and objects that move.

Locating objects demands being able to identify how far away and in what direction the objects are. Infants locate the distance of objects from themselves by using both monocular cues (cues available to each eye even if the other is closed) and binocular cues (cues to depth based on the difference in images on the two retinas when both eyes are used). Monocular depth cues based on motion are effective quite early, whereas the pictorial monocular cues are not effective before 6 or 7 months. Binocular depth perception (stereopsis) emerges quite suddenly at about age 4 months, apparently due to maturation of the visual pathways connecting the eye and the brain. In addition to infants' being able to perceive the depth of objects from cues in the immediate display, they can also use their memories of the true size of objects to infer how far away the objects must be.

The levels of auditory perception shown by young infants are at least ✓ as impressive as their achievements in visual perception. Infants are especially attentive to speechlike sounds. This appears to be due to their being interested in the speechlike sounds, rather than to their being able to detect them more easily than other sounds.

Infants' identification of both speech and musical tones is categorical, much like their color perception. The categorical perception is not due to the particular language infants hear; infants may set categorical boundaries at points different from those that appear in their native language. In addition to being able to discriminate between specific sounds, newborns also are able to identify more-general speech characteristics. For example, they can discriminate their mothers' voices from those of other women. They also show a preference for motherese, a form of speech characterized by high-pitched sounds and exaggerated intonations.

Auditory localization shows a U-shaped function. At birth and after 4 months of age, localization is quite accurate. During the interim, the ability is less acute. The pattern, like infants' pattern of visual attention, may reflect a shift from subcortical to cortical dominance.

Intersensory integration seems to be present from the earliest days. Vision, audition, and reaching are used together to attend to, identify, and locate objects and events.

Perceptual development research also has yielded practically-important discoveries for diagnosing and treating infants. Research on visual acuity has led to techniques for diagnosing whether infants with suspected visual abnormalities can see well enough to avoid corrective surgery. On the treatment side, sonar aids show great potential for helping blind children navigate around their environments. These devices substitute sounds for the sights that blind people cannot experience. The sonar aids provide information about the distance of the objects, their direction, and the type of object involved. Some researchers have hypothesized that the aids should be introduced during the first year, but they seem to be effective even when introduced considerably later.

## RECOMMENDED READINGS

**Banks, M. S. (In press). How optical and receptor immaturities limit the vision of human neonates. In C. E. Granrud (Ed.), *Visual perception and cognition in infancy*. Hillsdale, NJ: Erlbaum.** An elegant and persuasive analysis of the physical limits of infant visual perception; probably the most sophisticated analysis of infant perception performed to date.

Granrud, C. E., Haake, R. J., & Yonas, A. (1985). **Infants' sensitivity to familiar size: The effect of memory on spatial perception.** *Perception and Psychophysics, 37,* 459–466. Provocative demonstration of infants' ability to integrate knowledge about the sizes of objects to perceive how far away they are.

Haith, M. M. (1980). *Rules that babies look by.* **Hillsdale, NJ: Erlbaum.** This book presents an appealing description of how infants choose where to look, and how their visual scanning patterns change.

Humphrey, G. K., Dodwell, P. C., Muir, D. W., & Humphrey, D. E. (1988). **Can blind infants and children use sonar sensory aids?** *Canadian Journal of Psychology, 42,* 94–119. Heartening description of blind children's use of sonar aids to maneuver around their environments.

Maurer, D., & Maurer, C. (1988). *The world of the newborn.* **New York: Basic Books.** This book won the American Psychological Association book award for 1988. The award was well deserved, because the book is both readable and informative in describing how newborns see, hear, feel, and think.

# 5

# *Language Development*

Where you going
I'm going
Shoe fixed
Talk to mommy
Shoe fixed
See Antho
Anthony
Good night
See morrow morning. (Weir, 1962)

The preceding monologue was obtained from a tape recording of a 2½-year-old talking in his crib before going to sleep. The child's statements exemplify several key properties of language development. First, they communicate meaning. It is easy to understand most of what is being said, even though the phrases are not the ones that older individuals would choose. Second, the statements are cryptic. When children first learn to speak, they include only the essentials. They omit many of the articles, prepositions, adverbs, and adjectives that lend precision, color, and grammatical structure to the language of older individuals. Third, the language is internally motivated. No one else was in the room during Anthony's monologue; thus, there was no hope of reinforcement or even response to his speech. Nonetheless, he found talking sufficiently interesting that he spoke anyway.

Children's acquisition of language raises fundamental questions. Perhaps the most basic question parallels one alluded to in the previous chapter on perceptual development: How do children make sense of the "blooming, buzzing, confusion" of speech sounds? Simply hearing clearly what is said is quite demanding; no computer program yet devised can do it very well. Comprehending other people's statements requires additional abilities: understanding not only the meanings expressed directly but also unspoken implications. Speaking correctly requires yet further abilities: enunciating the individual sounds, ordering words within sentences, and organizing sentences in ways that communicate coherent thoughts.

In response to these demands, children engage in a variety of mental activities that enable them to comprehend and produce speech. Their well-developed auditory perception system, described in the previous chapter, allows them to hear clearly what other people say. This accurate perception of other people's speech, and their ability to imitate, helps them learn to pronounce words correctly. They pay attention to and remember the order of words that they hear in particular phrases, while also searching for generally applicable grammatical rules.

Above all, they attend to meanings, both the meanings they wish to convey and the meanings other people are trying to get across. Emphasizing meanings is an intelligent approach to language acquisition. Language is a tool for adapting to the social world. Sentences that express intended meanings will further that adaptation, even given serious shortcomings in pronunciation and grammar. Sentences that do not express intended meanings will not be adaptive, even if grammar and pronunciation are perfect.

Given language's complexity, how do children learn it so rapidly? As with perceptual development, young children's production of language, and especially their comprehension of it, seem far more advanced than many of their other cognitive capabilities. This might mean that children are born with a special ability to learn language, above and beyond more-general learning abilities. Alternatively, given children's massive exposure to language, perhaps they could learn almost any skill by age 5 if they were given comparably intense experience.

The question boils down to which *mechanisms* enable children to learn language. Are the mechanisms especially designed for language learning, or are they the same mechanisms that lead to other types of learning?

The issue of language-specific versus general learning mechanisms was at the heart of a famous argument between two giants of modern intellectual life: B. F. Skinner and Noam Chomsky. Chomsky's (1959) review of Skinner's (1957) book *Verbal Behavior* sparked the debate. The core of the argument concerned how children learn grammar. Skinner argued that children learn grammar in the same way they learn everything else:

through modeling and reinforcement. In his view, they start the learning process by imitating sentences of adults and older children. If a young child's statements are comprehensible, parents do what the child wants, thus reinforcing the statements. If the child's statements are inaccurate or incomprehensible, the parent does not do what the child wants, thus not reinforcing them. Skinner also presumed that parents shape their children's language by correcting the grammatical form of understandable but ungrammatical statements, so that children learn the desired form.

Chomsky strongly contested this view. He based his case on the indisputable fact that even 3-year-olds create thousands of statements that they never have heard anyone else say. Illustratively, I once heard a 3-year-old boy say, "What is that truck doing, washing the street for?" Neither adults nor other children would have been likely to produce this exact statement in the child's presence, due to the rarity of the event and the awkwardness of the grammatical form. Thus, the boy almost certainly did not learn it through simple imitation. Nor would he have been likely to learn it through reinforcement. If he never produced the sentence before, the response could not have been reinforced. However, the comprehensibility of the sentence, and the fact that children produce many sentences like it, suggest that it was not simply a random mistake.

Rather than learning specific responses, Chomsky argued, children form grammatical *rules*. Data on children's learning of past-tense forms support this position. Many of the most common verbs do not follow the usual verb + ed formula: *came, went, put, broke,* and *hit,* to name a few. At first, children say these past-tense forms correctly, apparently imitating what they hear adults say. Once they learn the standard rule for producing past-tense forms, however, they try to apply the rule to these irregular verbs as well as to regular ones. They wind up producing such terms as *goed, eated,* and *thinked* (Brown, 1973), as well as such double past-tense forms as *wented, ated,* and *thoughted* (Kuczaj, 1981). These errors indicate that language learning involves analysis of input and application of rules, rather than involving only imitation and reinforcement.

Chomsky went much further than simply criticizing Skinner's position, however. He proposed a rich and complex alternative theory that soon became far more influential. The central tenet of Chomsky's initial theory, and of all of the subsequent versions that have emerged over the past 35 years, is that people are born with innate knowledge of a *universal grammar.* By the term "universal grammar," Chomsky meant "the system of principles, conditions, and rules that are elements or properties of all human languages" (Chomsky, 1976, p. 29). The view emphasizes the characteristics that the grammars of the world's languages have in common and assumes that variability among the grammars derives from variations in a few basic properties. Reflecting this assumption, Chomsky sometimes referred to language learning as a process of "parameter setting" and other times as a process of "tuning," on an analogy to tuning in one of a few stations on a radio.

Chomsky further proposed that the mind in general can be viewed as being divided into a moderate-size group of semi-autonomous faculties that constitute "mental organs." The analogy was to physiological organs that perform functions within the circulatory or pulmonary system. Each mental faculty would be governed by its own principles and have its own acquisition devices. Thus, grammar would not be learned through the same mechanisms as other acquisitions such as mathematics or logic. In fact it would not be learned at all, so much as recognized. Innate knowledge of the universal grammar would allow children to grasp a language's grammar, and to grasp it quickly, despite its inherent complexity and the limited input that children would obtain from hearing other people speak.

A variety of types of evidence support Chomsky's view that language acquisition has special properties (Maratsos, 1989). The anatomical base of language differs from that of other cognitive skills. Many of the inferences about the relevant anatomy are based on studies of people who have suffered brain damage. Generally, damage to the left hemisphere of the brain harms language use more than damage to the right hemisphere. This is true of sign language as well as spoken language, which indicates that the problem is general to language functioning, rather than being specific to the auditory modality. In addition, within the left hemisphere, damage to one region (Broca's area) interferes with correct grammar but leaves the ability to express meanings relatively intact; damage to another region (Wernicke's area) allows grammatical but nonsensical speech (Maratsos, 1989). The parts of the cerebral cortex that seem most involved in language learning generally are not even present in species other than humans.

Another way in which language acquisition is special is its robustness. It occurs, and occurs quickly, across a wide range of environments. Children learn in cultures in which adults converse with children on topics of special interest to the children, in cultures in which adults refuse to discuss such topics, and in cultures in which they discourage young children from talking at all (Snow, 1986). Acquisition of other complex cognitive skills seems more dependent on favorable circumstances.

Another special characteristic of language acquisition is its self-motivating properties. Some children are interested in soldiers; others in dinosaurs, in dolls, or in music. In contrast, all children are sufficiently interested in language to master a very complex system in a relatively short time. Part of this is due to a desire to communicate. This desire is so characteristic of human beings that it is tempting to think it must apply to other animals as well. Interest in communicating information of no direct importance for survival seems to be uniquely human, though. Even chimpanzees that have learned to communicate quite well through sign language and symbols do not seem to have anything like the same interest as we do in communication for its own sake (Savage-Rumbaugh & Rumbaugh, 1980).

Desire to communicate is an important motivation for language acquisition, but the motivation extends even further. Consider why children strive to express themselves grammatically, even though they can communicate effectively using incorrect grammar. Beginning language learners often ask questions such as Anthony's "Where you going?" Other people understand such statements, respond appropriately to them, and rarely correct them (Brown & Hanlon, 1970). Yet children soon abandon such immature forms in favor of grammatically correct ones. This cannot be attributed to a general desire to imitate adults and older children. In dress, eating preferences, musical taste, and many other activities, young children show little interest in acting like adults. In sum, the desire to learn language, like the desire to be near other people and to understand the world around us, seems to be a basic part of people's makeup (Maratsos, 1989).

In line with Chomsky's theory, then, language acquisition appears to be special in many ways. However, his claims about the hypothesized language acquisition device, in particular that it operates through children's simply recognizing which of a few possible kinds of grammars they are learning, have fared less well. Comparisons among the world's languages reveal not one or a few grammars but large numbers of very different ones (Slobin, 1986). Even simple grammatical distinctions, such as that between *a* and *the,* are made in surprisingly many ways. In English, *a* and *the* are separate words, though both words are placed before the noun. In Finnish, a single word, *en,* is attached to the front of the noun when it plays the role of *the* and to the back of the noun when it plays the role of *a.* In Hungarian, the distinction can be signaled through the order of the verb and the direct object. In some African languages, tone patterns are used to make the distinction. In Chinese and Japanese, the distinction is inferred purely from context. Thus, language learning is far more complex than simply identifying and tuning in the type of language that is being heard. It seems to require both general learning abilities and abilities specific to language acquisition (Maratsos, 1989).

The discussion of language development in the rest of this chapter is divided into five main sections. The first four correspond to the four main aspects of language: phonology, meaning, grammar, and communication. *Phonology* concerns the ways in which people produce meaningful sounds, such as the sounds within words. *Meaning* emphasizes the correspondences between particular words and phrases on the one hand and particular objects, properties of objects, events, and ideas on the other. *Grammar* focuses on the system of rules through which people form sentences. *Communication* involves the way the rest of the language is used to convey messages that may not be present in the literal meanings of words. (For example, if I

**TABLE 5–1    Chapter Outline**

ask, "Do you know what time it is?" I am not looking for a "yes" or "no" answer, even though that is what the literal meaning of the words indicates.)

These four parts of language first assume prominent roles at different points in development. Phonology begins to develop early in infancy, as infants increasingly often make the sounds that appear in their language. Around their first birthday, infants produce their first understandable words, raising a variety of issues about word meaning. At roughly 18 months, toddlers begin to string together phrases of two or more words, and grammar becomes an issue. Finally, communication is complexly related to all the other aspects of language and could reasonably be placed at any point in the ordering. Because it can best be understood in the context of the other aspects of language, however, it is examined after them. Therefore, the focus of the discussion moves from phonology to meaning to grammar to communication. Finally, the chapter closes with a brief discussion of a general issue that affects all aspects of language: the relation between language and thought (Table 5–1).

## PHONOLOGY

### How People Speak

When people are silent, air passes freely through the windpipe, nose, and mouth. We speak by impeding the airflow. The two fundamental classes of speech sounds—vowels and consonants—are produced by two major classes of impediments. With vowels, the only impediment to the airflow comes in the vocal cords. There is no further blocking by the tongue, teeth, or lips. Consonants, on the other hand, include impediments

**TABLE 5–2    Location in Mouth Where Tongue is Placed for English Vowel Pronunciations**

|  | *FRONT OF MOUTH* | *MIDDLE OF MOUTH* | *BACK OF MOUTH* |
|---|---|---|---|
| High in mouth | m*ee*t<br>m*i*tt |  | c*oo*ed<br>c*ou*ld |
| Middle of mouth | m*a*te<br>m*e*t | glass*e*s | c*o*de<br>c*a*wed |
| Low in mouth | m*a*t | m*u*tt | c*o*d |

by the tongue, teeth, and lips, as well as by the vocal cords. The difference can be seen in pronouncing a vowel such as *a* or *i* and then making a *b* or *p* sound. With the vowels, we do not use our lips; with the consonants, we do. All languages include both vowels and consonants.

Different vowels are distinguished primarily by the placement of the tongue. As shown in Table 5–2, the *ee* sound is produced with the tip of the tongue high and quite far forward, near the irregular surface just above the top teeth, the *alveolar ridge*. In making the vowel sound in *mat*, however, the tongue is much lower. (Because people have little conscious awareness of the tongue's location within the mouth, it may be informative to use your fingers to determine your tongue's location when you make these sounds).

The main distinction among consonants is whether the flow of air is entirely halted by the placement of the tongue (*stops*) or whether the flow of air is largely but not entirely halted (*fricatives*). The typical *t* sound is a stop; the typical *s* sound is a fricative. Another major distinction among consonants is whether they are *voiced*. Voiced sounds are those where a strong vibration is evident when you place your finger on your Adam's apple. The voicing feature can be seen by contrasting pairs of sounds that are identical except for being voiced or unvoiced. For example, touching one's Adam's apple while saying the sounds reveals that the *zh* sound (as in *leisure*) is voiced, but the *sh* sound is not. Whether a sound is voiced or unvoiced, whether it is a stop or a fricative, and a handful of other features determine the exact sound that is made (Jakobson, Fant, & Halle, 1951).

### Development of Phonology

Infants produce a very wide variety of sounds. However, their assembly of the sounds into language is limited by difficulty in making the particular sound they want to make. Development comes in increasing ability to produce sounds at will and increasing skill combining them with other sounds to produce words and phrases.

How does the ability to make these sounds develop? Kaplan and Kaplan (1971) suggested that infants' phonology develops in four stages:

1. *Crying.* Infants cry from the day they are born. These sounds communicate that they would like something to be different. Many parents believe that they can infer what their infant would like sheerly from the sound of the crying. Given tape recordings of their infants' cries, however, parents quite often cannot tell what the infants want (Muller, Hollien, & Murray, 1974). At such times, parents infer the infant's desires from the context, rather than from the precise sound being made.
2. *Cooing.* By the end of the first month, infants make sounds other than cries. In particular, they coo by placing their tongue near the back of their mouth and rounding their lips. These coos resemble the *uh* sound that older individuals make in pronouncing the word *fun.*
3. *Babbling.* By 6 months of age, infants produce a wider variety of sounds. These include both consonant and vowel sounds. For the first time, infants also combine consonants and vowels, and thus produce syllables. These syllables are often repeated in sequences such as *babababababa.* The intonations of the babbling increasingly resemble those of speech.
4. *Patterned speech.* Near the end of the first year, infants say their first words. They also increase their production of sounds that appear in their language and decrease their production of sounds that are not part of it.

This sequence helps explain an otherwise surprising phenomenon. Even in languages that have nothing else in common, infants' first words are similar. They start with consonants, end with vowels, and often involve repetition of the same sounds. Thus, it is no accident that throughout the world, *dada, mama,* and *papa* are names for parents and are among the first words that children learn (Table 5–3).

In Table 5–3, the consonants *m* and *n* are associated with the meaning *mother,* but not *father.* This pattern is no coincidence; an examination of

**TABLE 5–3    Early Words for Mother and Father in 10 Languages**

|  | MOTHER | FATHER |
|---|---|---|
| English | mama | dada |
| German | mama | papa |
| Hebrew | eema | aba |
| Hungarian | anya | apa |
| Navajo | ama | ataa |
| Northern Chinese | mama | baba |
| Russian | mama | papa |
| Spanish | mama | papa |
| Southern Chinese | umma | baba |
| Taiwanese | amma | aba |

more than 1,000 terms drawn from the world's languages showed that 55 percent of the terms for mother included nasal sounds such as *m* and *n*, but only 15 percent of the terms for father did (Jakobson, 1981). Jakobson proposed an intriguing explanation for the difference. The only phonemes that can be produced when the lips are pressed to the breast and the mouth is full are nasal sounds, such as *m* and *n*. Later, infants may reproduce these sounds at the mere sight of food, to express an interest in eating, or to ask for any desired change. Thus, words including *m* and *n* would be especially convenient for naming the person who most often provides food and fulfills desires, the baby's mother. The use of such easy-to-make sounds to name mothers is a particularly nice example of cultures adapting to children's natures in a way gratifying to parent and child alike.

As infants' vocabularies expand, so do the phonological demands they face. They must identify the sounds within the words they wish to say, determine the order in which the sounds should be made, keep them in mind long enough to say them, and integrate them well enough to be understood. Development in the precision and consistency of these skills continues from the time children begin to produce words well into the elementary school period.

The difficulty of speaking clearly is especially apparent in the period from 18 months to 5 years. During this period, children use many words but often mispronounce them. Some of the problems that toddlers and preschoolers experience come from their failing to produce the sound they intend. Their pronunciation is inconsistent, in the sense that they sometimes mispronounce words that at other times they pronounce correctly. Another part of the problem stems from certain sounds' simply being difficult to make. Sounds such as *sh*, *th*, *s*, and *r* require precise coordination of vocal cords, tongue, teeth, and lips to be made correctly. Coping with other cognitive demands exacerbates the difficulty; children mispronounce more words when they try to produce more grammatically complex sentences (Panagos & Prelock, 1982).

Children cope with such challenges by selecting words carefully (Macken & Ferguson, 1983). Toddlers who know more than one term for a given meaning tend to select the term that is easier to pronounce. They avoid saying words they cannot pronounce (Ingram, 1986). Conversely, once they become able to produce a sound pattern, they increase their use of terms that make use of that phonological pattern (Vihman, in press). Such findings have been obtained for children learning many languages, including English, Finnish, Spanish, and Estonian.

The vocabularies of languages also tend to accommodate children by not using difficult-to-pronounce words for objects toddlers most want to talk about (people, animals, vehicles). For example, although *str* sequences are fairly common in English (e.g., strong, strap, straight), few are present in the names of objects that particularly interest young children.

Even toddlers seem to be quite conscious of their pronunciation difficulties. For example, in one experiment, a 3-year-old was presented a number of sentences ("I 'mell a 'kunk") and asked whether that was the way he would say it or the way his father would. On all 30 trials, the boy was correct in identifying the person who would use that pronunciation (Kuczaj, 1983). Such knowledge is an early example of *metalinguistic awareness*—awareness of what you know, and don't know, about language. To make concrete this metalinguistic awareness, consider the following conversation between a psycholinguist and his 2½-year-old son:

| | |
|---|---|
| *Father:* | Say "jump." |
| *Son:* | Dup. |
| *Father:* | No, "jump." |
| *Son:* | Dup. |
| *Father:* | No. "Jummmp." |
| *Son:* | Only Daddy can say "Dup!" (Smith, 1973, p.10). |

## MEANING

### Early Words and Word Meanings

*One-word phrases.*    When children begin to talk, they speak in single words. Presumably they do this because correctly combining the sounds needed to form a word demands all of their limited cognitive resources. Toddlers' frequent long pauses between the syllables of a single word contrast sharply with older children's fluent expression of whole sentences. Clearly, speech takes quite a bit of practice, and perhaps maturation, to become automatized.

Young children effectively compensate for their limited speech proficiency by choosing single words that convey larger meanings. These single words are often called *holophrases*, because they express the meaning of an entire phrase. When 1-year-olds say *ball*, the word seems to imply an entire thought such as "Give me the ball," "That is a ball," or "The dog took the ball." Context and intonations help adults and older children interpret these single-word statements.

Toddlers' choices of single words also help to convey their meanings. Greenfield and Smith (1976) found that children in the one-word stage who wanted a banana said *banana* rather than *want*. Because of the many things the child could want, and the relatively few aspects of bananas about which the child could be commenting, *banana* was the more informative term. However, when offered a banana they did not want, children said *no* rather than *banana*, presumably because saying *banana* could be misinterpreted.

*A child's first words.* The similarity between children's babbling and their early words makes it difficult to identify just when they produce their first word. Parents often discern words months before even sympathetic friends and relatives can. It is unclear whether the discrepancy reflects parental hopes and pride or whether the parents are simply more skilled in understanding their child. In any case, most dispassionate observers place the typical age of the eagerly awaited first word between 10 and 13 months, though deviations in both directions are common.

By 18 months, a vocabulary of 3 to 100 words is typical. These words seem to many observers to have a characteristically childlike flavor. One-year-olds use words like *ball, doggie,* and *more;* they almost never use words like *stove, animal,* and *less.* These choices reflect tendencies for children's first words to refer to objects and actions that interest them, that are relatively concrete, and that they want.

Children throughout the world refer to the same types of objects with their earliest terms. They talk about people: *dada, papa, mama.* They talk about vehicles: *car, truck, train.* They also talk about food, clothing, and household implements, such as keys and clocks. Table 5–4 lists the terms that Nelson (1973) found to appear most frequently among U.S. children's first 50 words.

*Overextensions, underextensions, and overlaps.* The fact that young children use a word does not guarantee that they mean the same thing by it that older individuals do. Clear deviations from standard meanings are quite common up to about 2 years of age (Rescorla, 1976), and more subtle ones continue for a considerable time thereafter.

Children's deviations from standard meanings fall into three categories: overextensions, underextensions, and overlaps. Anglin (1986) observed each of these in the speech of his oldest daughter, Emmy. *Overextensions* involve using a word to refer not only to the standard referents but to others as well. For example, Emmy used the term *doggie* not just to refer to dogs, but to refer to lambs, cats, wolves, and cows. *Underextensions* involve limiting the use of a word to a subset of its standard referents. For example, Emmy used *bottle* to refer only to her plastic drinking bottles; she would not use it with other bottles, such as Coke bottles. *Overlaps* involve overextending a term in some ways and underextending it in others. Emmy underextended the term *brella* by refusing to apply it to umbrellas that were folded rather than open, but simultaneously overextended it to kites and to a leaf used to keep off rain by a monkey in her storybook.

Overextensions are the most dramatic of these errors; almost everyone notices when a child calls a cat *doggie.* Underextensions are much less dramatic; in everyday situations, it is often impossible to know whether a child who does not say *doggie* upon seeing a particular dog underextends the term or simply does not feel like talking about the particular dog. This

**TABLE 5–4  Words Most Commonly Appearing in the First 50 Words Children Use (after Nelson, 1973)**

| CATEGORY AND WORD[a] | FREQUENCY[b] | CATEGORY AND WORD | FREQUENCY |
|---|---|---|---|
| FOOD AND DRINK: | | VEHICLES: | |
| Juice | 12 | Car | 13 |
| Milk | 10 | Boat | 6 |
| Cookie | 10 | Truck | 6 |
| Water | 8 | FURNITURE AND HOUSEHOLD ITEMS: | |
| Toast | 7 | Clock | 7 |
| Apple | 5 | Light | 6 |
| Cake | 5 | Blanket | 4 |
| Banana | 3 | Chair | 3 |
| Drink | 3 | Door | 3 |
| ANIMALS: | | PERSONAL ITEMS: | |
| Dog (variants) | 16 | Key | 6 |
| Cat (variants) | 14 | Book | 5 |
| Duck | 8 | Watch | 3 |
| Horse | 5 | EATING AND DRINKING UTENSILS: | |
| Bear | 4 | Bottle | 8 |
| Bird | 4 | Cup | 4 |
| Cow (variants) | 4 | OUTDOOR OBJECTS: | |
| CLOTHES: | | Snow | 4 |
| Shoes | 11 | PLACES: | |
| Hat | 5 | Pool | 3 |
| Socks | 4 | | |
| TOYS AND PLAY EQUIPMENT: | | | |
| Ball | 13 | | |
| Blocks | 7 | | |
| Doll | 4 | | |

[a]Adult form of word used. Many words had several variant forms, in particular the animal words.
[b]Number of children (of 18) who used the word in the 50-word acquisition sequence.

created an initial impression that overextensions were more common than underextensions. Testing 1- and 2-year-olds' word meanings more directly (by showing them objects and asking "What's this?" or "Is this a _____?") has revealed a different picture, though. These studies have shown that underextensions actually are more common than overextensions (Kay & Anglin, 1982). Thus, beginning language learners tend to be conservative in extending newly acquired words to novel referents. They more often err by forming word meanings that are too narrow than ones that are too broad (MacWhinney, 1989).

*Form and Function.*   What features play the largest roles in early word meanings? Two that have been proposed as especially important are the functions that objects serve and their form (perceptual appearance).

Nelson (1973) proposed that the functions objects serve are the largest determinant of which words children learn first and what they think the words mean. She based this conclusion on an analysis of the 50 most common early words (Table 5–4). She noted, for example, that children often referred to clocks, blankets, and keys, but rarely to stoves, tables, and floors. Nelson characterized the difference as being that the household items children named either moved by themselves or could be moved by the children. Thus, she argued, children talk about these objects because of their function, that is, what they do or allow the children to do.

Clark (1973) proposed the alternative view that form exerts the greatest influence on early word meanings. She based her argument largely on children's overextension errors. Children throughout the world call round things, such as walnuts, stones, and oranges, *balls*. These objects share few functions with balls, but they do share a similar appearance. Many children also label kittens, lions, and leopards as *kitty-cats*, despite the different functions of these animals. Even Nelson's data on the importance of motion could be reinterpreted as supporting Clark's position, since movement is a perceptually salient quality.

After carefully considering evidence for both positions, Bowerman (1980) reached an intuitively sensible resolution: form, function, and other properties *can* dominate early word meanings. She illustrated the point with observations of her own two daughters' early meanings. Both Eve and Christy overextended many of their early words. Typically, their overextensions were consistent with the particular instance from which they first learned the term. The overextensions emphasized a variety of notable features of the objects and actions they named, though perceptual appearance and function (in that order) were the most common.

Table 5–5 presents an instructive example. Eve learned the term *kick* in the context of kicking a ball. She later overextended the term to describe activities with similar forms and functions, even though many of the events she referred to are not ordinarily labeled *kicks* in English. For example, she

**TABLE 5–5    Some Early Words and Their Referents (from Bowerman, 1982, p. 284)**

1. Eva, kick.

*Prototype:* kicking a ball with the foot so that it is propelled forward.

*Features:* (a) waving limb; (b) sudden sharp contact (especially between body parts and other object); (c) an object propelled.

Selected samples. Eighteenth month: (first use) as kicks a floor fan (Features a, b); looking at picture of a kitten with ball near its paw (all features, in anticipated event?); watching moth fluttering on a table (a), watching a row of cartoon turtles on television doing can-can (a). Nineteenth month: just before throwing something (a, c); "kick bottle," after pushing bottle with her feet, making it roll (all features). Twenty-first month: as makes ball roll by bumping it with front wheel of kiddicar (b, c); pushing teddy bear's stomach against Christy's chest (b), pushing her stomach against a mirror (b); pushing her chest against a sink (b), etc.

used *kick* to refer to sudden sharp contact between a part of the body and an object, to an object being propelled, and to the waving of a limb.

Such initial guesses about word meaning make sense. When children hear an unfamiliar word, they cannot be sure which aspect of the situation it labels. Some words refer mainly to functions (e.g., *helps*), others to perceptual attributes (e.g., *red*), others to actions (e.g., *hits*). Interesting forms and functions increase the likelihood of children's being sufficiently intrigued by an object or action to learn a label for it early on. Thus, both will characterize many of the first words children learn and will figure prominently in the meanings they assign to those words.

### Development Beyond the Earliest Words and Word Meanings

*The course of vocabulary acquisition.*    In the first six months of using words, between roughly 12 and 18 months, children slowly acquire new terms. After this, however, there is a "language explosion" during which vocabulary grows remarkably quickly. As shown in Table 5–6, after increasing gradually until 18 months, vocabulary more than doubles between 18 and 21 months and again between 21 and 24 months. By 3 years, children know more than three times as many words as they did at 2 years. The rapid growth continues at least through age 5.

*Constraints on vocabulary acquisition.*    How do children acquire so many word meanings between 1½ and 5 years? Their problem is far from simple. Even if a parent points to a dog and says, "That's a dog," the lesson is unclear. Should the child conclude that the word *dog* means animal, collie, mammal, four-legged object, furry object, or any number of other possibili-

**TABLE 5-6  Size of Vocabulary at Various Ages (after M. E. Smith, 1926)**

| AGE | | NUMBER OF WORDS | GAIN |
|---|---|---|---|
| YEARS | MONTHS | | |
| | 8 | 0 | |
| | 10 | 1 | 1 |
| 1 | 0 | 3 | 2 |
| 1 | 3 | 19 | 16 |
| 1 | 6 | 22 | 3 |
| 1 | 9 | 118 | 96 |
| 2 | 0 | 272 | 154 |
| 2 | 6 | 446 | 174 |
| 3 | 0 | 896 | 450 |
| 4 | 0 | 1,540 | 318 |
| 5 | 0 | 2,072 | 202 |

ties? That people are able to make accurate inferences under such problematic circumstances has been called "the riddle of induction" (Quine, 1960).

Despite the many possible meanings a word might have, even 2- and 3-year-olds often can identify the correct meaning (or at least a good approximation) from a single exposure to the word (Carey, 1978; Heibeck & Markman, 1987). How can they do this? Markman (1984) proposed that children circumvent the riddle of induction by never considering the vast majority of logically possible hypotheses about word meanings. Instead, she suggested that young children's hypotheses are constrained in such a way that they focus on the most likely alternatives. Within her view, two constraints are especially important for learning word meanings: the taxonomic constraint and the mutual exclusivity constraint.

First consider the *taxonomic constraint*. When children as young as 18 months hear a new word in the context of an object whose name they don't know, they assume that the new word refers to the *class of objects* of which the term is a member. They assume the word does not refer to a part or property of the object or a relation that involves it (Markman, 1989). For example, if shown a picture of a German shepherd chewing a bone and told "This is a sud," they assume that *sud* refers to dogs as a class, rather than just to dogs chewing bones or to a dog's nose, body, or coat. The taxonomic assumption, together with context and linguistic cues, considerably narrows the possible meanings many words might have. In fact, Markman (in press) speculated that "the emergence of the taxonomic constraint may be what accounts for the very young child's sudden ability to acquire words rapidly."

Even if children assume that words used to describe objects refer to the category of which the objects are members, they still must determine the level of generality of the category. For example, when children in the previous example were told "This is a sud," how would they know whether *sud* meant German shepherd, dog, mammal, or animal? Part of the answer is that children (and adults) tend to assume, unless given evidence to the contrary, that unfamiliar words involve a basic level of description, that is, a level that conveys the main perceptual and functional properties of the object without being extremely specific. In the above example, children would assume that the word meant *dog*, because knowing that an object is a dog tells us its main characteristics without getting into detailed distinctions among types of dogs. This assumption works out well, because language addressed to young children includes many more basic-level terms, such as *dog*, than more-abstract or specific terms, such as *animal* and *German shepherd* (Anglin, 1977; Blewitt, 1983).

Sometimes, however, children do hear more-abstract or specific terms. How do they figure out what these mean? A large part of the answer is that older individuals explicitly indicate to young children when they are using a term at another level. For example, although parents introduce basic words by just pointing and labeling (e.g., "See the dog"), they introduce more-general words by defining them in terms of basic ones (Callanan, 1985). Thus, they might introduce the term *vehicle* by saying, "See the car; cars are a kind of *vehicle*." This strategy is effective in helping 3- to 5-year-olds understand that the new word involves a more-general level of description (Callanan, 1989).

Another issue raised by the taxonomic constraint is how children learn words that refer to properties, such as color and shape, if they assume that words name classes of objects rather than their properties. Again, one means is for the person introducing the new term to contrast it explicitly with already-known terms within the same category. Even a single statement such as "It's not gray, it's celadon" is sufficient for 5-year-olds to realize that "celadon" is the color of the object being described, as long as the contrastive term (gray in this example) is the one that children themselves would have used (Au & Laframboise, in press). Such explicit contrasting of old and new terms also helps 3- and 4-year-olds, but the younger children require two presentations of the contrast rather than just one.

The other key constraint that Markman posited—the *mutual exclusivity constraint*—involves the belief that words refer to non-overlapping sets of referents. That is, children assume that each object has one and only one name (Markman, 1989). Like the taxonomic constraint, the assumption of mutual exclusivity is not invariably correct. For example, the same animal might be described as a dog, as a pet, or as a bad girl. Nonetheless, when children encounter an unfamiliar word in a context in which the word might refer to one of the two objects, and they already know a name for one of the objects, they assume that the unfamiliar word refers to the unfamiliar object. Thus, if 3-year-olds already know the word *spoon* and not the word *tongs*, and they are told "Show me the gug," they consistently choose the tongs rather than the spoon (Golinkoff, Hirsh-Pasek, Lavallee, & Baduini, 1985; Markman & Wachtel, 1988).

The mutual exclusivity constraint seems especially important for reducing overextensions of word meanings. Recall that young children sometimes use words too broadly; for example, a child might call all four-legged mammals *doggie*. If such a child also followed the mutual exclusivity assumption, hearing an adult say "See the cat" would lead the child to narrow the previous definition of *doggie* so that it no longer included cats and other animals that were more like cats than dogs. In this way, *doggie* would eventually be restricted to dogs.

The mutual exclusivity constraint appears to be present by the time children are 2½ years old, though perhaps not earlier (Merriman & Bowman, 1989; though also see Markman, 1989). The consistency with which children apply the constraint increases in the next few years, but it clearly is present by 2½.

What accounts for children's increasingly consistent reliance on the mutual exclusivity constraint? One source of development may be an increasing ability to simultaneously keep in mind the apparent meanings of both previously known and new words, and thus to perceive the implications of a new word's apparent meaning for the likely meaning of an old one (Merriman & Bowman, 1989). Another likely source of development is a desire among children to fill gaps in their mental dictionaries (Clark, 1987). If you encounter an unfamiliar word and two objects to which the word might refer, why not guess that the new word refers to the object whose name you do not know rather than the one that you can already talk about? Two other possible sources are increasing willingness to accept adults' authority in matters of language use and increasingly ability to perceive features that distinguish the referents of old and new words (Mervis, 1989).

These constraints are not the only factors that help children home in on word meanings without much trial and error. By the time children are 2 or 3 years old, they understand quite subtle cues available in the language. They know that words introduced by saying "This is X" are usually proper names, that words introduced by saying "This is some X" usually refer to undifferentiated masses such as liquids, and that words introduced by saying "This is an X" usually refer to classes of objects such as dogs or cars (Gelman & Taylor, 1984; Macnamara, 1982). Adults also provide corrective feedback when word meanings are incorrect (Bohannon & Stanowicz, 1988). Further, not only are young children quite conservative in extending words beyond the contexts in which they initially hear them, they also spontaneously stop overgeneralizing terms if they do not hear them used by others in the way that they themselves use them (Merriman & Bowman, 1989). All these influences seem to contribute to the vocabulary explosion.

*Linguistic analysis.*   What of more-complex word meanings? Do children ever reorganize their initial knowledge of word meanings to reflect a later, more-mature general level of thinking, as might be suggested by a Piagetian analysis of cognitive development?

Apparently they do. Consider how 2-to-6-year-olds learn which verbs can be preceded by *un* (Bowerman, 1982). At first glance, terms such as *uncover, undress, unlock,* and *unstaple* would not seem to have anything in common that distinguishes them from nonwords such as *unbreak* and *unspill.* Careful analysis of these words, however, suggests a pattern. *Un* often can be attached to verbs that involve contact between objects (*unlock, unfasten,* and *unstaple*) or covering (*undress, unveil,* and *uncover*). In contrast, *un* almost never can be attached to other verbs.

Bowerman found that children's first use of these terms involved correct repetition of words they had heard other people use, such as *unbuckled* and *untangled.* Later, children began to attach the prefix in new and often incorrect ways. For example, one child said to her mother, "I hate you! And I'll never unhate you or nothing!" Such errors indicate that the child realized that *un* was a separate part of a verb, but had not figured out where it could be used. Later errors showed greater understanding that they were limited to verbs that involved covering or contact. For example, the same child who vowed never to unhate her mother recited a ghost story eight months later and said, "He tippitoed to the graveyard and *unburied* her." Although *unburied* does not happen to be a word in English, it does conform to the rule that *un* often can be attached to terms involving covering. Thus, both rote learning of specific words and detection of regular patterns influence children's acquisition of word meanings.

*Linguistic creativity.*   Children face many situations in which they do not know what a word means or do not know a word to express the meaning they intend. However, they show considerable creativity in transcending their limited knowledge. First consider a clever strategy 2-year-olds use for overcoming a particular difficulty in comprehension, the distinction between *in* and *on.* Clark (1973) described two ways in which children use the physical context to discriminate between the meanings of such statements as "Put object 1 *in* object 2" and "Put object 1 *on* object 2."

1.  If object 2 is a container with an open side up, put object 1 into it.
2.  If object 2 is a container with a closed side up, put object 1 on top of it.

Clark found that toddlers followed these rules when they heard *in* and *on.* They seemed to know that both words referred to locations, but not to know the distinction between them. Note that in most situations, children's understanding of *in* and *on* would have appeared perfect from an early age. Ordinarily, when we say to a child "Put 1 *on* 2," 2 is a surface, and when we say "Put 1 *in* 2," 2 has an opening on the top. Thus, children's context-based strategies for comprehending language serve them in good stead as far as behaving appropriately, even when they do not perfectly understand the words' exact meanings.

Children also show considerable creativity in inventing words to express meanings for which they do not know any appropriate term. Clark (1981) cited such examples as *fire-man* (someone who burns things), *hitter-man* (someone who hits things), and *hugging machine* (thing for hugging people). As these examples suggest, children's innovative uses of language are far from random. They seem to reflect rules for forming new words, such as combining words that are meaningful in their own right, using component terms that can be applied widely (*man, machine*), and using component words that have an unambiguous meaning.

Another base of the colorful character of children's language is their use of nonliteral expressions. At roughly 2 years of age, they begin to produce metaphors, for example calling a piece of string "my tail" (Winner, 1988). Most of these early metaphors are based on perceptual similarity, as in the tail example. More-abstract metaphors take much longer to master. Consider the metaphorical expression "The prison guard had become a *hard rock*." At around age 6 or 7 years, most children interpret this sentence to mean "A witch turned the guard into a rock" (Winner, Rosensteil, & Gardner, 1976). Later, at around age 9, they deny the meaningfulness of the sentence entirely, by saying, "A person can't be a rock." Still later, at around age 10 or 11, they interpret the sentence metaphorically and modify their usual interpretation of the one description so that it makes sense in the context of the other.

At first glance, the early magical interpretation about the witch having turned the guard into a rock would seem either to stand in the way of a correct interpretation or to be simply a wrong turn. The process that leads to the early and later interpretations may be quite similar, though. Children may as a matter of course first try to interpret statements literally. If the literal interpretation does not make sense, they may then search for an interpretation that is sensible. One resolution that is almost always applicable, but that usually is not especially compelling, is to take the statement as literally given, but to assume that it applies to a magical world where the usual constraints of reality are suspended. Another, more-sophisticated, strategy is to identify any clear relations that exist between the features of the two terms that are being compared. Focusing on the qualities of rocks and some prison guards as cold, unfeeling, and unresponsive exemplifies this strategy. With metaphors where the qualities that are needed to interpret the sentence sensibly are easily accessible, such as many perceptual metaphors, even 4-year-olds often interpret the sentences correctly. With metaphors where the relevant qualities are obscure, even adults sometimes resort to magical explanations (Reyna, 1985). Thus, construction of magical and of metaphorical interpretations emerge as two strategies that can be used when literal interpretations fail; development seems likely to be due to increased knowledge of attributes of the entities being compared, and to increased ability to keep in mind multiple features of the entities long enough to identify the points of similarity.

## GRAMMAR

### The Earliest Grammars

*From sequences to sentences.*   When children are about 1½ years old, they start to speak in two-word phrases. This is the true beginning of grammar, because it represents the first occasion where word order is an issue. During the next half-year or so, children develop a variety of skills culminating in the ability to speak in true sentences, the basic unit of all languages.

Sentences are more than simple strings of words. They are structured, cohesive units that express meaning and that follow conventions regarding word order, intonation, and stress. So basic are they that Anisfeld (1984) commented, "In a real sense, sounds and words exist to be used in sentences" (p. 113). Although the number of sounds and words in any language is finite, the number of sentences that can be produced from those sounds and words is infinite.

Children's earliest two-word phrases seem somewhere between lists of individual words and true sentences. The two words in each phrase express related meanings, but they are not very cohesive, often are separated by long pauses, and lack a unifying intonational contour. They are often referred to as *sequences* (of words), to distinguish them from true sentences. Thus, one 20-month-old boy produced such phrases as "train/bump," "cow/moo," and "beep/beep/trucks" (Anisfeld, 1984; the slashes indicate pauses between words). These expressions seemed to indicate meanings comparable to those of simple sentences ("The train bumped." "Cows say moo." "Trucks beep."). However, they lacked the intonational patterns and cohesion of sentences. Gradually, children progress to expressions that are sentencelike within phrases, but that depart from standard form across phrases, as in a 23-month-old girl's statement "I want cereal/that kind" (Anisfeld, 1984).

Along with these sequences, children begin to produce true sentences. At first, the sentences are a minority of all utterances, but within a few months, they become dominant. The cognitive effort needed to construct them is evident in the halting way in which young children talk. Braine (1971) estimated that 30–40 percent of 24-to-30-month-olds' statements are "replacement sequences," in which children build on earlier statements until they succeed in producing the desired form and meaning. Thus, Braine observed a 25-month-old say in succession, "Want more. Some more. Want some more." and a 26-month-old say, "Stand up. Cat stand up. Cat stand up table."

Children's early grammatical knowledge emphasizes meaning, rather than formal grammatical categories such as noun, verb, subject, and predicate. They understand grammatically identical sentences better when the sentences express typical meanings rather than unusual ones (Corrigan, 1988; Corrigan & Odya-Weis, 1985). Thus, they understand sentences with animate agents (e.g., "The boy washes the car.") better than ones with inanimate agents (e.g., "The soap washes the car."). With regard to the language that children themselves produce, children from very different language backgrounds emphasize the same meaningful relations in their two-word phrases: agent–action ("Mommy hit"), possessor–possessed ("Adam checker"), attribute–object ("big car"), recurrence ("more juice"), and disappearance ("juice allgone") (Anisfeld, 1984; Bloom, Lightbown, & Hood, 1975; Braine, 1976). Within each relation, children order words in a regular fashion. Thus, when describing an object that has disappeared, a child who said "juice allgone" would rarely if ever say "allgone juice." However, the consistency of the word ordering is specific to the meaning being expressed.

This initial specificity also is evident in learning of purely grammatical conventions. One such meaning-free grammatical convention in English involves different forms of the verb *to be* (e.g., *am, is, are*). When children start to use these forms, they include them only under specific circumstances. For example, Kuczaj (1986) observed that one of his two children initially used *are* only in declarative sentences starting with *these* or *those* ("Those are good toys."). His other child at first used *is* only at the end of sentences ("There they is."), before widening its use. This initial reluctance to extend newly acquired grammatical forms to novel contexts parallels children's conservatism about extending newly acquired word meanings.

### Later Grammatical Development

Once children produce true sentences, they begin to acquire many of the grammatical conventions used in adult language. For example, English-speaking children learn to indicate that an event happened in the past by appending *ed* to the verb. They learn to indicate that more than one individual was involved in an event by appending *s* or *es* to the noun. They learn to use *am, is* and *are* in the full range of circumstances to which they apply.

One task that illustrates how such acquisitions occur is learning to ask *wh* questions: questions starting with *who, what, when, where,* and *why.* Bellugi (1965) documented three stages in the development of such forms. At first, children not only fail to produce *wh* questions, they do not even understand them. Consider the following example (from Dale, 1976):

| MOTHER | CHILD |
|--------|-------|
| What did you hit? | Hit. |
| What did you do? | Head. |
| What are you writing? | Arm. |

Later, children begin to answer *wh* questions appropriately. They also develop a simplified way of asking such questions: adding the *wh* term and the appropriate pronoun to the beginning of a simple statement. For example, when an adult said, "You bent that game," a child answered, "Why me bent that game?" (Brown, Cazden, & Bellugi, 1969). Children at this level of understanding do not use auxiliary verbs (e.g., *has, was, did*), which are crucial in many English questions. They thus ask questions such as, "Why not he eat?" and "Why he smiling?" which lack the usual auxiliaries *does* and *is*.

Still later, children begin to use auxiliary verbs, but not necessarily correctly. This is not surprising, considering the number of processing steps necessary to transform a simple statement into a *wh* question. Consider what a child needs to do to transform "He thinks *x*" into "Why does he think *x*?"

1. Adopt a questioning intonation.
   Result: "He thinks *x*?"
2. Add the *wh* term to the beginning of the sentence.
   Result: "Why he thinks *x*?"
3. Realize that *does* must be added after the *wh* term.
   Result: "Why does he thinks *x*?"
4. Delete the *s* from *thinks*.
   Result: "Why does he think *x*?"

In light of the number and complexity of these transformations, it should not be surprising that children continue to err when asking *wh* questions for several years beyond the time they first attempt them. By age 5, though, most children have mastered *wh* questions and a variety of other grammatical forms.

Why are such grammatical forms learned when they are, rather than earlier or later? Lenneberg (1967) raised one intriguing possibility: that the time between 18 months and puberty is a critical period, during which the brain is especially receptive to learning grammar.

Initial examinations of grammatical acquisition seemed to contradict Lenneberg's hypothesis. For example, comparisons of adults and preschoolers who were completing their first year of living in Holland indicated that the adults' mastery of Dutch grammar was superior (Snow & Hoefnagel-Hohle, 1978).

However, a recent study that focused on the end point of grammatical acquisition, rather than knowledge after one year, suggested that there actually is a sensitive period for learning grammar. Johnson and Newport (1989) examined knowledge of English grammar among Korean and Chinese immigrants who had come to the United States when they were between 3 and 39 years old and who had lived in the United States for between 3 and 26 years. Because age of arrival and number of years in the United States were only moderately correlated, the investigators could separate the influences of the age at which the immigrants began to learn English from the amount of time they had spent learning it.

Age of arrival was closely related to ultimate level of grammatical mastery. In contrast, number of years in the United States had little relation to degree of mastery. Immigrants who came before age 7 knew grammar as well as native-born adults; those who came between 8 and 10 knew it slightly less well; those who came between 11 and 15 knew it less well still. Within this age range, the earlier that people came to the United States, the better their mastery of English grammar. However, hardly any of those who came between ages 17 and 39 mastered English grammar very well. Only 1 of the 22 people who arrived between ages 17 and 39 showed as much grammatical knowledge as the least-knowledgeable of the 15 people who arrived before age 11. Further, among those who arrived after age 15, neither age at arrival nor number of years in the United States correlated highly with degree of mastery. It appears, then, that grammatical acquisition is something like the proverbial race between the hare and the tortoise. Adults acquire grammar more quickly at first, but children eventually overtake them and in the end master grammar more completely.

### Explanations of Grammatical Development

As noted in the discussion of the Chomsky–Skinner debate, explaining grammatical development has proved very difficult. Currently, no one account qualifies as a generally accepted theory. However, several accounts do well at explaining particular aspects of grammatical development.

*Basic child grammar.*    Slobin (1986) proposed that there exists a basic child grammar that children impose on whatever language input they receive. Within this view, children anticipate that grammar will assume certain forms. They expect that certain meanings but not others are sufficiently important that they should be reflected in grammar, and also that particular meanings should be expressed in particular places within phrases. When meanings that children believe are important are marked by the grammar of the language, and when they are marked in the place within the sentence where children believe they should be, children learn them quickly. When the grammatical markings are in different places, or when children do not expect the meaning to be important at all, they learn slowly and make many errors.

One general principle of basic child grammar is, "An operator that affects a whole phrase or clause should not be placed within that phrase or clause, nor should it require changing of elements within that phrase or clause" (Slobin, 1983, p. 6). Illustratively, negatives affect the meaning of the entire clause they modify. When we say, "He didn't run to the store," the negative *didn't* modifies the meaning of the entire clause "run to the store." Children's errors indicate that they try to keep the negative outside of the clause even when the language they hear places it inside. In Turkish, correct grammar involves specifying the verb, then indicating whether the meaning is negative, and then completing the verb phrase (as in "He run didn't to the store."). Children often err, however, by moving *didn't* outside the verb phrase, as is done in English. Thus, children's expectations can, for a time, override the language to which they are exposed, leading to grammatical errors.

Children's expectations about what is important do not always conform to those of adults. For example, Polish toddlers find it easy to learn a difference that to most American adults seems very subtle: the difference between *perfective* and *imperfective* tenses. Perfective forms indicate that an action was executed once and completed; imperfective forms indicate that an action was executed repeatedly. In English, we might say "He opened the door" either when we intended a perfective meaning ("He opened the door once.") or an imperfective one ("The doorman opened the door again and again."). In Polish, the verb would need to have a particular ending to indicate which of the two meanings was intended. Slobin reported that in languages such as Polish, in which this difference is explicitly noted as part of the verb, children quickly and easily learn the distinction. Thus, the fit between children's expectations and the language they hear influences their learning of grammatical conventions.

*Semantic bootstrapping.* As noted earlier, children's early sentences usually follow standard orders of meanings such as agent–action–recipient (e.g., "Billy hit me."). Eventually, however, they produce sentences such as "Going to school sure is fun," in which the grammatical subject ("going to school") is not an agent, the verb ("is") is not an action, and the grammatical object ("fun") is not a recipient of any action. They also become able to recognize that a meaningless sentence can still be grammatically correct (e.g., "Frequent exercise prevents restless windows."). A full explanation of grammar must explain how people reach such abstract competence and what role their initial understandings play in the process.

Pinker (1984) proposed that the transition is based on a process of *semantic bootstrapping.* The basic idea is that children first identify the meanings that are most commonly reflected in sentences they hear, then use them to form meaning-based categories and rules for ordering words in sentences, and then correct these meaning-based categories and rules to purely grammatical categories and rules.

Grammatical categories generally are correlated strongly, though imperfectly, with meanings. Names of persons or things usually function as nouns, actions as verbs, and attributes of persons or things as adjectives. These relations provide a basis for early analysis of sentences. For example, from frequent exposure to sentences such as "Jim hit Mary," children can learn that the agent who engaged in the action is typically named at the beginning of the sentence, that the action itself is typically in the middle, and that the recipient of the action is typically at the end. This provides a basis for the child to order words within sentences according to the agent–action–recipient framework.

These early sentence frames may not only allow children to produce grammatical sentences, they also may provide a basis for learning grammatical rules not based on meaning. Within Pinker's theory, grammatical categories such as noun, verb, subject, and predicate are innate to human beings. Children's learning task is to identify how these grammatical categories function within their own language. They do this by establishing correspondences between the meanings they initially represent and the innately known grammatical categories. For example, they map the grammatical category "subject" onto the meaning-based concept of "agent." They also map the grammatical category "verb" onto the meaning-based category of "action." Once they categorize the language they hear in terms of these grammatical categories, they note regularities of ordering, phrasing, and intonation that allow them to extend the grammatical categories to cases where the grammatical subject is not an agent and the verb is not an action. Gradually, they elaborate these and other grammatical categories to include the full range of language that fits within the categories.

*Regularity detection.*    Maratsos (1982) took a different approach to explaining the formation of grammatical categories and rules. Rather than assuming that the basic grammatical categories are innate, he argued that they are formed through detecting regularities within the language input itself. He illustrated how this could work in the context of the German article system.

In German, all nouns are either masculine, feminine, or neuter. Different articles accompany each type of noun. When speakers wish to say *the,* they use *der* with masculine nouns, *die* with feminine nouns, and *das* with neuter nouns. Similarly, to refer to a noun as "it," German requires *er* when referring to masculine nouns, *sie* with feminine nouns, and *es* with neuter nouns.

How do German speakers know which form to use with which noun? Meaning is not as useful a guide as might be supposed. For example, the word for *spoon* is a masculine term, the word for *fork* is feminine, and the word for *knife* is neuter. Nor are endings or other phonological cues reliable guides to the noun's gender.

Maratsos proposed a three-stage model of how children learn the German gender system. First they learn arbitrary associations between particular nouns and sex-linked articles such as *die* and *das* that people use with them. Then children induce rules that underlie these associations. If children know that *die* is used with *fork*, they deduce that *sie* also will be, since nouns modified by *die* are also modified by *sie*. Following this, the several other aspects of German that depend on whether the noun is masculine, feminine, or neuter are induced through the same process. Thus, according to Maratsos, children learn particular cases, abstract the rules underlying them, and apply the rules to new cases.

How can we evaluate these alternative accounts of children's acquisition of grammar? In many ways, they resemble the proverbial story of the blind men feeling different parts of the elephant. Each grasps part of the truth, but none the totality. Slobin's and Pinker's emphasis on the role of meaning in formation of early grammatical categories seems well founded. Pinker's semantic bootstrapping idea is an attractive transition mechanism. Maratsos's idea that grammatical categories are formed through detection of regularities within the language that children hear also seems attractive. Yet the views are sufficiently different that it is unclear how they could be integrated into a single theory. In sum, Skinner's and Chomsky's original task of coherently depicting grammatical development continues to challenge the best minds in the field.

## COMMUNICATION

The ultimate purpose of language is communication. At first impression, communication might simply seem to be an aspect of meaning. In a sense it is, but the types of meaning included under the heading often depend on cultural convention as well as on literal definitions of words. For example, if I ask my daughter's teacher, "Is she doing well in school?" I am not looking for a "yes" or "no" answer, even though such an answer would be consistent with the meanings of the individual words and of the phrase as a whole. Even preschoolers respond to the intent of questions, rather than to their literal meaning, which shows they have mastered some of the communicative conventions of their language (Shatz, 1978).

Communication can be accomplished either through verbal means or through gestures and signs. Each of these modes of communication is considered in the following section.

## Communication Through Oral Language

Primitive communication skills are present even in the first months. One that may be particularly important for infants is motivating older people to talk to them. Although infants cannot respond with words, having other people talk to them helps them learn to talk.

Even 3- and 4-month-olds act in several ways that motivate adults to speak to them. In particular, when an adult talks to them, they move in rhythm with the adult's intonations and make sounds at points where the adult is about to stop talking (Condon and Sanders, 1974). Such behaviors create a rhythm akin to that of typical conversations. They encourage adults to talk more with the infants than if the infants remained motionless or behaved in ways uncorrelated with what the adult was saying. By 10 to 12 months, infants also use a variety of other ways to persuade older individuals to talk to them, such as pointing at objects or bringing them to adults (Bates, Benigni, Bretherton, Camaioni, & Volterra, 1979).

Adults, in turn, speak to infants in ways that encourage them to listen. As noted in the previous chapter, they use a form of speech known as motherese, in which they speak in high registers, exaggerated intonations, short simple sentences, and elongated vowels (as when saying "Wheeee"). The style of speech is sufficiently distinctive that preschoolers abstract its form and use it in speaking to yet younger children (Shatz, 1983).

Why do older individuals talk to infants and toddlers in motherese? One reason is that it clearly increases the infants' and toddlers' attention to what is being said. Another is that infants seem to enjoy it. A third reason is that the simplified sentences and exaggerated intonations may promote learning. Recall the moderate discrepancy hypothesis from the previous chapter. If children learn most efficiently from input just beyond their current level of understanding, then short, simple sentences, spoken slowly and with exaggerated intonations, may be ideal for learning pronunciations and establishing correspondences between grammar and meaning. For example, one way that motherese may simplify the task of detecting correlations between meaning and grammar is by avoiding constructions such as passive sentences (e.g., "Mary was hit by Jim.") that violate the typical pattern of the agent of the action also being the grammatical subject (Hochberg & Pinker, 1987).

When children begin to speak, they add new attention-getting strategies. Some of these strategies seem to be unique to beginning language users. For example, some toddlers repeat entire phrases with only minimal grammatical alterations (Billman & Shatz, 1981; Keenan, 1977). When I once asked my then 2-year-old son, "Are you a great big boy?" he responded, "I are a great big boy." The early responses to *wh* questions that were described previously provide another example of such imitations. The imitations often are considerably longer than the child's typical sentences at that time. Thus, they may provide a steppingstone for constructing longer and more-complex sentences than the child previously generated (Schlesinger, 1982).

Young children also are surprisingly adept at understanding the unspoken conversational rules of their language communities. By age 2, children seem to know that they should speak immediately after their conversational partner stops talking (Bloom, Rocissano, & Hood, 1976). One manifestation is that they speak more often after being spoken to than when the other person has not spoken. When asked a question, their replies are more closely related to the topic of the question than are their responses to other statements. This follows the conversational convention that questions demand a relevant answer, whereas declarative sentences can be followed by the introduction of new topics.

Toddlers' knowledge of conversational rules also extends to differences among types of questions. Two-year-olds more often say "yes" or "no" after questions that begin with "Did you" than after questions that begin with "What" or "Where" (Crosby, 1976; Rodgon, 1979). This occurs even when the rest of their answers show no understanding of the question whatsoever. Similarly, they often begin their replies to "Why" questions with "Because," even when that is the only appropriate part of their answer (Ervin-Tripp, 1970).

Although 2-year-olds know they should answer questions, their parents' active intervention often is necessary to keep conversations going beyond a single question–answer sequence. One way parents accomplish this goal is by building new questions into their responses to their children's statements (Kaye & Charney, 1980). Parents also ask "What?" when they do not understand what their children mean, as well as when they do not hear what was said. Even children under 2 at times respond to being asked "What?" by revising their earlier statements (Gallagher, 1981). Such parental strategies can have positive impact on children's language development. As one example, the frequency with which mothers ask 2-year-olds questions and repeat parts of their children's previous sentences in their own succeeding ones is positively correlated with grammatical development over the next six months (Hoff-Ginsburg, 1986). In sum, children and parents communicate quite well, even when the children's language is limited.

### Communication Through Gesture and Sign Language

Children communicate through gestures as well as speech. This is true of hearing children as well as deaf ones, though the gestures play especially large roles in the deaf children's communication.

*Deaf children's gestural communication.* The development of gestural language among deaf children illustrates that the motivation for language, and many of its particular features, does not depend on hearing speech.

Consider one study of the language development of 10 deaf children, all of whom had hearing parents who did not know sign language (Goldin-Meadow & Morford, 1985). Despite this unpromising-sounding language environment, all 10 children invented signing systems to express themselves. The children did not only convey meanings; most also developed simple grammars for ordering the signs. For example, when transferring an object to a person, they consistently named the object being transferred before the recipient (e.g., "Coke Johnny").

Further analyses indicated similarities between the meanings expressed in these first gestures and the meanings expressed in the first words of hearing children. The gestures and words both referred to toys, animals, clothing, vehicles, and people. Both also seemed to reflect the same goals: to note the existence of objects and to comment on or request actions relevant to the objects. Further, older deaf children, like older hearing children, use considerable amounts of nonliteral language such as metaphor, simile, and invented words (Marschark & West, 1985; Marschark, West, Nall, & Everhart, 1986).

In addition to the signs they invent, deaf children also often learn formal gestural systems, such as American Sign Language (ASL). Stokoe (1960) described three dimensions that determine meaning within ASL. One is the location at which a sign is made. The most common locations, in order of frequency, are the area in front of the body where the hands ordinarily move, the chin, the trunk, the cheek, the elbow, and the forehead. These also are the locations at which young children find it easiest to produce signs, one more instance of languages' having evolved to facilitate learning by young children (Bonvillian, Orlansky, & Novack, 1983). A second dimension that distinguishes signs is hand shape. Several common hand shapes are shown in Figure 5–1. The third dimension of variation among signs is hand movement. For example, in the "vehicle wandering upward" sign, the active hand moves upward in a winding pattern.

The ASL that children learn varies greatly in sophistication. One influential factor is whether the child comes from a home with hearing or with deaf parents. The large majority of deaf children are born to hearing parents. In such homes, children and adults often invent simple gestural languages for communicating before they are exposed to any more-formal sign language. Such "home sign" languages typically lack grammatical markings. Even when these children of hearing parents later are taught ASL, they often fail to learn much of its grammar (Newport, 1982).

The people who most frequently acquire the more-elaborate features of ASL, including a sophisticated grammar and flexible means of expression, are deaf children born to deaf parents. They are exposed to a formal sign language from infancy onward. Interestingly, though, the sign language that they usually see their parents using is the relatively simple form used by first-generation deaf people. How these children progress

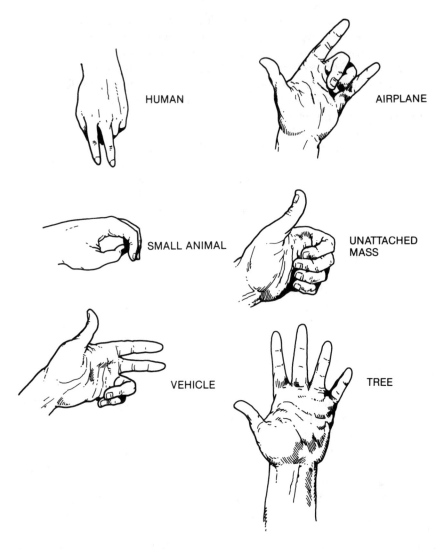

**FIGURE 5–1**    Some signs used in American Sign Language (from Newport, 1982).

beyond the language they see their parents use remains a challenge to our understanding.

*Hearing children.* Children who are not deaf also communicate through gestures and signs. Between 12 and 18 months, when children know relatively few words, gestures play a particularly important communicative role. Acredolo and Goodwyn (1985) examined in detail the verbal and nonverbal communication of Acredolo's daughter Kate. Kate's first consistent gesture appeared at 12 months, when she had produced three words verbally. It involved sniffing to refer to flowers. The next month, she began to lift her arms over her head to indicate *big* and to lift her nose and touch it with her finger to indicate *elephant.* Verbal and gestural language continued to develop in tandem for the next few months; at 15 months, 51 percent of Kate's vocabulary consisted of signs and 49 percent of verbal words. At that point, Kate's acquisition of verbal vocabulary accelerated; in the next month it more than doubled, whereas her gestural vocabulary increased only slightly. However, she continued to use the gestures to communicate for many months beyond that point.

Most hearing children are like Kate in using gestures much as they use words. They use the same gestures over extended periods of time, refer with them to a variety of particular objects from the same class, and use them even when not looking at the object to which they are referring (Acredolo & Goodwyn, 1989). The timing of the initial gestures also resembles that of the initial words; the two typically occur within one month of each other. Most of the gestures are acquired when children's spoken vocabulary is very small, between 0 and 25 words. Thus, they considerably enlarge children's ability to communicate at a time when their spoken vocabulary severely limits the ideas they can express. As Goldin-Meadow and Morford (1985) commented, "Communication in humans is a resilient phenomenon; when prevented from coming out of the mouth, it emanates almost irrepressibly from the fingers" (p. 146).

## LANGUAGE AND THOUGHT

Many Westerners know that Japanese society is technologically very advanced. Many also know that Japanese students score very highly on mathematics achievement tests. However, far fewer know that the Japanese language has an unusually extensive system of number words. As shown in Table 5–7, Japanese includes separate words for counting people, birds, four-legged animals, long thin objects such as pencils, and broad thin objects

**TABLE 5–7 Japanese Words for Counting Different Types of Objects**

| GENERAL OR UNKNOWN | PEOPLE | BIRDS | 4-LEGGED ANIMALS | PLANAR OBJECTS | LONG, THIN OBJECTS |
|---|---|---|---|---|---|
| 1. ikko | hitori | ichiwa | ippiti | ichimai | ippon |
| 2. niko | futari | niwa | nihiti | nimai | nihon |
| 3. sanko | sannin | samba | sambiki | sanmai | samhon |
| 4. yonko | yonin | yonwa | yonhiki | yonmai | yonhon |
| 5. goko | gonin | gowa | gohiki | gomai | gohon |

such as sheets of paper. On rainy days, Japanese mothers and their young children will play games such as "Let's count birds" (Hatano, 1989).

Observations such as these have stimulated considerable controversy about the relation between language and thought. Everyone agrees that people have concepts within which they categorize objects and events, and that they also have words for describing the objects and events. But how are they related? The issue is absolutely essential for understanding cognition. Do people throughout the world think in basically similar ways? Or are languages a sufficiently strong distorting lens that people who speak different languages experience the world differently? Similarly, does children's learning of new words trigger the formation of new concepts, or does ability to understand new terms demand that the relevant concepts already be in place? Consider three possible relations:

1. *Language shapes thought.* This position, known as the Sapir–Whorf hypothesis (after its two leading exponents), is based on the view that language shapes thought so profoundly that "the 'real world' is to a large extent unconsciously built up by the language habits of the group" (Sapir, 1951, p. 164). Its basic assumptions are that a culture's language shapes the way members of the culture interpret information about the world, and that differences among languages spoken in different cultures produce parallel differences in the way that members of the culture view the world.

2. *Thought shapes language.* As noted in Chapter 2, Piaget believed that the development of representational abilities at the end of the sensorimotor period makes possible the development of language, as well as other forms of representation such as drawing and mental imagery. Thus, he saw language development as depending on and awaiting cognitive development, rather than causing it. Within this view, "the linguistic input received by the child appears to have little importance either in determining that a category will be established or in determining the composition of a category" (Mervis, 1987, p. 225).

3. *Language and thought influence each other.* The Russian theorist Vygotsky, a contemporary of Piaget's, is especially identified with this position. According to Vygotsky (1962), language and thought begin developing independently. By age 2, however, their development becomes intertwined, and they mutually influence each other thereafter. The child's cognitive understanding of the world is expressed increasingly precisely in language, and language becomes increasingly effective in directing thought and action. Eventually, much of thought becomes internalized language.

A great deal of evidence has been collected on all sides of the issue. First consider evidence for thought's influencing language. Infants and toddlers throughout the world seem most interested in certain types of objects and events. The names of these objects and events become their first words, regardless of the particulars of their language (Barrett, 1986). Thus, they learn words for what they like to think about.

Another type of evidence for the influence of thought on language comes from the meanings that young children assign to the first words they learn. These meanings differ in characteristic ways from the meanings of the same words for adults. For example, when children are first learning to speak, they often refer to objects such as walnuts and round candles as "balls." These unusual uses reflect children's classification of objects overwhelming the influence of the language that they hear.

Nonlinguistic preferences and perceptions also influence later language learning. For example, children's guesses about the meanings of some new words reflect influences that have no particular linguistic base, but rather reflect general cognitive predispositions (e.g., they guess that both *top* and *bottom* refer to the upper surface of objects and that both *more* and *less* mean more) (Clark, 1983). Similarly, members of a tribe in New Guinea whose language did not include color terms beyond words for bright and dull learned words to label good examples of the basic colors (e.g., bright green) more easily than borderline examples (e.g., blue-green) (Rosch, 1973). The salience of basic colors within the perceptual system led to tribe members finding it especially easy to learn words to represent them.

The influence is by no means all in one direction, however; language also influences children's concepts and categories. When adults apply a word to an unfamiliar object, the labeling can lead children thereafter to think of the object as a member of the category referred to by the word (Mervis, 1987). Similarly, adults' use of a word to label an object for which a child does not know a word may lead the child to form a new category that includes objects like that one (Markman, 1987). Learning a label for a category also can result in children becoming more consistent in assigning objects with that label to the category and not assigning other objects to it, thus stabilizing the membership of the category (Schlesinger, 1982).

Together, these findings support the conclusion that language and thought mutually influence each other. Direct evidence supporting this position was provided by a study of the effects of grouping and labeling unfamiliar objects (Kuczaj, Borys, & Jones, 1989). Teaching 3-, 4-, and 5-year olds names for objects improved the children's ability to group the objects into categories. Thus, learning language that was relevant to the objects influenced the children's thinking about the objects. Conversely, prior experience in grouping the objects into categories led to more effective learning of their names. Here, thinking about the objects promoted the learning of language relevant to them. As Vygotsky suggested, language and thought may at first develop separately. A 6-month-old may have many thoughts without any corresponding language. By the second year, however, the development of thought and language seem inextricably intertwined.

## SUMMARY

The acquisition of language in the first few years of life is one of children's greatest achievements. They learn phonology, meanings, grammar, and communication. Phonology refers to the production and comprehension of speech sounds. Meaning refers to relations between words and the objects and events they describe. Grammar involves the ordering of words within statements, as well as the specification of tense and number. Communication is the way phonology, grammar, and meaning are used together to express desires and intentions, elicit reactions, and provide information.

Speech sounds are produced by impeding the usual flow of air. Different sounds are distinguished by the particular type of impediment. With vowels, the only impediments are produced by the vocal cords; with consonants, the tongue, teeth, and lips produce additional impediments. Phonological development proceeds in a regular sequence. First infants cry, then they coo, then they babble, and then they produce words. Languages throughout the world take advantage of the types of first syllables that babies produce by making these names of caretakers: *mama, papa, dada,* and so on. The ease of understanding what beginning speakers say is improved both by their avoidance of words with difficult-to-make sounds and by the tendencies of languages to use relatively easy-to-pronounce words to name objects that young children most wish to discuss. Later phonological development occurs in ability to control the sounds that are made and in the clarity of pronunciation.

The first words and word meanings of children throughout the world are quite similar. They refer to people, animals, toys, vehicles, and other objects that interest children, that are relatively concrete, and that the children want. Even when beginning language users say the same words as adults, they may not assign the words the same meaning. At first, children underextend some meanings, overextend others, and develop some meanings that are underextended in some ways and overextended in others. Form, function, and other striking characteristics of objects are the main components of early meanings. The rate of acquisition of new words is at first gradual, but it speeds up greatly at about age 18 months. Assumptions that unknown words refer to classes of objects (the taxonomic constraint) and that their referents are distinct from those of already-known words (the mutual exclusivity constraint) seem to facilitate this language explosion. Children also use a variety of clever strategies, both to infer the meaning of statements they do not entirely understand and to invent words for expressing meanings when they do not know any appropriate standard word.

Children's initial statements involve only one word. They are often called *holophrases,* because the single word expresses a larger unit of meaning. Somewhat later, children produce two-word phrases. This marks the true beginning of grammatical development, because it is the first time children need to order words in their statements. At first they base their ordering of words on the words' meanings. The orders follow standard meaningful patterns such as agent–action and possessor–possessed object. As with word meanings, children at first tend to be conservative about applying newly acquired grammatical constructions to novel contexts. After the two-word period, children learn to form a wide variety of grammatical constructions, many of them based on categories that have no clear correspondence to meanings. Among the factors that contribute to formation of purely grammatical categories and rules are children's expectations about the forms grammars should take, bootstrapping from early meaning-based categories to later grammar-based ones, and detection of regular patterns within the language. Although adults at first learn new grammars more rapidly than children, the children overtake them and eventually learn the new languages' grammars more completely.

Children communicate both through verbal language and through gestures. Long before infants say words, they motivate older people to talk to them by moving in synchrony with speech intonations and making sounds when the other person stops talking. Slightly later, infants direct conversation to particular objects by pointing to them and bringing them to adults. Adults and older children motivate infants and very young children to listen by adopting the conversational style known as motherese, involving high pitches, exaggerated intonations, and simple sentences. By age 2 or 3, children master a wide variety of conversational conventions. They know that they should answer "Did you" questions with "yes" or "no" and that they should answer "Why" questions with "because," even when they do not understand the meaning of the remainder of the sentence. Both deaf and hearing children use gestures as well as verbal language to communicate. With hearing children the use of gestures is most important between ages 1 and 2½, but with deaf children their importance continues throughout life.

Language and thought may begin their development separately, but beyond the first year, they are complexly intertwined. Each affects the other's development. Learning names for objects facilitates grouping them into categories, and categorizing objects makes it easier to learn their names. Language may also influence thought by stabilizing the membership of categories, and thought may also influence language by making it easier to learn words that correspond to preexisting categories.

## RECOMMENDED READINGS

Goldin-Meadow, S., & Morford, M. (1985). Gesture in early child language: Studies of deaf and hearing children. *Merrill-Palmer Quarterly, 31*, 145–176. Charming description of how deaf children invent signs to express themselves.

Johnson, J. S., & Newport, E. L. (1989). **Critical period effects in second language learning: The influence of maturational state on the acquisition of English as a second language.** *Cognitive Psychology, 21,* 60–99. Unusual study that examines the relation between age at the outset of immersion in a language and the degree to which people master the language's grammar. Makes a strong case for a critical period in grammatical acquisition.

Kuczaj, S. A., II, Borys, R. H., & Jones, M. (1989). **On the interaction of language and thought: Some thoughts on the developmental data.** In A. Gellatly, D. Rogers, & J. A. Sloboda (Eds.), *Cognition and the social world.* New York: Oxford University Press. Kuczaj and his colleagues present an intriguing consideration of the relation between language and thought.

Maratsos, M. P. (1989). **Innateness and plasticity in language acquisition.** In M. L. Rice & R. L. Schiefelbusch (Eds.), *The teachability of language* (pp. 105–125). Baltimore, MD: Brookes-Cole. Clear, convincing description of reasons for viewing language acquisition as a special process, not identical to the processes used for other types of learning.

Markman, E. M. (1989). *Categorization and naming in children: Problems of induction.* Cambridge, MA: MIT. This book provides a comprehensive integration of Markman's important and influential work on constraints on language learning and categorization.

Merriman, W. E., & Bowman, L. L. (1989). **The mutual exclusivity bias in children's word learning.** *Monographs of the Society for Research in Child Development, 54,* Serial No. 220. A thoughtful analysis of how constraints on acquisition of word meaning might operate and what it means to say that a child has such a constraint.

# 6

# Memory Development

*Memory is the mother of all wisdom.* (Aeschylus, fifth century B.C.)
*Memory is the treasury and guardian of all things.* (Cicero, first century B.C.)

Greek playwrights and Roman orators are not the only ones who have noted the centrality of memory to human civilization. The many movies and television shows that focus on amnesiacs reflect popular recognition of how our very identities depend on our memories: Lose your memory, lose your identity. People's fascination with mnemonists, individuals who perform prodigious memory feats, attests to a similar recognition. But how does memory operate, and how does it develop?

A number of basic characteristics of memory can be grasped by taking part in the following two experiments. To obtain the maximum benefit, participate as a subject in them. Write down your answers on a sheet of paper, for reference in the discussion after the experiments. Be sure to follow the instructions carefully.

*Experiment 1.* Read the following 12 words, proceeding from the top to the bottom of one column and then from the top to the bottom of the other. Do this twice. Then cover the words, and write them in any order:

| | |
|---|---|
| ball | bird |
| chair | cord |
| hammer | comb |
| cup | tree |
| typewriter | ghost |
| book | meat |

Now do the same thing with the following list:

| | |
|---|---|
| couch | orange |
| table | banana |
| lamp | dog |
| rug | rat |
| pear | horse |
| pineapple | sheep |

*Experiment 2.* Read the following group of numbers once, cover them, wait for 15 seconds, and write them in order:

3428670159

Now do the same thing with the following list:

212 467 9032

In Experiment 1, almost all people remember more words from the second list than from the first. They typically divide the 12 words in the second list into three categories—furniture, fruit, and animals. Then, when they attempt to recall the words, they use the category names to help them remember. They might say to themselves, "Furniture, let's see, did I see 'carpet,' no, did I see 'table,' yes, OK, 'table,' did I see 'lamp,' yes, 'lamp,' " and so on.

In contrast, the words in the first list cannot be organized into simple categories. Therefore, recalling each word is a new problem. People are flexible, and they often take advantage of whatever opportunities a task affords. Thus, in the first list, they might note that *typewriter* is followed by *book*, and might link the two by thinking to themselves, "Typewriters can be used to write books." They also might link *bird* and *tree*, or *cup* and *meat*. Such insights typically aid memory for the first list, but not enough to overcome the advantage of the more easily organized second list.

The fact that people can organize to-be-remembered material into categories is no guarantee that they will do so. Young children might not notice that *couch, table, lamp,* and *rug* are all furniture. If they did not, they might not benefit from the categorical structure. The ability to recognize potentially useful organizations may be a potent source of memory development.

Memory in this situation and others depends on two broad classes of processes: encoding and retrieval. As discussed in Chapter 3, *encoding* refers to the cognitive activities used to represent information on a particular occasion. One of these activities might be to note that the first four words in the second list are furniture, that the next four are fruits, and so on. *Retrieval* refers to the cognitive activities that the memorizer performs when trying to recall material that was presented earlier. A person trying to retrieve a list might use category names as *retrieval cues* and think, "Let's see. There were three categories. What were they? Oh yeah, one was furniture. . . ."

In the second experiment, you were asked to recall in order two lists of numbers. You probably remembered more from the second than from the first. The key difference was that you could draw an analogy between the second list and a long-distance phone number. Knowledge of the phone number form increases the efficiency of the rehearsal process most people use in this situation and thus helps them remember more of the numbers.

The influence of knowledge on memory is obvious in the phone number example. However, even in situations in which people lack knowledge directly relevant to the material they are trying to remember, they often find indirect ways to use it. Ericsson, Chase, and Faloon's (1980) case history of S. F. vividly illustrates this point.

Before the experiment began, S. F. was a seemingly unremarkable college sophomore. His grades were average, and he did not appear to be of unusual intelligence. One fact about him was unusual, however, and this proved to be important: He was an accomplished cross-country runner.

S. F. participated in a forward digit-span experiment. The task is similar to the one you performed on list 1 of Experiment 2. The experimenter presents a randomly ordered list of numbers at a rate of one per second; the participant needs to repeat the numbers in order. A frequent assumption in interpreting performance on digit-span tests is that recall of each digit requires one unit of memory capacity. Thus, the number of digits recalled is interpreted as indicating the capacity of working memory.

Previous research indicated that college students can correctly repeat lists of seven or eight digits, but not much longer ones (Dempster, 1981). A person who correctly repeats the 10 digits in the first list in Experiment 2 would be unusual, and would be thought to have an exceptional memory. S. F. was not exceptional in this regard. He could recall only seven digits when the experiment started. Yet by the end, he could recall more than 75 digits, a length that exceeds the achievements of professional mnemonists who perform on late-night television.

S. F. was not given special instructions in how to be a memory expert. He was, however, given extensive practice. For one hour per day, three to five days per week, for more than one and a half years, he practiced recalling lists of randomly ordered digits. If he correctly recalled all the digits in a list, his next list was one digit longer. If he failed to recall all of them, his next list was one digit shorter. Given this practice, his digit span improved from 7 to 79 digits, 10 times that of the average college student.

How did he do it? S. F.'s verbal reports were revealing. He said that he drew on his familiarity with cross-country racing to encode groups of three or four numbers as running times. For example, he encoded 3492 as "3 minutes 49.2 seconds, near world-record time (for the mile)." On those numeric combinations that he could not code as running times, he employed supplementary strategies, such as viewing the numbers as ages (e.g., 893 was encoded as 89.3, "a very old man"). These coding strategies, together with complex organizations of the three- and four-digit units, led to the great improvement.

Later, D. D., another cross-country runner, was taught S. F.'s memory strategies. He learned them so well that he eventually recalled more than

**FIGURE 6–1** Mean digit span for S. F. and D. D. as a function of practice. By the end of training, S. F., the first memory-span expert, could remember more than 75 digits. D. D., who was taught S. F.'s strategies, eventually was able to remember more than 100 digits (data provided courtesy of James Staszewski).

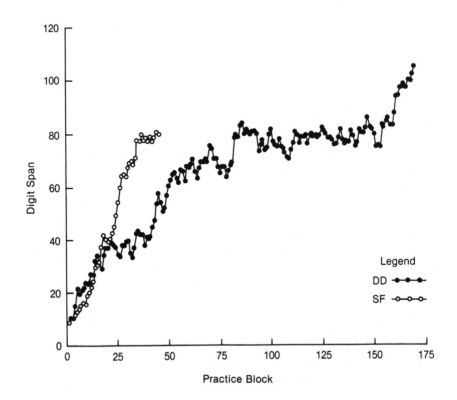

100 digits, surpassing S. F.'s record (Figure 6–1). Thus, the usefulness of the strategies was not limited to S. F. (Staszewski, 1988).

Aside from testifying to what people can accomplish with sufficient practice and determination, S. F.'s case history also illustrates several notable characteristics of memory. First, it demonstrates the pervasive influence of strategies and of prior knowledge of the content being remembered. Memory span traditionally has been thought of as a straightforward measure of memory capacity. Even there, S. F. demonstrated that strategies and content knowledge enter in.

Second, the case illustrates the role of meaning in memory. S. F. chose to encode numbers as running times and ages because these were especially meaningful to him. D. D. benefited from the same strategies for the same reason. In general, memory for meaningful material far surpasses memory for material that is not so meaningful.

A third lesson is that memory skills are often highly specific to particular content. Despite S. F.'s proficiency at recalling long sequences of numbers, his proficiency at recalling sequences of letters hardly changed. When, after three months of practice, he was asked to recall letters rather than numbers, his span for the alphabetic materials was a very average six consonants. This specificity makes it very difficult to say in the abstract how large a person's memory capacity actually is.

Fourth and finally, the data in Figure 6–1 show that neither S. F. nor D. D. ever reached a brick wall beyond which their memory could not improve. As Ericsson, Chase, and Faloon (1980) concluded, "There is seemingly no limit to improvement in memory skill with practice" (p. 1182).

The phenomena illustrated in these experiments create a basis for understanding a crucial question about children's memory:

## WHAT DEVELOPS IN MEMORY DEVELOPMENT?

Given an older child, a younger child, and a situation that both are seeing for the first time, the older child almost always will remember more. This is the central fact of memory development. The difference can be explained in four ways.

One possibility is that older children have superior *basic capacities.* Translated into terms of a computer analogy, this view suggests that what develops is the hardware of memory—its absolute capacity or its speed of operation—rather than the software—the particular procedures used to memorize material. A second possibility is that what develops is memory *strategies.* Older children know a greater variety of memory strategies and use them more often, more efficiently, and more flexibly than younger children. A third possibility is that *metacognition*—knowledge about one's own cognitive activities—is a main source of memory development. Older children better understand how memory works; they may use this knowledge to choose strategies and allocate memory resources more effectively. Finally, older children have greater prior knowledge of the types of content they need to remember; this greater *content knowledge* may explain their superior memory. Of course, these four hypotheses are not mutually exclusive; all of them, or any combination of them, could contribute to the superiority of older children's memory.

In this chapter we consider what is known about the contributions to memory development of changes in basic capacities, strategies, metacognition, and content knowledge (Table 6–1). Just to preview what will emerge, it appears that some of the sources of development contribute more than others, and that some sources play large roles in certain periods of childhood but not others. It may be worthwhile to apply your intuitions about memory development and what you have learned about children's thinking generally, to predict which of these potential sources of memory develop-

---

**TABLE 6–1   Chapter Outline**

   I.   What Develops in Memory Development?
  II.   The Role of Basic Capacities
        A.   Recognition
        B.   Association, Retrieval, and Generalization
        C.   Infantile Amnesia
        D.   Processing Capacity
        E.   Processing Speed
        F.   Evaluation
 III.   The Role of Strategies
        A.   Searching for Objects
        B.   Rehearsing
        C.   Organizing
        D.   Elaborating
        E.   Deploying Cognitive Resources
        F.   Evaluation
  IV.   The Role of Metacognition
        A.   Explicit Metacognitive Knowledge
        B.   Implicit Metacognitive Knowledge
        C.   Evaluation
   V.   The Role of Content Knowledge
        A.   Effects on How Much Children Remember
        B.   Effects on What Children Remember
        C.   Content Knowledge as an Explanation for Other Memory Changes
        D.   How Does Content Knowledge Aid Memory?
        E.   Evaluation
  VI.   What Develops When In Memory Development?
 VII.   Summary

---

ment will be most influential in infancy and early childhood, in middle childhood, and in late childhood and adolescence.

## THE ROLE OF BASIC CAPACITIES

Basic capacities are frequently used, rapidly executed memory processes such as recognition, association, and retrieval. They are building blocks of cognitive activity, in the sense that all more-complex cognitive activities are built up by combining them in different ways. Because they are so frequently used, development differences in them could account for an enormous number of other developmental differences in memory performance.

The role of basic processes in memory functioning is especially dominant early in life. Infants do not possess memory strategies, lack knowledge of the world, and are ignorant about the workings of their own memory. Still, they manage to learn and remember a great deal. Their relatively skillfull execution of basic processes is what allows this learning to occur.

### Recognition

It is difficult to even imagine cognitive development taking place without the ability to recognize. Fortunately, this ability is present from birth. When newborn *preterm* infants are presented a picture repeatedly, their looking at it gradually falls off; when they are shown a different picture, their looking immediately increases (Werner & Siqueland, 1978). No one knows whether the infants' recognition of the repeatedly shown picture is conscious; it may well be *implicit* rather than *explicit*. Either way, however, the recognition is sufficient that it leads infants to turn their attention elsewhere when the familiar picture is shown.

Infants' recognition of familiar objects also is surprisingly durable. Even two weeks after they are habituated to a particular form, 2-month-olds continue to prefer a different form (Fantz, Fagan, & Miranda, 1975). Further, as noted in Chapter 1, the rate at which 7-month-olds habituate to stimuli predicts their later IQs quite accurately (Fagan, 1984). This may either be due to people who quickly recognize objects having more time and energy to learn about other aspects of the world, or may be due to the rapid habituation in infancy being indicative of generally more efficient information processing.

On what basis do infants recognize objects as familiar? To answer this question, Strauss and Cohen (1978) habituated 5-month-olds to an object with a particular form, orientation, size, and color (for example, a large, black, right-side-up arrow). Later, the infants were shown the original object plus another one that varied in one or more of the attributes. The alternative object could be a white, large, right-side-up arrow. In the example, for the infants to prefer the new object, they would need to remember the color of the original, for this is the only dimension that differentiates the new object from the old one.

Immediately after 5-month-olds were shown the original stimulus, they remembered all four attributes. Fifteen minutes later, they remembered only form and color. Twenty-four hours later, they remembered only the object's form. Thus, infants' recognition of the type of object they saw (e.g., a dog) is quite durable, but their memory for its properties, such as size and color, is less enduring.

Recognition is strikingly accurate from early in life; 2-year-olds recognize pictures more accurately than adults recall them (Perlmutter & Lange, 1978). By 4 years, the accuracy of recognition is truly remarkable. In one study, 4-year-olds answered correctly 100 percent of questions concerning whether they had seen a picture earlier or not, despite their having seen as many as 25 pictures between their two exposures to the picture (Brown & Scott, 1971). Even when preschoolers were asked to recognize quite subtle differences—for example, when the only difference between two pictures was whether a dog they had seen was sitting or standing—they still recognized correctly on 95 percent of the trials (Brown & Campione, 1972). Ability to recognize very subtle distinctions improves even further beyond the preschool period (Sophian & Stigler, 1981), but in general, recognition is excellent from early in development.

### Association, Recall, and Generalization

Ability to associate stimuli and responses also seems to be present from birth. Siqueland and Lipsitt (1966) set newborns a simple task involving a buzzer and a tone. When the buzzer sounded, the newborns received a sweet solution for turning to the right. When the tone sounded, they received it for turning to the left. The newborns quickly learned to respond correctly, indicating that they were able to associate one sound with turning one way and the other sound with turning the other way.

Infants also can associate stimuli and responses when the reinforcement is less tangible than food. Rovee and Fagen (1976) placed a mobile above 3-month-olds' cribs and attached a string to one of their ankles and to the mobile. Kicking made the mobile move in interesting ways. The infants' rate of kicking increased considerably when they learned the connection between their action and the mobile's movements. Often, the recognition came quite abruptly; infants suddenly began kicking much more often. The abruptness of the change suggested that infants, like adults, may from time to time have insights.

In a later study, the infants' memories of the connection between their kicking and the mobile's movements were shown to be quite durable;

3-month-olds still remembered it two weeks after the initial experience (Enright, Rovee-Collier, Fagan, & Caniglia, 1983). The memories also proved to be quite precise. When a new mobile was substituted for the familiar one, infants at first did not transfer their learning to it. However, given exposure to several similar mobiles, the 3-month-olds learned to generalize to other mobiles (Rovee-Collier, 1989). Thus, even infants less than 6 months old associate stimuli and responses, generalize the learning to new situations, retain memories for an extended period of time, and have simple insights into connections between their behaviors and the consequences they produce.

Infants also possess the invaluable ability to recall objects and events that are not physically present. The capability is evident in their imitating at a later time activities that they saw earlier. Piaget (1951) contended that infants were incapable of such imitation until 18- to 24-months, because they could not form internal representations. In fact, however, infants as young as 9 months have been found capable of imitating novel activities such as pressing a recessed button on a box to trigger a beeping sound. After a 24-hour delay, 50% of infants who had seen an adult model this and 2 other actions repeated at least 2 of the 3 actions, versus 19% of infants who had not seen the adults model the activities (Meltzoff, 1988a). Similar findings have been obtained with 14-month-olds repeating truly novel activities, such as pressing one's forehead against a panel to make a light go on, after a 1-week delay (Meltzoff, 1988b). Such early imitation provides infants a way of learning from other people, as well as demonstrating that infants are capable of forming internal representations and of using them to recall the corresponding activities considerably later.

## Infantile Amnesia

If infants can recognize, associate, and learn, why are adults almost never able to remember specific events that happened to them during infancy and very early childhood? Think about it; what is the first thing that you remember, and what if anything, can you remember that happened before you were 3? Even when people claim to remember early occurrences, for example when under hypnosis, checks on the accuracy of their statements often reveal that they are recalling stories they heard later, rather than the actual event. The phenomenon is not limited to human beings; rats also show little recall of events that occurred in their infancy (Spear, 1984).

How might this inability to recall the earliest experiences be explained? It is not due simply to the sheer passage of time; recall from Chapter 3 people's excellent recognition of pictures of people who attended high school with them 35 years earlier. Another seemingly plausible explanation, that infants do not form enduring memories at this point in development, also is incorrect. Children between 2½ and 3 years old remember experiences that occurred in their first year (Myers, Clifton, & Clarkson, 1987). Nor does Freud's (1905/1953) hypothesis that infantile amnesia reflects repression of sexually charged episodes explain the phenomenon. While such repression may occur, people cannot remember any other events from infancy either.

Two other explanations seem more promising. One involves the possibility of physiological changes relevant to memory. In particular, maturation of the frontal lobes of the brain continues throughout early childhood, and this part of the brain may be critical for remembering particular episodes in ways that can later be retrieved (Boyer & Diamond, in press; Schacter, 1987). A variant of this view is that there are two memory systems, one explicit and one implicit, that mature at different rates. The explicit memory system, which gives rise to conscious experiences of recall and recognition, is believed to mature more slowly than the implicit system, which facilitates learning and memory, but on an unconscious level. Consistent with this view, when 9-year-olds are shown pictures of children with whom they attended preschool six years earlier, they show physiological reactions characteristic of memory even when they do not consciously recognize the other child (Newcombe, Fox, & Prime, 1989). This implicit memory resembles that shown by adult amnesiacs, who cannot consciously recognize familiar faces, but react with physiological responses characteristic of remembering. Since no one has discovered a way of measuring the consciousness of infants, it is quite possible that most or all findings on recognition and recall in the first 6 months reflect implicit rather than explicit memory.

The other likely explanation for infantile amnesia involves incompatibilities between the ways in which infants encode information and the ways in which older children and adults retrieve it. Whether people can remember depends critically on the fit between the way in which they earlier encoded the information and the way in which they later attempt to retrieve it. The better able the person is to reconstruct the perspective from which the material was encoded, the more likely that recall will be successful.

Supporting this view are the variety of factors that work against older children's and adult's retrieval efforts closely matching infants' and toddlers' encoding. The spatial perspective of a person whose head is usually five or six feet above the ground is very different from that of a person who is only two feet tall even when standing. Older children and adults often try to retrieve the names of things they saw, but infants would not have encoded the information verbally. Time of day and season of the year are meaningful retrieval cues for adults ("I remember it happened on a warm summer afternoon."), but again are unlikely to closely match the way in which they encoded their experiences when they were infants. These incompatibilities between early encoding and later retrieval efforts seem likely to provide at least part of the explanation for infantile amnesia. Whether they are the whole story remains to be seen, though.

### Processing Capacity

One of the most controversial issues about children's thinking is whether their memory capacity, particularly their working-memory capacity, changes with age. There is little question about the potential importance of such changes. If young children cannot hold as much information in memory as older ones, their ability to learn and remember would be seriously impaired. But are such differences in fact present?

As noted earlier, this question has been addressed by examining how many randomly selected numbers or letters children of different ages can remember. Figure 6–2 illustrates that the number increases steadily with age. Most 5-year-olds can correctly recall lists of four digits, but not longer ones, whereas most adults can recall lists with seven digits. Such data have

**FIGURE 6–2** Improvement with age in memory span for numbers and letters (after Dempster, 1981). Copyright 1981 by the American Psychological Association. Adapted by permission.

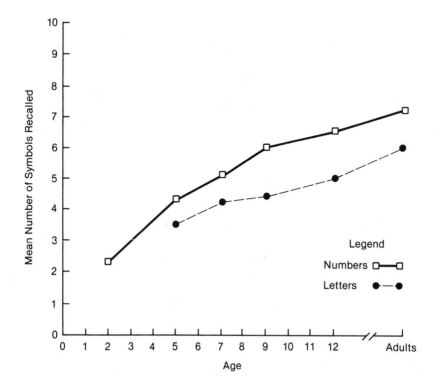

led a number of investigators, among them Pascual-Leone (1970, 1989), to propose that the absolute number of symbols that people can hold in working memory more than doubles from infancy to adulthood.

Although the data are clear, the implications for whether working memory capacity changes with age are not so obvious. The demand on cognitive resources that a task imposes reflects both the child's resources and the demands of the task. Developmental improvements in performance can be produced either by an increase in the child's resources or by a decrease in the resources the child expends in doing the task. Consider some reasons why older children might remember longer lists of numbers, even if the absolute capacity of their working memory did not differ from that of younger children. The older children know more about numbers. This greater familiarity could help them remember the numbers more efficiently. They also know more strategies, such as rehearsal, for enhancing their recall. They also are more skillful in choosing when to use the strategies they know. Thus, it is clear that older children can store more material in working memory, but it remains unknown (and perhaps unknowable) whether this is due to change in the actual capacity of working memory or to changes in knowledge and strategies that allow more material to be stored within the same capacity (as in the car trunk analogy in Chapter 3).

### Processing Speed

Speed of information processing, like the number of numbers that can be held in memory, increases greatly with age. This has been found for immediate processing (Hoving, Spencer, Robb, & Schulte, 1978), processing of information in working memory (Hale, 1990; Kail, 1986, 1988; Keating & Bobbit, 1978), and retrieval of information from long-term memory (Hale, 1989; Kail, 1986, 1988; Keating & Bobbitt, 1978; Whitney, 1986). Again, however, considerable controversy has arisen over whether the increased speed is due to greater use of more-efficient strategies, to greater familiarity with the items being processed, or to increases in speed per se.

Recent evidence suggests that speed of processing per se, as well as greater knowledge and more-efficient strategies, contributes to the faster processing. Kail (1986) examined 8-to-21-year-olds' processing rates on two tasks. On both of them, the increase with age in processing speed was best described by the same mathematical equation—one that differed from the equation that best describes improvements that come with practice (Newell & Rosenbloom, 1981). The same type of result has been obtained since then on five other, quite different tasks, as well as emerging again on the two original ones (Hale, 1990; Kail, 1988.) Absolute speed of processing thus does seem to increase with age, above and beyond the large increases attributable to practice and superior strategies.

**Evaluation**

Evaluating the contribution of basic processes to memory development is not a simple task. Depending on the perspective taken, it can legitimately be argued that basic processes contribute to memory development (1) in large and direct ways; (2) little, if at all; or (3) indirectly, but importantly.

First consider the perspective within which basic processes are large and direct contributors to memory development. From the initial days out of the womb, infants recognize, associate, generalize, and perform other basic processes. These capacities allow them to learn and remember a tremendous amount before they possess strategies, understanding of memory, or content knowledge. Further, without basic capacities, all other memory activities would be futile. For example, rehearsing a phone number would be pointless if we could not associate the phone number with the person whose number it was. In sum, understanding how basic processes operate is essential to understanding how children's memories work at all ages.

Now consider the perspective from which basic processes appear to contribute little if anything to memory development. Because these processes are present so early, and because they function quite well even in the beginning, most *improvements* in memory with age cannot be attributed to improvements in the basic capacities. From this perspective, basic processes are essential for memory, but contribute little to memory development (though the recent work on changes in speed of processing may lead to changes in this view).

Finally, consider a third perspective—that basic processes exert a large but indirect effect on memory development. From this perspective, basic processes not only are critical to memory in general but also allow children to acquire useful strategies and content knowledge. These improved strategies and content knowledge are viewed as the direct causes of most improvements in memory. Without the basic processes, though, the strategies and content knowledge would never have been learned. Thus, the contribution of basic processes to developmental improvements in memory is seen as absolutely essential, but indirect.

Fortunately, there is no need to choose among these three perspectives. Each one holds a considerable amount of truth, and a full appreciation of the contribution of basic processes to memory development requires all three.

## THE ROLE OF STRATEGIES

Strategies have been defined as "cognitive or behavioral activities that are under the deliberate control of the subject and are employed so as to enhance memory performance" (Naus & Ornstein, 1983, p. 12). Children employ strategies in all phases of memorization: when they encode material, when they store it, and when they retrieve it. Age-related improvements in memory are in large part due to acquisition of new strategies, refinement of existing ones, and extension of existing strategies to new situations.

Although many particulars vary with the strategy, certain features characterize the development of all strategies (Waters & Andreassen, 1983). When children first acquire a memory strategy, they use it in only some of the situations where it is applicable. They limit it to materials where the strategy is easy to use and to situations that are relatively undemanding. They also are quite rigid in applying the strategy and often fail to adapt to changing task demands. All of this changes with development. Older children and children more experienced in using a strategy more actively initiate it; use it in more diverse situations, including ones that make the strategy difficult to execute; use higher-quality versions of the strategy; and become more flexible in tailoring the strategy to the particulars of the situation. We next consider some strategies that even very young children use, and then turn to strategies used mainly by older children.

### Searching for Objects

Even before their second birthday, children begin to use rudimentary strategies. Several of these strategies are evident in the way they search for hidden objects. In one study (DeLoache, Cassidy, & Brown, 1985), 18-to-24-month-olds saw a Big Bird doll hidden under various objects such as pillows. They then had to wait three or four minutes until the experimenter asked them to find the doll. The toddlers engaged in a variety of strategic activities to keep alive their memories of the doll's location. While waiting, they looked at the hiding place, pointed to it, and named the hidden object. They did not engage in these activities nearly as frequently when Big Bird was placed in plain sight, thus indicating that the activities were limited to situations where memory loss was a potential problem.

Very young children's use of such strategies is fragile; they use them only under the most favorable circumstances. Thus, when an object was hidden under one of three identical cups, rather than under a more distinctive object such as a pillow, 2-year-olds did not engage in strategic activities such as watching or touching the correct cup. In contrast, 3-year-olds behaved with the identical cups as 1 ½-year-olds had with the pillow and other more distinctive objects (Wellman, Ritter, & Flavell, 1975). In general, familiarity with the task setting leads to more consistent and efficient searching (Schneider & Sodian, 1988).

Development of strategies for finding hidden objects does not stop in early childhood; it continues for many years. For example, when asked to find an object hidden under one of six identical cups placed on a spinning turntable, 8-year-olds spontaneously used the strategy of picking up from the table a gold star or a paper clip and placing the marker on the relevant cup; 5-year-olds usually required hints from the experimenter to use this strategy; 3-year-olds either did not use the strategy at all or did so only after a great deal of prompting (Beal & Fleisig, 1987; Ritter, 1978).

### Rehearsing

When verbatim recall is essential, reciting the information over and over can help children greatly. School-age children often use this strategy to good advantage. Consider the following report:

> A 9-year-old boy memorized the license plate number of a getaway car following an armed robbery, a court was told Monday. . . . The boy and his friend . . . looked in the drug store window and saw a man grab a 14-year-old cashier's neck. . . . After the robbery, the boys mentally repeated the license number until they gave it to police. (*Edmonton Journal*, January 13, 1981, cited in Kail, 1984)

Without rehearsing the license number, the boys almost certainly would have forgotten it before they could tell the police.

Children younger than age 6 or 7 rehearse considerably less often than older children. In one study, 5- and 10-year-olds were shown seven pictures and saw the experimenter point to three of them. The children knew they would need to point to the same three pictures in the same order, but they had to wait 15 seconds before doing so. Far more 10- than 5-year-olds moved their lips or audibly repeated the pictures' names in the 15 seconds between when the pictures were presented and when the children were asked to name them. Those children who rehearsed in this way recalled more than those who did not (Flavell, Beach, & Chinsky, 1966).

The quality of rehearsal continues to improve well beyond the age at which children first rehearse. When 9-year-olds were presented a list of words to remember and asked to rehearse aloud, they typically rehearsed each new item in isolation. For example, asked to remember a list that started "desk, lawn, sky, shirt, cat," most said "cat, cat, cat" after hearing *cat* (Ornstein, Naus, & Liberty, 1975). In contrast, most 13-year-olds used a more-sophisticated version known as *cumulative rehearsal*, in which they combined the past few words with the newly presented one. After hearing *cat*, they said "desk, lawn, sky, shirt, cat." This latter approach proved considerably more effective in aiding subsequent recall.

Rehearsing helps both older and younger children remember material that they must later repeat verbatim. Children of a given age who use even the simpler forms of rehearsal recall more than peers who do not.

When original nonrehearsers are taught to rehearse, their recall improves. When children who use relatively simple rehearsal strategies are taught more-sophisticated ones, their recall also benefits (Naus, Ornstein, & Aivano, 1977). Some demonstrations of the potential usefulness of teaching children to rehearse have been especially dramatic. Providing retarded children with extensive training and practice in rehearsal has led to their recall becoming as accurate as that of untrained adults with average IQs (Belmont & Butterfield, 1977).

These successes are only half the story, however. Getting young children to generalize their training to new situations is much more difficult than getting them to rehearse in the original situation. This is true even when the strategy improved recall in the first case. Unless given explicit instructions to use the strategy in later situations, children often do not do so (Hagen, Hargrove, & Ross, 1973; Keeney, Cannizzo, & Flavell, 1967).

Why would children not use a helpful strategy? Initial attempts to explain this finding focused on two possibilities. One was that young children fail to use rehearsal and other strategies because they have a *mediational deficiency* (Reese, 1962). In this view, they do not rehearse because rehearsal does not have the same beneficial effect on their recall as it does on older children's. The other proposed explanation was that their failure to use such strategies was due to a *production deficiency* (Flavell, 1970). Within this view, young children's failure to rehearse was due to their simply not knowing the strategy or when to use it.

Today, neither of these positions seems tenable. The mediation deficiency hypothesis fails to explain why young children benefit from being taught strategies. The production deficiency hypothesis fails to explain why, even when young children have been taught a strategy, their recall rarely reaches the level of older children's, and why they often fail to transfer strategies to new situations.

What seems necessary is a deeper appreciation of the costs as well as the benefits of using a strategy. In many cases, young children both realize fewer benefits from using strategies and incur greater costs. When people first learn a strategy, the costs in mental effort required to use it are greater than they will later be. For example, rehearsing a set of numbers while simultaneously performing another task (such as tapping one's index finger on a table as fast as possible) produces greater decrements in performance on the other task for younger than for older children (Guttentag, 1984, 1985; Kee & Howell, 1988). The greater decrease in tapping rate seems to be due to the greater mental resources the younger children need to expend to rehearse. Complementarily, when an experimenter reduces the mental effort needed to use a strategy, differences between older and younger children's recall decrease (DeMarie-Dreblow & Miller, 1988).

This perspective suggests that young children's use of a helpful strategy can be raised by either increasing their benefits from using the strategy or decreasing the cost to them of using it. Consistent with this prediction, children more often rehearse, and rehearse in more-sophisticated ways, when the benefits to them of using a strategy are increased, for example by paying them money for successful recall (Kunzinger & Wittryol, 1984). Strategy use also increases when costs of using the strategy are decreased, for example by presenting material that is relatively easy to rehearse (Ornstein, Medlin, Stone, & Naus, 1985; Ornstein & Naus, 1985). Children's use of a strategy thus is sensitive to both its costs and its benefits. Increases with age in strategy use reflect both greater benefits and lower costs to the older children.

### Organizing

When people need to recall material, but not necessarily in the original order, they often reorganize it into easier-to-remember form. Experiment 1 at the beginning of the chapter illustrated this tendency. Most people organize the second list into furniture, fruit, and animals, which allows them to recall more items.

The development of organizational strategies parallels the development of rehearsal. As with rehearsal, 5- and 6-year-olds use the strategy considerably less often than do 9- and 10-year-olds. Also as with rehearsal, the quality of older and younger children's organizations differ. Younger children divide lists into a greater number of categories, each having fewer members. Their categories are less stable, with considerable reorganization often occurring from one trial to the next (Moely, 1977). Executing the strategy also requires more of their available cognitive resources (Bjorklund & Harnishfeger, 1987).

A final parallel involves learning new strategies. Children as young as 4 or 5 years can learn organizational strategies (Moely, Olson, Halwes, & Flavell, 1969). Learning the strategy helps them remember more. On the other hand, they often do not transfer the learning to new situations, even to ones that are relatively similar to the original one (Williams & Goulet, 1975). As with rehearsal, this may be due to children's expending greater cognitive resources on executing organizational strategies and not recalling as much when they use them.

Children's organization of material raises an issue that goes to the very heart of the question "What is a strategy?" This issue concerns whether organization is a voluntary strategy or a product of involuntary associations. Consider two types of behavior that look like identical examples of organization, but that differ in their reason for occurring. One conforms closely to the definition of strategies that was provided earlier in the chapter: a behavioral activity that is "under the deliberate control" of the child. A girl trying to recall a list of words that included *hammer, nail,* and *screw* might think, "OK, there were some tools. Was 'hammer' one of them? Yes.

Was 'chisel'? No. Was 'nail'? Yes. Was 'screw' on the list? Yes." The girl would recall all of the tools together, and this *clustering* would reflect the organization that she in fact imposed on the terms. (The consistency with which members of a category are recalled consecutively [clustered] is a widely used measure of how consistently the category is being used to organize the material.)

Now consider a second sequence of behavior, in which only involuntary associations between different members of a category are operating. Suppose another girl needed to remember the same list. If she first thought of "hammer," she might next say "nail," because hammers reminded her of nails. Having said "nail," she might next recall "screw" because she associated nails and screws. This use of associations between items does not meet the previously-cited definition of a strategy, because it is not under the child's deliberate control. Behaviorally, however, the pattern of recall would be identical to that produced by the voluntary process.

The problem is more than a logical possibility. Much of the clustering of category members that is evident in young children's recall seems due to associations between different members of a category rather than to intentional organization. Young children mainly show clustering in situations in which they are memorizing highly associated items. They often recall only those category members that are strongly associated with each other. For example, in the category "birds," they might consecutively recall robins, blue jays, and sparrows but not remember ostriches, chickens, and other atypical birds (Lange, 1973, 1978; Schneider, 1986). Adolescents and adults are much more likely to recall the atypical birds along with the typical ones. Thus, they appear to proceed from the category to its individual members, rather than relying exclusively on associations among the individual members.

It seems, then, that organization can reflect either voluntary, strategic processes or involuntary, associative ones. Actually, the situation is even more complex. Strong associations among category members facilitate the use of voluntary strategies in which the category itself is used for remembering. Hearing *ostrich* and *chicken* does not quickly bring to mind the category "birds"; hearing *robin* and *bluejay* does. Thus, involuntary, associative processes can trigger voluntary, strategic ones, as well as voluntary, strategic processes' aiding the recall of weakly associated items. We can distinguish conceptually between strategies and associative knowledge, but their workings in children's memory are complexly interrelated.

### Elaborating

People often need to remember material that cannot be organized into neat categories. One way to achieve this goal is to think about or create connections among the items that must be remembered. Thus, a girl who needed to remember her schoolbook, her lunch, and her arithmetic assignment might form an image of two pieces of bread sandwiching the book, with the book's pages holding the assignment. Such elaborative imagery facilitates recall (Pressley, 1982).

Elaborative images are not the only useful elaborations; elaborative verbal phrases also can be memorable. In my sophomore year in high school, my English teacher told the class to remember what *alliteration* meant by thinking of the phrase "apt alliteration's artful aid." The phrase must have been an effective memory aid for me to have remembered both it and the meaning of alliteration for this long.

Elaboration is a relative latecomer among the strategies. It is used primarily by older elementary school children and adolescents. Even when younger children generate elaborations, they typically are not as useful as those of older children. For example, asked to remember the words *lady* and *broom*, older children usually generate sentences involving active interactions among the terms, such as "The lady flew on the broom on Halloween." If younger children generate elaborations at all, they tend to be static ones, as in "The lady had a broom" (Buckhalt, Mahoney, & Paris, 1976; Reese, 1976). The active elaborations are more helpful, probably because they more directly suggest memorable mental images. The difference in quality of the elaborations is also evident in children's benefits from their own elaborations versus ones suggested by the experimenter. Older children benefit more from elaborations that they make up themselves (Reese, 1977); younger ones benefit more from ones suggested by the experimenter (Turnure, Buium, & Thurlow, 1976). Apparently, older children elaborate in ways especially meaningful to them, thus producing superior recall. Young children, when they elaborate at all, usually do so in unmemorable ways, thus producing less good recall.

### Deploying Cognitive Resources

As noted in the discussion of perceptual development (Chapter 4), much of infants' attention has an elicited, involuntary feel to it. Within a few years, however, children begin to attend more selectively. For example, 4-year-olds who are told that they later will need to remember some toys tend to name those toys more during the waiting period (Baker-Ward, Ornstein, & Holden, 1984). This suggests that they selectively attend to the toys they need to remember.

The development of selective attention continues for many years. In one series of studies (Hagen & Hale, 1973), 5-to-15-year-olds were presented with a series of cards, each with two pictures. One picture on each card was identified as the important one. However, after presenting all of the cards, the experimenter surprised the children by asking them to remember both objects previously labeled unimportant and ones that they had been told were important.

It should not be surprising that 14- and 15-year-olds remembered more items that they had been told were important than 5- and 6-year-olds. What is surprising, though, is that the younger children remembered just as many of the items previously described as unimportant. In some experiments, younger children actually remembered more "unimportant" items than did older ones. It seems that a large part of the reason older children generally remember more is that they focus their attention more sharply.

Older children also are less at the mercy of the *salience* (perceptual strikingness) of the particular stimuli they encounter. They do what the task calls for, even if the context does not make it easy to do so. In one experiment, Odom (1978) presented 4- and 6-year-olds with a version of Piaget's matrix classification task. As in the Piagetian task, the matrix included three rows and three columns. Eight of the boxes were filled in; children needed to infer the contents of the ninth. Some children were presented matrices that differed on two salient dimensions, such as size and color. Other children were presented matrices whose stimuli differed on two less-salient dimensions, such as texture and orientation. When the stimuli differed on dimensions of low salience, the 4-year-olds performed much less well than the older children. However, when the dimensions were highly salient, the 4-year-olds performed nearly as well. The finding was especially striking given the difficulty 4-year-olds usually have on the matrix task.

Part of older children's superior deployment of attention rests on its more-systematic character. This was demonstrated in an analysis of 4-to-8-year-olds' eye movements (Vurpillot, 1968). The children were shown pictures of houses with six windows, like those in Figure 6–3. They needed to determine whether the house on the left was identical to that on the right, and if not, where they differed. Ideally, children would scan a window in the house on the left, then the corresponding window in the house on the right, then another window in the first house, then the corresponding window in the second house, and so on until they either found a difference or had examined all windows of the houses. Systematically proceeding through the different windows, for example from top to bottom and left to right, also seemed a desirable way to deploy attention, because it would assure that all windows would be compared without repetitions.

With age, children's visual scanning became increasingly systematic. Older children more often looked back and forth between corresponding windows in the two houses and more often proceeded down a column or across a row within a house. They also were more likely to examine all windows before answering that the houses were identical. To summarize, with age, children's attention becomes more focused on relevant features, less at the mercy of perceptual salience, and more systematic.

**FIGURE 6–3** Sample of stimuli used by Vurpillot (1968) to study development of visual attention. Children needed to find whether houses were different (as in the top pair) or identical (as in the bottom pair).

### Evaluation

Age-related improvements in the frequency of use and quality of children's strategies play a large role in memory development. Between ages 5 and 15, frequency and quality of rehearsal, organization, elaboration, and attention deployment improve greatly. Use of strategies has a large beneficial effect on children's ability to remember in many situations. Children younger than those who generally use strategies spontaneously can learn them, though such learning often fails to generalize to new situations. Finally, development of memory strategies is not limited to changes in how often the strategies are used. Older children also use more-effective versions of the strategies, derive greater benefits and fewer costs from using the strategies, and use them in difficult as well as easy contexts.

One of the more-intriguing findings about memory strategies is that training children to use such strategies is no guarantee of their continued use. This raises the question, "How do they decide which strategy to use?" Children often are quite sensible about these decisions. For example, when items remain visible, 8-to-11-year-olds use high-quality versions of rehearsal in which they rehearse many different items. When items do not remain visible, the same children adopt the lower-quality but easier-to-execute strategy of rehearsing one item at a time (Guttentag & Ornstein, 1985). Children make use of their *metacognitive knowledge* (that is, knowledge of their cognitive capacities, strategies, and tasks) to make such decisions.

## THE ROLE OF METACOGNITION

Metacognition can be divided into two types of knowledge: explicit, conscious, factual knowledge (often called "declarative knowledge") and implicit, unconscious, behavioral knowledge (often called "procedural knowledge") (Brown, Bransford, Ferrara, & Campione, 1983; Paris & Lindauer, 1982). As an example of explicit metacognitive knowledge, even preschoolers are consciously aware that it is easier to remember a few items than many. However, much other metacognitive knowledge is unconscious; the knowledge influences behavior without our being aware of it. Such implicit metacognitive knowledge is exemplified in the reading of good students who slow down their reading when material becomes difficult without even knowing they are doing so. In the following paragraphs, we examine the development of both explicit and implicit metacognitive knowledge and how they affect children's ability to remember.

### Explicit Metacognitive Knowledge

People possess a variety of knowledge about cognition in general and memory in particular. This knowledge includes information about tasks (Is it easier to remember the main point of a passage or to remember the passage verbatim?), about strategies (Is it better to rehearse a phone number or just to try hard to remember it?), and about people (Are younger children better or worse than older ones at remembering?). Much of this information seems to be acquired between ages 5 and 10.

Probably our most-basic knowledge of memory is that it is fallible. Almost all children beyond age 6 know that they forget, but a substantial minority of 5-year-olds (30 percent) deny that they ever do (Kreutzer, Leonard, & Flavell, 1975). Young children's overoptimism about their memory capacities can be seen in other contexts as well. For example, when 4-year-olds were asked how many of 10 pictures they would remember, most thought they would remember all 10 (Flavell, Friedrichs, & Hoyt, 1970). Their estimates of what they would remember were higher than those of older children, even though they actually remembered less. With age and experience, appraisals of one's memory capabilities become considerably more sober.

Factual knowledge about many aspects of memory develops greatly once children enter school. For example, 6-year-olds know much better than 4-year-olds that noise impairs ability to learn, that studying improves memory, and that memory is more accurate when there is less to remember (Yussen & Bird, 1979). The improvement may be due to the large amount of remembering children need to do at school.

Development continues beyond the early elementary school period as well. Approximately half of first graders know that it is easier to remember the main themes (the gist) of a story than it is to remember the story verbatim; virtually all fifth-graders do (Kreutzer et al., 1975; Kurtz & Borkowski, 1987). Similarly, approximately half of first graders know that recognition is easier than recall, whereas virtually all fifth-graders do (Speer & Flavell, 1979). During elementary school and beyond, children and adolescents acquire a wide range of knowledge about how tasks, strategies, and characteristics of learners affect memory (Schneider & Pressley, 1989; Weinert, 1986).

Much research on this type of explicit factual knowledge of cognition has been motivated by the plausible assumption that children's increasing knowledge about memory and about the general cognitive system leads them to choose better strategies and to remember more effectively. Evidence for this intuitively reasonable position has been surprisingly long in coming. Early investigations revealed only weak relations (Cavanaugh & Perlmutter, 1982). More-recent analyses of the results of many studies have yielded evidence of somewhat stronger relations between metamnemonic knowledge and memory performance (Schneider, 1985). However, the relation still does not appear as strong as many people's intuitions suggest it should be (Schneider & Pressley, 1989).

### Implicit Metacognitive Knowledge

In contrast to the relatively slow acquisition of explicit, factual knowledge about memory, even toddlers show impressive implicit knowledge. This is especially evident in their monitoring of their own cognitive activities. For example, 2-year-olds show that they monitor their use of language when they spontaneously correct their mistakes in pronunciation, grammar, and naming of objects. They also show such monitoring in comments on their own and others' use of language, and in their adjusting what they say to listeners' knowledge and general cognitive level (Clark, 1978). For example, my then 2½-year-old-daughter once told me, "You're a 'he,' Todd's a 'he,' and girls are 'she's.' " Two weeks later, she encountered difficulty pronouncing the word *hippopotamus* and explained, "I can't say it because I can't make my mouth move the right way."

Such self-monitoring enables even young children to experience a *feeling of knowing* that can help them anticipate how well they will later remember. Illustratively, when 4- and 5-year-olds were shown photographs of children they knew to varying degrees, they accurately predicted whether they would identify the child from being given his or her name, even when they could not recall the child's name on their own (Cultice, Somerville, & Wellman, 1983).

Despite this early ability to monitor thought processes well enough to experience feelings of knowing, and despite the fact that such monitoring improves further during the elementary school period (Zabrucky & Ratner, 1986), the skill is far from perfectly developed even among older students (Ghatala, Levin, Foorman, & Pressley, in press; Zabrucky & Ratner, 1986) and adults (Baker & Anderson, 1982; Glenberg & Epstein, 1987). Problems are especially persistent in monitoring one's understanding well enough to detect a lack of understanding of what other people are saying. For example, even a fairly large percentage of college students failed to detect the blatant contradictions in the following paragraph:

> Some snakes have a poisonous bite, but some snakes are harmless and even help us. The garter snake, for example, helps us by keeping bad insects away from our gardens. Garter snakes eat these insects. They find the insects by listening for them. The insects make a special noise. Garter snakes do not have ears. *They cannot hear the insects. They can hear the sounds of the insects.* That is how they are able to find the insects (Elliott-Faust, 1984; cited in Schneider & Pressley, 1989, p. 167) [italics mine].

Ability to monitor one's own comprehension seems to be one of the key differences between good and poor readers. Older and better readers slow down and often return to the place in the text where comprehension difficulties began. In contrast, younger and poorer readers rarely return to problem spots (Garner & Reis, 1981; Whimbey, 1975). The situation is paradoxical; the younger and less-skilled readers have more reason to re-read (because they typically understand less well on the first reading), but they do so less often.

Self-monitoring skills are especially critical for choosing what and how much to study. Not surprisingly, older children are more-effective students. The amount of time children study before saying that they know the material increases steadily from age 4 at least through age 12 or 13 (Dufresne & Kobasigawa, 1989; Flavell, Freidrichs, & Hoyt, 1970). During roughly the same age range, children derive increasing benefits from being given extra study time (Brown & Smiley, 1978). They also more often use active strategies such as turning away from the material and testing themselves (Dufresne & Kobasigawa, 1989; Leal, Crays, & Moely, 1985). Further, they focus more of their attention on material they have not yet mastered (Bisanz, Vesonder, & Voss, 1978).

Allocating study time is a tricky business, though. Consider just the dilemma posed in studying for later examinations after receiving the results of earlier ones on the same material. Is the best strategy to concentrate primarily on the topics that caused the most errors earlier, or is it better to distribute study time over other topics as well? Focusing on the sections that you didn't remember should help performance on that material, but might lead to worse performance on the material you correctly recalled the first time. On the other hand, reviewing the better-learned portions might be a waste of time.

Not surprisingly, children who are just learning to study have difficulty making these choices. In one study where children were given a chance to study after performing partially correctly on an initial memory test (Masur, McIntyre, & Flavell, 1973), 7- and 9-year-olds took different paths. The 9-year-olds focused on the items they had not remembered; the 7-year-olds distributed their attention more widely. The 9-year-olds' strategy sounds more sophisticated, but in fact it did not help them. Those children who focused on the previously missed items remembered no better on a later test than those who reviewed a broader range of items. Apparently, the items they forgot between the first and second testings canceled out the items that they previously had not remembered but later learned. Some problems do not have a good solution.

### Evaluation

Metacognition is at the same time intriguing and frustrating. Part of the appeal resides in the plausibility of its central premise—that what children know about their memories influences how they attempt to remember. Another part lies in the potential generality of the influence of metacognitive skills and knowledge. For example, knowing the relative usefulness of strategies on various types of material could potentially improve children's strategy choices. Yet another part of the appeal resides in the potential benefits of teaching metacognitive knowledge and skills. Unlike basic processes, which are very difficult if not impossible to change, and unlike any particular strategy or area of content knowledge, which will only be useful under specific circumstances, metacognitive knowledge and skills are potentially both instructible and broadly applicable. For example, teaching children to monitor their comprehension can have broadly beneficial effects on their learning (Baker & Brown, 1984; Borkowski, Johnston, & Reid, 1987; Ghatala, et al., in press; Palincsar & Brown, 1984; Paris, Wixson, & Palincsar, in press).

The frustrating aspect of metacognition becomes apparent when we try to determine whether children's increasing metacognitive knowledge is generally related to their remembering better. Both memory performance and knowledge about memory improve with age. However, the relation between which children remember best and which know the most about memory is not especially strong. This raises the question of how much impact metacognition actually has on memory development.

One useful way of thinking about the issue is summarized in the proverb, "Many a slip twixt the cup and the lip." Metacognition may influence memory performance only when each of a relatively long series of conditions is met. Otherwise, more-automatic processes may dominate strategy choices and recall. Consider what might be involved in a girl's using metacognitive knowledge to choose a strategy for remembering verbatim a long list of numbers. The girl would need to know that her memory was not perfect and that there was a chance that she would not remember all of the numbers. When she heard the particular list of numbers, she would need to monitor her own memory well enough to recognize that her storage of the numbers was insufficient to hold them in memory without using some strategy. She also would need to know a relevant strategy, such as rehearsal, and would need to choose it rather than a less-effective alternative. Finally, for her to use the relevant strategy more often in the future, she would need to attribute whatever benefit she derived to using the strategy rather than to some other factor such as trying harder.

This perspective makes understandable both the considerable success that can be gained from teaching children metacognitive skills, and the frequent findings of weak relations in the everyday environment between metacognitive knowledge and memory performance. If all links in the chain are present, as would often occur in carefully planned instructional programs, metacognitive knowledge can considerably aid memory performance. If even one is missing, however, as would often occur in the everyday environment, the effect can be nullified.

Consider how this seems to operate in one area—the transfer of strategies to new situations. Even if children know a strategy, use it, and witness improved memory as a result, they rarely transfer the strategy to new situations unless they also attribute the improvement in memory to use of the strategy (Borkowski, Carr, & Pressley, 1987; Fabricius & Hagen, 1984; Pressley, Levin, & Ghatala, 1984). Children and adults who have been taught to use a strategy that improves their memory often attribute the improvement to factors other than the strategy itself. For example, Fabricius and Hagen created a situation in which 6- and 7-year-olds sometimes used an organizational strategy and sometimes did not. Using the strategy almost always improved their later recall. Although all children had the opportunity to make this observation, only some of them attributed the improvement to using the strategy. Others attributed their success to looking longer, using their brain more, or slowing down. The children's attributions accurately predicted whether they employed the same type of strategy a week later in a slightly different situation. Fully 99 percent of children who earlier attributed their success to the use of the organizational strategy used the strategy on the second occasion, compared with 32 percent of those who thought other factors responsible.

Whatever the theoretical status of metacognitive knowledge, its potential practical importance is clear. In the discussion of children's reading in Chapter 9, we will encounter a remarkably successful training program initiated by Palincsar and Brown (1984) to teach poor readers to understand better what they are reading. The program teaches them to effectively monitor their comprehension while reading and also supplies strategies for dealing with failures to comprehend. Anything that works as well as this program is well worth learning more about.

## THE ROLE OF CONTENT KNOWLEDGE

Older children know more than younger ones about almost everything. In general, the more that people know about a topic, the easier it is for them to remember new information about it. Therefore, greater content knowledge would lead older children to remember more even if there were no other differences between them and younger children.

Prior knowledge of related content affects memory in several ways. It influences how much and what children recall. It influences their execution of basic processes and strategies, their metacognitive knowledge, and their acquisition of new strategies. Under some circumstances, it exerts a greater influence than all other factors combined. Evidence concerning each of these points is discussed next.

### Effects on How Much Children Remember

The fact that older children regularly recall more than younger ones may in large part be due to the older children's knowing more about the material they are trying to remember. Content knowledge exerts such a large impact that more-knowledgeable children can remember more than less-knowledgeable adults. In particular, when asked to reconstruct chess positions from memory, 10-year-old chess experts outperformed adults who were novices at the game (Chi, 1978). This finding was not attributable to the children's being generally smarter or possessing better memories. When the children and adults were given a standard digit-span task, the adults, as usual, remembered more (Figure 6–4). Children also remember more than adults about other types of content that they know better, such as titles of children's TV programs and books (Lindberg, 1980). Thus, differences in content knowledge can outweigh all of adults' other memory advantages.

Differences in content knowledge also can overwhelm differences in IQ. Schneider, Korkel, and Weinert (1989) examined memory for a story about a fictitious young soccer player and his experiences in "the big

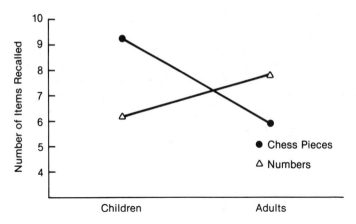

**FIGURE 6–4** Number of chess pieces and digits recalled by 8- to 10-year-old chess experts and adult chess novices immediately after presentation (after Chi, 1978).

game." The children who heard the story included equal numbers of children with high soccer knowledge and above-average IQs, high soccer knowledge and below-average IQs, low soccer knowledge and above-average IQs, and low soccer knowledge and below-average IQs.

As might be expected, children with high soccer knowledge remembered more about the stories, drew a greater number of correct inferences, and noticed more inconsistencies within the story than those with lower knowledge. Surprisingly, however, at each level of expertise, higher-IQ children did not remember any more about the soccer game than lower-IQ children. They also were no more likely to draw correct inferences about it or to notice contradictions. High IQ-children may acquire expertise faster, and may be knowledgeable about more topics; however, when knowledge is equivalent, memory for new information also seems equal.

### Effects on What Children Remember

If content knowledge influences memory, then detailed analyses of what people already know should help us anticipate what they will remember. This has been examined in the context of memory for baseball (Spilich, Vesonder, Chiesi, & Voss, 1979). The investigation began with consideration of what a person knowledgeable about baseball might know. As shown in Table 6–2, the analysis stressed *goals*, which ranged from the top level of winning the game to the bottom level of avoiding strikes and accumulating balls, and *setting events*, which defined the immediate situation. More-knowledgeable people were hypothesized to differ from less-knowledgeable ones primarily in their understanding of these goals and setting events.

**TABLE 6–2  Baseball Knowledge Structure (from Spilich et al., 1979)**

*SETTING*

General:  Teams playing, team at bat, team in field, inning, miscellaneous conditions
Specific:  Relevant: teams' records as related to goal structure, players' records as related to goal structure
           Irrelevant: team attributes, player attributes
Enabling:  Batter at bat and pitcher ready to pitch

*GOAL STRUCTURE*

| TEAM AT BAT | LEVEL | VARIABLES | VALUES | TEAM IN FIELD |
|---|---|---|---|---|
| Winning game | 1 | Game outcome | Win–lose | Winning game |
| Scoring runs | 2 | Score | Domain of game scores | Preventing runs from scoring |
| Getting runners on base and advancing runners | 3 | Pattern of base runners | Eight possible patterns | Preventing runners from getting on base or advancing by making outs |
|  |  | Outs | 0, 1, 2, 3 |  |
| Having "balls," | 4 | "Balls" | 0, 1, 2, 3, 4 | Getting "strikes," |
| Avoiding "strikes" |  | "Strikes" | 0, 1, 2, 3 | Avoiding "balls" |

*NONGAME ACTIONS*

Relevant nongame actions
Irrelevant nongame actions

197

College students high and low in baseball knowledge were presented a fictitious baseball game and then asked questions about it. They differed not only in how much but also in what they remembered. Knowledgeable students focused on the important information. They most often recalled events relevant to goals at the top of the hierarchy and least often information at the lowest levels. In contrast, the less-knowledgeable students recalled unimportant details as often as the critical facts. They actually recalled a greater number of actions that were irrelevant to the progress of the game than did their more-knowledgeable peers.

The two groups also made different types of errors. Unknowledgeable students often recalled sequences inconsistent with the rules of baseball, such as the first batter of an inning hitting into a double play. Those knowledgeable about baseball never made such errors. Instead, they tended to substitute one plausible detail for another. It is not hard to imagine why knowledgeable people's memory for new material takes the shape it does. Existing knowledge provides a framework for organizing new information, serves as a point of comparison against which to check the plausibility of recalled sequences, and facilitates inferences about future events.

Like the adults who were knowledgeable about baseball, children regularly draw inferences that go beyond the information given. For example, when young children heard a story about a helpless creature with a broken wing, they had no trouble identifying the creature as a bird, despite this information's never having been stated (Paris, 1975). With age and increased knowledge, children draw a greater number and variety of inferences (Paris & Lindauer, 1977). However, the basic inference-drawing capability is almost certainly an innate part of children's thinking. Note that drawing inferences is closely related to memory focusing on the central message of events (the gist) rather than the details. Inferences are formed to fill the gaps and to make events coherent—that is, so there will be a gist to remember.

With large enough changes in children's knowledge, their memory for a previous event can actually become *more* rather than *less* accurate with the passage of time. Piaget and Inhelder (1973) presented 5-to-8-year-olds a row of sticks, ordered from shortest to longest. The children needed to remember the row for a later recall test. A week later, they were asked to draw the row of sticks they had seen. Six to eight months later, the test was repeated.

Surprisingly, children's reproductions were more accurate on the second testing than on the first. That is, they were more likely to draw a correctly ordered row half a year after they saw the original row than a week after they saw it.

Liben (1975) suggested that the improvement might be due to children's better understanding the idea of ordering rather than to their better remembering the initial configuration of sticks. To test this hypothesis, she asked children to imagine and draw 10 sticks standing up straight in a row, without their having seen any row previously. Five-year-olds drew rows ordered perfectly by size on 19 percent of trials, whereas 8-year-olds did so on 82 percent. Thus, the improvement that Piaget and Inhelder observed over the six-month period between their two tests may not have stemmed from improved memory for the original situation, but rather from ordering becoming a more-prominent idea in the children's thinking.

These results are most interesting for the questions they raise about the nature of memory. By most definitions of memory, it is logically impossible for an internal representation of an event to improve over time. If children do not store information in memory initially, they cannot retrieve it later. From this viewpoint, children in the Piaget and Inhelder experiment may simply have been inferring what the row probably looked like rather than remembering it. However, in arguing against this view, Piaget and Inhelder distinguished between two types of memory. One was memory in the strict sense, which they defined as memory for the attributes of stimuli shown in the particular situation. The other was memory in the broad sense, defined as the operation of intelligence and knowledge on new and old information. They argued that memory in the broad sense inevitably influences memory in the strict sense: All remembering involves both memory for literal details and also inferences and abstractions. Given the inherent importance of inferences and of memory for gist in people's remembering, Piaget and Inhelder's position becomes increasingly plausible the longer it is considered.

### Content Knowledge as an Explanation for Other Memory Changes

Changes in basic capacities, strategies, and metacognition often are used to explain age-related improvements in children's ability to remember specific content. This equation can be reversed, however. Increasing knowledge of specific content influences efficiency of basic processes, acquisition and execution of strategies, and metacognitive knowledge.

First consider the effect on basic processes. At least from age 5, children automatically encode the relative frequency of events, and do so very accurately. However, 5-year-olds' encoding of frequency information is even more accurate when the content is familiar (pictures of classmates) than when it is not (pictures of children who are strangers) (Harris, Durso, Mergler, & Jones, 1990). Similarly, the more that people know about the content they are trying to keep in memory, the more material they can store in working memory (Huttenlocher & Burke, 1976).

Next consider how content knowledge influences the use and efficiency of memory strategies. Children use strategies such as organization more often for remembering groups of familiar items than for remembering groups of less familiar ones (Bjorklund, Muir, & Schneider, 1990). Moreover, the greater efficiency when strategies are executed with familiar content is sufficient so that 8-year-olds who rehearse familiar items subsequently remember as much as 11-year-olds who rehearse unfamiliar ones (Zember & Naus, 1985).

Familiar content also facilitates learning of new strategies. Chi (1981) examined a 5-year-old's learning of an alphabetic retrieval strategy for her classmates' names. (First think if any names start with A; then think if any names start with B, etc.). Although the strategy was novel, the girl learned it and applied it to recalling her classmates' names rather easily. However, the same girl could not then apply the alphabetic strategy she had already learned in the familiar context to remembering a new set of names of people she had never met.

These results may hold an important implication for how children learn to use new strategies. Early in the acquisition process, they may employ strategies effectively only on familiar content. Practice using the strategies with the familiar content may lead to execution of the strategies becoming automatized and making fewer demands on the children's processing resources. This automatization, in turn, allows children to apply the strategies to more-demanding, unfamiliar content. Thus, the familiar content may serve as a kind of practice field upon which children exercise emerging cognitive skills, such as new memory strategies.

Now, consider how content knowledge influences metacognition. Since memory functioning itself depends heavily on knowledge of specific content, it is not surprising that knowledge *about* memory functioning also depends on it. Content knowledge influences both explicit and implicit metacognition. With regard to explicit knowledge, the child chess experts studied by Chi (1978) not only remembered more about the chess positions they saw, but also more accurately predicted the relatively large number of viewings required before they would be able to perfectly reconstruct from memory the positions on the board. The difference was in the opposite direction of the usual greater optimism/lesser realism that younger individuals show in predicting their memory performance. With regard to implicit knowledge, the feelings of knowing (or not knowing) of the soccer experts in the Schneider et al. (1989) study were more accurate than those of the novices. Clearly, all aspects of memory are influenced by content knowledge.

### How Does Content Knowledge Aid Memory?

Two mechanisms that help explain why people better remember new information when they are knowlegeable about other, related information are spreading activation and encoding of distinctive features.

*Spreading activation.*    One way of thinking about people's limited attentional resources is as a finite ability to activate information in memory. When people focus their attention entirely on one topic, that topic is strongly activated and therefore can be recalled quickly and easily. When they divide their attention among several topics, each of those topics becomes somewhat active, and recall is not quite as quick or easy. It is not just the particular topic that becomes active; activation automatically spreads from each topic that is receiving attention to others that are associated with it. For example, thinking about dogs not only makes the concept of dogs more active; activation spreads to topics such as animals, cats, bones, and so on, so that they too are remembered more quickly and easily.

One way of representing people's content knowledge and the spread of activation across various aspects of that knowledge involves *semantic networks*. Such networks typically include relevant concepts, their relations to other concepts, and how strongly the concepts are associated with each other. For example, a semantic network model of a young child's knowledge about dogs might include the information that dogs are animals, that they have four legs, that they eat bones, that they chase cats, that they are friendly, and so on. Increasing experience leads to additional concepts being added to the network, for example that dogs like to catch frisbees. Experience also leads to stronger connections among concepts already in the network, such as that between "dogs" and "animals." The increasing variety and strength of these connections facilitates acquisition of further information. For example, knowing that dogs like to retrieve sticks and balls makes it easier to learn that they also like to retrieve frisbees.

The role of spreading activation can be seen in thinking about why older children use organizational strategies more effectively and with a greater variety of material (Rabinowitz & Chi, 1987). Consider what would happen if younger and older children encountered within a list *chicken, hawk,* and *penguin.* Both older and young children would associate *bird* with *hawk,* but the connection would be stronger for the older children. Younger children might not associate *chicken* and *penguin* with birds at all, whereas older children probably would. Thus, the older children would more likely see that all three items were birds. Further, even if a younger and an older child both had this realization, thinking of the "bird" category would aid the older child's recall to a greater extent, because more activation would spread from the category name to the individual category members. Thus, spreading activation within a semantic network would lead older children to more often use organizational strategies and to be more successful when they used them.

Chi and Koeske (1983) illustrated in an especially charming context the usefulness of viewing the role of content knowledge in terms of spreading activation within a semantic network. They studied a 5-year-old budding dinosaur expert. Many young children are fascinated by dinosaurs, but this particular boy knew more than most. He could name 40 types of dinosaurs and was intimately familiar with the contents of the nine books about them that he owned. His mother spent an average of three hours per week reading him these books.

How would it be possible to get inside the boy's head to find out how his knowledge of dinosaurs was organized? Chi and Koeske used two procedures to do so. First, on six separate occasions, the boy was asked to name all the dinosaurs he knew. The dinosaurs the boy consistently clustered together in recall were viewed as being grouped in his memory. Second, the experimenter and the boy played a game in which she named two or three traits of a dinosaur, and he guessed which dinosaur it was.

Based on what they learned about the boy's knowledge of dinosaurs, Chi and Koeske developed a semantic network model of what he knew. Part of this model is shown in Figure 6–5. One main part of the representation includes the types of dinosaurs. As can be seen in the figure, Chi and Koeske hypothesized that the child divided dinosaurs into two main categories: armored dinosaurs (the group on the bottom left part of the figure) and giant plant eaters (the group at the top right). Links between a pair of dinosaurs indicate that the child recalled that pair in order on at least one of the six occasions; the more links, the more times the child showed that ordering (and presumably, the more closely he connected the two dinosaurs).

The representation also includes properties of the dinosaurs. The properties named in Figure 6–5 are the clues that were effective in the second game in helping the boy figure out which dinosaur the experimenter had in mind. These properties are indicated in small letters. The *di* in the middle of the figure is particularly interesting. It indicates that a number of dinosaurs shared a particular diet and that this diet was a useful cue to all of their identities. Thus, diet seemed to be a central feature in the boy's representation of these dinosaurs.

Chi and Koeske hypothesized that the boy would be most adept at remembering dinosaurs that were associated strongly with other dinosaurs and their properties. The boy's recall of dinosaurs from a list that the experimenter presented supported this prediction. He remembered more of the dinosaurs that had many links to other dinosaurs (many paths through which activation could spread) than of the dinosaurs that had few such links.

Thus, the boy's existing knowledge made understandable not only how many dinosaurs he remembered, but which specific ones he recalled. It also suggested a plausible learning mechanism. If he read about an unfamiliar dinosaur, he could relate it to the dinosaurs he already knew about, could infer many of its properties from his knowledge of their properties, and could contrast its unique features to theirs. He also could later remember the new dinosaur by first recalling the better-known ones associated with it and having activation spread from them. These processes

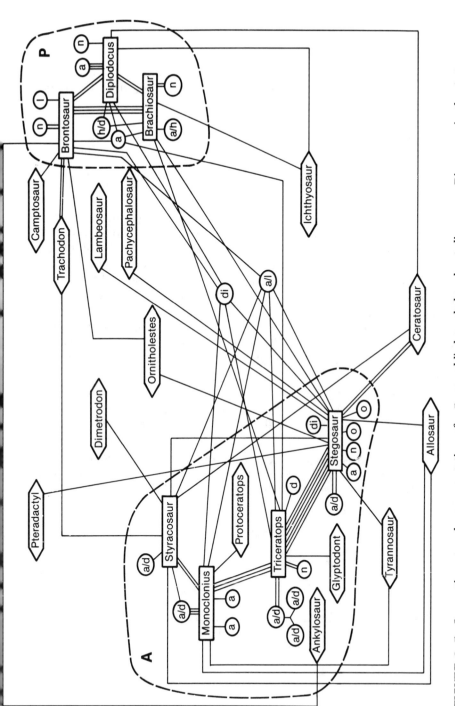

**FIGURE 6-5** Semantic network representation of a 5-year-old's knowledge about dinosaurs. Dinosaurs in the A group are armored. Those in the P group are giant plant eaters. Multiple lines between dinosaurs indicate especially close connections. Small letters connected to dinosaur names indicate known traits: a, appearance; d, defense mechanism; di, diet; n, nickname; h, habitat; and l, locomotion (from Chi & Koeske, 1983).

would make it easier for the boy to learn about new dinosaurs than it would be for a child who knew less about them.

*Encoding of distinctive features.*  By focusing attention on distinctive features, content knowledge also helps children distinguish between different entities. Such distinctive features play a particularly clear role in reading. Letters of the alphabet closely resemble each other. Ordinarily, all are black, stationary, close together, and about the same height and width. To see the situation from a young child's perspective, imagine how hieroglyphics look to you.

Letters in our alphabet are distinguished by the presence or absence of a small number of critical features, among them whether the letter includes a vertical segment, whether it includes a curve, and whether it is symmetrical. Illustratively, *H* differs from *F* in that *H* is symmetrical around both horizontal and vertical axes, while *F* is not symmetrical around either. In addition, *F* has two horizontal lines; *H* has two vertical ones.

Do children use these critical features to distinguish among the letters? Apparently they do. When 7-year-olds see pairs of letters presented on a screen, the more features that differentiate the letters, the faster they can tell whether the letters are the same or different (Gibson, Schapiro, & Yonas, 1968). Thus, letters that differed on many features (e.g., *G* vs. *W*) were judged different more rapidly than letters that differed on only one (e.g., *P* vs. *R*).

Gibson and her colleagues used a statistical technique known as hierarchical cluster analysis to determine which features the 7-year-olds used to discriminate among letters. As shown in Figure 6–6, the first division that

**FIGURE 6–6**  Letters 7-year-olds most easily discriminate from other letters. Divisions closer to the top of the tree indicate easier discriminations. Thus, discriminating C and E was easier than discriminating C and G. (Data from Gibson, Schapiro, & Yonas, 1968).

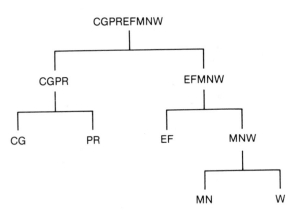

children made, reflected in the top division in the tree diagram, was whether the letter included a curved segment. They quickly distinguished all letters that included curved segments from all letters that lacked such segments. Within the set of letters that had curves, children were quickest at distinguishing those letters that also had a straight line from those that did not. Within the set of letters that lacked a curve, children were quickest at discriminating those letters that included a diagonal line from those that did not.

Sometimes the physical appearances of objects lead children to hone in quickly on the distinctive features, even if they do not know anything about the objects. In other cases, learning is necessary before they discover the distinctive features. The alphabet seems to fall into the latter category. Nodine and Steurle (1973) examined the eye movements of 5-year-olds who did not know how to read and of 6-year-olds who did. They found that the 6-year-olds focused more often on the distinctive features of letters. This focusing helped them memorize sequences of letters more rapidly. Thus, encoding distinctive features, like forming networks of associations, contributes to prior knowledge aiding memory for new information.

### Evaluation

Any explanation of memory development must reserve a large place for increasing knowledge of specific content. Content knowledge increases greatly with age. It is clearly related to how well children remember, as was evident in the studies of memory for chess positions, for soccer, for baseball, and for dinosaurs. It provides a context within which children can place new information, serves as a check on the plausability of their memories for particular events, facilitates their drawing of inferences, and helps them encode distinctive features. It also contributes to the development of other competencies that have been proposed as explanations of memory development, such as basic capacities, strategies, and metacognition. Much remains to be learned about how content knowledge helps children remember, but it seems clear that changes in content knowledge play a large role in memory development.

### WHAT DEVELOPS WHEN IN MEMORY DEVELOPMENT?

Different aspects of memory may not only contribute different amounts to memory development, but also may make their greatest contributions at different times. Table 6–3 summarizes the contributions of basic capacities, strategies, metacognition, and content knowledge during several periods of life.

Many basic capacities, such as the ability to recognize familiar objects and to associate objects with each other, are present at birth. These capaci-

**TABLE 6–3  Contributions of Four Aspects of Memory During Several Periods of Development**

| SOURCE OF DEVELOPMENT | AGE | | |
|---|---|---|---|
| | 0–5 | 5–10 | 10–ADULTHOOD |
| Basic Capacities | Many capacities present: association, generalization, recognition, etc. By age 5, if not earlier, absolute capacity of the sensory store and of short-term memory at adultlike levels. | Speed of processing increases. | Speed of processing continues to increase. |
| Strategies | A few rudimentary strategies such as naming, pointing, and selective attention. | Acquisition of many strategies: rehearsal, organization, etc. | Increasing use of elaboration. Continuing improvement in quality of all strategies. |
| Metamemory | Little factual knowledge about memory. Some monitoring of ongoing performance. | Increasing factual knowledge about memory. Improved monitoring of ongoing performance. | Continued improvements in explicit and implicit knowledge. |
| Content Knowledge | Steadily increasing content knowledge helps memory in areas where the knowledge exists. | Steadily increasing content knowledge helps memory in areas where the knowledge exists. Also helps in learning of new strategies. | Continuing improvements. |

ties are crucial in enabling children to learn and remember from the first days of life. At least from age 5, the absolute capacity of memory seems to be constant. However, the speed of processing does increase, and this helps to enable the functional capacity of memory to increase.

Memory strategies begin to contribute to memory development somewhat later than basic capacities. The earliest strategies appear in the second year, but many other important strategies, such as rehearsal, organization, and elaboration, become prominent around age 6 or 7. The quality of the strategies, their frequency of use, and the flexibility with which they are tailored to the demands of specific situations continue to develop well into later childhood and adolescence.

Two types of metacognitive skills, explicit factual knowledge about memory and implicit procedural knowledge, seem to have different developmental courses. Even before age 5, considerable implicit knowledge is evident. Children monitor their ongoing comprehension in some situations, though the range of situations in which they do so continues to grow for many years thereafter. The monitoring seems to influence memory procedures throughout childhood. In contrast, factual knowledge about memory appears to develop primarily between ages 5 and 15, perhaps in response to attending school and needing to remember a considerable amount of arbitrary information. The factual metacognitive knowledge may exert most of its effects on memory procedures, in late childhood and adolescence some years after it is first acquired.

Content knowledge contributes to memory development from early in life. It influences both how much and what children remember. It also affects the efficiency of execution of basic processes, the ability to acquire new strategies, and the metacognitive knowledge that children possess. Together, basic capacities, strategies, metacognition, and content knowledge account for the two essential features of memory development: first, that even infants in the first two weeks of life have the ability to remember, and second, that the efficiency and effectiveness of memory continue to improve throughout early childhood, middle childhood, and adolescence.

## SUMMARY

Memory development can be explained in four ways: changes in basic capacities, in strategies, in metacognition, and in content knowledge. Some of these factors seem to exercise larger effects that others. Some also seem to contribute more during some age periods than during others.

Even infants and younger children possess basic memory capacities. Newborns can form associations and recognize objects as familiar. By age 3 months, infants possess a wide range of memory skills. They generalize, remember the gist of events, and even show insight. The number of symbols that can be held in memory improves throughout childhood and adolescence, but it is unclear whether this is due to changes in the actual capacity of memory or to improvements in strategies, metacognition, and content knowledge. Processing speed also increases throughout childhood and adolescence. Improving strategies, metacognition, and content knowledge contributes to this change, but the speed of processing per se also seems to increase.

The use of broadly applicable strategies such as rehearsal, organization, and elaboration changes greatly with age. Rudimentary strategic activities can be seen even among 1½-year-olds, but use of strategies increases especially rapidly between 5 years and adolescence. Children who use such strategies typically remember more than those who do not. Changes in the quality of strategies and the range of situations in which they are used continue well beyond the time at which they are first adopted. As strategies become better adapted to the demands of particular tasks, their effectiveness also increases. Young children can learn to rehearse, organize, and elaborate. However, these children often fail to use the strategies in later situations, and they use them less effectively than do older children. This may be due to a combination of lesser benefits and greater costs to the children of using the strategies, as well as to the children's not perceiving the connection between using the strategy and remembering better. Overall, learning of these strategies seems to account for an important part of memory development, particularly in middle childhood and beyond.

Metacognition includes two distinct types of knowledge: explicit, factual knowledge about memory, and implicit, unconscious knowledge such as that involved in monitoring and regulating memory activities. Implicit, unconscious metacognitive knowledge is already evident among toddlers. Explicit, factual knowledge is not evident as early, but between ages 5 and 10 it too becomes quite extensive. Development of both types of metacognitive knowledge continues throughout life. At present, exactly how metacognition influences memory activities is not well understood. Whatever the theoretical difficulties, though, children's understandings of their own memories seem to have important ramifications for their educational achievement, particularly their reading comprehension.

Knowledge of related content seems to greatly affect children's memory. Content knowledge guides children's memory for specific events, influences their ability to learn strategies, and helps them make plausible inferences. Under some circumstances, content knowledge can more than balance the influence of all other changes in memory that come with age and experience. Children who are experts on topics such as chess, soccer, and dinosaurs exhibit truly impressive memory in their area of expertise. Formation of networks of related associations and encoding of distinctive features appear to be two of the mechanisms that help children with high content knowledge to better remember new information.

# RECOMMENDED READINGS

Chi, M. T. H., & Koeske, R. D. (1983). **Network representation of a child's dinosaur knowledge.** *Developmental Psychology, 19,* 29–39. Charming in-depth analysis of a young boy's expert knowledge about dinosaurs.

Guttentag, R. (1989). **Age differences in dual-task performance: Procedures, assumptions, and results.** *Development Review, 9,* 146–170. Thoughtful analysis of the effects of mental effort on strategy choices and strategy efficiency.

Kail, R. (1986b). **Sources of age differences in speed of processing.** *Child Development, 57,* 969–987. Intriguing evidence that the basic speed of information processing increases with age. Such an increase, if present, could have extremely broad ramifications for theories of cognitive development.

Lange, G. (1978). **Organization-related processes in children's recall.** In P. A. Ornstein (Ed.), *Memory development in children.* Hillsdale, NJ: Erlbaum. An article that questions whether children's seemingly strategic behavior is in fact strategic. Raises fundamental questions about what we mean when we say that children use strategies.

Schneider, W., & Pressley, M. (1989). *Memory development between 2 and 20.* **New York: Springer-Verlag.** This book provides a comprehensive and up-to-date summary of what is known about memory development.

# 7

# *Conceptual Development*

Experimenter: *It's twelve o'clock in the afternoon and the sun is shining really bright. You already ate something today, but you're still very hungry, so you decide to eat pancakes with syrup, orange juice, cereal, and milk. Could that be lunch?* Kindergartner: *No . . . because lunch you have to have sandwiches and stuff like that.* E: *Can you have cereal for lunch?* K: *No.* E: *Can you have pancakes for lunch?* K: *No . . . No.* E: *Well, how do you know if something is lunch or not?* K: *If the time says 12:00.* E: *This was 12:00* K: *Well, I don't think so.* E: *(Repeats story.) Is that lunch?* K: *I know . . . that one is not lunch . . . you have to eat sandwiches at lunch.* E: *Can you have anything else?* K: *You can have drinks, but not breakfast.* (Keil, 1989, pp. 77, 291)

This child's concept of lunch clearly differs from that of older children and adults. But what can we conclude from the difference? Is it simply an isolated confusion between typical and essential characteristics of lunch? Or is it symptomatic of a more-general tendency of younger children to understand concepts superficially and not to grasp their core meaning?

Concepts involve grouping together different entities on the bases of some similarity. The similarity can either be quite concrete (a concept of balls) or quite abstract (a concept of justice). We need concepts because they allow us to draw inferences in situations in which we lack direct experience. If told that malamutes are dogs, a child immediately also knows that they have four legs, a tail, fur; that they are animals; that they probably are friendly to people; and so on. Concepts also save us mental effort by allowing us to bring to bear previous knowledge in new situations. Once we have the concept "doberman," we do not need to think hard about this particular tall, black, sharp-toothed dog that we see running loose to know that we would do well to go elsewhere.

Conceptual understanding is so basic to our thinking that it is difficult to consider it in isolation. It influences, and is influenced by, perception, language, memory, problem solving, reasoning—in short, by every aspect of our thinking. It is no accident that the discussion in Chapter 5 of the relation between language and thought was largely a discussion of the complex interconnections between word meanings and conceptual understanding. Similarly, our concepts reflect our perceptions, and our perceptions are influenced by our concepts; we remember in terms of known concepts, and we use memory to build new concepts; and so on.

The tendency to form concepts is a basic part of human beings. Infants form them even during their first months (Quinn & Eimas, 1986). Within a few years, children acquire a huge number and variety of concepts. Consider a few concepts that most 5-year-olds in the United States possess: tables, chairs, animals, trees, Nintendo, dirt bikes, running, birthdays, winter, fairness, time, and number. Some of these concepts involve objects, others events, others ideas, others activities, and yet others dimensions of existence. Some of the objects are part of nature; others are artifacts made by people to serve a specific purpose. Some of the concepts are possessed by children throughout the world and have been throughout history. Others are specific to children living in advanced industrial societies of the late twentieth century. Some concepts are acquired in infancy; others much later. Some are used constantly; others only rarely.

In this chapter, we look at conceptual development from two perspectives. One focuses on conceptual representations in general; the other focuses on the development of specific concepts of particular interest (Table 7–1).

**TABLE 7–1   Chapter Outline**

I.   Conceptual Representations in General
   A.   Defining-Features Representations
   B.   Probabilistic Representations
   C.   Exemplar-Based Representations
   D.   Theory-Based Representations

II.   Development of Some Particularly Important Concepts
   A.   Time
   B.   Space
   C.   Number
   D.   Mind

III.   Summary

The approach that emphasizes the development of conceptual representations in general is based on the assumption that the nature of people's minds leads them to represent most or all concepts in a particular way. The nature of this representation is of primary interest; the details of the particular concepts are secondary. This approach has been most common in studying object concepts such as tools, furniture, and vehicles, where the particulars of the concept are less important than the concept's representativeness.

If the nature of people's minds leads them to impose a certain type of representation, and if young children's minds differ fundamentally from the minds of older individuals, then young children's concepts may also differ fundamentally. For example, young children's concepts may be concrete, whereas those of older children may be abstract. Many of the most prominent developmental theorists have subscribed to this *representational development hypothesis*. Table 7–2 lists some of the contrasts between younger and older children's concepts that they have proposed.

The other main approach has been to focus on the development of particular, inherently important concepts. Certain concepts, such as space, time, number, and mind, are so basic to our understanding of the world that their development is important in its own right. They are among the basic dimensions along which we encode our experience. As such, they have played central roles in the theories of philosophers such as Kant and psychologists such as Piaget. They also may develop quite differently than other concepts. Unlike most concepts, they are universal across cultures and historical periods, are present in rudimentary form even in infancy, and are constantly used. It is hard to imagine how people could learn such concepts if there were not some relatively specific biological basis for them. For example, if people did not code events according to when they occurred, what experiences could lead to their doing so? Understanding of these basic concepts often changes dramatically during development, but their core seems to be part of our inheritance as human beings. In the sections that follow, we first consider the development of conceptual representations in general, and then the development of a few particularly important concepts.

**TABLE 7–2**

| *DESCRIPTION OF YOUNG CHILDREN'S CONCEPTS* | *DESCRIPTION OF OLDER CHILDREN'S CONCEPTS* | *THEORIST(S)* |
|---|---|---|
| Concrete | Abstract | Piaget (1951) |
| Perceptual | Conceptual | Bruner, Goodnow, & Austin (1956) |
| Holistic | Analytic | Werner & Kaplan (1963) |
| Thematic | Taxonomic | Vygotsky (1934, 1962) |
| Global | Specific | Inhelder & Piaget (1964) |

## CONCEPTUAL REPRESENTATIONS IN GENERAL

How do people represent concepts? Four main possibilities have been proposed: defining-features representations, probabilistic representations, example-based representations, and theory-based representations. The differences among the proposed representations can be seen in the Figure 7–1 depictions of the concept "uncle." *Defining-features representations* are like the simplest and most straightforward dictionary definitions. They include only the necessary and sufficient features that determine whether an example is or is not an instance of the concept. *Probabilistic representations* are more like the articles in encyclopedias. Rather than just representing a few features that must always be present, people may represent concepts in terms of a large number of properties that are somewhat, but not perfectly, correlated with the concept. Thus, uncles tend to be nice to their nieces and nephews, though they are not necessarily so. *Example-based representations* can be compared to pictures in a photo album. People may store in memory the particular examples of a concept they have encountered and draw general inferences directly from this data base. Finally, *theory-based representations* are akin to chapters in a science textbook, in that they emphasize causal relations among elements of a system. Children's conceptual representations may include explanations for why their uncles tend to be nice, why they tend to be about as old as their parents, and so on.

Are young children capable of generating all of these types of representations? As previously noted, some of the most eminent developmental theorists—Piaget, Vygotsky, Werner, and Bruner, among others—have thought not. Although they used different terminology, all hypothesized that young children cannot form what we are calling defining features representations. We next consider the evidence on which they based this view and whether they were correct.

### Defining-Features Representations

What would it mean for people to represent concepts in terms of defining features? First, they would know the concept's necessary and sufficient features. Second, they would use these features to determine whether particular examples were instances of the concept.

Piaget, Bruner, and others largely based their view that young children could not form such concepts on observations of children's play with objects. They presented children objects from several categories, such as animals, toys, and furniture, and observed which ones children put together. They found that older children typically divide the objects into straightforward *taxonomic* categories (categories defined by shared characteristics): They put animals with animals, toys with toys, and so forth. In contrast, a typical preschooler might put together a dog and a frisbee

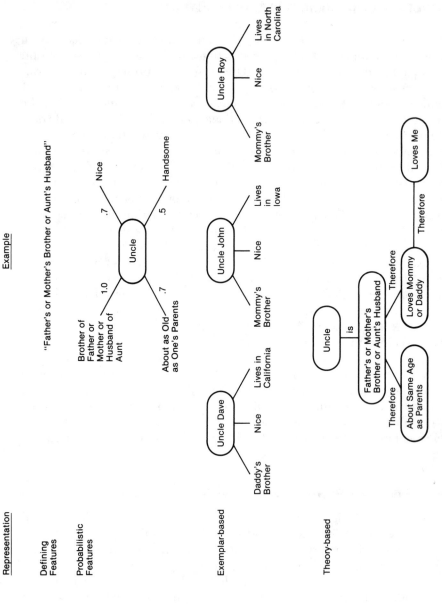

Representation | Example

Defining
Features | "Father's or Mother's Brother or Aunt's Husband"

Probabilistic
Features

Brother of
Father or
Mother or
Husband of
Aunt — 1.0 — Uncle — .7 — Nice

About as Old — .7          .5 — Handsome
as One's Parents

Exemplar-based

Daddy's — Uncle Dave — Lives in California
Brother        Nice

Mommy's — Uncle John — Lives in Iowa
Brother        Nice

Mommy's — Uncle Roy — Lives in North Carolina
Brother        Nice

Theory-based

Uncle — is — Father's or Mother's Brother or Aunt's Husband

About Same Age — Therefore — Loves Mommy or Daddy — Therefore — Loves Me
as Parents

**FIGURE 7-1**  Ways in which the concept "uncle" might be represented within defining features, probabilistic, exemplar-based, and theory-based approaches.

(because dogs like to catch frisbees), a cat and a chair (because cats like to curl up in chairs), and a game and a shelf (because games belong on shelves). Such groupings led Bruner, Olver, and Greenfield (1966) and Inhelder and Piaget (1964) to conclude that preschoolers' concepts were *thematic*, whereas older children's were *taxonomic*.

Vygotsky (1934, 1962) used a similar task. He presented children a number of blocks that differed in size, color, and shape, and asked them to group together those that went together. Children 6 years and older who were given this sorting task typically chose a single quality as the defining feature. For example, they might choose color as necessary and sufficient for membership in a group, and put all the red blocks together, all the green blocks together, and so on. Preschoolers, however, seemed to form what Vygotsky called *chain concepts*. These were concepts in which the basis of classification changed from example to example. Thus, the grouping lacked any single defining feature. The following type of evidence led Vygotsky to hypothesize that preschoolers form chain concepts rather than true ones.

> The child might pick a few triangular blocks until his attention is caught by, let us say, the blue color of a block he has just added: he switches to selecting blue blocks of any shape—angular, circular, semicircular. This in turn is sufficient to change the criterion again: oblivious of color, the child begins to choose rounded blocks. . . .The chain formation strikingly demonstrates the perceptually concrete, factual nature of complex thinking. (p. 64)

These types of observations led Vygotsky to hypothesize that children pass through three stages of conceptual development. Very early, they form thematic concepts, stressing relations between particular pairs of objects. Later, they form chain concepts, by momentarily classifying on the basis of abstract dimensions such as color or shape, but often switching the basis of categorization, as in the previous quotation. Still later, during the elementary school period, they form true concepts, based on stable necessary and sufficient features.

*Evaluation.*    The defining-features view of concepts has led to a number of interesting discoveries about preschoolers' conceptual understanding. Among these are the findings that young children often do not sort objects along a single consistent dimension and that they tend to arrange objects according to how the objects interact, rather than according to their categorical relations.

Should we believe the broader theoretical claim that young children's concepts differ fundamentally from those of older children and adults? I think not. Research conducted to test the claim that young children cannot form certain types of concepts has consistently shown that they actually can do so. For example, Bauer and Mandler (1989a; Experiment 3) tested whether children well below 5 or 6 years rely on thematic and chain concepts to the exclusion of taxonomic ones. They presented 1-year-olds(!) with sets of three objects. The target object was placed in the middle, and children were asked, "See this one? Can you find another just like this one?" Of the remaining two objects, one was related to the target object thematically and the other taxonomically. For example, in one problem, the object in the middle was a monkey, the taxonomically related object was a bear, and the thematically related object was a banana. More than 85 percent of the 1-year-olds chose the taxonomically related objects (the monkey and the bear) as being more similar than the thematically related ones (the monkey and the banana).

If even 1-year-olds understand taxonomic relations, why would the impression have arisen that 4- and 5-year-olds cannot understand them? Much of the reason may lie in children's interests rather than their capabilities. Young children may put dogs and frisbees together, rather than dogs and bears, because they find the relation between dogs and frisbees more interesting. Supporting this interpretation, Smiley and Brown (1979) found that preschoolers who sorted objects thematically could, when asked, explain perfectly the categorical relations among the objects. Cole and Scribner (1974) reported similar findings with tribespeople in Africa. Experimenters could elicit the ostensibly more-sophisticated categorical sortings from the tribespeople only by asking, "How would a stupid man do it?" Both the children and the tribespeople possessed the relevant concepts, but they chose not to apply them in the particular situation.

Another contributor to the misimpression has been underestimating the role of specific content knowledge in conceptual understanding. Although young children represent some concepts in terms of defining features, they do not know what the defining features are for many other concepts. Consider an experiment in which 5- and 9-year-olds heard two stories describing a particular object, and then were asked whether that object could be an example of the concept (Keil & Batterman, 1984). As shown in Table 7–3, one story indicated that the object included many features people associate with the concept, but also indicated that it lacked the defining feature. The other story indicated that the object included the defining feature for the concept, but that it lacked many features people typically associate with it.

The 9-year-olds generally emphasized the defining features; they usually said that the story at the top of Table 7–3 did not describe an island, but that the story at the bottom did. The performance of 5-year-olds was in some ways similar and in other ways different. The 5-year-olds did not rely on the defining feature on as many concepts as the 9-year-olds. However, on some relatively familiar concepts, such as "robbers," the 5-year-olds did rely on defining features, and on other, relatively unfamiliar concepts, such as "taxis," the 9-year-olds did not consistently do so. (The fact that the study

**TABLE 7–3    Stories from Keil and Batterman (1984)**

*CHARACTERISTIC FEATURES BUT NOT DEFINING FEATURES*

*Island*
There is this place that sticks out of the land like a finger. Coconut trees and palm trees grow there, and the girls sometimes wear flowers in their hair because it's so warm all the time. There is water on all sides except one. Could that be an island?

*DEFINING FEATURES BUT NOT CHARACTERISTIC FEATURES*

On this piece of land, there are apartment houses, snow, and no green things growing. This piece of land is surrounded by water on all sides. Could that be an island?

was conducted in Ithaca rather than New York City probably had a lot to do with the particular concept *taxi* being unfamiliar.) The same trend occurs with periods of time and events (e.g., winter) and with objects (Sera & Reittinger, 1989). There, too, 5-year-olds showed understanding of the critical role of defining features on some concepts, but not on nearly as many as 9-year-olds. The most reasonable overall conclusion seems to be that both younger and older children can form defining-features representations, but that knowledge about and interest in defining features increases with age.

## Probabilistic Representations

From the time of Aristotle until relatively recently, most concepts have been viewed as having defining features. Children and adults might or might not know the defining features, but they were there to be known. Today, however, the prevailing view among philosophers and others interested in concepts is that most concepts do not have defining features. The following argument of the philosopher Ludwig Wittgenstein exemplifies this perspective:

Consider for example the proceedings that we call "games." I mean board games, card games, ball games, Olympic games, and so on. What is common to them all? If you look at them, you will not see something that is common to *all*, but similarities, relationships, and a whole series of them at that. . . . In ball games there is winning and losing; but when a child throws his ball at the wall and catches it again, this feature has disappeared. Look at the parts played by skill and luck; and at the difference between skill in chess and skill in tennis. Think now of the game of ring-a-ring-a-roses; here is the element of amusement, but how many other characteristic features have disappeared! And we can go through the many, many other groups of games in the same way; can see how similarities crop up and disappear. (Wittgenstein, 1970, pp. 31–32)

Wittgenstein's example points to the possibility that all of us, adults as well as children, may represent most concepts in terms of probabilistic relations between the concept and various features, rather than in terms of a few defining features. Eleanor Rosch, Carolyn Mervis, and their associates have developed an appealing theory based on this view of concepts. The central theme is that members of most concepts are united by family resemblances rather than by defining features. The individual examples of the concept resemble each other to varying degrees and in varying ways, much like different family members do, but there is no set of features that all of them possess. Rosch and Mervis' theory is built around four powerful ideas: cue validities, basic-level categories, nonrandom distributions of features, and prototypic examples.

*Cue validities.*    How might children decide whether objects are examples of one concept or another? Rosch and Mervis (1975) suggested that they do so by comparing *cue validities*. The basic insight is that the degree to which the presence of a feature makes it likely that an object is a member of a concept depends on the frequency with which that feature accompanies that concept, and on the infrequency with which the feature accompanies other concepts. For example, the feature of flying makes it likely that an object is a bird in proportion to the frequency with which flying is found in birds and in proportion to the infrequency with which flying is found in other things. Because most (though not all) birds can fly, and because most (though not all) other things cannot fly, ability to fly is a highly valid cue for an object's being a bird.

The idea of cue validities helps the probabilistic approach to explain a phenomenon that proved troublesome for the defining-features approach: that some instances of a concept seem like better examples of the concept than others. Within the framework of the defining-features approach, if both examples have the necessary and sufficient features, why would one be considered a better example than the other? The probabilistic approach suggests that objects perceived as better examples are ones whose features have higher cue validities for that concept. Thus, people view apples as better examples of fruits than pineapples, because the size, shape, and texture of apples have higher validities for the fruit category. More generally, the probabilistic approach envisions people considering a large number of features of a newly encountered object, summing the cue validities of the features of that object for different concepts, and viewing the object as a member of whichever concept achieves the highest sum.

*Basic-level categories.*    Rosch, Mervis, Gray, Johnson, and Boyes-Braem (1976) noted that many categories are hierarchical, in the sense that all instances of one category are necessarily instances of another. They proposed that these hierarchies typically include at least three levels (Table 7–4): a very

**TABLE 7–4    Examples of Superordinate, Basic, and Subordinate Category Members**

| SUPERORDINATE LEVEL | BASIC LEVEL | SUBORDINATE LEVEL |
|---|---|---|
| Furniture | Table | End table |
| Animal | Bird | Canary |
| Food | Vegetable | Asparagus |
| Tool | Hammer | Tack hammer |
| Vehicle | Car | Fiero |

general one (*the superordinate level*), a very specific one (*the subordinate level*), and one of middling generality (*the basic level*). The basic level is the level at which cue validities are maximized. For example, "chair" is a basic-level category, because it has certain features with very high cue validities, among them legs, a back, and a seat. Superordinate categories, such as "furniture," do not have features with comparably high cue validities. Some pieces of furniture have legs and others do not; some pieces have backs and others do not. Conversely, subordinate categories, such as "kitchen chairs," share all the features of the basic-level category, but lack features that clearly discriminate them from other instances of the basic-level category. What features cleanly discriminate kitchen chairs from chairs in general, for example? Rosch et al. concluded that basic-level categories such as "chair" are more fundamental classifications than either superordinate or subordinate categories.

The idea of basic-level categories has several important developmental implications. If such categories are indeed basic, children should learn them first. To test this implication, Rosch et al. asked 3-year-olds to identify which two toys, from a set of three, were most alike. Sometimes the two similar toys were from the same basic category (two airplanes). Other times they were from the same superordinate category (an airplane and a car). The third object in either case came from an entirely different category—for example, a toy dog. When the two similar objects came from the same basic-level category, the 3-year-olds put them together on 99 percent of their choices. By contrast, when the two most similar choices had in common only a superordinate category, the 3-year-olds chose them 55 percent of the time.

Language development shows a similar pattern. Children learn words that name basic-level categories before words that name superordinate or subordinate ones (Anglin, 1977). Both hearing speakers of oral languages and deaf speakers of American Sign Language show this ordering (Rosch et al., 1976). Parents seem sensitive to the priority of basic-level categories in their children's development and base their introductions of new superordinate terms on known basic-level terms. For example, when they introduce the term *mammal*, they point to foxes, sheep, raccoons, and other animals and say, "These are mammals." Use of such multiple basic-level examples seems to help children learn the superordinate terms (Callanan, 1985).

Although basic-level categories play prominent roles in early conceptual understanding, some of the particular categories differ considerably from those that adults consider basic. Illustratively, the objects that 1-year-olds label "balls" often include such objects as round candles, round coin banks, and multisided beads. Their "ball" category seems to correspond to the adult category "things that can be rolled." Mervis (1987) labeled such notions as *child-basic categories*. The particulars of "child-basic" and standard-basic categories often differ, but Mervis argued that the principles by which they are formed are the same. Both young children and adults include in their basic categories objects that can be used to achieve similar functions or that have similar overall appearances. Differing perspectives on what constitutes an interesting function lead to the differences in the categories that are produced at different ages.

How do children move from child-basic to standard-basic categories? Grasping the role of perceptually insignificant but functionally important attributes may be critical in the transition process (Tversky & Hemenway, 1984). For example, young children seem to initially ignore the slots in round coin banks and the wicks on round candles, and focus on the more perceptually striking round shape. Once the child understands the correlation between an object's form and its function (e.g., between presence of a wick and the function of burning), conceptual distinctions become easier to understand. In keeping with this interpretation, an experimenter's identifying perceptually subtle attributes that are critical to category membership, and then explaining the function of those attributes, helped 24-month-olds move from child-basic to standard-basic categories (Banigan & Mervis, 1988).

*Correlations among features of natural concepts*    Conceptual understanding involves more than knowing cue validities of individual features. Correlations among features are at least as essential. One of Rosch et al.'s main arguments about the nature of concepts was that features of objects in the world are not randomly distributed, but rather tend to cluster together. Things that slither along the ground also tend to have scales, to be long and thin, to be difficult to see in their natural environments, and so on. Fortunately, even babies less than 1 year old are adept at noting correlations among features and at using the correlations to form new concepts.

Younger and Cohen (1983) demonstrated this point. They showed 10-month-olds pictures of four fanciful beasts, one by one (Figure 7–2). The body and tail in each picture were correlated, in the sense that if a beast had a certain type of body, it also had a particular type of tail. Thus, if you knew what type of body the beast had, you could predict its type of tail.

Following these four exposures, the dishabituation trial was presented. On it, the 10-month-olds saw an animal whose body and tail were

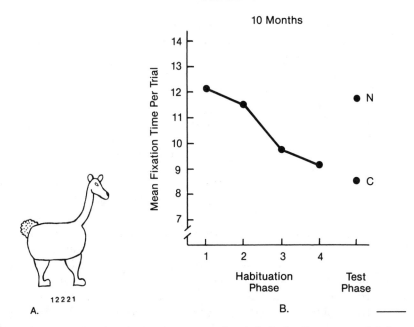

A.    B.

**FIGURE 7–2**   A. Example of stimuli presented to infants by Younger and Cohen (1983). B. Times spent looking at fanciful beasts during the habituation and dishabituation phases of the experiment. Note the recovery in looking time for the novel stimulus group (N) in which the body-tail relation was reversed. Note also the lack of recovery in the control group (C) in which the body-tail relation was maintained.

not those that previously had appeared together, though each had been seen earlier with a different body or tail. Presumably, babies would find such a combination surprising if they detected the earlier body–tail relation, but not if they only attended to the body and tail as separate parts. In fact, babies did show renewed attention to this novel body-tail combination (Figure 7–2B). Thus, even infants note correlations among features and use them in forming concepts.

The correlational patterns that children detect change considerably with age. This is evident in representations of information about quantifiable dimensions, such as size, loudness, pitch, and brightness (Smith, Sera, & Goodrich, 1989). The magnitudes of some pairs of dimensions, such as the size and the darkness of an object, are seen as more strongly correlated by 2-year-olds than by 4-year-olds or adults. In contrast, the magnitudes of other pairs of dimensions, such as an object's loudness and its size, are seen as more strongly correlated by the older children. The pattern seems to reflect the combined effect of two factors: an early general quantitative representation within which children attempt to locate a variety of individual dimensions, and a developing knowledge of the actual correlation patterns present in the world and reflected in particular word meanings.

*Prototypes.* A fourth concept introduced by Rosch and her colleagues was that of prototypes. Prototypes are the most representative instances of concepts—that is, the examples that have the highest cue validities. Lassie was a prototypical dog, not only because she was familiar, but because she had qualities (e.g., size, shape, type of bark) representative of dogs in general.

Both children and adults are very adept at abstracting the prototype from examples they encounter. In fact, they are so adept that when they are shown the examples surrounding a prototype but not the prototype itself, they often are more confident that they have seen the prototype, which was not shown, than the objects surrounding it, which were (Bransford, 1979).

Infants as young as 3 months abstract prototypical forms. Bomba and Siqueland (1983) showed 3- and 4-month-olds a variety of dot patterns generated by randomly transforming an original "prototype" pattern of dots (Figure 7–3). During this initial phase of the experiment, the infants were not shown the prototype. However, exposure to the examples derived from the prototype led infants later to act as if they had seen it. When the prototype was shown to them along with another, unfamiliar pattern, they preferred looking at the other pattern; they acted as if they had seen the prototype often and were bored with it. Over time, as memory for the particular dot patterns decreased but the general concept remained, the 3- and 4-month-olds actually showed more interest in previously shown exam-

**FIGURE 7–3** From top to bottom on the left, the prototypic triangle, diamond, and square. From left to right, increasingly large distortions of each prototypic shape (after Bomba & Siqueland, 1983).

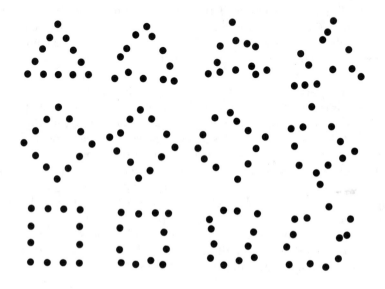

ples, which they had seen but apparently did not remember, than in the prototype, which they had not seen but did "remember." By 7 months, infants can abstract considerably more-complex prototypes than at 3 months (Younger & Gotlieb, 1988), but the basic ability to form prototypes is clearly present even at the younger age.

*Evaluation.*    Viewing conceptual representations in terms of probabilistically related features has much to recommend it. Even in the first year, infants abstract prototypical patterns, form basic-level categories, and notice cue validities and correlations among features. With development, they form increasing numbers of superordinate and subordinate level categories, move from child-basic to standard-basic categories for those concepts on which they started with child-basic categories, and become sensitive to more-complex and subtle correlational patterns.

The probabilistic-features approach also has some weaknesses, though. One that it shares with the defining-features approach is vagueness about what constitutes a feature. For example, what features make up the concept "a beautiful face"? They clearly are much more complex than a nose of a certain size, eyes of a certain shape, lips curved at a certain angle, hair of a certain color, and so on. Much more important than these tangible features are relations among the features, such as how the parts of the face fit together. Yet it is unclear whether relations such as "fitting together" can usefully be viewed as features; given that many beautiful faces strike us as unique, it also is unclear whether they are based on probabilistic relations at all.

Another weakness, related to the previous one, is that the approach is vague about the very early phases of concept formation. In particular, it does not specify how children determine which features of unfamiliar objects and events they should encode. As discussed in Chapter 3, determining which features to encode is often quite difficult; even quite simple scenes offer an infinite number of possible encodings. Yet, unless children encode the important features and relations, they cannot learn their cue validities.

Children may overcome this problem by assuming, when they are first learning a word or concept, that a wide variety of properties of the examples they encounter are potentially relevant. Their conceptual representations at that point, and perhaps for some time after, may be closely tied to the examples they have encountered. The role of examples in children's conceptual representations is explored in more detail in the next section.

### Exemplar-Based Representations

In some ways it seems unlikely that examples could play a prominent role in conceptual representations. Even a 2-year-old has encountered so many examples of objects and events that representing all of them seems impossible. How much memory capacity would be required to store all this information? What speed would be required to zoom through the many stored examples to find the particular one of immediate interest?

These difficulties may be less serious than they initially appear, though (Farah & Kosslyn, 1982). Space for storing examples may not be a problem, because the long-term memory capacity of the human brain is for all practical purposes unlimited. Searching through large numbers of examples also seems to be less difficult than might first be assumed. College students who have been briefly shown as many as 2,500 pictures can quickly discriminate those they have seen previously from those they have not (Standing, Conezio, & Haber, 1970).

Carey (1978) suggested several reasons why children would find representing examples especially useful for constructing new concepts. Consider the concept "tall." The first three statements in which a child heard this term might refer to a tall building, a tall lady, and a tall drink. The three absolute sizes would be wildly discrepant. Further, children probably would not realize quickly that even among objects that are the same height, "tall" is more likely to be applied to thin ones. If concepts in general are this complex (and "tall" does not seem like an unusually complicated notion), retaining detailed information about the first few examples encountered seems essential for inferring the abstract properties of the concept. This is the same logic that led Klahr and Wallace to postulate the time line as a detailed record of processing (Chapter 3).

Consistent with this analysis, examples do seem to play more-prominent roles in younger than in older children's conceptual representations. Kossan (1981) found that 7-year-olds learned more effectively under conditions that promoted careful attention to particular examples than under conditions that promoted learning of a rule for classifying new instances. In contrast, 10-year-olds learned equally well under the conditions that promoted learning of the rule. Kossan concluded that the 7-year-olds were more accurate in the example-based condition because it was closer to the style in which they habitually learned.

Similarly, 4-year-olds have been found to grasp unfamiliar concepts in an example-by-example way in a situation in which 10-year-olds understand the same concepts more in terms of abstract rules (Tighe, Glick, & Cole, 1971). Also, 5-year-olds have been found to more easily acquire concepts that are most easily thought of in terms of individual examples than in terms of rules; 7-year-olds, like adults, show the reverse pattern (Kendler & Kendler, 1962). These findings suggest that young children's conceptual representations emphasize particular examples more heavily than do the representations of older individuals.

*Evaluation.* Representations of particular examples clearly play a role in conceptual development. The role may be especially large among young children. At all ages, however, such information seems very unlikely to be the sole content of conceptual representations. The reason is evident when we consider what children need to do to decide whether a new object is an example of a concept. How do they compare the new object with known examples? Since the new object almost never will be identical to the old one, they must have some basis of comparison beyond a simple "matches/doesn't match." The only obvious way of performing such comparisons is to note correspondences among the features and relations within the examples. This analysis implies that the conceptual representation must include a description of the important features and relations as well as the example as a whole.

A second difficulty with example-based approaches is lack of specificity about what constitutes an example. When people see a honeybee buzzing around their backyard, do they remember the particular honeybee, do they remember just that it was a honeybee, or do they remember just that it was a bee? The simplest assumption for an example-oriented approach—that the individual bee is represented—seems unlikely. Recall that the objects people are most sure that they have seen (the prototype) are sometimes objects they have never actually encountered. This finding seems difficult to explain if people remember specific examples but not more-abstract characterizations.

In sum, representations of particular examples are a) almost certainly a part of conceptual representations at all ages; and b) almost certainly not the entirety of conceptual representations at any age.

### Theory-Based Representations

What concept has the following members: children, portable TVs, jewelry, photo albums, and paintings? The question seems extremely strange until we hear the answer: things we would take out of the house first in case of fire. Suddenly, the strangeness of the concept disappears (Barsalou, 1985).

As this example suggests, there is more to concepts than examples, correlations among features, and defining features. Concepts also embody theoretical beliefs about the world and the relations of entities to each other (Carey, 1985; Murphy & Medin, 1985). These theoretical beliefs influence our conceptualization of new events. Contrast your reaction to the statement "Today, I saw a car with orange wheels" with your reaction to the statement "Today, I saw a car with square wheels." Both situations are extremely unfamiliar; people would not have had an opportunity to calculate cue validities or feature correlations for either the orange or the square wheels. Neither is in the least prototypical. Yet our theoretical beliefs lead us to react differently to the two statements. When we hear that a car had orange wheels, we infer that the owner may be a prankster or a hippie, that the rest of the car may also be brightly painted, and that the car probably functions normally. When we hear that a car had square wheels, we infer that it was standing still, that it was not intended to function normally, and that it may be a sculpture intended to elicit reactions of surprise. Such inferences reflect our informal theories about how cars work and about why people do strange things.

Keil (1989) proposed a particularly intriguing theory of the role that such causal beliefs play within conceptual development. The following are among the main principles he suggested:

1. Most concepts are partial theories, in that they include explanations of relations among their parts and of their relations to other concepts.
2. Theories are complexly tied to people's associative knowledge; they do not stand apart from it.
3. Causal relations are basic within these theories; they are more useful than other types of relations.
4. Hierarchical relations also are especially informative.

The import of these assumptions can be illustrated with regard to a hypothetical situation. Suppose a girl was asked, "Why do yaks have four legs rather than three or five?" She might retrieve memories of horses and cows running and then answer that four legs can be moved in pairs, which allows yaks to run relatively fast and still maintain their balance. This answer suggests that the child possessed a partial theory that allowed her to go beyond defining features, probabilistically-related features, and particular examples to explain _why_ the world is as it is. The answer also illustrates the relation between associative knowledge and theoretical beliefs, in that it reflects both specific memories of the running of other four-legged animals and an informal theory of how running works. The role of causal relations is evident in the child's explaining four-leggedness in terms of what it allows yaks to do. Finally, the fact that the child knew that she could reason from her knowledge of animals in general to yaks, since they are a type of animal, attests to the usefulness of hierarchical relations.

Keil proposed that theories are not limited to adults' and older children's concepts. They also are present in many of the concepts of very young children. This is not to say that the conceptual representations are the same at all ages. The depth and interconnectedness of the theoretical beliefs, the frequency with which they are relied on, and their relative dominance within conceptual representations all increase with development. Viewed from another perspective, Keil hypothesized that at all ages, concepts include both theoretical connections and isolated factual information. However, as theories become increasingly sophisticated, they explain an increasingly broad range of the factual knowledge.

The types of theory-laden relations depicted within Keil's approach exist at all levels of generality, from very specific to very encompassing. One of the most encompassing conceptual divisions divides the world's objects and events into a fairly small number of categories. The existence of these categories is evident within language use when we consider *predicability* (the types of predicates that can be used in various types of sentences). As may be recalled from long-ago grammar lessons, the predicate is the part of the sentence that includes the verb and its complement. In the sentence "The monster is now alive," *The monster* is the subject, and *is now alive* is the predicate.

The phenomenon that motivated Keil's interest was children's ability to distinguish between statements that contain nonsensical predicates and statements whose predicates render the sentence untrue but sensible. Even if the speaker is mistaken in saying, "The monster is now alive," the sentence still is comprehensible. However, it is more than false to say, "The monster is now an hour"; it is meaningless. The predicate *is now alive* can be used to describe living creatures, whereas the predicate *is now an hour* describes events. Even preschoolers discriminate between the two types of statements. The question is how they do so.

Keil (1979, 1981) hypothesized that children innately divide their experiences into certain fundamental categories and that they assume that these categories are hierarchically related. The fundamental categories that Keil hypothesized are denoted by the capital letters in Figure 7–4. In a sense, these categories function as implicit divisions of the world into domains that we can theorize about: physical objects, living things, animals, plants, and so forth. Paralleling these fundamental categories are classes of predicates that can be used to characterize the category members. Since the categories are hierarchically organized, so are the classes of predicates that can be used to comment on them.

The Figure 7–4 hierarchy divides both the fundamental categories and their potential predicates into classes of decreasing generality. The classes toward the top apply very widely. Any object, event, or idea can be said to be interesting, for example. The classes of predicates toward the bottom, in contrast, apply much more narrowly. Only humans and perhaps a few other mammals can be said to "feel sorry" or to "be honest."

Keil's claim was not that the full predicability tree shown in Figure 7–4 is present at birth. Rather, he argued that the form of the conceptual organization is always a treelike hierarchy, and that children make basic distinctions within the hierarchy (objects versus events, animals versus plants) before they make more-subtle ones (intentional versus unintentional events, sentient versus nonsentient animals).

How would such predicability trees contribute to conceptual development? Keil advanced the following scenario. Suppose an older girl who did not know the word *tempest* encountered the sentence "The tempest lasted for an hour." If she possessed the full Figure 7–4 tree, which Keil suggested was typical by sixth grade, the predicate *lasted for an hour* would indicate

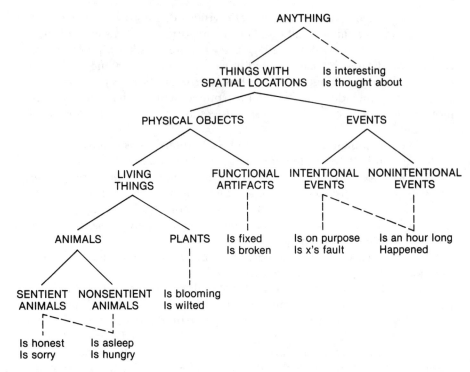

**FIGURE 7–4**  Part of Keil's (1981) predicability hierarchy indicating which categories of objects can be described by which types of predicates. Categories of objects are in capitals; predicates that can be used to describe words in that category are in lowercase letters. Early in development, children only make distinctions shown at top of tree. Gradually, they make distinctions found lower and lower in the tree. The full tree represents adults' knowledge of predicability.

that tempests are unintentional events of some type. By contrast, Keil suggested that a younger child with a less-detailed predicability tree would not be able to constrain the potential meaning of the unfamiliar term to as great a degree. For example, since younger children do not seem to discriminate between the types of predicates that can be used to describe intentional and unintentional events, they could not infer from "The tempest lasted for an hour" that tempests are unintentional. Generally, the more-detailed predicability tree, and the more-detailed categorization that underlies it, would allow older children to draw more-precise inferences than younger ones, and thus help them learn faster.

Theoretical knowledge also helps young children overcome the influence of immediate perceptions to see deeper similarities. In one study (Gelman & Markman, 1987), 3- and 4-year-olds were told a fact that they did not know before. For example, they were shown a picture of yellow oil and told, "When you put some of this in water, it floats up to the top." Then the children were told the names and shown pictures of several other objects and asked whether those objects also would float to the top. The most-interesting cases were objects from the same category that looked different (e.g., brown oil) and objects from a different category that looked similar (e.g., yellow honey). When asked whether each object would float, both 3- and 4-year-olds answered affirmatively much more often to the object from the same category that looked different (the brown oil). Thus, young children know that members of categories are united by properties that allow generalization from one member to another, even when the category members look quite different.

When do children first possess implicit theories? Spelke (1988) speculated that infants begin life with the theory that the world is composed of physical objects that are cohesive, have boundaries, have substance, and continue to exist over time and movement. As one source of evidence for her view that infants possess a primitive theory of objects, she cited Baillargeon's finding that 4-months-olds look for a long time when an object appears to swing through a space that they previously saw was occupied by another object. She argued that the infants' prolonged looking indicated that they were surprised and that this surprise indicated that they view objects as permanent and as having substance; why else would they show surprise at an object moving through a space that another, now hidden object had occupied earlier? From such findings, Spelke concluded:

> The spontaneous development of physical knowledge is a process of *theory enrichment*, in which an unchanging core conception of the physical world comes to be surrounded by a periphery of further notions. It is not difficult to see in outline how theory enrichment could occur. If an initial theory of the physical world allows children to single out objects, then children will be able to acquire further knowledge about objects by following them through time and observing their behavior. The initial theory will perpetuate itself over the learning process, because the entities the child learns about will be just the entities that his initial theory has specified. (p. 181)

*Evaluation.* The theory-oriented approach to conceptual development is bold and promising. Concepts are at their heart relational; causal relations are often especially critical. Children seem to focus on these causal relations from early in life. Knowing the causal relations helps children realize which information to encode from among the infinite number of possibilities they might encode. The causal knowledge also helps them to draw inferences, to generalize, and to understand their experience. This insight of theory-based approaches is an important one.

Critical problems remain before it will be possible to evaluate the contribution of the approach as a whole, however. One problem is a lack of definition of what qualifies as a theory. A physicist's theory of matter differs profoundly from that of a typical adult, much less that of a child or an infant. Within scientific theories, internal consistency, parsimony, and formalization are important qualities. It is not clear which of these qualities, if any, are shared by the concepts of infants and young children. This vagueness about what qualifies as a theory has led to people using the term *theory* in very different ways. For example, Carey (1985) proposed that very young children possess only two theories: a theory of physics and a theory of psychology. She suggested that they eventually differentiate these two into roughly a dozen theories, corresponding to major physical, biological, and social science disciplines that are taught at universities: physics, chemistry, biology, psychology, economics, and so on. In contrast, Keil (1989) argued that concepts in general are theoretical and that young children have large numbers of theories. Without definition of what constitutes a theory, it is impossible to know whether children have a few "privileged" theories or vast numbers of concepts that include theoretical aspects. Is a child's "theory" of biology qualitatively different from the child's "theory" of baseball, and if so, how?

A related problem involves lack of clarity about what evidence can be used to test whether a child possesses a theory. For example, does an infant's lengthy look at an object swinging through a location previously occupied by another object really mean that the infant has a theory that such an event is impossible? An anecdote illustrates the problem. A few months ago, I was on my back porch, and I saw a bird turn its head 180 degrees so that it was looking directly back at its tail. I was not surprised that the bird could do this, since I had read that birds possess this capacity. I was extremely interested in seeing it, though. Anyone measuring my looking time would have recorded a very long fixation. The point is that long looking times do not necessarily indicate surprise, and are a very long way from indicating that the looker has a theory that the event is impossible. More generally, it is unclear how we can tell whether a child has a theory, much less what the theory includes and how it changes over time.

On balance, though, viewing concepts in terms of theory-based representations is an innovative new perspective. A number of problems remain to be resolved, but the approach's emphasis on the role of causal relations within conceptual understanding seems a large step forward. The propensity to try to explain what we see and what happens to us is a basic property of human beings, and it seems to play a central role in the concepts we form from very early in development.

*Summary.*    What can we conclude about children's conceptual representations? From very young ages, children seem to represent concepts in terms of all four types of information that have been discussed: defining features, probabilistically related features, examples, and informal theories. The relative prominence of the different types of information and the frequency with which children rely on them may change, however.

When children are just beginning to form a concept, memory for specific examples may play an especially large role. As they come to encode the relevant features of the concept, they begin to compute cue validities that link the encoded features to the concept. Eventually, for concepts that have defining features, children distinguish between those features that are definitional and those that are only characteristic. And, throughout the period, children seek to establish causal relations, both among different aspects of the concept and between the concept and related ideas.

At any age, people understand different concepts at different levels. Some concepts are included in rich explanatory networks that include connections to many other concepts. Others are quite isolated. Similarly, children's representations of some concepts emphasize defining features; their representations of other concepts emphasize probabilistic features; and so on. Further, an individual child's representation of a single concept often includes all four types of information. In sum, no one type of information seems to consistently dominate children's conceptual representations at any age. Numerous types are always present.

## DEVELOPMENT OF SOME PARTICULARLY IMPORTANT CONCEPTS

Some concepts are so important, and so pervasive in our representation of reality, that they merit special attention. Among them are time, space, number, and mind.

### Time

The concept of time includes three fundamental subcategories: experiential time, logical time, and conventional time (Friedman, 1978). *Experiential time* refers to our subjective experience of the order of events and their duration. It provides the basis for all other understandings. *Logical time* involves time as a continuous dimension that can be reasoned about. An event that starts later and ends earlier than another even must have taken a shorter time. *Conventional time* concerns days of the week, months of the year, and other societal devices for dividing the temporal continuum into discrete periods.

*Experiential time.* Piaget (1969) hypothesized that infants possess some sense of time, but only as it affects their own movements. Their sense of time was viewed as not extending beyond what they themselves did until the end of their first year. It now appears, though, that younger infants have a sense of the time taken by other people's activities as well as by their own. This is evident in interactions between infants and adults. Infants between 3 and 5 months organize their behaviors in ways that react to the timing of their mothers' activities (Lester, Hoffman, & Brazelton, 1985). The strength of the relation increases between 3 and 5 months, but some adjustments in the timing of the infants' actions are already evident at 3 months. Moreover, 2-month-olds discriminate between identical sequences of notes when they are played in different rhythms. This indicates an even earlier sense of the timing of external events within auditory perception (Fraisse, 1982).

Another aspect of experiential time is ability to estimate the durations of events. By 5 years, children can estimate durations of 3 to 30 seconds quite well, especially if given feedback on the true length of the intervals (Fraisse, 1982). Older children become increasingly adept at using counting to help them estimate durations. However, counting only produces accurate estimates if the units of time being counted are themselves of equal duration; counting quickly to 10 does not take the same amount of time as counting slowly. Many 5-to-7-year-olds count with units of varying length, which results in their inaccurately estimating the passage of time when they use counting strategies (Levin, 1989).

*Logical time.*    To measure logical understanding of time, Piaget (1969b) presented children two trains that ran in the same direction along parallel tracks; the question was which train traveled for the longer time. Although the two trains started and stopped at the same times, children below 6 or 7 consistently said that the train that stopped farther down the track traveled the longer time, as well as the longer distance and the faster speed. Piaget concluded that preoperational children lacked a logical understanding of time, speed, and distance.

Subsequent studies have replicated Piaget's observations but cast doubt on his interpretation. For example, when 5-year-olds observed cars moving in circular paths, rather than along straight lines, they had little difficulty deducing from the starting and ending times which car traveled for the greater total time (Levin, 1977). They also showed understanding of logical properties of time in comparing the sleeping times of two dolls that were said to fall asleep and wake up at the same or different times (Levin, 1982). In these cases, there were no strongly interfering cues, such as unequal stopping points, on which children could base incorrect judgments. It thus appears that 5-year-olds understand the logical relations among beginning, ending, and total time, but that their grasp is sufficiently fragile that interfering cues can lead to their not relying on it.

Young children are not the only ones who do not always use the logical understanding of time, speed, and distance that they possess. Older children and adults have the same problem. Think about this situation: When a race car travels around an oval track, do both its doors move at the same speed? Almost everyone's intuition is that of course they do, but in fact they do not. The door toward the outside of the track is covering a greater distance in the same time, and therefore is moving faster. The reason that the problem is so difficult is that it flies in the face of what Levin, Siegler, and Druyan (1990) labeled the *single-object/single-motion intuition*. This is the belief that all parts of a single object must move at the same speed. Young children, older children, and college students alike share this intuition. They all consistently say that all parts of an object moving in a circular path travel at the same speed.

Despite the single-object/single-motion intuition's ordinarily persisting at least from third grade through college, it can be overcome through physical experiences that dramatically contradict it. Levin et al. presented sixth-graders a six-foot-long rod that was attached at one end to a pivot. The child and the experimenter both held the rod while walking around the pivot on four trials. On two of the trials, the child held the rod near the pivot, and the experimenter held it at the opposite end; on the other two trials, their positions were reversed. The difference in the speed at which children needed to walk while holding the inner and outer parts of the rod was sufficiently dramatic for them not only to learn that the outer part was moving faster, but also to generalize their new understanding to other problems in which different parts of a single object moved at different speeds. This physical experience accomplished what years of informal experience and formal science instruction usually fail to do. As one boy said, "Before, I hadn't experienced it. I didn't think about it. Now that I have had that experience, I know that when I was on the outer circle, I had to walk faster to be at the same place as you" (Levin et al., 1990). Such physical experiences may help children understand concepts at a deeper level than standard classroom instruction usually does.

*Conventional time.* Not until they go to school do most children learn the conventional time system of seconds, minutes, hours, days, months, and years. Understanding of this system seems to involve three types of representations: associative, ordered verbal list, and mental image.

The earliest knowledge of conventional time appears to be isolated *associations,* such as knowledge of the date of one's birthday or the day of a favorite television show (Friedman, 1989). Then children learn that these specific times are embedded within larger systems. Such systems could be represented either as *ordered verbal lists,* which proceed from earlier to later, or as *mental images,* which can be scanned equally easily in both directions. To determine which type of representation children use, Friedman (1986) presented such questions as "If one goes forward (backward) from Wednesday, will Saturday or Monday come first?" If children represent the days of the week as an ordered list, they presumably would find it easier to go forward than backward (since the list goes forward). In contrast, if they form a mental image of the seven days, they should as easily go in one direction as the other.

Second-graders did not answer either type of question consistently correctly, indicating that they possessed neither type of representation. Fourth- through eighth-graders did well on the forward task but not on the backward one, indicating that they used the ordered-list representation. College students did equally well on both tasks, indicating that they either relied consistently on a mental image or used whichever representation was easiest. Almost identical results were obtained when questions concerned the months of the year.

These results do not mean that through eighth grade, children are incapable of forming mental images of conventional time units. Rather, the findings seem to reflect the time units' having been learned originally as ordered lists, and the knowledge remaining in that form until people need to convert it to other forms to solve specific problems (Friedman, 1986). For example, having to figure out whether you become hungry at an earlier or a later time the spring morning after daylight savings time goes into effect and clocks were set ahead might lead children to form images of clock times and sun angles on mornings before and after the change. This, in turn, might lead to a greater general appreciation of the usefulness of images in thinking about time.

### Space

We live in a world of locations and distances. We can represent these locations and distances in at least three ways: in relation to our own position, in relation to landmarks, or in relation to an abstract framework (Huttenlocher & Newcombe, 1984). *Egocentric representations* involve the relations between our own location and that of one or more objects of interest (targets). Thus, a target's position might be represented as "10 paces to my left." *Landmark-based representations* relate the position of the target to that of one or more objects in the environment. Thus, we could represent a location by thinking, "I parked the car on the yellow level near the Section B sign." *Allocentric representations* depict the spatial layout relative to some abstract frame of reference, such as that provided by a map or coordinate system. The name *allocentric* reflects the fact that such representations are sufficiently flexible that any position within one can serve as the center or reference point for thinking about the surrounding space.

The three types of spatial representations are not as separate in people's minds as these definitions might suggest. For example, landmarks provide useful reference points within egocentric representations and also provide convenient points of origin within allocentric representations. Further, in everyday spatial reasoning, children of a variety of ages flexibly use knowledge of specific routes, as well as overall representations of space, to figure out where things are. Nonetheless, each of the three types of representations is widely used and each emphasizes different aspects of the spatial environment, so it seems useful to distinguish among them.

*Egocentric representations.*    Piaget (1971) suggested that before infants are 1 year old, they exhibit a kind of sensorimotor egocentrism. Recall from Chapter 2 that egocentrism refers to young children's tendency to view the world solely from their own perspective. Piaget claimed that in infancy, the egocentrism is quite literal, and that infants represent locations of objects only in relation to themselves. For example, they might continue to represent an object as being a right turn away from themselves even after they moved to the opposite side of the object, resulting in its being on their left.

Piaget's hypothesis was supported by subsequent findings that 6- and 11-month-olds frequently fail to compensate for changes in their own spatial position (Acredolo, 1978). They continue to turn in the direction that previously led them toward the target but that no longer does so. Not until 16 months do they compensate for the change in their position relative to the target.

This sensorimotor egocentrism is not absolute, even at such young ages. Infants' difficulty in adjusting to changes in spatial position can be mitigated if either distinctive landmarks or gravity provide cues to the object's location (Rieser, 1979). Under such conditions, 6-month-olds usually turn in the appropriate direction, even when it differs from the direction that previously led to the object. Adjusting to changes in position also seems to be less of a problem when testing is done in the infant's home than when it is done in an unfamiliar environment (Acredolo, 1979). This may be due either to infants' knowing the landmarks better in the familiar livingroom setting, or to their simply feeling more comfortable there.

How do infants learn to represent space in a way not tied to their own position within it? Experience moving around the environment seems to be one formative influence. Eight-month-olds who can crawl or who have extensive experience in a walker succeed considerably more often in locating objects' spatial positions than infants of the same age who neither crawl well nor have experience with walkers (Bertenthal, Campos, & Barrett, 1984). The longer children have been locomoting, the greater their advantage (Kermoian & Campos, 1988). The source of locomotion also matters. Just as it is easier for adults to learn a spatial layout when they are the driver rather than the passenger in a car, infants learn spatial layouts more effectively when they walk around them than when they are carried. The reason seems to involve differences in how attention is deployed. When 12-month-olds walk to the other side of a layout and have the opportunity to look at all times at the point where a prize has been hidden, they both look at it more than children who are carried and subsequently do better in turning toward the object from the new position. In contrast, when they cannot see the prize as they walk from one position to the other, they subsequently are no better in turning toward it than children who were carried (Acredolo, Adams, & Goodwyn, 1984). Thus, one benefit of self-produced motion is that it leads to more-effective deployment of visual attention.

By 1½ to 3 years, depending on the task, children consistently show nonegocentric spatial representations on tasks that involve searching for objects from different starting points. For example, they turn toward the object's location regardless of whether they walked to the new position themselves or were carried to it. They also know that people who occupy a different location in space than they do see different things. In particular, they realize that people see what can be connected with their eyes by a direct line (Flavell, Everett, Croft, & Flavell, 1981).

Despite these improvements, children continue to rely on egocentric representations in a number of situations in which they need to take a spatial perspective different than their own. One such situation is Piaget and Inhelder's (1967) *three mountains problem*. On this task, children are shown a display like that in Figure 7–5 and asked to describe or construct a model of what a doll sitting on the other side of the table would see. Children below age 9 or 10 often err by describing what *they* see, rather than what the doll would. Thus, if they see the tallest mountain on their right, they think the doll also would see it on its right.

Several surprising factors have been found to contribute to children's

**FIGURE 7–5** Piaget's three-mountain task. The child is asked how the scene appears to a doll sitting across the table (after Piaget, 1967).

difficulty on this task. That dolls cannot actually see is one; children do better when depicting the perspective of a seeing person sitting on the other side of the table than in depicting the perspective of a doll or a blindfolded person sitting there (Cox, 1975; Fehr, 1979). Children also do better when they move to the position of the other observer (with the display covered), before describing what the observer would see. Moving to the other person's position allowed 4-to-6-year-olds to succeed consistently on the problem (Shantz & Watson, 1971). Moreover, 2½-year-olds who were shown an arrangement of four toys on a floor, each toy standing on an identical dot, could put each toy back where it had been after they crossed to the other side of the arrangement (Huttenlocher & Newcombe, 1984). On the other hand, when the places on which the toys had stood were not specified, the same 2½-year-olds did poorly, not even maintaining the overall shape of the arrangement. The young children's success on the one task but not the other may have been due to the spots on the floor, and one or more features of the external room, serving as landmarks with which toys could be aligned. Following we consider the role of landmarks more extensively.

*Landmarks.* We often give directions in terms of landmarks, as in "You go through the Fort Pitt Tunnel, turn off at the Banksville Road exit, and go south until you hit MacFarlane Road." We do this because landmarks provide a way of dividing the environment into more-manageable segments. In a sense, they allow people to apply a divide-and-conquer strategy to solving the perennial problem of how to get from here to there.

Representation of spatial locations in terms of landmarks begins in the first year. As noted previously, 6-month-olds' representations of an object's position survive a change in perspective if a distinctive landmark is near the object (Rieser, 1979). People as well as objects can provide such landmarks; 9-month-olds at times use their mothers' location as a landmark for locating interesting objects near her (Presson & Ihrig, 1982). The usefulness of landmarks is evident at all ages. For example, adding an external landmark, such as a toy horse in a fixed position, helps elementary school children succeed on the three mountains problem (Fehr & Fishbein, 1976; Huttenlocher & Presson, 1973).

The use of landmarks appears to undergo considerable refinement beyond this initial period (Huttenlocher & Newcombe, 1984). Before children's first birthday, only landmarks immediately adjacent to the target usually lead to accurate location of targets. By about 2 years, landmarks that are more distant from the target also help. By age 5, children can represent an object's position relative to multiple landmarks, a much more powerful procedure for establishing exact locations.

Development involves changes not only in how landmark information is used, but in which landmarks are brought to bear. Almost anything can be used as a landmark. Our own location, that of objects in the room, and that of the walls of the room all can be thought of as landmarks. When Acredolo (1976) pitted these three types of landmarks against each other, she found 3-year-olds relied most heavily on the relation of the target to their own position; 5-year-olds relied most on the relation of the target to an object (a desk) in the room; and 7-year-olds relied most heavily on the relation of the target's position to the framework provided by the walls of the room. The first representation might be viewed as egocentric, the second as landmark-based, and the third as allocentric, but all can also be viewed as relating the location of the object to that of landmarks.

*Allocentric representations.*   Frequently, we can neither see nor go directly from here to there. Such situations demand integration of spatial information from multiple perspectives into a common abstract representation. Such representations are perhaps the most purely spatial of the three types. Egocentric and landmark-based representations can be reduced to a verbal form relatively easily (e.g., the restaurant is near DuPont Circle). In contrast, allocentric representations, which include all relations among the entities within the space, can be reduced to verbal form only with great difficulty.

Most 4-to-6-year-olds can form allocentric representations, though the precision of the representations increases considerably with development. Lockman and Pick (1984) examined 4-to-6-year-olds, 8- and 9-year-olds, and adults who lived in a housing complex in identical two-story townhouses. The task involved shining a light pen to indicate the location of a target relative to one's own position within such a townhouse. For example, children might stand in the kitchen and be asked to point to their bedroom on the second floor. The target's location could never be seen; it was always hidden behind a wall, floor, or ceiling.

When the question involved rooms on the same floor, performance was very accurate at all ages (Figure 7–6). When the question involved rooms on a different floor, there was substantial improvement with age. Even the 4-to-6-year-olds were reasonably accurate, though. Their average deviation of 50 degrees meant that their estimates were generally within the right part of the house. This ability to estimate hidden positions in three-dimensional space without direct routes to link the locations suggests that 4-to-6-year-olds can form allocentric representations.

How does the capacity to form such representations develop? Landau, Spelke, and Gleitman (1984) claimed that children innately represent spatial layouts, along with information about Euclidean distances among landmarks, in terms of an abstract reference system. However, methodological criticisms of their study (Liben, 1988), along with some recent, striking data on the spatial representations of visually impaired people (Rieser, Hill, Talor, Bradfield, and Rosen, 1989), render this claim questionable. Reiser et al. contrasted the spatial representations of adults who developed severe

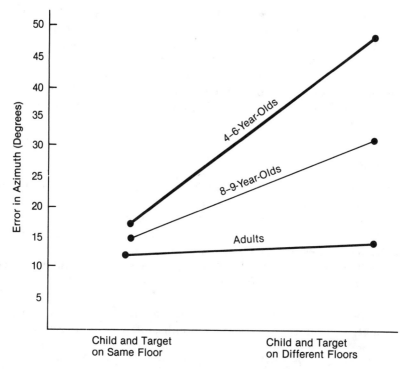

**FIGURE 7–6**  Average angular errors of children and adults when pointing at out-of-sight locations on the same floor as the child's location or on a different floor (after Lockman & Pick, 1984).

visual impairments either early in life (before age 3; almost always before birth) or later in life (after age 5; usually after age 10). All of the visually impaired people suffered from generally poor visual acuity; some also had restricted peripheral vision. The task was to imagine standing at a particular landmark facing in a particular direction in a familiar part of one's neighborhood and to point toward where other imagined landmarks would be.

Those whose visual impairments began early in life and included difficulties with peripheral vision represented the spatial layout much less accurately than those whose impairments started later or whose peripheral vision was intact. If space was innately represented in a Euclidean form, there would be no reason to expect these differences within the visually impaired population. Instead, the finding appeared to be due to early perceptual learning being critical for geometrically accurate spatial representations. Rieser et al. argued persuasively that the critical contributor to an abstract understanding of space was the opportunity to correlate two types of information that accompany self-produced movement: bodily sensations and the flow of visual information from a wide spatial area. These two types of information allow the individual to learn which spatial relations remain invariant and which undergo changes when the person moves, and thus allow formation of allocentric representations of space. The interpretation is consistent with the previously noted findings of the beneficial effects of self-produced movement in enabling infants to form nonegocentric representations of space, especially when they watch the target as they move to the new location.

### Number

Understanding of numbers involves two basic types of knowledge: understanding of cardinality and understanding of ordinality. *Cardinality* refers to absolute numerical size. A common property of people's arms, legs, eyes, and feet is that there are two of them. The cardinal property of two-ness is what these sets share. *Ordinality* refers to relational properties of numbers. That someone is the third-prettiest girl in the class and that five is the fifth number of the counting string are ordinal properties.

*Cardinal properties of numbers.* Understanding of cardinality begins surprisingly early in infancy. By age 4 months, infants can discriminate one object from two, and two objects from three (Antell & Keating, 1983; Starkey & Cooper, 1980; Strauss & Curtis, 1981). This was learned through the use of the habituation paradigm. Infants were shown sets of objects that differed in a variety of ways but that all had the same number (e.g., two objects). Once the infants habituated to displays with this number of objects, they were shown a set with a different number. Their renewed looking testified to their having abstracted the number of objects in the previous sets.

Discriminating among larger numbers of objects poses greater difficulty for infants. Those below 1 year do not appear to discriminate four objects from five or six (Starkey & Cooper, 1980; Strauss & Curtis, 1981). This finding suggests that infants identify cardinalities through *subitizing*, a quick and effortless perceptual process that people can apply only to sets of one to three or four objects. When we see a row of between one and four objects, we feel like we immediately know how many there are; in contrast, with larger numbers of objects we usually feel less sure, and often feel a need to count. Adults and older children are similar to infants in being able to very rapidly identify the cardinal value of one to three or four objects, but not larger sets, through subitizing (Chi & Klahr, 1975).

Between 2 and 4 years of age, children become proficient in another means of establishing the cardinal value of a set—*counting*. This allows them to assign numbers to larger sets than can be subitized. Gelman and Gallistel (1978) pointed to the rapidity with which children learn to count and hypothesized that the rapid learning was possible because it was guided by knowledge of *counting principles*. In particular, they hypothesized that even before age 2, children knew:

1. The *one–one principle:* Assign one and only one number word to each object.
2. The *stable order principle:* Always assign the numbers in the same order.
3. The *cardinal principle:* The last number assigned indicates the number of objects in the set.
4. The *abstraction principle:* The other principles apply to any set of objects.
5. The *order irrelevance principle:* The order in which objects are counted is irrelevant.

Several types of evidence persuaded Gelman and Gallistel that children understood all of these principles by age 5, and most of them by age 3 or 4. Even when children erred in their counting, they showed knowledge of the one–one principle, since they assigned exactly one number word to most of the objects. For instance, they might count all but one object once, either skipping or counting twice the single miscounted object. These errors seemed to be ones of execution rather than of misguided intent. Children demonstrated knowledge of the stable order principle by almost always saying the number words in a constant order. Usually this was the conventional order, but occasionally it was an idiosyncratic order such as "1, 3, 6." The important phenomenon was that even when children used an idiosyncratic order, they used the same idiosyncratic order on each count. The 2-to-4-year-olds demonstrated knowledge of the cardinal principle by saying the last number with special emphasis. They showed understanding of the abstraction principle by not hesitating to count sets that included different types of objects. Finally, the order irrelevance principle seemed to be the most difficult, but even here 5-year-olds demonstrated understanding. Many of them recognized that counting could start in the middle of a row of objects, as long as each object was eventually counted. Although few children stated the principles, their counting suggested that they understood and used them.

Gelman and Gallistel argued that one reason the principles were important was that understanding of them guided children's acquisition of counting skill. This argument rested on the assumption that children understood the principles before they could count accurately. However, a variety of subsequent findings have indicated that children actually count skillfully *before* they understand the principles that underlie the counting (Briars & Siegler, 1984; Frye, Braisby, Lowe, Maroudas, & Nicholls, 1989; Wynn, in press). Experience with counting may provide a data base from which children can distinguish essential features of the usual counting procedure (e.g., counting each object once and only once) from incidental ones (e.g., starting at the leftmost or rightmost end of a row).

A central feature of cardinality is that it is maintained over some transformations but not others. Piaget's number conservation task was designed to assess when children acquire such understanding. As described in Chapter 2, this number conservation task begins with two rows that have equal numbers of objects, at least six objects per row. One row is lengthened or shortened but is not otherwise changed. Then the child is asked whether the two rows still contain the same number of objects. Before age 6 or 7, children usually say that the longer row has more objects.

This number conservation task can be placed in a broader context. As Klahr and Wallace (1976) and Halford (1982) noted, a sophisticated understanding of conservation implies understanding of three transformations, not just one. The child should understand not only that certain transformations do not influence quantity, but also that transformations involving addition increase number and transformations involving subtraction decrease it. Further, early understanding of conservation might apply to small sets of objects but not to large sets. In sum, understanding of conservation involves understanding of the effects of at least three transformations on both small and large sets of objects.

Children acquire understanding of these different conservation problems at different points in development, but they acquire the understandings in a consistent order (Siegler, 1981). The earliest understandings involve the effects of addition and subtraction on small sets. Children as young as 4 years know that adding an object to a row with a small number of objects results in more objects and that subtracting an object from such a row results in fewer objects. However, if the number of objects in the two rows is large, or if the only transformation is to elongate or compress a row, 4-year-olds judge the longer row to have more objects.

Gradually, children extend their knowledge to other transformations and to larger sets. First they learn that merely lengthening or shortening a row with a few objects leaves the number of objects unchanged. Next they learn that adding an object to a set with many objects increases its number, and that subtracting an object decreases the number. Finally they learn that lengthening or shortening a large set leaves its number unchanged. Interestingly, this last type of problem to be mastered was the very one used by Piaget in his number conservation task.

At this point, which most children reach at around age 6 or 7, they can correctly solve all number conservation *problems*. Understanding of the number conservation *concept* is not yet complete, though. At first, children solve the problems by counting the number of objects in each row after the transformation or by placing the objects in the rows in one-to-one correspondence and seeing if either row has anything left over. Later, they solve the problems without counting or pairing. Instead, they rely on the type of transformation that was performed. If one row had an object added, it necessarily has more; if one row had an object subtracted, it necessarily has less; if nothing was added or subtracted, the two rows continue to have the same amount.

This last discovery is important, because it allows children to transfer knowledge from number conservation to other types of conservation problems. Counting and pairing are useful for solving number conservation problems, but cannot be applied to other conservation tasks. For example, how could counting be used to determine whether pouring water into a differently shaped glass changed the amount of water? On the other hand, relying on the type of transformation allows children to solve all conservation problems. Adding to the relevant dimension always results in more, subtracting always results in less, and neither adding nor subtracting results in the same amount. Consistent with this analysis, children who solve number conservation problems by counting or pairing rarely answer liquid-quantity or solid-quantity conservation problems correctly. Also consistent with it, children who solve number conservation problems by relying on the type of transformation usually also solve liquid- and solid-quantity conservation problems through the same reasoning (Siegler, 1981).

An interesting general implication of this sequence is that ability to solve all problems correctly does not always mark the end point of development. At times, more-general or more-efficient ways of solving problems may exist. Under these circumstances, conceptual understanding may continue to develop even after children can solve all problems in a domain.

*Ordinal properties of numbers.* Ordinality refers to the relative positions or magnitudes of numbers. A number may be first or second in an order, or it may be greater or less than another number. Mastery of ordinal properties of numbers, like mastery of cardinal properties, begins in infancy. However, it seems to begin later, between 12 and 18 months.

The most-basic ordinal concepts are *more* and *less*. To test when infants understand these concepts as they apply to numbers, Strauss and Curtis (1984) repeatedly presented 16-to-18-month-olds with two squares—one containing one dot, the other containing two dots. They reinforced the babies for selecting the square with two dots. Then they presented two new squares (e.g., squares with four dots and three dots). The babies more often chose the set of dots that maintained the "larger" relation, thus indicating understanding of this ordinal property (see also Cooper, 1984).

In the preschool period, children learn to compare numbers apart from the objects they represent. For example, they learn to solve such problems as "Which is bigger, 6 or 3?" To study the process by which they do so, Siegler and Robinson (1982) asked 3-, 4-, and 5-year-olds to compare the magnitudes of all 36 possible pairs of the numbers 1 through 9. The 3-year-olds' performance was at chance level, whereas both 4- and 5-year-olds were correct on more than 80 percent of trials. Also, the 3-year-olds' errors were evenly distributed among problems, whereas those of the older children were concentrated on problems with relatively large numbers and relatively small differences between numbers (e.g., 8 versus 7). Interestingly, these are the same problems that adults find most difficult, as evidenced by their relatively long solution times on them. In sum, substantial progress is made between ages 3 and 5 in understanding numerical magnitudes.

How do preschoolers make such progress? Despite numbers' representing an inherently quantitative dimension, children seem to divide them into qualitative categories when they are first learning about them. In particular, they divide the numbers into very small, small, medium, and large subcategories. Since they know that large anythings are bigger than medium-sized anythings, and that medium-size anythings are bigger than small anythings, this strategy allows quite a good understanding of numerical magnitudes. Classifying numbers into subcategories seems to serve the same function as dividing space into regions around landmarks. It allows children to divide a single difficult task into several simpler ones and thus to conquer the challenges of the domain.

### Mind

We live in a world not only of space, time, and number, but also of mind. Basic understanding of our own minds and the minds of other people is essential for us to understand the human environment. Consciousness helps us gain this understanding; we are aware of some of the workings of our minds, and this provides a basis for generalizing to the minds of others (Johnson, 1988). How is it, though, that consciousness comes to have the vocabulary that it does? In particular, how do we come to think about our thinking in terms of purposes, beliefs, knowledge, intentions, desires, and so forth?

Wellman (1990) proposed that from roughly 3 years onward, children have a naive theory of how the mind works, which he labeled a *belief–desire theory*. It was a theory, because it divided the world into coherent categories and provided potential explanations for why events occur. It was a belief–desire theory, because its central tenet was that internal beliefs and desires lead to actions. The theory's basic organization is outlined in Figure 7–7.

Wellman hypothesized that 3-year-olds' theory of mind was built on a foundation of four types of understanding:

1. Understanding of the basic distinction between the mind and the world.
2. Understanding of the existence and nature of beliefs and desires.
3. Understanding of relations among mental entities.
4. Understanding that the contents of the mind represent those of the world.

With regard to the first point, most 3-year-olds realize that thoughts, dreams, and memories differ both from typical physical objects, such as

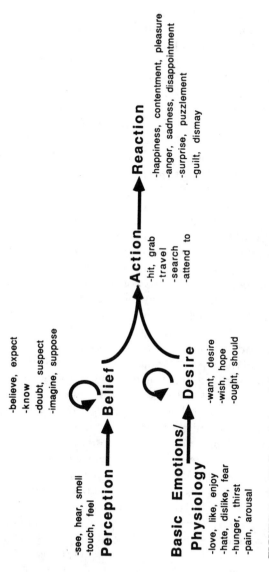

**FIGURE 7-7** Wellman's (1990) depiction of children's theory of mind.

chairs and tables, and from insubstantial physical entities, such as smoke and sounds. When asked to explain why it was impossible to touch thoughts and dreams, 3-year-olds often advanced mental explanations ("Cause it's her imagination; Cause it's in his mind"). In contrast, they rarely advanced such explanations in accounting for why they could not touch sounds (Wellman, 1990). They demonstrated understanding of the relations among beliefs, desires, and actions by indicating that other people's beliefs and desires would determine what the people did, even when those beliefs and desires differed from the child's own (Wellman & Bartsch, 1988). The 3-year-olds also showed understanding of relations among some mental entities, such as perceptions and beliefs. In particular, they knew that perceiving something directly produces beliefs about the perceived object, and that merely being near the perceiver does not (Pillow, 1988). Finally, 3-year-olds evidenced a

degree of understanding of the relation between mental representations and the physical environment; for example, they knew that mental images are a representation of objects that exist in tangible form in the outside world (Wellman, 1990).

Wellman hypothesized that this belief–desire theory is not children's first concept of mind, though it is the first, in his view, that is sufficiently elaborate to qualify for the title "theory." Preceding the belief–desire theory is an understanding of the role of desire without an understanding of the role of belief. Two-year-olds consistently predict that characters in stories will do as they wish, even when the child would make a different choice. However, 2-year-olds are considerably less consistent in predicting that characters will act in accord with their own beliefs, for example beliefs about where a hidden object is located, when those beliefs differ from the views of the child (Wellman & Wooley, in preparation).

The origins of the concept of mind may go back even before age 2. One potential origin involves the concept of "agency," the idea that people's actions are self-caused and that other people, like oneself, are the authors of their own actions. Implicit in this idea is that there is something within the person that is causing the action; eventually, this something is labeled "the mind." Such a concept of agency may be present even in infancy (Poulin-Dubois & Shultz, 1988). A related possibility is that understanding of the mind grows from observing relations between intentions and physical causality (Leslie, 1988). For example, it could grow out of observations of the similarities and differences between a glass of milk toppling off the edge of the table and the child deciding to topple a glass of milk over the

edge. Similarly, a likely precursor of the concept of mental representation is the tendency, starting at about 1 year, to engage in pretend play, in which an object is used to represent another, quite different object (Bretherton, 1984; Leslie, 1987). This provides children an opportunity to reflect on how their minds can at least temporarily change what objects mean to them.

Development of the child's theory of mind also continues beyond age

3. Children distinguish increasingly clearly between their own knowledge and that of others. When 4- and 5-year-olds are shown what an object is, then shown a small, uninformative patch of the object, and finally asked whether someone who saw just that small patch would know what the object was, they usually say yes; 6-year-olds less often make such mistakes, and 8-year-olds almost never do (Taylor, 1988). Similarly, 5-year-olds usually know that if another person sees a box full of red markers and is told that one of the markers has been transferred to a different box, the person will know what color the marker is. Younger children generally think the other person will not know, despite the fact that they themselves correctly assume the marker will be red (Sodian & Wimmer, 1987).

After age 3, children also distinguish increasingly clearly between appearance and reality. Flavell, Flavell, and Green (1983) presented 3-, 4-, and 5-year-olds with certain imitation objects, such as a spongelike object that looked just like a rock. The children were encouraged to play with the objects so that they knew the objects were not what they appeared to be. Then they were asked questions aimed at establishing whether they differentiated between what the objects looked like and what they "really, really were." The children were asked similar questions about the objects' color and size. Here, they viewed the objects through a blue plastic sheet or through a magnifying glass.

The majority of 4- and 5-year-olds could distinguish between what the object currently looked like and what its identity, color, and size really were. The 3-year-olds, on the other hand, did considerably less well on this and on a variety of other tasks that measured their understanding of the difference between appearance and reality. For example, they at times claimed that a cloth that smelled like an orange really was an orange. Similarly, many of them, unlike 4-year-olds, claimed that the images on television screens represented tangible objects inside the set (Flavell, Flavell, Green, & Korfmacher, in press). An effort to teach 3-year-olds the appearance–reality distinction was unsuccessful (Flavell, Green, & Flavell, 1986). Thus, understanding of the appearance–reality distinction increases a great deal beyond age 3.

The inherent importance of people's everyday concept of mind may be less self-evident than the importance of the concepts of time, space, and number. After all, it is the superficiality and incorrect assumptions of our everyday theories of the mind that make scientific research on cognition necessary. To the extent that everyday psychological theories affect our actions, however, we can only understand human behavior by understanding the concepts and theories that influence it. The importance of these everyday theories is evident in thinking about how we play games involving direct competition with other people. Regardless of whether the game is bridge, chess, football, poker, or tennis, we base much of our behavior on analyses of our opponents' goals and beliefs and what actions they are likely to take given those goals and beliefs. Similar analyses influence our behavior whenever we interact with other people. In short, just as we could not understand the physical environment without concepts of time, space, and number, we could not understand the social environment without a workable concept of mind.

## SUMMARY

Conceptual development can be approached either by considering conceptual representation in general or by focusing on particular concepts of special importance. Conceptual representations in general can assume at least four forms. Defining-features representations depict concepts in terms of a few necessary and sufficient features. Probabilistic representations include many features that are associated with the concept to varying degrees, but no feature that is necessary and sufficient for category membership. Exemplar-based representations include particularly memorable or important instances of the concept. Finally, theory-based representations focus on causal relations among different aspects of conceptual understanding.

A number of prominent developmental theorists, including Piaget, Vygotsky, Werner, and Bruner, have formulated versions of the representational development hypothesis. Within this view, young children cannot form representations based on necessary and sufficient features. However, even 1-year-olds have proved capable of relying on necessary and sufficient features with familiar concepts. Young children do appear to rely on defining-features representations less often than do older individuals, but they clearly can form them.

Both children's and adults' representations often emphasize probabilistic relations rather than necessary and sufficient ones. Even infants abstract prototypical forms, detect cue validities and correlations among features, and generate basic-level categories. Within a relatively short time, children also begin to form subordinate and superordinate concepts, move from child-basic to standard-basic concepts, and abstract increasingly complex correlational patterns.

Examples also play an important role in conceptual representations. Because of the complexity of many concepts and the difficulty of deciding what to encode, it seems extremely useful for children to retain detailed information about early-encountered examples of a concept. Examples may play an especially large role when a concept is just being formed.

Theory-based representations emphasize the role of causal and hierarchical relations. A wide variety of children's concepts seem to have theoretical aspects that facilitate inferences, explanations, and generalizations, and that help children overcome the influence of superficial perceptual similarity. There may also be certain special theories, such as theories of biology and of the mind, that have different qualities than concepts in general; the ways in which such theories differ from others, however, are not yet clear. Some concepts seem to have theoretical aspects from early in life, but the depth and scope of theory-based concepts clearly increases greatly with development.

Another perspective on conceptual development is provided by focusing on the particulars of the development of concepts of special importance. Among such special concepts are time, space, number, and mind. These concepts are worthy of unusual attention because they are used to represent a vast range of experiences, because they are present in some form from infancy to old age in all of the world's cultures, and because our thinking about the world would be so drastically different without them.

Understanding of the concept of time includes an understanding of experiential time, logical time, and conventional time. Infants as young as 3 months organize their behavior in ways that react to the rhythm of their mother's activities, thus showing a sense of experiential time. By age 5 years, children know the logical relations among beginning, ending, and total times, though their grasp is tenuous and can easily be disrupted by misleading cues. Children acquire understanding of conventional time during the school years. It develops from early isolated associations with particular events to representation of the system that provides the context for the events.

Locations and distances within space can be represented in terms of relations to oneself, in terms of relations to landmarks, or in terms of an abstract system. Egocentric representations lead infants younger than 1 year to continue turning in the direction that previously led to a goal, even when their position relative to the goal changes. Even during this period, however, landmarks immediately adjacent to the goal help infants overcome their propensity to turn in the direction that had worked earlier. The variety of objects that can serve as landmarks and the distance over which they are effective increase considerably in the next few years. Early experience correlating the flow of visual information with one's own movements may be critical for forming more-abstract, allocentric representations of space.

Representations of number include cardinal and ordinal information. Even infants understand certain cardinal and ordinal properties of numbers. This is evident in their habituating to sets with a given number of objects and in their learning to choose the set with the larger number of objects. By the end of the preschool period, children supplement their early understanding of cardinality with understanding of counting and number conservation. They also supplement their understanding of ordinality with knowledge of numerical magnitudes.

By age 3, children seem to understand the mind in terms of a system of desires and beliefs that lead to actions. Before this age, the role of desire is understood, but the importance of belief may not be. In the years after age 3, children come to understand increasingly deeply the distinction between appearance and reality. They also more clearly distinguish between what they themselves know and what other people do.


## RECOMMENDED READINGS

Huttenlocher, J., & Newcombe, N. (1984). The child's representation of information about location. In C. Sophian (Ed.) *Origins of cognitive skills.* Hillsdale, NJ: Erlbaum. This article presents a well-reasoned analysis of the way in which children use egocentric perspectives, landmarks, and perceptual patterns within layouts to locate objects in space.

Keil, F. C. (1989). *Concepts, kinds, and cognitive development.* Cambridge, MA: MIT Press. A thoughtful and interesting presentation of the theory-based-representations approach to conceptual development.

Levin, I., & Zakay, D. (Eds.) (1989). *Time and human cognition: A life span perspective.* New York: North-Holland. This up-to-date collection of articles summarizes what is currently known about the development of understanding of time.

Mervis, C. B., & Rosch, E. (1981). Categorization of natural objects. *Annual Review of Psychology, 32,* 89–115. Reviews the accumulated evidence for the roles of basic-level categories, correlations among features, and cue validities in children's conceptual development. One of the most-interesting and influential lines of work in the study of thinking.

Wellman, H. M. (1990). *Children's theories of mind.* Cambridge, MA: MIT Press. Summarizes the rapidly growing body of research on the development of understanding of how the mind works, and puts forth intriguing proposals about the development of theoretical understanding of the mind.

# 8

## *Problem Solving*

Georgie (a 2-year-old) wants to throw rocks out the kitchen window. The lawnmower is outside. Dad says that Georgie can't throw rocks out the window because he'll break the lawnmower with the rocks. Georgie says "I got an idea." He goes outside, brings in some green peaches that he had been playing with, and says: "They won't break the lawnmower." (Waters, 1989, p. 7)

Georgie's triumph over those who would spoil his fun illustrates the essence of problem solving: a goal, an obstacle, and a strategy for circumventing the obstacle and reaching the goal. In Georgie's case, the goal was to throw things out the window; the obstacle was his father's disapproval; the solution strategy was "throw peaches, not stones." The 2-year-old's end run around his father's prohibition illustrates how clever early problem solving can be.

Problem solving is a central part of all our lives. Deciding what courses to take next semester, what word will complete a crossword puzzle, how to find our keys, and how to answer a brain teaser all demand problem solving. Probably not a day goes by without our trying to solve some problem.

Problem solving also provides much of the purpose of other cognitive processes such as perception, language, memory, and conceptual understanding. If we ask why evolution would result in people's being able to perform these processes, a large part of the answer must be that they enhance people's ability to solve problems that the environment presents. That is, they help people adapt to changing circumstances. As suggested by this view, problem solving is not distinct from perception, language, memory, and conceptual understanding, but rather is the orchestration of these capabilities to overcome obstacles and reach goals.

As important as problem solving is in adults' lives, it probably is even more important in the lives of children. With age and experience, people learn ways of circumventing many obstacles so that situations that once posed problems no longer do. For example, when a child first goes to a friend's house a few blocks away, figuring out the best way to walk home represents a real problem. With repeated visits, however, it poses no problem at all. Because children encounter so many situations that are new to them, they are constantly moving from one problem to another.

It is no accident, then, that the two main theoretical approaches to cognitive development—the Piagetian and information-processing approaches—both place great emphasis on problem solving. This emphasis seems well deserved. Children's frequent problem solving teaches them a great many lessons; through solving problems, children contribute to their own development. In addition, problem solving requires children to invent solutions for themselves, rather than parroting ideas they have heard or relying on well-practiced routines. Thus, it often reveals unique characteristics of children's thinking that are less evident when they can fall back on what they have heard from others.

*Organization of the chapter.*     This chapter includes two main sections. The first provides an overview of children's problem solving. The initial part of the section describes several general themes that have emerged from research on children's problem solving. Then, a number of these themes are illustrated in the context of development of problem-solving capability on a single task: the balance scale.

The second section of the chapter focuses on several specific problem-solving processes: planning, causal inference, analogy, tool use, and logical deduction. These processes were chosen for special attention because children frequently use them, because changes in their effectiveness have much to do with changes in the overall effectiveness of problem solving, and because they provide a sense of the varied ways in which children solve problems. They are not the only problem-solving processes that children use—children utilize far too many processes for all of them to be discussed in a single chapter—but they do seem to be among the largest contributors to development. The chapter's organization is summarized in Table 8–1.

**TABLE 8–1    Chapter Outline**

## AN OVERVIEW OF PROBLEM SOLVING

### Central Themes

*Task analysis.*   The processes used to solve a problem largely reflect the problem that is being solved. Think about the following anecdote:

> We watch an ant make his laborious way across a wind-and-wave-molded beach. He moves ahead, angles to the right to ease his climb up a steep dunelet, detours around a pebble, stops for a moment to exchange information with a compatriot. Thus he makes his weaving, halting way back to his home. . . . Viewed as a geometric figure, the ant's path is irregular, complex, hard to describe. But its complexity is really a complexity in the surface of the beach, not a complexity in the ant. On that same beach another small creature with a home at the same place as the ant might well follow a very similar path. (Simon, 1981, pp. 63–64)

Simon went on to argue that, as in the ant's journey across the beach, much of the complexity we observe in people's thinking is really a reflection of the complexity of the environment. Only by performing a careful *task analysis* of the demands of particular problems can problem solving be understood, since so much of it is an effort to adapt to the task. In situations where people solve problems efficiently, detailed analyses of task requirements can indicate what they are doing. In situations where people cannot solve problems efficiently, analyses of the task provide a background against which to evaluate exactly where the processing difficulty lies. Thus, task analyses can help distinguish actions people take because the actions are adaptive from actions they take because of their own information-processing limitations.

Consider how task analyses can lead to insights about children's problem solving. Klahr (1985) presented 5-year-olds a puzzle in which a dog, a cat, and a mouse needed to find their way to a bone, a piece of fish, and a hunk of cheese, respectively. To solve the puzzle, children needed to move all three animals to the locations with the appropriate food. Superficially, the greater the number of moves needed to reach the goal, the harder the problem would seem.

Klahr's task analysis, however, indicated that different problems created varying degrees of conflict between the child's immediate goal of getting a given animal to the desired food and the child's higher goal of getting all three animals to the right positions. Some problems required children temporarily to move an animal already at its goal away from the goal, so that another animal could reach its goal. These problems were more difficult for the preschoolers to solve than problems that required more moves but that did not entail any conflict among goals. Other problems required children to resist the temptation to move an animal directly to a goal and instead to make a different move. These problems were even more difficult than the problems that required the 5-year-olds to move an animal away from a goal it had already reached. The detailed analysis of the task and the conflicts it created between immediate and longer-term goals enabled Klahr to identify the approach that many children used: trying on each move to increase the fit between the current and the desired arrangement of pieces. This seems to be a quite widely used problem-solving strategy.

*Encoding.*    As discussed in Chapter 3, encoding involves identifying the critical information in a situation, and using it to build an internal representation. Children often fail to encode important features of a task, because they do not know what the important features are, because they cannot comprehend them, or because they do not know how to encode them efficiently. This failure to encode critical information can prevent children from learning from potentially useful experiences. If they are not taking in the relevant information, they cannot benefit from it.

Misencoding often dooms problem solving efforts to failure. In one such case, 4-to-11-year-olds and college students watched a moving electric train carrying a ball on a flatcar. At a predesignated point, the ball dropped through a hole in the moving flatcar and fell several feet to the floor. The task was to predict the trajectory of the ball as it fell (McCloskey & Kaiser, 1984).

More than 70 percent of the 4-to-11-year-olds, and a sizable minority of the college students, predicted the ball would fall straight down. After they advanced this hypothesis, the experimenter ran the trains so that subjects could see what actually happened. (The ball fell in a parabolic trajectory.) The children and the college students were faced with reconciling their predictions with the outcome they saw.

Their explanations revealed how misencoding can influence problem solving and reasoning. Some said that the ball fell straight down just as they thought it would. Others said that the train gave the ball a push forward just before it was released. Interestingly, a number of the college students who encoded the ball as having fallen straight down had previously taken and passed college physics courses. Apparently, this experience was insufficient to change either their expectations or their encoding of what they saw. As will be demonstrated in this chapter, changes in encoding play a critical role in the development of a variety of types of problem solving.

*Mental models.* Much of the purpose of encoding is to build an appropriate *mental model* of the task (Gentner & Stevens, 1983; Johnson-Laird, 1983). Halford (1990) identified a number of central characteristics of such mental models. The most important is that the model accurately represent the structure of the problem. That is, relations among components of the mental model should parallel the essential relations in the problem. When the model's structure parallels that of the situation depicted in the problem, people feel that they understand; otherwise, they feel they do not, even if they can generate a solution by other means, such as by remembering it. The structure depicted within a mental model includes not only static features but also dynamic ones, such as the moves and operations that are possible. Thus, mental models constrain the problem-solving process by ruling out many classes of moves. The mental modeling process also involves abstraction, in which nonessential features of the problem are stripped away and are not represented within the model. This stripping away of incidental features facilitates generalization from the mental model of the original problem to related problems with different superficial characteristics but a parallel structure.

These properties of mental models can be seen by considering the simple question: Why can't you see the back of your head without a reflecting device such as a mirror? As soon as we think about this question, we become aware of our mental model of the locations of facial features on the human head, the constraints on their movements, and the way the head as a whole moves and carries its features with it. Constructing such mental models is both a form of understanding in its own right and a means of making future events more understandable.

*Domain-general and domain-specific knowledge.* One of the basic issues about problem solving is the relation of domain-general and domain-specific processes. The distinction involves the range of situations in which a given problem-solving process can be applied. As the names suggest, domain-general processes can be applied relatively broadly, whereas the range of applicability of domain-specific processes is narrower.

At first, it might sound like domain-general processes must make a larger contribution than domain-specific ones. The issue is not so simple, however, because there is a trade-off between the breadth of applicability of a process and its efficiency in solving any particular type of problem. Processes that are broadly applicable tend not to be as efficient in solving a specific class of problems as are processes more precisely tailored to fit the particulars of that class of problems. Thus, even though the general problem-solving skills of adults are undoubtedly greater than those of children, the specific chess strategies of the child chess experts studied by Chi (1978) allowed them to solve chess problems more effectively than inexperienced adult players.

Although the relative importance of domain-specific and domain-general processes has often been debated (e.g., Liben, 1987b), it almost certainly is more useful to think about how the two work together than to compare their independent contribution (Ceci, 1989; Sternberg, 1989). The reason can be understood by returning to the anecdote about Georgie and the peaches. Without the specific knowledge that peaches are softer than stones, Georgie could not have generated his solution. Without general problem-solving skills, such as the understanding that there may be different routes to the same goal, he also could not have done so. Problem solving relies on knowledge and processes of many levels of generality. The real issue is how children integrate such diverse information into efficient problem-solving procedures, rather than whether specific or general knowledge is more important.

*Developmental differences.* Perhaps the most-frequent theme of this chapter might be given the paradoxical title "young children's competence and older children's incompetence." Many of the best-known claims regarding cognitive development involve problem-solving processes that young children supposedly cannot perform. For example, Piaget (1970) and Inhelder and Piaget (1964) claimed that preoperational children were incapable of transitive inference and hierarchical classification. In contrast, the problem solving of adolescents and adults was idealized as deductive and rational (Inhelder & Piaget, 1958).

More recent investigations, however, have shown that this discontinuity is more apparent than real. Young children, supposedly unable to engage in certain kinds of problem solving, actually are more competent than had been realized. The key to revealing these competencies has been simplifying problems by eliminating sources of difficulty extraneous to the process being examined. Complementarily, adolescents and adults have proved to be far less logical and rational than once was believed. Their planning, scientific reasoning, and powers of deduction all fall short of the ideal of the formal operational reasoner.

These findings do not imply that problem solving is similar in early childhood and adolescence. In fact, it differs profoundly. The change, however, is not typically from being absolutely unable to execute a process to being able to do so. Instead, most changes seem to be in the range of situations in which children successfully execute the problem-solving processes. Older children can fight their way through thickets of memory demands, linguistic subtleties, and misleading cues that utterly defeat younger children. They also learn how to solve new problems much more quickly. Thus, although young children are more competent and older ones less so than was once thought, plenty of development still is evident.

### An Example of the Development of Problem Solving

To obtain a feel for the development of problem solving, it is helpful to consider changes from infancy to adulthood on a single task. The balance scale provides one convenient context for considering these changes. Even infants in their first half-year can solve some balance scale problems; even college-educated adults usually fail to solve others. Changes occur along a wide variety of dimensions relevant to problem solving: children's untutored strategies for solving the problem, their ability to learn from experience with it, and their encoding of the problem, among them. Further, development of balance scale problem solving exemplifies a number of themes applicable to problem solving in general.

*Rules for solving problems.* Figure 8–1 illustrates a type of balance scale on which children's problem solving has often been examined. The scale includes a fulcrum and an arm that can rotate around it. The arm can tip left or right or remain level, depending on how weights (metal disks with holes in them) are arranged on the pegs on each side of the fulcrum. However, a lever (not shown in the figure) is typically set to hold the arm motionless. The child's task is to examine the arrangement of weights on pegs and to predict which (if either) side would go down if the lever were released.

A task analysis of this problem, together with Inhelder and Piaget's observations of children's thinking about balance scales, indicated that the task had two relevant dimensions—weight on each side and distance of the weight from the fulcrum—and that the challenge was to attend to both relevant dimensions and combine them appropriately. This analysis, to-

**FIGURE 8–1** The balance scale. Metal disks were placed on a peg on each side of the fulcrum. Children needed to decide which side of the balance would go down, given the particular configuration of weights on pegs (from Siegler, 1976).

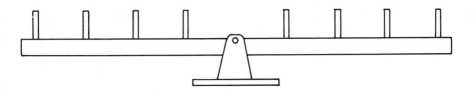

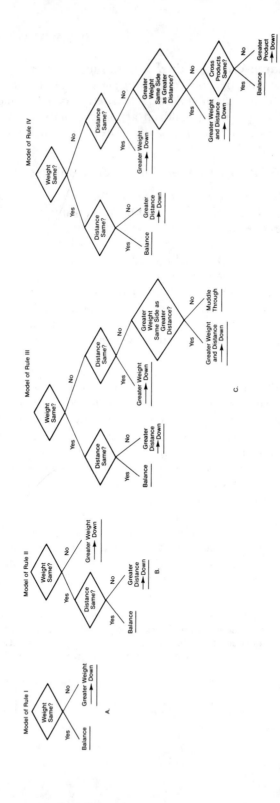

**FIGURE 8–2** Rules for solving balance-scale problems (from Siegler, 1976).

gether with the known tendency of young children to focus on a single relevant dimension, led Siegler (1976) to hypothesize that children would solve such problems by using one of the four rules depicted in Figure 8–2:

- *Rule I:* If the weight is the same on both sides, predict that the scale will balance. If the weight differs, predict that the side with more weight will go down.
- *Rule II:* If one side has more weight, predict that it will go down. If the weights on the two sides are equal, choose the side with the greater distance (i.e., the side that has the weight farther from the fulcrum).
- *Rule III:* If both weight and distance are equal, predict that the scale will balance. If one side has more weight or distance and the two sides are equal on the other dimension, predict that the side with the greater value on the unequal dimension will go down. If one side has more weight and the other side more distance, muddle through or guess.
- *Rule IV:* Proceed as in Rule III unless one side has more weight and the other more distance. In that case, calculate torques by multiplying weight times distance on each side. Then predict that the side with the greater torque will go down.

But how could it be determined whether children use these rules to solve balance scale problems? Asking children how they solved the problems would be the simplest strategy, but answers to such questions could either overestimate or underestimate their knowledge. The answers would give a misleadingly positive impression if children simply repeated information they heard at home or in school but did not understand. The answers would give a misleadingly negative impression if children were too inarticulate to communicate knowledge they in fact possessed. Such difficulties often limit the usefulness of children's verbal explanations as indexes of their reasoning (Brainerd, 1973).

In light of these difficulties, I formulated the *rule assessment method* to determine which, if any, rule a given child used. This rule assessment method involved generating problems for which different rules yielded specific patterns of correct answers and errors. As shown in Table 8–2, the types of problems used to assess children's rules were:

1. *Balance problems:* The same configuration of weights on pegs on each side of the fulcrum.
2. *Weight problems:* Unequal amounts of weights, equidistant from the fulcrum.
3. *Distance problems:* Equal amounts of weights, different distances from the fulcrum.
4. *Conflict–weight problems:* One side with more weight, the other side with its weight farther from the fulcrum, and the side with more weight goes down.
5. *Conflict–distance problems:* One side with more weight, the other side with "more distance," and the side with more distance goes down.
6. *Conflict–balance problems:* The usual conflict between weight and distance, and the two sides balance.

**TABLE 8–2   Predicted Percentage of Correct Answers on Each Problem Type for Children Using Each Rule**

| PROBLEM TYPE | RULE | | | |
| --- | --- | --- | --- | --- |
| | *I* | *II* | *III* | *IV* |
| *Balance* | 100 | 100 | 100 | 100 |
| *Weight* | 100 | 100 | 100 | 100 |
| *Distance* | 0 (Should say "Balance") | 100 | 100 | 100 |
| *Conflict-Weight* | 100 | 100 | 33 (Chance Responding) | 100 |
| *Conflict-Distance* | 0 (Should say "Right Down") | 0 (Should say "Right Down") | 33 (Chance Responding) | 100 |
| *Conflict-Balance* | 0 (Should say "Right Down") | 0 (Should say "Right Down") | 33 (Chance Responding) | 100 |

Children who used different rules would produce different patterns of responses on these problems (Table 8–2). Those using Rule I would always predict correctly on balance, weight, and conflict–weight problems and always predict incorrectly on the other three problem types. Children using Rule II would behave similarly, except that they would answer correctly on distance problems. Those adopting Rule III invariably would be correct on all three types of nonconflict problems and perform at a chance level (33 percent correct) on the three types of conflict problems. Those using Rule IV would solve all problems.

The large majority of children age 5 to 17 years consistently used 1 of the 4 rules (Siegler, 1976). Five-year-olds most often used Rule I, 9-year-olds most often used Rule II or III, and 13- and 17-year-olds usually used Rule III. Few children of any age used Rule IV. Similar sequences of rules on the balance scale task have been observed in a number of subsequent studies (Damon & Phelps, 1988; Ferretti & Butterfield, 1986; Ferretti et al., 1985; McFadden, Dufrense, & Kobasigawa, 1986; Strauss & Ephron-Wertheim, 1986; Surber & Gzesh, 1984; Zelazo & Shultz, 1989).

The expected developmental changes in performance on the six problem types also emerged. For example, consider performance on conflict-weight problems. As shown in Table 8–2, children using Rule I consistently solve such problems correctly. They predict that the side with more weight goes down, which, as previously noted, is by definition correct on conflict–weight problems. In contrast, children using Rule III, who realize that both weight and distance are important, muddle through or guess on conflict problems. They therefore would not usually solve conflict–weight problems correctly. Consistent with this analysis, the 5-year-olds in Siegler (1976), most of whom used Rule I, were correct on 89 percent of conflict-weight problems. In contrast, 17-year-olds, most of whom used Rule III, were correct on only 51 percent. Percentage correct decreased from age 5 to age 17 on all 6 conflict–weight problems, but on none of the other 24 problems. Developmental decrements in performance are sufficiently rare that this data pattern was strong support for the rule analysis that predicted it would occur.

Development of the ability to solve balance scale problems actually begins well before age 5. Some such ability emerges in infancy. Case (1985) presented infants a balance scale with a bell beneath one end. Pushing down on that end would make the bell ring. By 4 to 8 *months,* infants who saw an experimenter produce the ringing sound by hitting that end of the arm responded by reaching to strike or touch that end themselves. By 12 to 18 months, infants imitated the experimenter's solution to a harder problem: depressing one end of the beam so that the other end would go up and ring a bell above it. By 2 to 3½ years, children could figure out the solution to this problem without seeing the experimenter solve it first. By 4 to 5 years, children could even make the bell ring when they were given a heavy and a light block and needed to put a block on each end of the scale in such a way that the bell above one would ring.

Turning to much older children, an anecdote may convey just how specific problem-solving skills often are. In the original Siegler (1976) study, we almost decided not to include the 16- and 17-year-olds. We were told by the headmistress of the school that the students would all perform perfectly, since they had learned about balance scales in *two* previous science courses. Thus, we were surprised when less than 20 percent of students used Rule IV.

A later conversation with a science teacher in the school proved revealing. The teacher pointed out that the balance scale used in classes in this school was a pan balance, whereas the balance scale in the experiment was an arm balance. Retesting of a few students indicated that they indeed could solve comparable problems when they were presented on the pan balance! This limited generalization is, unfortunately, the rule rather than the exception in problem solving; similar findings have arisen in many domains (Chipman, Segal, & Glaser, 1985).

*Learning and encoding.* One reason for identifying both the typical development sequence of rules and the rules used by individual children is to predict which instructional experiences will help particular children learn. To illustrate this point, Siegler (1976) identified 5- and 8-year-olds who used Rule I on the balance scale task. The children were then presented feedback experience. In this feedback experience, children first were given a problem and asked which side of the balance would go down. Then the lever that ordinarily held the arm motionless was released, and children saw whether their prediction was correct. Each child received such feedback on one of three types of problems. Some received balance and weight problems, problems that their existing approach (Rule I) would solve correctly. Others received distance problems, which their existing rule would not solve but which they would be able to solve when they acquired the next rule in the typical developmental sequence. Yet others received conflict problems, which they would not understand even qualitatively until they reached Rule III.

The *moderate-discrepancy hypothesis* (Chapter 4) suggested how the children would react to these problems. This hypothesis indicates that the most effective problems for promoting learning are somewhat, but not greatly, beyond the child's initial level. Thus, distance problems would help these children most, because they were solvable by Rule II, the next rule that Rule I children typically would acquire.

As expected, most children who were presented distance problems, one level above their existing approach, succeeded in learning Rule II. Also as expected, both 5- and 8-year-olds who received feedback problems that Rule I could solve continued to use Rule I. Reactions to the conflict problems were unexpected, however. The 5- and 8-year-olds, both of whom used Rule I initially, reacted differently to the same experience. As expected, most 5-year-olds made no progress. Unexpectedly, however, most 8-year-olds benefited from feedback on conflict problems. They often advanced to Rule III, which entailed qualitative understanding of the roles of weight and distance on all problems.

Why might 5- and 8-year-olds, all of whom used Rule I initially, have reacted differently to the same experience with the conflict problems? Subsequent detailed examination of a few children suggested that encoding of the balance scale configuration played a critical role in whether they learned. The 8-year-olds seemed to encode information about both weight and distance. In contrast, 5-year-olds seemed to see each configuration solely in terms of two piles of weights, one on each side of the fulcrum. They did not appear to encode distances of the weights from the fulcrum.

If 5-year-olds' encoding was limited in this way, their failure to learn from the conflict problems would not be surprising. They simply would not be taking in the relevant information about distance.

To understand the evidence that suggested this hypothesis, consider a 5-year-old girl's response to the problem: four weights on the first peg to the left of the fulcrum versus four weights on the fourth peg to the right.

Experimenter: What do you think'll happen?
Lisa: Stay the same.
E: Yeah? Let's see if you're right (Releases lever. Scale tips right-down, with sharp rap as it hits table). Did they?
L: No!
E: No! No they didn't. Did they?
L: Plunk. Plunk.
E: Plunk! Why do you think that was?
L: I don't know. They both had four. (Counts)
E: They both have four. Is that what made this side go down so much and this side go up so much?
L: No.
E: What do you think it was?
L: I don't know.
E: Think about it. What could it be?
L: I just don't know.
E: Just don't know. Look at it for a moment and try to figure out what it could be. Real carefully.
L: This one is far away (points right) and this one is close (points left).
E: Okay. Have any other ideas?
L: No. (Klahr & Siegler, 1978, pp. 108–109)

As this example illustrates, repeated suggestions to "think about it" and to look carefully seemed necessary before 5-year-olds even noticed the different distances of the weights from the fulcrum.

To test whether improved encoding was in fact related to learning, 5- and 8-year-olds who used Rule I were presented an encoding test. They saw an arrangement of weights on pegs and then, after that arrangement was hidden behind a board, needed to reproduce the problem on an initially empty balance scale. Putting the right number of weights on the two sides indicated encoding of weight; putting the weights the right distances from the fulcrum indicated encoding of distance.

The 8-year-olds usually placed the correct number of weights on the correct peg, showing that they encoded both weight and distance. The 5-year-olds, in contrast, usually put the right number of weights on each side, but generally put them on the wrong peg. They showed little if any encoding of the weights' distance from the fulcrum.

Following this, other 5-year-olds who used Rule I were taught to encode distance as well as weight. Then they were given feedback on the same conflict problems that previously had not produced learning in children of this age. The instruction in encoding made a large difference in ability to learn. Although none of the 5-year-olds without encoding training had benefited previously from feedback on such conflict problems, 70 percent who had received encoding training now did.

*Generality.*    Children approach a variety of problems in ways similar to those they use on the balance scale. Consider development of ability to solve projection of shadows problems (Siegler, 1981). On this task (Figure 8–3), each of two T-shaped bars was located between a light source and a screen. The question was which object would cast the larger shadow on the screen if the light sources were turned on. Typically, 5-year-olds based their judgments on a single dimension; they judged that the larger object always cast the larger shadow. This parallels their basing all of their balance scale judgments on the single dimension of the amount of weight on each side. Among 8- and 9-year-olds, the most common approach was Rule II, in which children relied on the dominant dimension (here the size of the objects) unless its value for the two choices was equal; if so, they considered a second dimension, the distance of the objects from the light source. Among 12- and 13-year-olds and adults, Rule III predominated; they consistently consider both dimensions, but did not know the proportionality formula for integrating them. Finally, as with the balance scale, few people

**FIGURE 8–3**    Projection of shadows apparatus used by Siegler (1981). Turning on the point light sources led to different-size shadows on the screen, with the shadows' sizes depending on the length of the T-shaped bars and their distances from the light sources and the screen.

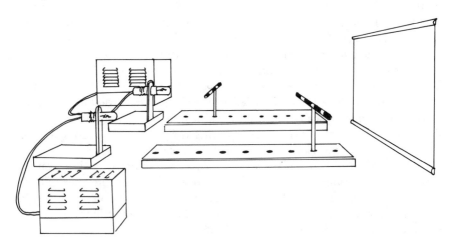

of any age knew Rule IV, the proportionality rule that solves all problems correctly. Similar sequences of rules have been found on a wide variety of problems, among them problems involving temperature and sweetness (Strauss, 1982), happiness and fairness (Case, Marini, McKeough, Dennis, & Goldberg, 1986), fullness (Bruner & Kenney, 1986), inclined planes (Ferretti et al., 1985; Zelazo & Shultz, 1989), causal reasoning (Shaklee & Mims, 1981), and concept formation (Case, 1985).

One especially common finding has been that 4-to-6-year-olds base many of their problem-solving approaches on only a single dimension on problems where two or more dimensions are relevant. This is the case not only with the problems just listed but also with liquid and solid quantity conservation problems; time, speed, and distance problems; probability problems; class inclusion problems; spatial reasoning problems; problems involving social dilemmas; and use of quantitative adjectives (Dean, Chabaud, & Bridges, 1981; Inhelder & Piaget, 1958; Levin, Wilkening, & Dembo, 1984; Ravn & Gelman, 1984; Siegler, 1981; Siegler & Richards, 1979; Surber & Gzesh, 1984; Wagner, 1981).

These findings do not mean that 4-to-6-year-olds cannot consider more than one dimension in solving a problem. They can, and often do. Nor is it the case that young children are the only ones who rely on unidimensional rules in situations where more than one dimension is relevant. Adults also often do this (e.g., Neisser & Weene, 1962). However, children of this age do appear to have especially strong preferences for such rules. Persuading them that such rules are incorrect can be very difficult.

The finding of developmental differences in learning on the balance scale also is typical of learning in many situations. A number of the most-venerable constructs regarding cognitive development have been based in large part on observations of developmental differences in learning: stages, critical periods, the problem of the match, and readiness, among them. For example, consider the following observation from the first decade of this century about *reading readiness:*

> Much that is now strenuously struggled for and methodized over in these early years of primary reading will come of themselves with growth, and when the child's sense organs and nervous system are stronger. . . . Reading will be learned fast when the time comes. Valuable time is wasted on it in the early years. (Huey, 1908, pp. 303, 309)

Although the language sounds quaint, the basic observation—that older children learn faster and more easily than younger ones—remains true. This was evident on balance scale problems: 8-year-olds learned more effectively than 5-year-olds. It also is true on many other problems. For example, 4-to-7-year-olds can learn to solve conservation problems if given any of a variety of types of training. However, when the learning of older and younger children within this age range is compared, the older children almost always learn faster and more completely (Beilin, 1977; Field, 1987; Langer, 1974/75; Strauss, 1972). Among the many types of problems where older children have been shown to learn more effectively are conservation of number (Field, 1981; Kingsley & Hall, 1967), conservation of liquid quantity (Halford, 1970; Strauss & Langer, 1970), analogical reasoning (Brown, 1989), class inclusion (Inhelder, Sinclair, & Bovet, 1974), separation of variables (Case, 1974), and moral judgments (Turiel, 1966).

How can we explain such differences in learning, which emerge even when younger and older children's initial performance is identical? We already have seen how differences in one problem-solving process, encoding, contribute to older children's greater learning about balance scales. We now examine the contributions of a number of other critical processes to many other types of problem solving.

## SOME IMPORTANT PROBLEM-SOLVING PROCESSES

### Planning

Scene: 6-year-old and father in yard. Child's playmate appears on bike:

> *Child:* Daddy, would you unlock the basement door?
> *Daddy:* Why?
> *Child:* Cause I want to ride my bike.
> *Daddy:* Your bike is in the garage.
> *Child:* But my socks are in the dryer. (Klahr, 1978, pp. 181–182)

This conversation illustrates a number of characteristics of planning. One is that planning, like problem solving as a whole, can be thought of in terms of goals, obstacles, and solutions. Here, the child's plan seems to include the goal of riding her bike; recognition of the obstacles of having neither her socks nor her bike; and the solution of going to the basement, getting her socks from the dryer there, and then getting her bike from the garage.

Despite this parallel structure, planning and problem solving are not identical. Two differences seem especially important (Scholnick & Friedman, 1987). First, planning necessarily refers to the future, whereas problem solving involves both the present and the future. Second, planning necessarily refers to actions, but problem solving may not involve any particular action. If I try to figure out what a friend meant by an ambiguous comment, I am trying to solve a problem, but I am not planning. Thus, planning is often a part of problem solving, but the two are not identical.

Planning has several general characteristics. It seems to occur most often when the situation is complex and novel. In such situations, we lack well-trodden paths to follow and are likely to make mistakes if we do not plan. Even in such novel situations, however, people often act without planning, at times to their regret (Pea, 1982).

When we do plan, we tend to do so opportunistically. Rather than formulating a complete plan and then executing its steps, we usually make relatively abstract plans with many gaps. We revise the plan as we execute it, basing revisions on how well the plan is working out and what opportunities for improvement we see.

A third important characteristic is that planning has both benefits and costs. It can save us from making foreseeable mistakes and wasting effort, but it also takes time and can be cognitively demanding. Effective problem solving demands not acting impulsively but also avoiding unnecessary hesitation (Pea & Hawkins, 1987).

*Means-ends analysis.* Means-ends analysis is an especially useful and widely applicable form of planning. It involves comparing the goal we would like to attain with the current situation, and reducing differences between the two until the goal can be met. The process demands shifting attention among our subgoals, our procedures for meeting the subgoals, and discrepancies between the current state and the overall goal.

The previously-noted success of 4-to-8-month-olds in ringing the bell above the balance scale suggests that even infants use means-ends analysis to solve problems. Case (1985) hypothesized that after seeing the balance scale's arm ring the bell, infants form a goal of reinitiating the movement that produced the interesting event (Figure 8–4). However, they cannot

**FIGURE 8–4**  Case's (1985) analysis of infants' reasoning about how to make one end of the balance scale ring the bell.

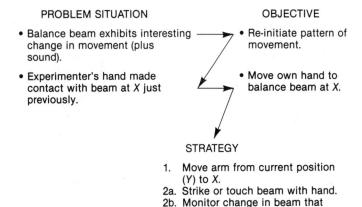

PROBLEM SITUATION

- Balance beam exhibits interesting change in movement (plus sound).
- Experimenter's hand made contact with beam at *X* just previously.

OBJECTIVE

- Re-initiate pattern of movement.
- Move own hand to balance beam at *X*.

STRATEGY

1. Move arm from current position (*Y*) to *X*.
2a. Strike or touch beam with hand.
2b. Monitor change in beam that results.

achieve this objective directly. This leads them to try to remember what the experimenter did. Once they succeed in recalling that the experimenter pushed one end of the balance down with her hand, they form a subgoal of doing the same thing. This allows them to realize their original goal by moving their hands to the same end of the balance, pushing it down, and observing the interesting result.

Infants exhibit means–ends planning on other tasks as well. Willatts (1984) presented 9-month-olds with a foam rubber barrier, behind which was hidden a cloth. For some of the babies, a small toy rested on the far end of the cloth. Other babies encountered the same arrangement, except that the toy was beside, rather than on top of, the cloth. Babies who saw the toy on the cloth were much more likely to push the barrier aside and pull the cloth to them than were babies who saw the toy next to the cloth. Pushing the barrier aside would have been more likely among the babies in this group than among the babies in the other group only if they planned to get the toy, since its value was only as a means toward that end.

The development of means–ends analysis in subsequent years involves large changes in the number and complexity of subgoals that children can keep in mind at once and in their ability to resist the lure of short-term goals to pursue longer-term ones. The changes can be seen in 3- to 6-year-olds' approaches to the Tower of Hanoi problem (Figure 8–5). The game is to make one's own stack of cans into the same configuration as the experimenter's stack in as few moves as possible. There are only two rules: Move only one can at a time, and never place a smaller can on a larger one (because it would fall off). (To appreciate the planning that is necessary to solve such problems, try to find the optimal [7 move] solution to the problem in Figure 8–5.

Not surprisingly, older children can solve longer problems. Most 3-year-olds solve two-move problems (i.e. problems that require two moves to progress from the initial arrangement to the goal); most 4-year-olds solve four-move problems; and most 5- and 6-year-olds solve five- or six-move problems (Klahr & Robinson, 1981). More interesting than these changes in the length of problems children can solve are changes in the strategies they use in planning which moves to make. The 3-year-olds' strategies seem limited almost exclusively to direct efforts to move disks to their goal. When they cannot move a can to its goal because another can is on top of it, they often simply break the rules and put the can there anyway. The older children react to such situations by establishing subgoals that move them in promising directions for fulfilling their original goals (though directions that sometimes do not work out). They also look further ahead in planning their moves. Even at age 6, however, children have difficulty solving problems that require them to make a move away from attaining a short-term goal, just as age peers had on the dog–cat–mouse problem described earlier (Klahr, 1985).

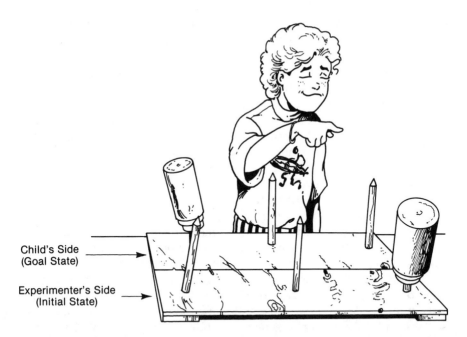

Child's Side
(Goal State)

Experimenter's Side
(Initial State)

**FIGURE 8-5** Three disk Tower of Hanoi problem. The task is for the child to move the three cans on his side to match the three on the experimenter's side, moving only one can at a time and never putting a smaller can on top of a larger one. The problem can be solved in seven moves.

*Route planning.* One of the most-common uses of planning is to choose the most-efficient route for reaching a destination. For example, when ordered to put away possessions that they have strewn about the house, children try to minimize the distance they must travel. This might mean moving to the staircase all of the clothes, games, books, and cassettes scattered around the first floor before hauling the collection to their bedroom on the second floor.

Ability to plan such routes starts very early. For example, children near their first birthday often walk or crawl to rooms they cannot see at the beginning of the trip, in order to get toys they also cannot see in the beginning (Benson, Arehart, Jennings, Boley, & Kearns, 1989).

Not surprisingly, considerable development in route-planning skills occurs beyond this early period. Even in the short time between ages 4 and 5, children's ability to engage in such planning increases considerably. The 5-year-olds do less backtracking, consider more alternative routes, and more quickly correct their errors than do 4-year-olds (Fabricius, 1988).

With age, children also show greater flexibility in adjusting strategies to circumstances. In one study of 4-to-10-year-olds (Gardner & Rogoff, 1985), some children were told that the only important consideration in planning a route was avoiding wrong turns. Others were told that speed as well as directness was important. When both speed and directness mattered, both 4-to-7-year-olds and 7-to-10-year-olds planned some of the route in advance and the rest as they came to choice points. The younger children did the same when only directness mattered, but the older ones did not. Instead, they often planned the entire route before they began, which helped them avoid wrong turns. The older children thus realized the benefits of planning when time spent planning was unimportant, and avoided the time cost of planning when speed was important. The younger children's not planning under the condition where speed was irrelevant deprived them of the benefits the planning could bring.

How do children learn to plan effectively? The social world of adults and other children is one important source of information. However, not everyone is equally effective in promoting better planning. In particular, adults are more effective than 9-year-olds in helping 5-, 7-, and 9-year-olds learn to plan efficient routes (Ellis & Rogoff, 1982; Gauvain & Rogoff, 1989; Radziszewska & Rogoff, 1988). Their effectiveness is greater even when the 9-year-olds are trained to insure that they, like adults, know the best routes to take (Radziszewska & Rogoff, 1989).

The adults' superiority as teachers appears due to the way they interact with the learners. They discuss planning strategies more and involve the learners more in making decisions. In contrast, when children teach, they rely more on just telling learners what route to take, without explaining the reasons. Consistent with this interpretation of why adults are more effective than children as teachers, adults who share responsibility to a relatively large extent promote more-effective learning than adults who do not involve the child as much (Gauvain & Rogoff, 1989). Such results regarding effective teaching skills are not limited to planning spatial routes; they also have been found in learning of arithmetic (Reeve, 1987). By involving children more in the planning process, adults may also help children learn to plan more effectively themselves.

### Causal Inference

Much problem solving is an effort to determine the causes of events. For example, when a child takes a clock apart to see how it works, the child is trying to find out what causes each part to move. Two-year-olds' endless "Why" questions, such as "Why do dogs bark?" also sometimes are efforts to understand causes. (At other times, they are simply efforts to annoy their parents.)

Why people infer causal connections among events has long intrigued philosophers and psychologists. There is nothing in the external world that forces such inferences. It might seem obvious to us that when one pool ball hits another, and the second ball begins to roll, that the rolling of the first ball caused that of the second. But is this inference logically justified?

Couldn't the second ball simply have begun rolling for some other reason? Would we draw the same inference if we opened the trunk of a car and the car's radio suddenly turned on?

*The Humean variables.*    British philosopher David Hume (1739–1740/ 1911) described three features that could lead people to infer that two events are causally related: The events occurred close in time and space (*contiguity*); the event labeled the "cause" preceded the event labeled the "effect"; and the cause and effect regularly occurred together on past occasions. Each of these variables—contiguity, precedence, and covariation— has been found to influence children's (and adults') causal inferences.

Infants in their first half-year already seem to use contiguity to infer that events are related. Four- and 5-month-olds look longer than usual when they see an object start moving without any collision; they also look longer when the object does not start to move until half a second after a collision (Leslie, 1982). The longer looking times suggest that they are surprised to see such events. During early childhood, contiguity so strongly influences causal inferences that it often overrides all conflicting cues (White, 1988).

By age 5, perhaps earlier, children also use the order of events to infer that one event caused the other. When 3- and 4-year-olds are shown three events in the order A B C and then asked, "What made B happen?" they tend to choose event A, which preceded event B, rather than event C, which followed it (Bullock & Gelman, 1979; Kun, 1978). It should be noted, however, that 3-year-olds show this understanding of precedence in fewer situations than older children. In a variety of situations, as many 3-year-olds say that the second event caused the first as say the reverse (Corrigan, 1975; Kuhn & Phelps, 1976; Shultz, Altmann, & Asselin, 1986; Sophian & Huber, 1984). All studies, however, find that by age 5, children consistently choose the earlier event as the cause.

The importance of consistent covariation of events seems to be the last of the three Humean variables to be understood. Young children are especially likely to ignore this variable when it conflicts with contiguity. For example, 5-year-olds do not attribute a causal connection to a sequence in which one event always follows 5 seconds after another event (Mendelson & Shultz, 1976). In contrast, 8-year-olds and adults do see the delayed but consistent relation as indicating that the two events are causally connected. To summarize the development of understanding of the Humean variables, contiguity is influential even in infancy; precedence is sometimes considered in attributing causes by age 3 and consistently by age 5; and covariation becomes increasingly influential after age 5.

*Beyond the Humean variables.*    Children's (and adults') causal inferences extend beyond Hume's analysis in at least one important respect: They place considerable emphasis on mechanisms that they believe generate relations among events. Shultz (1982) provided a particularly clever demonstration of this. Three-year-olds were shown a yellow and a green lamp, both of which could produce a spot of light on the wall. Before turning on either lamp, the experimenter placed a mirror between the green lamp and the wall. Then the experimenter turned on the green lamp. Because of the placement of the mirror, this did not produce any light on the wall. After five seconds, the experimenter simultaneously slid the mirror in front of the yellow lamp and turned that lamp on. Now a spot of light appeared on the wall, since there was no barrier between it and the green lamp.

The experimenter asked which lamp made the spot on the wall. Temporal contiguity suggested the yellow lamp, since it had been turned on at the same time as the light appeared on the wall. However, the 3-year-olds usually chose the green lamp as the cause. Shultz argued that they did this because they understood how lamps transmit light and how barriers can block the transmission. Their knowledge about the mechanisms that connected the events was sufficiently powerful to outweigh the fact that the yellow lamp was turned on at the same time that the light appeared on the wall.

Different situations present varying types of information relevant to drawing causal inferences. Sometimes these sources of information point to the same conclusion, but other times they do not. Much of the challenge that children face in deciding among alternative potential causes is to decide which type of information to weigh most heavily. At least from age 3 onward, children seem to use a set of strategy choice rules for making these decisions (Shultz, Fisher, Pratt, & Rulf, 1986). When information about generative mechanisms is available, children use it. When it is not, they rely on the types of information that are most perceptually striking and that impose the least information processing load. Spatially and temporally contiguous causes have these qualities and thus are frequently influential. Only when none of these types of information is available do children consider less striking factors that are correlated with the effect's occurrence. This framework suggests that preschoolers' frequent failure to consider delayed but regular connections in inferring causation is due to the regular but delayed connections in those situations not being explainable by obvious generative mechanisms, not being very perceptually striking, and not being easy to maintain in memory for the amount of time required.

*Scientific reasoning.* Children often have been likened to scientists. Both ask fundamental questions about the nature of the universe. Both also ask innumerable questions that seem utterly trivial to others. Finally, both are granted by society the time to pursue their musings. This "child as scientist" metaphor has motivated a great deal of examination of how children form hypotheses, generate experiments to test them, and reach conclusions concerning the meaning of the data.

Much scientific reasoning is aimed at identifying causal relations. Examination of children's efforts to establish such relations has indicated that despite some global resemblances to the problem solving of scientists, there also are large differences. One such difference is in separating theory and evidence. Children often fail to distinguish conclusions based on evidence about the situation from conclusions based on their prior beliefs (Dunbar & Klahr, 1988; Kuhn, 1989; Kuhn, Amsel & O'Loughlin, 1988; Kuhn & Phelps, 1982; Metz, 1985). Children also have difficulty designing experiments that can yield informative conclusions and in interpreting experiments that yield results inconsistent with their prior beliefs.

Schauble (1990) performed a particularly interesting study of the interplay of prior beliefs, experiments yielding new evidence, and conclusions based on the new data and prior beliefs. Children aged 9–11 were presented a computer-generated microworld involving toy race cars. The task was to determine the causal impact on the race cars' speed of five factors: engine size, wheel size, presence of tailfins, presence of a muffler, and color. Tests of the children's initial beliefs indicated that they expected a large engine, large wheels, and presence of a muffler to cause the cars to go quickly. They did not think tailfins or the color of the car would matter. In fact, within this particular microworld, a large engine and medium-sized wheels made the car go more quickly, muffler and color were irrelevant, and absence of tailfins increased the car's speed when the engine was large and had no effect when the engine was small.

The children were presented a series of eight sessions in which to learn about the cars. In each session, they could put whatever features they wanted on different cars, to try to learn the effect of each feature. The task was not inherently difficult. By varying one feature and holding all others constant, children could establish the role of each variable. An adult scientist who was presented the task identified the causal roles of all features in one short session.

The children were much slower to identify the causal relations. One reason was that more than half of their experiments were invalid. In such invalid experiments, the cars that children designed often varied in two or more ways, so that it was impossible to determine which factor caused any observed difference in their speeds. Even when children performed valid experiments, they often drew conclusions inconsistent with the evidence but consistent with their prior beliefs. Further, even after hypothesizing a correct role for a variable and observing evidence consistent with their hypothesis, they vacillated between the correct new hypothesis and the incorrect expectation produced by their prior views. They were particularly reluctant to abandon previous beliefs until they formulated an alternative explanation that could account for an unanticipated observation.

The picture of the 9-to-11-year-olds' problem solving was not altogether bleak. In spite of often performing invalid experiments, and often not drawing correct conclusions from the data their experiments yielded, the children showed substantial learning in the eight sessions of the experiment. Their predictions of the race cars' speeds became considerably more accurate. An increasing percentage of their experiments were valid. They drew appropriate conclusions increasingly often. Thus, with practice in scientific reasoning, children's experimental methods and their ability to identify causal relations both improve considerably. (See Kuhn et al., 1988, for related findings.)

Adults also often fall short of the ideals of scientific problem solving. Their errors come about for many of the same reasons as children's: performing invalid experiments, incorrectly interpreting data, and clinging to existing theories even when the evidence argues against them (Shaklee, 1979; Shaklee & Elek, 1988; Wason & Johnson-Laird, 1972). Even professional scientists make similar errors under some circumstances (Greenwald, Pratkanis, Lieppe, & Baumgardner, 1986). Thus, identifying causes through valid experimentation and data interpretation remains a challenge throughout our lifetimes.

### Analogy

When people face novel problems, they often interpret them in terms of better-understood ones. For example, consider the following version of Duncker's (1945) X-ray problem:

> A physician needs to destroy a patient's tumor, and the only way to do so is with large doses of X-rays. Unfortunately, the required dose of radiation would also destroy healthy tissue that the X-rays passed through on the way to the tumor. One half of the amount of X-rays would not destroy the healthy tissue but would not destroy the tumor either. What would you do?

Most people find this problem difficult. They are more likely to find a solution, however, if they first learn to solve a problem in which an attacking army cannot travel in one large group, because the attack route is too narrow, but instead must divide into separate units that travel from different directions and converge at the enemy's location. Having learned to solve this army problem, many students generate the parallel solution of giving half the dose of X-rays from each of two directions, with the two paths converging at the tumor. Such extrapolation from a better-understood to a less-well-understood problem is the essence of analogical problem solving.

The development of analogical problem solving resembles that of causal inference. Even very young children can draw successful analogies under some circumstances, yet under other circumstances, even college-educated adults fail to do so. This resemblance is no coincidence. Drawing appropriate analogies depends critically on understanding and identifying parallels in the relations, especially the causal relations, in the situations being compared.

*Developmental similarities.* First consider a study that illustrates 3-to-5-year-olds' ability to solve problems analogically (Brown, Kane, & Echols, 1986). The children heard a story in which a genie needed to transport jewels across a wall and into a bottle. The genie solved the problem by rolling up a piece of paper to make a tube, placing the tube so that it ended at the mouth of the bottle, and then rolling the jewels through the tube into the bottle. After hearing this story, children were given an analogous problem, in which an Easter bunny needed to transfer eggs across a river and into a basket. Some 5-year-olds but very few 3-year-olds solved the second problem unaided. However, when the children were asked questions that required them to recall the central facts of each story (who had the problem, what goal they were trying to achieve, what obstacle stood in their way, how they circumvented it), both older and younger children consistently solved the new problem. Interestingly, both younger and older children who without help accurately recalled the goal structure of the genie story consistently were able to analogize from it to the Easter bunny story. The difference between the age groups was in how many children of each age organized the original story in terms of its basic structure—the aspect that could be transferred to the new situation.

Although preschoolers recognize some relevant analogies, older children and adults fail to see many others. Without being given a hint that two problems are related, college students often fail to recognize analogies that they readily apply when the parallel is called to their attention (Gick & Holyoak, 1980).

The same variables influence children's and adults' success in solving problems analogically. People of all ages are more likely to recognize relevant analogies between two situations when superficial characteristics (such as the characters' names) as well as deep characteristics (such as goals, obstacles, and potential solutions) are similar (Brown & Campione, 1984; Gentner & Landers, 1985; Holyoak, Junn, & Billman, 1984). They also are more likely to analogize when they have encountered several previous problems with the same solution principle, rather than just one (Crisafi & Brown, 1986; Gholson, Emyard, Morgan, & Kamhi 1987). Useful analogies are also more likely when people know a great deal about the content area of the original problem than when they do not (Inagaki & Hatano, 1987). Complete encoding of relevant structural features is similarly important to analogical problem solving at all ages (Chen & Daehler, 1989; Sternberg & Nigro, 1980; Sternberg & Rifkin, 1979).

*Developmental differences.*    These similarities should not obscure the profound changes that occur with age in analogical problem solving. Young children require explicit hints to draw analogies that older children draw without such hints (Crisafi & Brown, 1986; Brown et al., 1986). Their analogizing is hindered by superficial perceptual dissimilarities that do not influence the analogizing of older children and adults (Gentner & Toupin, 1986; Goldman, Pellegrino, Parseghian, & Sallis, 1982; Holyoak et al., 1984). Their execution of processes involved in analogizing, such as encoding and inference, is less efficient than that of older children (Bisanz, 1979; Pellegrino & Goldman, 1983; Sternberg & Rifkin, 1979).

An especially striking development comes in the range of situations in which children can recognize analogies despite superficial dissimilarities between the situations. When 4-to-6-year-olds are given problems where only the deep structure unites the problems, they rarely recognize the analogy (Gentner & Toupin, 1986). In contrast, 8-to-10-year-olds do not require such superficial similarities to recognize these same analogies; parallel sets of relations are sufficient for them to do so.

A comparable developmental trend is evident in interpretation of metaphors (Gentner, 1988). Children correctly interpret metaphors based on appearances of the objects being compared (a superficial feature of the metaphor) before they correctly interpret metaphors where only relational structures are parallel. Further, with age, children become increasingly likely to interpret relationally those metaphors that can be viewed either in terms of similarities between objects or in terms of similarities between relations. Preschoolers *can* recognize analogous relations across situations. However, the ability to penetrate beneath the surface clearly increases greatly during the course of development.

## Tool Use

Children do not solve problems in a vacuum. They use available tools to help them. Some of these tools, such as spoken language, written language, and mathematics, are extremely pervasive. They help children solve many problems (Bruner, 1965). A large number of other tools are useful in more delimited situations, but are invaluable when applicable.

*Tools for solving problems directly.*    Children do not wait long to begin using tools. In one study, 1- and 2-year-olds saw an experimenter reel in an attractive toy by using a rake or cane (Brown, 1989). Then the toddlers were asked to get the toy themselves. They were strapped into a seat so that they could not move, but had available a variety of potential tools. For example, a child who had seen the toy reeled in with a long cane might have within reach a long rake, a short cane, a long straight tube that was the same color as the original cane, and a long, squiggly, flexible object. The toddlers were quick to choose, and their choices were almost always good ones. They chose tools that were rigid, that had an end that was appropriate for pulling, and that were long enough to reach the toy. They were indifferent to whether the tool was the same color as the one they had seen used originally. They also were perfectly willing to substitute rakes for canes and vice versa. Thus, they understood the causal properties that led to the tools being appropriate for solving the problem.

*Symbolic representations as tools.* Not all tools are used to solve problems directly. Some, such as maps and scale models, are used to symbolize an external environment and thus to guide problem-solving activities.

Toddlers demonstrate considerable facility in using this type of tool, just as they do with more directly useful tools such as canes and rakes. DeLoache (1987) created a situation in which 2½ and 3-year-olds saw a small toy hidden in a scale model of a room. Then the child was asked to find the toy in a room that was a life-size version of the scale model. If the toy in the scale model was hidden under a miniature chair, it could be found under the corresponding life-size chair in the room. All children were explicitly told about the correspondence between the scale model and the larger room.

Despite the small (7-month) difference in average age of children in the two groups, they differed greatly in ability to use the scale model. The 3-year-olds found the hidden object without error on more than 70 percent of trials; the 2½-year-olds found it without error on fewer than 20 percent. This was not attributable to failure to understand the situation or to remember what had been done with the model. Children of both ages consistently recalled where the miniature object was hidden within the model when they were asked about it later. Rather, the difference was in ability to use the scale model to infer the object's location in the larger room. Examination of children between 2½ and 3 years indicated that most children first could use the model at between 33 and 35 months, and that as soon as they did so, they usually did so perfectly (DeLoache, 1989).

What was the source of the 2½-year-olds' difficulty in using the scale model to solve the problems? One possibility was that they did not understand how any type of representation could be used as a tool to solve this type of problem. To test this interpretation, DeLoache (1987) showed 2½-year-olds either line drawings or photographs of the larger room. The same children who could not use the scale model to find hidden objects were able to use the line drawings and photographs to do so. Thus, they could use some representations as tools for solving problems.

The source of young children's difficulty with the scale model may be difficulty in simultaneously viewing it as an object in itself and as a representation of another object. Within this view, the photographs and line drawings are easier to use than the scale model because they are interesting only as representations of another object. Consistent with this interpretation, having children first play with a scale model, which would make them think of the model more as an object in itself, decreased their later success in using it to find hidden objects. Conversely, eliminating any potential interaction with the model—by putting it in a glass window where it could be seen but not touched—allowed children to find the hidden objects more successfully than usual (DeLoache, 1989).

Children create their own symbolic tools, as well as using ones given to them. For example, 7-to-11-year-olds can generate informal maps to guide their problem solving. In Karmiloff-Smith (1979), 7-to-11-year-olds played the part of ambulance drivers who needed to transport a sick patient to the hospital. The patient's home was a picture at one end of a 40-foot roll of paper; the hospital was a picture at the other end. In between were 20 choice points. Each choice point involved two choices, one of which led to a dead end. Children were told to make the trip once without the patient, so that they could find the fastest route. They were also encouraged to mark up the paper to help them remember which route to take later.

Within the one-hour session, children often changed the types of marks they made, even when the original marks were optimally informative. One 7-year-old's marks are depicted in Figure 8–6. At first, she indicated the dead end simply by placing a bar perpendicular to the path. Then she began augmenting this representation by putting both the bar and an "X" on the wrong path and an arrow on the right one. Finally, she returned to the original, sparer notation.

Why would children abandon a correct approach that allowed them to perform effectively? The issue is not unique to map-drawing; we have seen

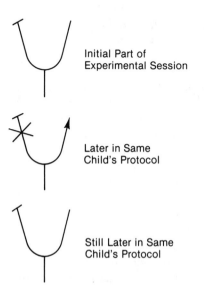

Initial Part of Experimental Session

Later in Same Child's Protocol

Still Later in Same Child's Protocol

**FIGURE 8–6**  Maps drawn by a 7-year-old at three points during a session. Note how redundant features are added in the second representation but eliminated in the third (after Karmiloff-Smith, 1986).

the same phenomenon in children's number conservation and class inclusion strategies and in their use of past tense and causal verbs. Karmiloff-Smith suggested that the process reflects a drive that children have to understand *why* their strategies work. Children's first goal seems to be to perform correctly. Attaining that goal does not necessarily satisfy them forever, though. If they do not understand why an approach works, or suspect that another approach might be more effective, efficient, or elegant, they may abandon the original, at least temporarily. Understanding this type of cognitive motivation, and the way in which children decide when to experiment with alternative approaches, is one of the deeper challenges confronting current theories of cognitive development.

*Tools for measuring.*    Measurement procedures such as counting, weighing, and using rulers and yardsticks are an especially useful type of tool for solving many problems. Like all of the other problem-solving techniques, however, these measurement procedures are two-edged swords. Used appropriately, they can enhance problem solving. Used inappropriately, they can lead it down erroneous paths.

Consider how inappropriate use of measurement techniques, in particular inappropriate counting, can lead children astray (Miller, 1984; 1989). Three- to 10-year-olds were asked to give two turtles equal amounts of food. Most of the children used a distributive counting strategy, in which they divided the food by giving one piece to one turtle, the next piece to the other turtle, and so on. This resulted in an equal division of the number of pieces of food, but not necessarily of the amount of food, since the pieces varied in size. Belief in the effectiveness of the counting procedure ran sufficiently deep that when several preschoolers found they had given one more piece of food to one of the turtles, they simply cut in half a piece that belonged to the other turtle, and gave one piece to each, thus equalizing the numbers. With age, children more often attempted to create equal-size pieces, but they still counted out equal numbers for each turtle, even when the attempt to standardize their size failed. Not until age 9 did most children divide the food into equal amounts. The difficulty is reminiscent of 5- to 9-year-olds misestimating the passage of time because they did not count in units of equal duration (Levin, 1989). Measurement tools expand children's capabilities, but they also can seduce children into making mistakes.

### Logical Deduction

Logical deduction can be used to solve problems whenever the information provided in the initial statement of the problem is sufficient to ensure that a particular solution is correct. Geometric and logical proofs are classic examples of this type of problem solving. Given a set of premises, students can deduce consequences until they arrive at a conclusion.

Deduction is used in many other contexts as well. Try this brain teaser: A car travels the 100 miles from town A to town B, always traveling at a speed of 25 mph. A bird that always travels 50 mph first flies away from town B until it meets the car, then flies back to town B, then flies away from Town B until it meets the car, then flies back to Town B, and so on. The question is how far the bird flies before the car reaches town B.

The answer is 200 miles. Since the bird flies at all times at 50 mph, and it takes the car 4 hours to reach town B, the bird's distance must be 200 miles. All the necessary information was present in the original problem. The trick was discarding the irrelevant information and deducing the solution (Halford, 1990).

Two deductive processes that are especially widely applicable for solving problems are transitive inference and hierarchial classification.

*Transitive inference.*    Transitive inference involves extrapolating ordinal relations to new cases. For example, if Bill is taller than Susan, and Jim is taller than Bill, we can deduce that Jim is taller than Susan. Children below age 6 or 7 often have difficulty solving these problems. Piaget (1970) attributed this failure to the young children's not understanding the basic logic of transitive inference. More recently, two alternative interpretations have been proposed. One attributes the young children's difficulty to their not remembering the premises. The other suggests that it is due to their not forming an appropriate representation or mental model.

First consider the memory-difficulty hypothesis. To deduce answers to transitivity problems, children need to remember the pairwise relations (e.g., A > B). Without such information, they cannot deduce the conclusion, regardless of their understanding of the logic.

If children in fact understand the basic logic underlying transitivity but fail to deduce solutions to transitivity problems because they often forget the premises, then ensuring that they remember the premises should allow them to deduce appropriate conclusions as well. To test this memory-difficulty interpretation, Bryant and Trabasso (1971) showed preschoolers five sticks of varying length, each of a different color. The children learned which stick in a given pair of adjacent-size sticks was longer and were asked about that pair repeatedly until they knew the order of the length of the two sticks. After children learned the relative lengths of each of the four adjacent-size pairs, they were presented the pairs in a random order until they answered all of them consistently correctly. Finally, children were questioned not only about the original pairs, but also about pairs of nonadjacent-size sticks whose relations they could only infer (e.g., the second and fourth longest sticks). Consistent with the memory-difficulty hypothesis, children who memorized the relative sizes of the original pairs generally drew appropriate transitive inferences.

What representation of the problem would allow children to draw such inferences? The answer seems to be that they represented the sticks as being in a row, arranged from longest to shortest. Given such a representation, answering the question, "Which is longer?" is easy; simply locate the two asked-about stimuli and choose the one closer to the tall end (Trabasso, Riley, & Wilson, 1975).

But why do young children have difficulty remembering the premises and forming such representations? As part of his more general theory of cognitive development, Halford (1990) proposed that three factors are influential: understanding of the basic logic of the task, choices among alternative strategies, and information-processing capacity.

Within Halford's theory, understanding of the logic underlying transitive inference originates in understanding of concrete situations. For example, children might first understand the basic logic of transitivity in the context of everyday activities such as playing with blocks. They might notice that if block A was bigger than block B, and block B bigger than block C, then block A invariably was also bigger than block C. This initial understanding could serve as a mental model, useful for deciding how to represent other orderings. For example, children could view the longest stick in the Bryant and Trabasso experiment as analogous to the largest block in a collection, the shortest stick as analogous to the smallest block, and so on.

Children also use several strategies for solving transitive-inference problems other than forming integrated linear representations. One alternative is to simply assume that if the information concerning the relative sizes of two entities is inconclusive, the more-recently mentioned object is larger (Halford, 1984). This simplification strategy reduces the information-processing load, but it does so at the risk of a wrong guess about the ordering (as illustrated in Figure 8–7). Another strategy that accomplishes the same goals—and has the same drawbacks—is remembering the gist of the premises but not their details, for example by forming an impression that a given stick is usually referred to as being longer than others (Brainerd & Reyna, 1990). Negative feedback concerning the outcomes generated by these alternative strategies would help children learn to form integrated linear representations when they could, and fall back on one of the other strategies when the information-processing demands of holding inconclusive evidence in memory were too great.

The final development involves increases in information-processing capacity. Greater capacity to hold both conclusive and inconclusive information in memory until clarifying information is available allows children to form integrated linear representations in more situations.

To summarize, Halford's theory suggests that development of skill in drawing transitive inferences depends on generation of adequate mental models of the situation, which in turn depends on knowledge of the underlying logic, feedback about the inadequacy of alternative strategies, and memory for the premises and their possible relations.

Representational Array

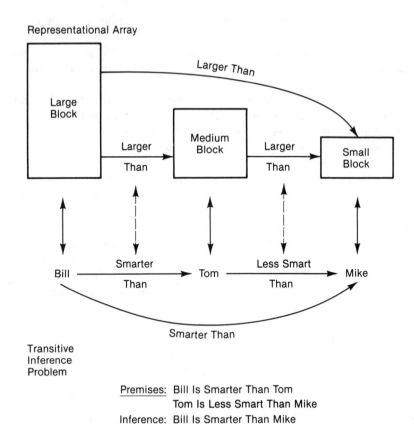

Transitive
Inference
Problem

Premises:  Bill Is Smarter Than Tom
          Tom Is Less Smart Than Mike
Inference: Bill Is Smarter Than Mike

**FIGURE 8–7**    Halford's (1990) analysis of how a child might solve a transitive inference problem through analogizing to prior knowledge about blocks.

These factors also influence children's success in solving other deduction problems, such as *syllogisms* (All *A* are *B;* All *B* are *C;* therefore, All *A*
are *C*). Many people form Venn diagrams to represent the information in
such problems (Oakhill, 1988). Consistent with the view that working-
memory demands are a critical limit on people's ability to use mental models to solve deductive reasoning problems, 9-to-12-year-olds' difficulty in
solving syllogisms increases with the number of mental models that need to
be considered and with the memory demands imposed by the ordering of
information within the problem (Johnson-Laird, Oakhill, & Bull, 1986).

*Hierarchical organization and class inclusion.* The Venn Diagrams that
are commonly used as mental models of syllogisms are instances of a more
general form of representation known as *hierarchical classification.* Hierarchies are organizations of sets in which the more general set includes all
members of the more specific ones. For example, within the hierarchy

"fruit, kind of fruit, subvariety of fruit," fruit includes all grapes, and grapes include all red seedless grapes.

Hierarchical organizations are useful in many contexts. They are basic to conceptual understanding. Superordinate, basic, and subordinate level concepts exemplify such hierarchical organizations. They are similarly central within memory. Recall how organizing a large number of words into a few superordinate categories (e. g., tools, types of furniture, and vehicles) helped children remember long lists of words. In general, knowing hierarchical relations promotes transfer, in that characteristics true at the more general level also will be true at the more specific levels. For example, if a child hears that helicopters are a type of vehicle, and the child knows that vehicles transport people, the child can infer that helicopters also do.

Children's language use and conceptual understanding show some ability to organize information hierarchically from age 1 onward (Bauer & Mandler, 1989a). However, using such hierarchical organizations to solve unfamiliar problems remains a challenge years later. We earlier encountered one test of such problem solving: Inhelder and Piaget's (1964) class-inclusion task. Recall from Chapter 2 that this task involves presenting children a number of objects that can be viewed as members of either a single set or two subsets. For example, children might be presented 4 bears and 6 lions, a total of 10 animals. Then they would be asked if there were more objects in the set or in the larger subset (more animals or lions). Children below age 8 usually answer that the subset contains more animals—that is, that there are more lions than animals. They compare the two subsets (bears versus lions) rather than the set and the larger subset (animals versus lions). Inhelder and Piaget believed that young children did this because they could not simultaneously view a single object as a member of both a set and one of its subsets. This inability to reason from a hierarchical organization would prevent them from solving class-inclusion problems.

It now appears, though, that ability to view objects as simultaneously belonging to a set and one of its subsets is only one of the factors that conspire to make this class-inclusion task difficult. The following are among the other major sources of difficulty: the wording of the question, the need to determine the number of objects in the subsets and the set, the need to compare the sizes of the larger subset and the set, and the complexity of the appropriate decision rule (Trabasso, Isen, Dolecki, McLanahan, Riley, and Tucker, 1978). Thus, in response to the question "What develops in class inclusion?" Trabasso et al. answered, only partly in jest, "Everything" (p. 178).

Consider how variables once thought to be irrelevant, because they have nothing to do with hierarchical organization, can influence children's class-inclusion performance. Class inclusion questions can either involve *class* nouns or *collection* nouns. A simple way of distinguishing between the two involves whether the same term can be used to refer to the set and the subsets. With class nouns, such as *tree*, both set and subset can be referred to by the same term. Thus, both two particular oak trees and trees in general can be labeled *trees*. With collection nouns, such as *forest* and *gang*, this is not the case. Two oak trees cannot be called a forest; two children cannot be called a gang. Both collection and class nouns can enter into hierarchical relations, though. Both the oak/forest and the oak/tree relations are hierarchical.

Young children react very differently to class-inclusion questions that differ only in whether they include class nouns or collection nouns. In one study (Markman, 1973), some 5- and 6-year-olds heard questions similar to Inhelder and Piaget's, in which class nouns were used. Illustratively, they saw five baby frogs, a mommy frog, and a daddy frog, and were asked: "Here are some frogs. . . .Who would own more, someone who owned the frogs or someone who owned the baby frogs?" Other children were asked about the same array of objects, but heard a collection noun used to describe them: "Here is a family of frogs. . . .Who would own more, someone who owned the family or someone who owned the baby frogs?"

The 5- and 6-year-olds who received the class nouns (baby frogs versus frogs) rarely answered correctly. This replicated Inhelder and Piaget's finding. However, their peers who received the collection nouns (baby frogs versus frog family) consistently answered correctly. Collection nouns seem to make such problems easier by focusing attention on hierarchical relations, since terms such as "family" always involve a part-whole relation whereas class terms such as "frogs" may or may not (Markman & Callanan, 1983).

*Escape from logic.*   Although hierarchical classification and transitivity problems are designed to elicit deductive reasoning, children often find ingenious ways of solving them without such reasoning. For example, 7-to-9-year-olds usually solve class-inclusion problems by counting the number of objects in the particular subset they were asked about, counting the number of objects in the whole set, and choosing the alternative whose count yields the larger number (Markman, 1978). Not until age 10 or 11 do they consistently solve class-inclusion problems by deducing the conclusion. That is, not until then do they rely on the reasoning that the set is inherently larger than the subset, regardless of the particular numbers involved.

Similar patterns have emerged on a number of other logical deduction tasks. For example, 5-year-olds avoid drawing transitive inferences when it is possible to solve such problems by other means (Jager-Adams, 1978). One way that they do this is by forming mental images of the different-length sticks and using the images to solve the problem (Brainerd & Kingma, 1985). In number conservation, 5-year-olds count the object in each row or place them in one–one correspondence, rather than deducing the result from the type of transformation that was performed (Siegler,

1981). Similarly, young children often refuse to accept the truth of simple tautologies without checking them. When an experimenter said, "Either the chip I am holding in my hand is blue or it is not blue," 7-year-olds insisted that the experimenter open her hand before they would accept the statement as correct (Osherson & Markman, 1975).

These findings do not mean that children cannot reason deductively. They clearly can. What, then, do the findings mean? One intriguing, though far from conclusive, interpretation is that young children can deduce conclusions, but they do not view the conclusions as being true by reason of logical necessity (Bereiter, Hidi, & Dimitroff, 1979; Cauley, 1985; Gellatly, 1987; Murray, 1987; Murray & Armstrong, 1976). Young children may view the products of deduction as being likely to be true, but no different in their logical status than lunch not involving cereal and orange juice. Such a failure to distinguish between logically-necessary and empirically-likely outcomes would explain young children's eagerness to verify by empirical means relations that older children and adults view as purely logical matters. It also would make more understandable the seemingly opposite tendency of young children to reach conclusions when the evidence does not logically allow them to do so (Acredolo & Horobin, 1987; Byrnes & Overton, 1986). If young children view these problems as ones of identifying the likely conclusion, rather than of deducing the one that logically must be true, their standards of evidence could be less strict.

Defining what it means to have a concept of logical necessity has proved very difficult (Murray, 1987), and some evidence of ability to discriminate between logically necessary and nonnecessary relations has been found in 6- (though not 5-) year-olds (Somerville, Hadkinson, & Greenberg, 1979). Thus, the difference between younger and older children may reflect, at least in part, different preferences for empirical and logical solutions rather than a different grasp of them. Nonetheless, a deeper understanding of the development of the concept of logical necessity may provide a clue as to why young children so often solve problems empirically rather than deductively.

## SUMMARY

The development of problem solving involves children's efforts to overcome obstacles and attain goals. It involves the orchestration of a large number of other processes toward this end. Much of children's problem solving reflects the structure of the task. How well children encode the critical information in the task and how well they can use the encodings to form mental models are among the key determinants of their success on many problems. Their success also depends critically on ability to integrate general and specific knowledge, and on their selection of the right process in the right situation. Recent research has indicated that younger children are more-competent, and older children less-competent, problem solvers than was once believed. However, profound development also is evident in the range of problems about which children can reason effectively and that they can solve.

These general patterns are evident in development of ability to solve balance scale problems. Task analyses suggested that children would use one of four solution rules, ranging from basing all judgments on the amount of weight on each side to computing torques when necessary. Application of the rule assessment approach indicated that children do indeed use these rules. Some of the rules, particularly the tendency of 4-to-6-year-olds to base judgments on a single salient dimension, have proved general across many tasks. Developmental differences in ability to learn about balance scale problems are due at least in part to the limitations of young children's encoding. Helping them encode relevant information helps them learn more effectively.

Among the most-prominent problem-solving processes are planning, analogical reasoning, causal inference, tool use, and logical deduction. Planning, like problem solving in general, involves consideration of goals, obstacles, and alternative solution strategies. It is used most often in complex and novel situations. One frequent type of planning is means-end analysis. This approach involves progressively reducing differences between goals and current states. Simple forms of it are evident in children's first year, both in solving balance scale problems and in obtaining distant toys. Development of planning occurs primarily in the number and complexity of subgoals children can maintain in memory, and in their ability to avoid the temptation of meeting short-term goals at the expense of longer term ones.

Many causal inferences are based on three variables whose importance was identified by the British philosopher David Hume: contiguity, precedence, and covariation. Even infants are influenced by contiguity. Precedence sometimes exerts an influence by age 3 and consistently does so by age 5. Covariation in the absence of contiguity becomes increasingly important beyond age 5. By age 3, identification of a mechanisim that explains how causes produce effects can have more impact than even contiguity. Preschoolers' choices among alternative causes reflect primary attention to potential mechanisms, secondary attention to information such as contiguity that is perceptually striking and easy to maintain in memory, and tertiary attention to other cues.

Very young children can form analogies in simple situations, yet even adults often fail to recognize other potentially useful analogies. Many of the same variables influence children's and adults' success in analogizing. However, older children and adults recognize many more analogies than do young children, especially when superficial features of problems obscure the relation between the old and new situations.

Use of tools to solve problems is also evident among very young children. Some of these tools, such as canes and rakes, can be used to attain goals directly. Others, such as maps and scale models, are effective in less-direct ways. Tools are not always advantageous, however. Their availability can lure children into mistakes, as well as helping them solve otherwise-difficult problems.

Among the most-prominent deductive processes are transitive inference and hierarchical classification. Preschoolers can solve transitive-inference problems when they can remember the premises and integrate them into rowlike representations. However, the range of situations in which they can do so is much more limited than is true of older children. Improvement with age may reflect improved ability to hold in memory uncertain relations between premises, rather than adopting simplification strategies that reduce memory load but at the cost of making assumptions of uncertain validity.

Preschoolers also can hierarchically classify sets of objects. Their ability to do so, however, depends on the familiarity of the relations and the particular language that is used. Their conclusions also are frequently based on empirical checking rather than on logical deduction. This may reflect the younger children's having only a limited concept of logical necessity, or may simply mean that they trust empirical observations more than their logical deductions.

## RECOMMENDED READINGS

DeLoache, J. S. (1989). *The development of representation in young children.* In H. W. Reese (Ed.) *Advances in child development and behavior. Vol. 22* (pp. 1–39) New York: Academic Press. DeLoache summarizes the fascinating changes that take place between 2½ and 3 years in ability to use scale models to represent spatial layouts and locations.

Halford, G. S. (1990). *Children's understanding: The development of mental models.* Hillsdale, NJ: Erlbaum. This book presents an integrative and cohesive account of how changes in mental models, working-memory capacity, and problem-solving experience together shape cognitive development.

Kuhn, D., Amsel, E., & O'Loughlin, M. (1988). *The development of scientific reasoning skills.* Orlando, FL: Academic Press. In some ways, children are like scientists; in others, they are not. This book explores the implications of the "child as scientist" metaphor and presents a number of intriguing studies of how children's scientific reasoning changes with prolonged experience in experimenting and drawing conclusions.

Rogoff, B. (1990) *Apprenticeship in thinking.* New York: Oxford University Press. Perhaps the most-sophisticated treatment to date of how children and adults combine to create the conditions under which cognitive growth occurs.

Simon, H. A. (1981). *The sciences of the artificial.* Cambridge, MA: MIT Press. A lucid presentation of the surprising similarities that unite problem solving in architecture, computer science, economics, and other fields. Page for page, one of the most worthwhile books I have ever read.

# 9

# *Development of Academic Skills*

I struggled through the alphabet as if it had been a bramble-bush; getting considerable worried and scratched by every letter. After that, I fell among those thieves, the nine figures, who seemed every evening to do something new to disguise themselves and baffle recognition. But, at last I began, in a purblind groping way, to read, write, and cipher, on the very smallest scale. (Pip, in Dickens's *Great Expectations*)

Traditionally, children's thinking in and out of school has been treated as two separate subjects. The study of thinking inside the classroom was labeled "educational psychology." The study of thinking outside the class-room was labeled "developmental psychology." Researchers considered themselves to be educational psychologists or developmental psychologists, but not both. They published in different journals. They attended differ-ent conferences. They studied different problems.

Recently, the walls separating the fields have been crumbling. Fields of psychology may be compartmentalized, but children are not. As dis-cussed in Chapter 8, what children know profoundly influences what they learn. This is true regardless of whether the knowledge was acquired inside or outside the classroom. Misconceptions about falling objects, acquired outside the classroom, influence college students' scientific reasoning in their physics courses (McCloskey & Kaiser, 1984). Complementarily, what children learn inside the classroom greatly influences their thinking in the outside world. This is true even when the knowledge is not explicitly taught. Memory strategies improve more for children who attend first grade than for age peers who do not, even though first-grade teachers rarely teach such strategies (Smith, 1989). Apparently, the need to remember a great deal of new information improves children's ability to do so, even without direct instruction in how to remember.

Practical decisions concerning children's educations, as well as theories about how they think, depend on the mutual influence of intra- and extra-classroom factors. One issue faced by many parents is whether to start children in school as soon as the district says they can begin, or to hold them back and have them start the next year. In many regions of the United States, it has become common to hold children, especially boys, back for a year. The logic is that they will be more mature and will be able to learn more when they are older. To test whether older children do in fact learn more in first grade, a team of investigators examined children in a locality where 95 percent of children still start school at the time the school district says they are ready to do so (Bisanz, 1989; Morrison, 1989). The study focused on children who either just missed the age cutoff or just made it. The two groups were within one month of each other in average age, but one group entered first grade a full year before the other. The question was whether attending first grade at the younger age would result in less learning.

The results were the same for reading and for math. Children who barely made the cutoff progressed just as much during first grade as children who barely missed it, despite the 11-month difference in ages. There may be other reasons to hold children back from starting school, such as manual dexterity, skill in athletics, and social maturity. In terms of how much the children learn, however, there seems to be no good reason to do so.

*Organization of the chapter.* This chapter focuses on children's learning of mathematics, reading, and writing. The discussion of mathematics proceeds from the arithmetic skills that are acquired in the early grades to more-complex arithmetic, to estimation, and finally to algebra. The discussion of reading first focuses on relevant skills that children acquire prior to formal instruction, then on how children read individual words, and finally on the development of comprehension—the true goal of learning to read. The discussion of writing first addresses the question of why writing is more difficult than speaking, then examines the initial drafting process, and finally describes how children revise (or fail to revise) already-written papers. Table 9–1 summarizes the chapter's organization.

*Common features across academic domains.* Superficially, it might seem that children's reading, writing, and mathematics are interesting topics in their own right, but ones that have little in common. It turns out, though,

**TABLE 9–1  Chapter Outline**

I.  Mathematics
    A.  Basic Arithmetic
    B.  More-Complex Arithmetic
    C.  Estimation
    D.  Algebra
II.  Reading
    A.  The Typical Chronological Progression
    B.  Prereading Skills
    C.  Identifying Individual Words
    D.  Comprehension
III.  Writing
    A.  The Initial Drafting Process
    B.  Revision
IV.  Summary

that the basic questions about how children learn in each area are quite similar.

1. How do children allocate attentional resources to cope with competing processing demands?
2. How do children choose which strategy to use from among the several that they might use?
3. Should instructors teach children directly the techniques used by experts in an area, or are indirect teaching approaches more effective?
4. What causes individual differences in knowledge and learning?

These questions have led to discovery of some striking unities in children's thinking in the different subject areas. Consider, for instance, children's strategy choices in addition, reading, and spelling. In all three areas, children need to choose whether to state answers from memory or revert to more time-consuming alternatives. To add, children need to decide whether to retrieve an answer and state it or to put up their fingers and count them. To read words, they need to decide whether to state a pronunciation that they have retrieved from memory or to sound out the word. To spell, they need to decide whether to write a retrieved sequence of letters or look for the word in a dictionary. Despite the differences among the subject areas, children seem to make all these decisions through the same strategy choice mechanism. In this chapter we consider both specific findings in, and general patterns across, mathematics, reading, and writing.

## MATHEMATICS

Learning mathematics demands acquisition of three types of competence: procedural, conceptual, and utilizational (Gelman, Meck, & Merkin,

1986). *Procedural competence* involves skill in solving problems through se-quences of actions. *Conceptual competence* involves understanding the princi-ples that underlie those sequences of actions. *Utilizational competence* in-volves knowing the appropriate circumstances for taking the actions. Thus, the three types of competence involve knowledge of *how* to solve problems, *why* they can be solved in that way, and *when* the techniques should be used.

Successful coordination of these three types of competence is what gives mathematics its power. A single well-chosen equation can describe the basic structure of many otherwise dissimilar situations. However, integrat-ing procedures for generating and solving such equations, rationales for why the procedures are legitimate, and knowledge of when the procedures should be applied is far from simple.

This difficulty can be seen in the context of a relatively straightfor-ward analogy—that between Dienes blocks and the base-10 system (Schoenfeld, 1986). Dienes blocks are commonly used materials for illustrat-ing what the base-10 system means. Within the Dienes system, each $1 \times 1$ block represents a unit of 1, each $1 \times 10$ block represents a unit of 10, and each $10 \times 10$ block represents a unit of 100. The blocks can be used to illustrate the relations among 1's, 10's, and 100's. Stacking 10 of the 1's units blocks (the $1 \times 1$ blocks) creates a column the same size as 1 of the 10's units (a $1 \times 10$ block) Similarly, pushing together 10 of the 10's unit blocks creates a block the same size as 1 100's unit block.

One common application of Dienes blocks is for explaining the long subtraction algorithm (Figure 9–1). The blocks are used to clarify why reducing the value of a column by 1 unit, and increasing the value of the column immediately to its right by 10 units, leaves unchanged the value of the original number. Students have little difficulty understanding the le-gitimacy of trading 1 of the $1 \times 10$ blocks for 10 of the $1 \times 1$ blocks. Understanding the implications of this correspondence for the standard subtraction algorithm often is less easy, however. Students who are taught the subtraction algorithm through use of Dienes blocks do fine in subtract-ing Dienes blocks from each other, but they often encounter the same types of difficulty using the standard subtraction algorithm with numbers as do children taught without such blocks (Resnick & Omanson, 1987). Paradoxically, the very straightforwardness of subtraction with Dienes blocks may lead children to see it as a different task than ordinary numeri-cal subtraction. The paradox is reminiscent of one of DeLoache's (1987) findings about 2-year-olds' use of scale models: The more that children viewed a model as a real object in and of itself, the harder it was to treat it as a symbol for something else. In sum, integrating mathematical proce-dures, the concepts that underlie the procedures; and the conditions un-der which the procedures are useful is a profoundly challenging task.

Next we consider the acquisition of several specific mathematical skills: basic arithmetic, complex arithmetic, estimation, and algebra.

| Procedure | Numerical Representation | Dienes Blocks Representation |
|---|---|---|

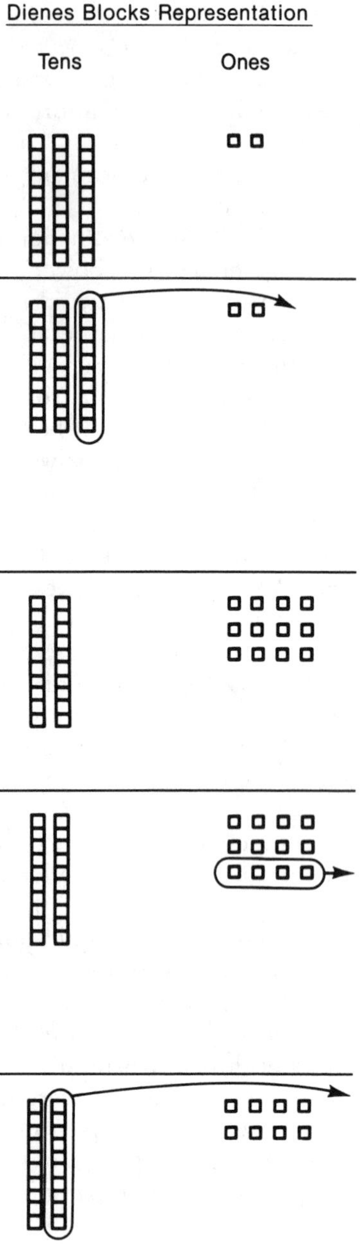

**FIGURE 9–1**   Use of Dienes blocks to explain the conceptual basis of borrowing in multidigit subtraction (after Resnick & Ford, 1981).

### Basic Arithmetic

*Early understanding.*    Children show some understanding of addition and subtraction, as they apply to small sets of objects, as early as age 2. This understanding was evident in a study in which an experimenter first placed several balls in a tube, then added or subtracted one, and then asked the child to reach in often enough to pull out all of the balls (Klein & Starkey, 1987). The construction of the tube allowed children to touch and pull out only one ball at a time; they could not feel if other balls remained.

When between one and three balls remained in the tube after the addition or subtraction, the 2-year-olds usually reached into the tube the right number of times. Thus, if there were three balls, they reached in three times. Since there was no way for them to have felt whether any balls remained in the tube, their stopping reaching at the right time indicated that they knew how many balls were present after the small-number addition and subtraction.

By the time children enter kindergarten, many have learned to solve most addition and subtraction problems with numbers below 10. Their learning of these problems may be accelerated by educational television programs such as "Sesame Street." Studies before the television era (e.g., Ilg & Ames, 1951) did not find similar competence until children were in first grade.

*Strategy diversity.*    When children learn to add and subtract, they use a variety of strategies, rather than always proceeding in a single way. This use of diverse strategies continues for several years for each arithmetic operation (Goldman, Mertz, & Pellegrino, 1989) and is evident among children with learning disabilities for an especially protracted period (Geary, Widaman, Little, & Cormier, 1987; Goldman, Pellegrino, & Mertz, 1988). To add, first- and second-graders sometimes count on their fingers from one, sometimes count from the larger of the two addends (on 3 + 6, counting "6, 7, 8, 9"), sometimes retrieve answers from memory, and sometimes infer answers from better-known answers of related problems (e.g., "6 + 5, hmm, I know, 5 + 5 = 10, so 6 + 5 must be 11") (Baroody, 1984; Geary & Burlingham-Dubree, 1989; Siegler & Robinson, 1982). To subtract, first- and second-graders sometimes count down from the larger number (on 12 − 3, they might count three counts down from 12 to 9 and advance 9, the stopping point, as the answer), sometimes count up (on 12 − 9, they might count "9, 10, 11, 12" and advance 3, the number of counts upward, as the answer), sometimes retrieve answers from memory, and sometimes base answers on knowledge of related problems (Carpenter, 1986; Fuson, 1984). The same phenomenon is evident in somewhat older children's multiplication. To multiply, third- and fourth-graders sometimes repeatedly add one of the multiplicands the number of times indicated by the other (solving 6

× 8 by adding eight 6's or six 8's), sometimes make hatchmarks and count or add them (solving 3 × 4 by making three groups of four hatchmarks each and counting or adding them), sometimes retrieve answers from memory, and sometimes base answers on those of related problems (Brownell & Carper, 1943; Siegler, 1988b).

As children gain experience with each arithmetic operation, the strategies they use change. The most striking change is toward increasing use of retrieval. After a few years of experience, most children consistently retrieve answers to all, or almost all, of the basic arithmetic facts. There also is change from less-sophisticated to more-sophisticated strategies other than retrieval. Thus, when children begin to add, they rely most often on putting up their fingers and counting from 1. As they gain increasing skill and understanding, they increasingly use more-sophisticated strategies, such as counting from the larger addend or decomposing a problem into two simpler ones (12 + 3 = 10 + (2 + 3) = 15).

During the same period, children also come to solve arithmetic problems increasingly quickly and accurately. The changes in speed and accuracy come about both because of changes in which strategies are used and because of changes in how efficiently each strategy is executed. The strategies that predominate in later use, such as retrieval and counting from the larger addend, are inherently faster than the strategies used most often initially, such as counting from 1. Within any given strategy, speed and accuracy also increase. Thus, Siegler (1987b) found that solving problems by decomposing them into simpler forms took an average of 6.9 seconds for kindergarteners, 4.1 seconds for first-graders, and 3.2 seconds for second-graders. Percentage correct generated by the strategy increased from 91 percent to 92 percent to 97 percent. During the same period, frequency of this relatively fast and accurate strategy increased from 2 percent to 9 percent to 11 percent of trials.

*Choices among strategies.*    One of the most-striking characteristics of children's arithmetic is how adaptively they choose among alternative strategies. The choices are adaptive in several senses. One involves the choice of whether to state a retrieved answer or to use a *backup strategy* (a strategy other than retrieval). Even among 4- and 5-year-olds, the harder the problem (measured either by large numbers of errors or long solution times), the more often children use a backup strategy to solve the problem (Siegler & Shrager, 1984). Use of the backup strategies does not cause the errors; children err more often when they are forbidden to use backup strategies than when they are allowed to use them. Instead, children choose backup strategies most often on the problems on which those strategies boost accuracy by the largest amount (Siegler & Robinson, 1982). Children make similarly adaptive strategy choices in subtraction and multiplication (Figure 9–2).

Using backup strategies most often on the hardest problems helps children balance concerns of speed and accuracy. Consider a 5-year-old's choice between solving an addition problem by stating a retrieved answer or by counting from 1. Retrieval is faster, but counting from 1 tends to be more accurate for young children, especially on difficult problems. Most 5-year-olds reconcile these goals by using retrieval primarily on relatively easy problems, where it can yield accurate answers, and by using backup strategies on the more difficult problems, where the backup strategies much more often yield correct answers. This allows fast and accurate performance on easy problems and slower but accurate performance on harder ones.

Children also choose adaptively among alternative backup strategies. For example, 6- and 7-year-olds count up from the larger addend most often on problems such as 2 + 9, where this strategy greatly reduces the amount of counting that is needed relative to alternative strategies such as counting from 1 (Siegler, 1987b). In general, children tend to choose the fastest approach that they can execute accurately.

*A model of strategy choice.* How do children choose so adaptively among the alternative strategies that they know? The Siegler and Shipley (1990) strategy choice model that was described in Chapter 3 focuses on this question. Here, we examine the way that the model makes a particularly common strategy choice in arithmetic: whether to state a retrieved answer or to use a backup strategy.

The mechanism by which the model makes this choice involves two interacting parts: a representation of knowledge about particular problems, and a process that operates on the representation to produce performance. First consider the representation. It involves associations of varying strengths between each problem and potential answers, both correct and incorrect, to that problem. For example, in Figure 9–3 (p. 298), the answer 6 is connected to the problem "3 + 4" with a strength of .19, the answer 7 is connected to "3 + 4" with a strength of .17, and so on.[1]

Representations of different problems can be thought of as varying along a dimension of peakedness. In Figure 9–3, the representation of "2 + 1" is a *peaked* distribution, because the preponderance of associative strength is concentrated in a single answer (the peak of the distribution).

---

[1] These estimated associative strengths are based on children's performance in a separate experiment. Four-year-olds received simple addition problems and were asked to "just say what you think the right answer is as quickly as possible without putting up your fingers or counting." The purpose of these instructions was to obtain the purest possible estimate of the strengths of associations between problems and answers. The numbers in the matrix indicate the proportion of trials on which children advanced a given answer to a given problem. Thus, the diagram for 3 + 4 indicates that children advanced the answer "6" on 19 percent of trials in this retrieval-only experiment.

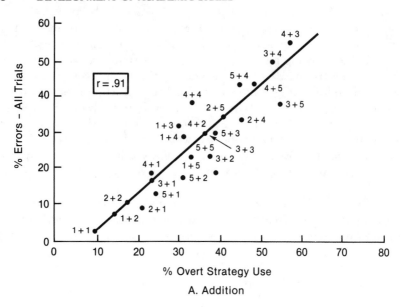

A. Addition

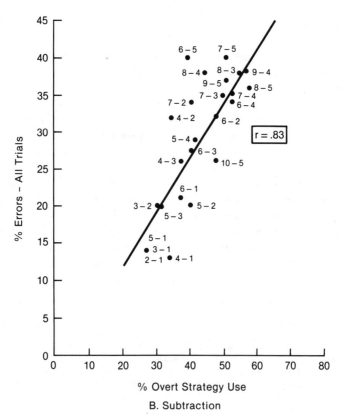

B. Subtraction

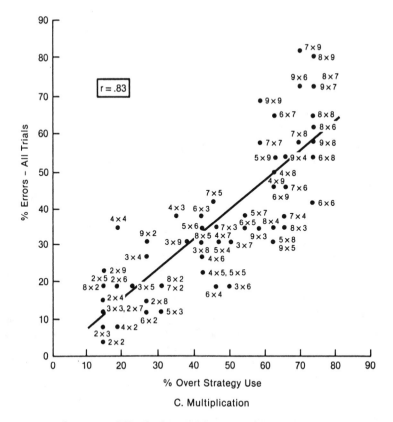

**FIGURE 9–2** The more difficult the problem, as measured by percentage of errors on it, the more often children use overt strategies (data from Siegler & Shrager, 1984; Siegler, 1987a; 1988b).

The representation of "3 + 4," in contrast, is a *flat* distribution because associative strength is distributed among a number of answers, with no one of them constituting a strong peak.

The process operates on this representation in the following way. First, the child sets a *confidence criterion.* This confidence criterion is a threshold that must be exceeded by the associative strength of a retrieved answer for that answer to be stated. The confidence criterion can assume any of a range of numerical values.

Once the confidence criterion is set, the child retrieves an answer. The probability of any given answer's being retrieved on a particular retrieval effort is proportional to the associative strength of that answer relative to the associative strengths of all answers to the problem. Thus, because in the Figure 9–3 example the associative strength connecting "2 + 1" and "3" is .82, and because the total associative strength connecting "2 + 1" with all

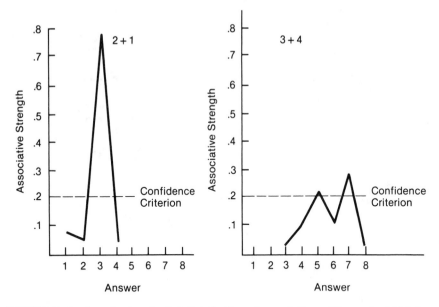

**FIGURE 9–3**   A peaked and a flat distribution of associations. The peaked distribution would lead to less frequent need for children to use overt strategies, fewer errors, and shorter solution times (from Siegler, 1986).

answers is 1.00, the probability of retrieving "3" as the answer to "2 + 1" would be .82.

If the associative strength of whatever answer is retrieved exceeds the confidence criterion, the child states that answer. Otherwise, the child may either again retrieve an answer and see if it exceeds the confidence criterion or abandon efforts to retrieve and instead use a backup strategy to solve the problem.

Within this model, the more peaked a given distribution, the more often that retrieval, rather than a backup strategy, will be used (because the greater the concentration of associative strength in one answer, the higher the probability that the most strongly associated answer will be retrieved, and the higher the probability that that answer's associative strength will exceed the confidence criterion and thus allow the retrieved answer to be stated). Similarly, because the answer with the greatest associative strength ordinarily is the correct answer, the greater the concentration of associative strength in that answer, the more probable that the retrieved answer will be correct. Thus, the high correlations between percentage of errors on a problem and percentage of backup strategies on the problem (Figure 9–2) emerges because both errors and strategy choices on each problem reflect the peakedness of that problem's distribution of associations.

How do some problems come to have peaked distributions and others flat ones? A basic assumption of the strategy choice model is that children associate the answers they state with the problems on which they state them. Answers that are stated most often become most strongly associated with the problems. This view implies that the problems that are easiest to solve by use of backup strategies will also be the easiest to solve via retrieval, because more-frequent correct execution of backup strategies will create more-peaked distributions of associations. Thus, a problem such as 2 + 1 comes to have a more-peaked distribution of associations than 3 + 4 because children are more likely to correctly count three fingers, and thus to associate the answer "3" with 2 + 1, than they are to correctly count seven fingers on 3 + 4. Consistent with this view, the problems that are most difficult to solve via backup strategies are generally the same ones that are most difficult to solve via retrieval (Siegler, 1988b). Also consistent with it, children who are more skillful in using backup strategies generally are also better able to efficiently retrieve correct answers to addition and subtraction problems.

*Individual differences in strategy choices.*    Individual children differ considerably in how they learn arithmetic. These individual differences are evident as early as first grade (Siegler, 1988a). Rather than everyone solving addition and subtraction problems in the same way, children seemed to fall into three groups: "good students," "not-so-good students," and "perfectionists."

The contrast between good and not-so-good students was evident along all of the dimensions that might be expected from the names. The good students were faster and more accurate on both retrieval and backup strategy trials on both tasks. They also used retrieval more often on both of them.

The differences between good students and perfectionists were more interesting. The two groups were equally accurate on both retrieval and backup strategy trials. However, the perfectionists used retrieval significantly less often than not only the good students but even than the not-so-good students.

The differences among good students, not-so-good students, and perfectionists were interpretable in terms of two key variables within the just-described strategy choice model: peakedness of distributions of associations and stringency of confidence criteria. In the terms of the model, perfectionists were children who possessed peaked distributions and set very high confidence criteria. Good students were children who also possessed peaked distributions but set somewhat lower confidence criteria. Not-so-good students were those who possessed flat distributions and set low confidence criteria. Within the computer simulation implementation of the strategy choice model, these combinations of distributions of associations and confidence criteria produce performance much like that of the three groups of children.

Subsequent evidence proved consistent with this analysis. Perfectionists and good students scored equally highly on standardized achievement tests four months after the experimental sessions. Both scored much higher than children classified as not-so-good students. Further, almost half of the not-so-good students either were assigned the next year to a learning disabilities class or were retained in the first grade, versus none of the perfectionists and good students. Thus, the differences between not-so-good students and the other two groups were apparent in standard measures of achievement. The differences between good students and perfectionists, however, would probably have gone undetected without the strategy choice model.

*Understanding of arithmetic principles.* As skill in adding, subtracting, and multiplying increases, so does understanding of the principles on which arithmetic is based. One such understanding involves the principle that adding and subtracting the same number leaves the original quantity unchanged. Development of understanding of this principle can be seen in performance on problems of the form "a + b − b" (e.g., 17 + 24 − 24). Children who solve such problems through applying the principle would not be influenced by the size of *b*. They would quickly state as the answer the number that corresponded to *a*, regardless of the size of *b*. In contrast, children who solve the problem by adding *b* and then subtracting it would take longer when *b* was large than when it was small.

Bisanz and Lefevre (1990) found that time required to solve these problems decreased greatly from 6 years to adulthood. This change reflected a combination of faster computation and more-frequent reliance on principles that eliminated the need to perform any computation. Between ages 6 and 9, the main change was in the speed of computation. Solution times became faster, but most 9-year-olds, like most 6-year-olds, took longer when *b* was large. In contrast, most 11-year-olds and almost all adults appeared to ignore the particular value of *b*, leading to equally fast performance with all values. It seems likely that understanding of the principle increased between ages 6 and 9 as well as later, but that concurrent increases in children's computational speed led many 9-year-olds who could have applied the principle instead to rely on computation.

*Effects of context.* The context within which arithmetic problems are presented exercises a substantial influence on children's ability to solve them. The well-known "Far Side" cartoon in which Hell's Library is stocked exclusively with arithmetic and algebra word-problem books attests to many people's phobia toward problems that require them to apply relatively simple mathematical procedures in strange context. Part of the difficulty is due to the baroque wording of many such problems (e.g., Joe has 23 marbles; he has 7 more than Bill had yesterday before he gave Joe half of his marbles; how many fewer marbles does Bill have today than yesterday?). Such phrasings burden working-memory capacity and contribute to the difficulty of the problems (DeCorte & Vershaffel, 1984: Kintsch & Greeno, 1985; Nesher, 1982).

Even when wordings are not convoluted, unfamiliar contexts often strain children's utilizational competence and thus lead them not to apply procedures that they use successfully in other contexts. This was illustrated in a study of 9-to-15-year-old Brazilian street children who were the sons and daughters of poor migrant workers who had moved to a large city (Carraher, Carraher, & Schliemann, 1985). The children contributed to the family financially by working as street vendors, selling coconuts, popcorn, corn on the cob, and other foods. Their work required them to add, subtract, multiply, and occasionally divide in their heads. (One coconut costs $x$ cruzeiros; five coconuts will cost . . . . ) Despite little formal education, the children could tell customers how much purchases cost and how much change they should get.

In the experiment, the children were asked to solve three types of problems. Some were problems that could arise in the context of customer–vendor transactions. ("How much do I owe for a coconut that costs 85 cruzerios and a corn-on-the-cob that costs 63?") Others involved similar problem-solving situations but did not involve goods carried by the child's stand. ("If a banana costs 85 cruzeiros and a lemon costs 63 cruzeiros, how much do the two cost together?") Yet others were numerically identical problems but presented without a problem-solving context (e.g., "How much is 85 + 63?"). The children solved 98 percent of the items involving questions that could arise at their stand, 74 percent of the items that involved selling unfamiliar goods, and only 37 percent of the items without a problem-solving context. These differences demonstrate the importance of utilizational competence. The children clearly knew how to add, but did not always know when to do so.

### More-Complex Arithmetic

*Buggy subtraction algorithms.* Once children have mastered basic arithmetic facts, they learn algorithms for solving problems involving larger numbers. However, many children encounter difficulty grasping the relation between the procedures they learn for long subtraction, multiplication, and division and the principles that underlie the procedures. The resulting memorization without understanding creates fertile ground for confusions to grow.

These confusions are exemplified by the "bugs" that show up in children's learning of the long subtraction algorithm. Brown and Burton (1978) investigated this problem using an error analysis method, much like the rule assessment approach that was used to study balance scale prob-

**TABLE 9–2    Example of a Subtraction "Bug"**

| 307 | 856 | 606 | 308 | 835 |
|-----|-----|-----|-----|-----|
| −182 | −699 | −568 | −287 | −217 |
| 285 | 157 | 168 | 181 | 618 |

lems. That is, they presented problems on which particular incorrect rules, which they labeled "bugs," would lead to predictable errors.

Many of children's errors reflected such bugs. Consider the pattern in Table 9–2. At first glance, it is difficult to draw any conclusion about this boy's performance, except that he is not very good at subtraction. With further analysis, however, his performance becomes understandable. All three of his errors arose on problems where the top number included a zero. This suggests that his difficulty was due to specific problems subtracting from zero, rather than general carelessness, ignorance, or lack of motivation.

Analysis of the three errors the boy made (the first, third, and fourth problems from the left) suggests the existence of two bugs that would produce these particular answers. When the problem required subtraction from 0, he simply reversed the two numbers in the column. For example, in the problem 307 − 182, he treated 0 − 8 as 8 − 0, and wrote "8" as the answer. The boy's second bug involved not decrementing the number to the left of the zero (not reducing the 3 to 2 in 307 − 182). This lack of decrementing is not surprising because, as indicated in the first bug, he did not borrow anything from this column. Thus, the three wrong answers, as well as the two correct ones, can be explained by assuming a basically correct subtraction procedure with two particular bugs.

Why do such bugs appear? Most seem to be due to students' encountering an *impasse*, a point in the problem where their understanding of the procedure does not point to a clear way to proceed. Under such circumstances, children attempt to repair their basic procedure and circumvent the impasse (Brown & VanLehn, 1980). For example, many students would find that the second column of 307 − 182 presented an impasse for them. Such an impasse might lead them to attempt any of a number of particular repairs to their basic procedure. They might reverse the two numbers in the column, might just write 0 as the answer, and so forth. Thus, successful remediation must identify not only the bugs but also the impasse that triggers them.

Brown and Burton (1978) wrote a computer program, known as "Buggy," to teach prospective teachers how to detect impasses and bugs. The program works in a tutorial fashion. It might first display the five problems and answers shown in Table 9–2. The teacher would be told to indicate when he or she knew what bug(s) were present in the student's performance. The next task would be for the teacher to generate new problems and to answer them the way the bug would suggest. The program would give the teacher feedback on each of the generated answers. Finally, once the teacher produced five consecutive correct answers to the self-generated problems, "Buggy" would design new problems where subtle differences between the teacher's understanding of the bug and the bug itself would manifest themselves. If the teacher answered these correctly, the program would offer congratulations for insight and persistence.

Working with "Buggy" helped teachers learn to design problems that more effectively discriminated among alternative bugs. All 24 of the student teachers who used it indicated that they gained something positive from the experience. To quote one of the testimonials: "I think this system is fantastic. It's a wonderful way to expose people (who are involved with children) to the problems children will probably have. It might be especially useful with special learning needs children" (Brown & Burton, 1978 p. 89). Computer programs such as "Buggy" seem to have the potential both to teach teachers about the specific problems children encounter in a given learning situation and, more generally, to make them aware of the need to be alert for subtle but systematic error patterns that reveal students' misunderstandings.

*Fractions.* When presented the problem $\frac{1}{2} + \frac{1}{3}$, many children answer $\frac{2}{5}$. They generate such answers by first adding the two numerators and then adding the two denominators. The problem is far from transitory. Many adults enrolled in community college math courses make such errors, too (Silver, 1983).

Why should such a simple error be so persistent? One reason seems to be that many children and adults think of addition of fractions in terms of an example used in many math textbooks to introduce the concept: a circle divided into sections, some of them shaded and some not (Figure 9–4). In this example, the sum can be found by counting the number of shaded parts and dividing the sum by the total number of parts of the circle (Silver, 1986). However, this model fails when dealing with problems in which the fractions represent different objects.

Much of the difficulty in performing arithmetic operations with fractions seems to arise from not thinking of the magnitudes represented by the fractions. This was evident in children's errors on a standardized test in estimating the answer to $\frac{12}{13} + \frac{7}{8}$ (Table 9–3). Fewer than one-third of 13- and 17-year-olds correctly estimated the answer to this simple problem.

A similar misunderstanding of the relation of symbols to magnitudes is evident in fourth-to-sixth-graders' attempts to deal with decimal fractions. Consider what children do in judging the relative size of two decimal fractions, such as 2.37 and 2.357. Examination of children in three countries—France, Israel, and the United States—revealed that the most-common approach on such problems was to judge that as long as the

1/8 + 3/8 = 4/8 = 1/2

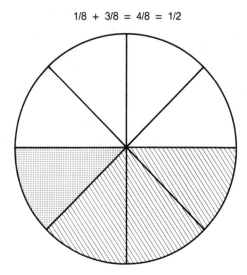

**FIGURE 9–4** Implicit model used by many children (and some adults) to think about addition of fractions.

numbers to the left of the decimal point were equal, the larger number was the one with more digits to the right of the decimal point (Resnick, Nesher, Leonard, Magone, Omanson, & Peled, 1989). Thus, 2.357 would be thought larger than 2.37. Almost half of the children who held this view believed it so strongly that they were willing to conclude that the number with more digits to the right of the decimal must be larger even when they were not allowed to see the particular digits there.

Resnick et al. suggested that such choices reflect the operation of a *Whole Number Rule*. This rule is based on an analogy between decimal fractions and whole numbers. Since a whole number with more digits is always larger than one with fewer digits, some children conclude that the number with more digits to the right of the decimal also must be larger. Consistent with this interpretation, several children who used the Whole Number Rule explicitly said that zeroes immediately after the decimal point were unimportant, as they are at the leftmost extreme of whole numbers.

Another group of children made the opposite responses. They consistently judged that the larger number was the one that had fewer digits to the right of the decimal. Thus, 2.43 would be larger than 2.436. Resnick et al. suggested that these children were using a *Fraction Rule*, based on a flawed analogy between decimal fractions and nondecimal fractions such as ⅝. Within this interpretation, children who know that numbers such as .67 are read as "67 hundredths" and that numbers such as .673 are read as "673 thousandths" correctly understand "thousandths" as connoting

**TABLE 9–3   Estimating the Sum of Two Fractions***

*ESTIMATE the answer to $^{12}/_{13}$ + $^7/_8$. You will not have time to solve the problem using paper and pencil.*

| ANSWER | PERCENTAGE CHOOSING ANSWER | |
| --- | --- | --- |
| | AGE 13 | AGE 17 |
| 1 | 7 | 8 |
| 2 | 24 | 37 |
| 19 | 28 | 21 |
| 21 | 27 | 15 |
| I don't know | 14 | 16 |

*From National Assessment of Educational Progress (Carpenter, Corbitt, Kepner, Lindquist, & Reys, 1981).

smaller parts than "hundredths." However, they go on from there to conclude incorrectly that the total value of the term with the larger denominator must be less (just as ⅝ is less than ⅚).

Consistent with the view that children base their answers on these interpretations, Resnick et al. found that in Israel and the United States, where nondecimal fractions are taught before decimal fractions, errors consistent with the Fraction Rule were quite common. In France, however, where decimal fractions were taught first, errors that conformed to the Fraction Rule were rare.

The difficulty in understanding decimal fractions does not quickly disappear. Zuker (1985; cited in Resnick et al.) found that one-third of Israeli seventh- and ninth-graders continued to use the Whole Number Rule or the Fraction Rule in comparing the sizes of decimal fractions. Thus, with decimal fractions as with long subtraction, failure to understand the relation between the procedure and its underlying rationale leads to systematic and persistent errors.

### Estimation

A number of national commissions (e.g., Romberg & Stewart, 1983) have recently attempted to answer the question, "Why is mathematics achievement in America so poor?" The commissions' reports suggest that several aspects of mathematics instruction in the schools should be changed. One of their primary suggestions is that more emphasis be placed on ability to estimate accurately, that is, knowing roughly what the answer must be even before computing an exact solution. This would help children avoid mistakes such as that with ¹²⁄₁₃ + ⅞, in which most 13- and 17-year-olds show an inability to estimate the results of fractional arithmetic problems typically taught to 10- and 11-year-olds (Table 9–3).

Children estimate much more effectively when dealing with small- and medium-size whole numbers. This was evident in their strategies for playing a computer game (Newman & Berger, 1984). At the bottom of the screen was the number 1; at the top was the number 23. Children were told that each vertical position between 1 and 23 corresponded to a specific number—the position just above the 1 would be position 2, for example. Since no numbers or marks appeared between the 1 and the 23, children could only estimate what the number for the position would be. On each trial, children saw a target appear somewhere between the 1 and the 23 and needed to estimate what number went with that position. A dart was then shot across the computer screen at the number the child chose. The process continued until the child chose the right number, at which point the dart would land on and destroy the target.

Children used a number of estimation strategies to help them send the dart to the right position. The most common strategy among 6-year-olds was to count from 1 to wherever the target appeared, estimating the sizes of the units. This worked quite well for targets in the lower part of the screen, but not for targets in the middle or top. The most-common strategy among 7-year-olds was to count from 1 when the target appeared in the bottom half of the screen and to count backward from 23 when it appeared in the top half. This worked well when the target was near the top or bottom, but not when it was near the middle. The majority of 9-year-olds adopted a third strategy. They counted from the top, from the bottom, or from an arbitrary benchmark they established in the middle, depending on which was most efficient. This approach worked well for all targets.

Why did different-age children adopt different strategies? Newman (1984) suggested that facility with numbers was critical. Even among children of a single age, those who generally knew more about numbers, even knowledge that had nothing obvious to do with this task, were better at estimating where the target would be. The practical implication is that providing children with a greater variety of experiences with numbers, not just calculation, might improve their ability to estimate. Improved ability to estimate, in turn, might eventually help children generally do better in mathematics by helping them know approximately what the correct answer must be and allowing them to infer that certain of their answers must be wrong.

### Algebra

Learning algebra greatly increases the power of children's mathematical reasoning. A single algebraic equation can be used to represent and reason about an infinite variety of situations. This power is frequently not realized, however. Even students who do well in algebra classes often do so by treating the equations as exercises in symbol manipulation, without any connection to real-world contexts. This limits the students' ability to solve problems using algebra, and can lead to a variety of misconceptions as well.

Many misunderstandings of algebra seem to arise from incorrect extensions of correct rules (Matz, 1982; Sleeman, 1985). For example:

Since the distributive principle indicates that

$$a \times (b + c) = (a \times b) + (a \times c),$$

some students extend the principle to all operations and represent it as

$a R_1 (b R_2 c) = (a R_1 b) R_2 (a R_1 c)$ (where $R_1$ and $R_2$ are arithmetic relations),

which leads to incorrect conclusions such as

$$a + (b \times c) = (a + b) \times (a + c).$$

Students use a variety of procedures to determine whether transformations of algebraic equations are appropriate. Among 11- to-14-year-olds, the most-frequent strategy for determining whether transformations are acceptable is to insert numbers into the original and new equations and to see if they yield the same result (Resnick, Cauzinille-Marmeche, & Mathieu, 1987). This procedure produces correct results, though it rarely indicates why the transformation is legitimate. Another common approach is to justify the transformation by citing a rule. Some students cite appropriate rules, but many others cite distorted versions of rules, as in the previous example of the incorrect version of the distributive law. Another of the most-common erroneous rules is to view $(a - (b - c))$ as equivalent to $((a - b) - c)$, apparently on a mistaken analogy to the associative principle that $(a + (b + c)) = ((a + b) + c)$.

These problems are not quickly overcome. Even college students encounter difficulty with them. For example, the following seemingly trivial algebra problem was correctly solved by fewer than 30 percent of engineering students at a major state university.

> Write an equation using the variables $C$ and $S$ to represent the following statement: "At Mindy's restaurant, for every four people who order cheesecake, there are five people who order strudel." Let $C$ represent the number of cheesecakes and $S$ represent the number of strudels ordered." (*Clement, Lochhead, & Soloway,* 1979 p. 46)

Most students represented this problem as $4C = 5S$. At first impression this seems logical. The impression crumbles, though, when one considers that the equation means that we should multiply the two smaller values (4 and the number of people who order cheesecake) to get a product equal to the one produced by multiplying the two larger values (5 and the number of people who order strudel).

Both Clement et al. and Resnick et al. reached the same conclusion: Children's and adults' difficulties on such problems stem from their not connecting equations with what they mean. Without such connections, algebra collapses into an exercise in remembering which arbitrary symbol manipulations are permitted and which are not. Thus, although the power of algebra ultimately comes from equations allowing abstraction over particular situations, learning to translate from particular situations to equations and from equations to particular situations is essential for mastery of the subject.

### Computer Programming

Students currently attending school receive far more exposure to computers than those in any previous generation. Advocates of such exposure have hoped that it would engender not only knowledge about and comfort with computer programming, but also generally enhanced problem solving skills (Papert, 1980). Planning, problem decomposition, and debugging are some of the high-level skills that might be acquired through programming experience with computer languages such as LOGO.

In general, the hopes of broad transfer of computer programming skills to other types of problem solving have not been realized. Simply learning to program does not seem to influence general problem solving and reasoning. However, a recent instructional program (Klahr & Carver, 1988) specifically designed to use experience with LOGO as a basis for creating general debugging skills demonstrated that programs deliberately aimed at producing such transfer can succeed.

The instructional program was based on a careful task analysis of what debugging entailed. Within this analysis, the debugging process begins with running a program and observing that the actual output deviates from what was planned. Following this, the skilled debugger describes the discrepancy between desired and actual outcomes, and proposes specific types of bugs that might be responsible. Then the debugger identifies parts of the program that could conceivably produce such bugs. This step demands representing the program in a way in which specific parts are identified with specific functions. Following this, the debugger checks the relevant parts of the program to see which, if any, of them are failing to produce the intended results; replaces the faulty component; and runs the debugged program to determine if it now produces the desired output.

Klahr and Carver used this analysis to teach debugging to 8-to-11-year-olds participating in a computer programming class. The instructional program succeeded in producing improved debugging. On tests of debugging skill, children who received the relevant instruction took barely half as long to solve debugging problems as children who had not encountered it. This improvement transferred to debugging standard English instructions for accomplishing such tasks as traveling to a destination, arranging furniture in a room, and ordering food. The improvement seemed due in large part to students who received the debugging instruction analyzing the nature of the discrepancy from the hoped-for results, hypothesizing possible causes, and focusing their search on relevant parts of the program rather than simply checking the program in an unfocused line-by-line manner. A second experiment showed that the children who improved most on the LOGO debugging task also improved most on the transfer task. The results illustrate the benefits of careful task analyses for designing instruction that produces both learning and transfer.

## READING

Children's reading can be viewed either chronologically (what happens at particular ages) or topically (how does competency $x$ develop). In this section, I first consider the main types of reading development that occur at different ages. Then I examine three crucial aspects of reading development in greater detail: prereading skills, identification of individual words, and comprehension of larger units of text.

### The Typical Chronological Progression

Chall (1979) hypothesized that children progress through five stages in learning to read. The stages oversimplify some complex and overlapping cognitive changes and make reading acquisition seem tidier and neater than it really is. However, they do capture the major developments that occur in learning to read and the ages at which each type of development seems most dramatic. They also communicate a sense of the multiple challenges that children must meet to become good readers.

In Stage 0, lasting from birth to the beginning of first grade, children master several prerequisites for reading. Many learn to identify the letters of the alphabet. Many learn to write their names. Some learn to read a few words, typically the names of products such as Coca-Cola and stores such as Sears. As was the case in arithmetic, young children's knowledge of reading seems to be considerably greater today than it was 40 or 50 years ago. The improvement may be due to educational programs such as "Sesame Street" and to often-repeated, attention-grabbing television commercials.

In Stage 1, which usually occupies first and second grade, children acquire *phonological recoding skill,* that is, skill involved in translating letters into sounds and in blending the sounds so as to produce words. Children also complete their learning of the letter names and sounds in this stage.

In Stage 2, most commonly occurring in second and third grades, children begin to read fluently. They do not need to spend as much time and mental effort to identify each word. However, Chall indicated that at this stage, reading is still not for learning. The demands of word identification on children's processing resources remain sufficiently great that acquiring new information through reading is difficult. The demands of keeping words and ideas simple, so as not to hopelessly overload processing capacity, may contribute to the uninteresting character of most early reading books. The existence of captivating books that children at this level can read, such as Charlotte's Web, Stuart Little, and the Pippi stories, demonstrates that the limit is not absolute. Nonetheless, it may be even more difficult to write a great story that 7- and 8-year-olds can read than to write a high-quality adult novel.

In Stage 3, which Chall identified with fourth through eighth grade, children become capable of obtaining new information from print. To quote her characterization, "In the primary grades, children learn to read; in the higher grades, they read to learn" (p. 24). At this point, however, according to Chall, readers only can comprehend information presented from a single perspective.

In Stage 4, which occupies the high school years, children come to comprehend written information presented from multiple viewpoints. This makes possible much more sophisticated discussions of history, economics, and politics than was possible previously. It also allows appreciation of the subtleties of great works of fiction, which are presented much more often in high school than in elementary school.

This chronology points to two major themes in children's acquisition of reading skills: the centrality of reading comprehension as the goal of learning to read, and the need for efficient word identification so that sufficient processing resources are available for comprehending. Before children can even acquire word-identification skills, though, they need certain prior capabilities. These are discussed in the next section.

### Prereading Skills

Children acquire certain important prereading skills effortlessly. They seem to simply absorb the knowledge that written language proceeds from left to right on a page, that text continues from the extreme right on one line to the extreme left on the next, and that spaces between letter sequences signal separations between words. Two other prerequisites for reading are considerably more difficult for most children to master, though: discriminating among letters and dividing words into component sounds. These relatively demanding prerequisites are discussed next, as are a group of children of special interest—precocious readers.

*Letter perception.* As discussed in Chapter 6, identification of distinctive features plays a critical role in letter recognition. Once children learn that each letter can be described as a unique combination of curves, horizontal segments, vertical segments, and diagonals, they can more quickly and accurately identify the letters. However, even after this initial learning, letters that differ only in orientation—*b* and *d*, and *p* and *q*, for example—are often confused with each other (Calfee, Chapman, & Venezky, 1972). Such confusions may arise because in contexts other than reading, orientation rarely affects identity. A boy's dog is his dog regardless of the direction in which it faces. In any case, by second or third grade, the large majority of children no longer confuse letters in reading (Kaufman, 1980).

Many parents and teachers, as well as researchers, have wondered whether learning letter names helps children read. The picture is complex, but a least a preliminary conclusion is possible. Kindergarteners' ability to name letters predicts their later reading achievement scores, at least into second and third grade, quite well (DeHirsch, Jansky, & Langford, 1966). At first glance, this would seem to indicate that learning letter names helps children. However, teaching letter names to randomly selected young children does not facilitate their learning to read (Venezky, 1978). Together, the two facts suggest that learning the letter names does not cause later superior reading. Rather, other variables—interest in print, general intelligence, perceptual skills, parental interest in their children's reading, or some combination of the above—probably are responsible both for some children's learning the letter names and for those children's later tending to read well.

*Phonemic awareness.* Another difficult prerequisite for reading is realizing that words consist of separable sounds. This realization has been labeled *phonemic awareness.* Even after several years of speaking a language, most children seem unaware that they are combining separate sounds to make words. Liberman, Shankweiler, Fischer, and Carter (1974) illustrated this point with 4- and 5-year-olds. The children were told to tap once for each sound in a short word. Thus, they were supposed to tap twice for "it" and three times for "hit." Performance on the task proved to be an excellent predictor of the child's early reading achievement (Liberman & Shankweiler, 1977). Further, training 4- and 5-year-olds to detect which of three words does not share a common phoneme (*cot, pot, hat*) led to improved reading and spelling performance as much as four years later (Bradley & Bryant, 1983). Children who are poor readers in first grade also benefit from such training (Vellutino & Scanlon, 1987).

Why should phonemic awareness be so closely related to, and so helpful in promoting, early reading achievement? Thinking about the process by which children learn to read suggests an answer. When children are taught to read, they learn the sounds that typically accompany each letter. Unless they can blend these sounds into a word, however, the knowledge of these sound–symbol correspondences does little good. Being able to divide a word into its component sounds, a skill required on phonemic awareness tasks, demands recognition of the sounds that must be blended. Thus, phonemic awareness may accurately predict early reading achievement because it measures how well children can blend sounds to form words.

Phonological awareness may originate, at least in part, from a rather charming source: nursery rhymes. How well children know nursery rhymes at age 3 predicts their later phonological awareness, even when the contributions of the child's age, the child's IQ, and the mother's educational level are statistically controlled (Maclean, Bryant, & Bradley, 1987). The minimal contrasts that often occur between words at the ends of lines within such rhymes (e.g., *horn* and *corn, Muffet* and *tuffet*) may help children isolate the separate sounds that are present within each syllable and recognize that words are made up of such separable sounds.

*Precocious readers.*    Some 2- and 3-year-olds can read. They are not in general the product of "better baby" schools or other instructional systems. Instead, they are simply children who, usually without any special teaching, have somehow cracked the alphabetic code.

What distinguishes precocious readers from other children? As a group, they tend to be of above average IQs, but their scores are not in general exceptional (Jackson, 1988). Conversely, studies of children with very high IQs have shown that about half could read by age 5 but that the other half could not (Roedell, Jackson, & Robinson, 1980; Terman & Oden, 1947).

Interviews with parents of children who read well when they entered first grade have indicated several precursors of exceptional early reading (Jackson, Donaldson, & Cleland, 1988). Most such children could recite the alphabet and identify some capital letters before age 3. By age 3, two-thirds recognized some words on signs. Most began to read simple books by age 4 and could sound out unfamiliar words by age 5.

Comparison of the reports of parents of early readers with those of parents of children who did not read so early suggests that the largest differences between the two groups involve interest in reading (Durkin, 1966). This includes both the interest of the children in learning to read and the interest of the parents in having their children read. Parents of both early readers and nonreading peers said that their children were interested in reading before starting school. However, the parents of the precocious readers noted several specific sources of interest that were not mentioned as often by the other parents: presence of reading materials in the home, availability of a blackboard for the child at home, and the child's being unusually interested in word meanings. Precocious readers tend to be from middle- or upper-class backgrounds (Briggs & Elkind, 1977). However, the child's interest seems to be the key. Interviews with the parents of superior readers in a school serving a lower-class black population also indicated that almost all of the children started learning to read before entering first grade (Durkin, 1982).

Contrary to the fears of a number of educators, precocious reading does not adversely affect later reading and general school performance. Children who know how to read when they enter school remain superior readers through at least sixth grade (Durkin, 1966; Mills & Jackson, in press). It cannot be concluded that the early reading caused the later superiority, however. Exposing randomly selected children to two years of reading instruction prior to first grade did not result in their reading better at the end of third grade (Durkin, 1974/75). Further, 5- and 6-year-olds' general verbal ability is at least as good a predictor of their later reading skill as is their initial reading skill (Mills & Jackson, in press). At minimum, though, precocious reading does children no harm and predicts good later reading.

### Identifying Individual Words

Reading development in the early grades is largely the development of skill at identifying individual words. Children use two distinguishable word identification procedures: *phonological recoding* (sometimes called decoding) and *visually based retrieval*. In both, children first examine printed words and later locate the entry for the word in long-term memory. The central difference concerns what happens in between. When children phonologically recode a word, they translate the visual form into a speechlike one, and use this speechlike representation to identify the word. When they visually retrieve a word, they do not take the intermediate step. The two approaches are not quite as distinct as this description suggests; for example, children sometimes phonologically recode the first letter or two and then are able to retrieve the word's identity without further recoding. Despite these mixed cases, the distinction still seems to correspond to a genuine difference in word-identification strategies.

The difference between the two word-identification processes is echoed in the difference between the two main approaches to reading instruction. The *whole-word approach* emphasizes visual retrieval; the *phonetic approach* emphasizes phonological recoding. Historically, educational practice has gyrated erratically between the two instructional approaches. At the beginning of this century, most teachers in the United States emphasized phonics. Between the 1920s and the 1950s, they emphasized visual retrieval. In the past 20 years, they again emphasized phonics. Two likely reasons for the switches are that both methods do eventually succeed in teaching most children to read, and that neither method succeeds in teaching every child to read. In addition, neither approach has to be pursued in pure form. Most teachers use both. The issue is not whether children need to learn letter–sound relations or whether they need to be able to retrieve words rapidly, but how early and to what extent each skill should be emphasized.

Another reason the debate has not been resolved is that plausible arguments can be made for each side. The whole-word argument: Skilled readers rely on visually based retrieval; the goal of reading instruction is to produce skilled readers; therefore, beginning readers should be taught to read like skilled ones. The phonics argument: For children to learn to read, they must be able to identify unfamiliar words; phonological recoding skills allow them to do this; therefore, beginning readers should be taught in a way that will allow them to read independently.

Understanding the processes by which children learn to read provides an informed basis for choosing between these two arguments. Next we examine phonological recoding, visually based retrieval, and the process by which children choose which of the two approaches to use to identify a particular word. The analysis suggests an explanation for why one of the two approaches to teaching children to read has proven more effective than the other.

*Phonological recoding.* Everyone who has observed children learning to read has heard them translate letters into sounds and combine the sounds into words. The technique allows them to "sound out" words that they otherwise could not read without help. This advantage underlies the persistent and continuing international trend toward use of alphabetic rather than pictorial writing systems (Gleitman & Rozin, 1977). Simply put, alphabetic systems are easier to learn.

The nature of the reading material that beginning readers encounter makes evident the advantage of having good phonological recoding skills. Firth (1972) examined the 2,747 words that occurred in a basal reader for first- and second-graders. More than 70 percent of the words were presented five or fewer times, and more than 40 percent of the words only once. Some basal readers repeat words more frequently, but more-repetitive material tends to degenerate into the remarkably boring "Look, look, see Spot" style so memorable to those who encountered it. As long as children must read large numbers of words that they have rarely seen, phonological recoding skill is essential.

Beyond allowing children to read independently, skillful phonological recoding also probably contributes to efficient visually based retrieval. Jorm and Share (1983) described how this might occur. Their basic assumption was that children learn the answers that they state; this was the same assumption made by Siegler and Shrager (1984) about arithmetic learning. If children lack good phonological recoding skills, they will be forced to rely more often on context to infer words' identities. Context is often an undependable guide, though; relying on it will lead to many errors. In contrast, accurate sounding out will increase the association between the printed and the spoken word, thus increasing the likelihood of the child's being able to retrieve the word's identity through purely visual processes. As Jorm and Share commented, "Phonological recoding may be the principal mechanism by which beginning readers learn to use the more efficient visual-retrieval route and eventually achieve skilled performance" (p. 114). This view is supported by numerous studies indicating that knowledge of phonetic relations predicts individual differences in reading even in later childhood and adolescence, when most readers no longer sound out many words (Johnson & Baumann, 1984).

*Visually based retrieval.* It is tempting to describe the development of word-identification skills by saying that at first children sound out words, and later they use visually based retrieval. In fact, the progression is not this simple. Many children can retrieve the identities of a few words even before they know any sound–symbol correspondences. Gough and Hillinger (1980) provided the example of a preschooler who learned to read two words: "Budweiser" and "Stop." The boy learned the first word from beer cans, the second from road signs. Context provided many clues to these words' identities. Some young children, however, also can read such words if they are typed on an index card. A girl might know that she knows two words and that "Budweiser" is the long one and "Stop" is the short one. Next, she might learn the word "Coors." The long–short distinction would no longer be sufficient. Now she might identify the words on the basis that if a familiar word was long, it was "Budweiser"; if it was short and started with a letter that had only one curve, it was "Coors"; if it was short and started with a letter that had two curves, it was "Stop."

Although the first uses of visually based retrieval may rely on one or two features, the retrieval process eventually incorporates parallel processing of a great many sources of information (McClelland & Rumelhart, 1981). Among these are information from the particular letters, from the word as a whole, and from the surrounding context. Such parallel processing allows older children and adults to identify a huge variety of words quickly and effortlessly.

*The role of context.* Context influences word identification from early in the learning-to-read process. In the large majority of cases in which first-graders substitute one word for another, the word that is substituted is consistent with the surrounding context (Weber, 1970). Children also spontaneously reread passages twice as often when their errors are inconsistent with the context as when they are consistent with it (Weber, 1970). Thus, context influences word identification even in the first year of formal instruction in reading.

*Strategy choices in word identification.*    As in arithmetic, children choose adaptively among alternative word-identification strategies. They use the fast retrieval approach when it can yield correct answers, and resort to backup strategies, such as sounding out, on the more difficult words, whose pronunciation and spelling they cannot accurately retrieve (Figure 9–5). This observation raises the issue of how children know whether to use phonological recoding or visually based retrieval to identify a particular word.

The way in which children decide whether to retrieve a word's identity or to sound it out seems to be analogous to the procedures they use in addition and subtraction. Through experience, they associate each word's visual appearance and its identity. Each time they encounter the word, they try to retrieve its identity. If the alternative they retrieve has sufficient associative strength, they say it. Otherwise, they resort to a backup strategy, such as sounding out the word or asking an older child or adult what it is.

Consistent with the proposed parallel between strategy choices in arithmetic and word identification, the same types of individual differences are present in both areas. Some readers are like the perfectionists in Siegler (1988a); they are slow, accurate, and likely to use backup strategies. Olson, Kleigl, Davidson, & Foltz (1985) referred to such children as "plodders." Other children follow the pattern of the good students; they are faster and more likely to use visually based retrieval rather than sounding out. Olson et al. referred to them as "explorers." Jackson et al. (1988) described similar individual differences in their sample of precocious readers.

This perspective, combined with Jorm and Share's (1983) position that children become able to use visually based retrieval through prior accurate use of phonological recoding, implies that phonics-based instruction should be superior to the whole-word approach in helping children identify words quickly and accurately. The logic is that accurate use of backup strategies, such as sounding out, will increasingly make possible fast and accurate retrieval. This is in fact what seems to happen. In both classroom and laboratory tests, phonics-based approaches have proven superior in promoting reading achievement (Chall, 1979; Lesgold & Curtis, 1981).

### Comprehension

Reading comprehension is arguably the most-important academic skill that children acquire. It allows them to master new information, to pursue all kinds of interests, and, perhaps most important for many children, to escape boredom.

Reading comprehension can be divided into four component processes: lexical access, proposition assembly, proposition integration, and text modeling (Perfetti, 1984). *Lexical access* is another name for word identification. It is the process by which children retrieve the meaning of a

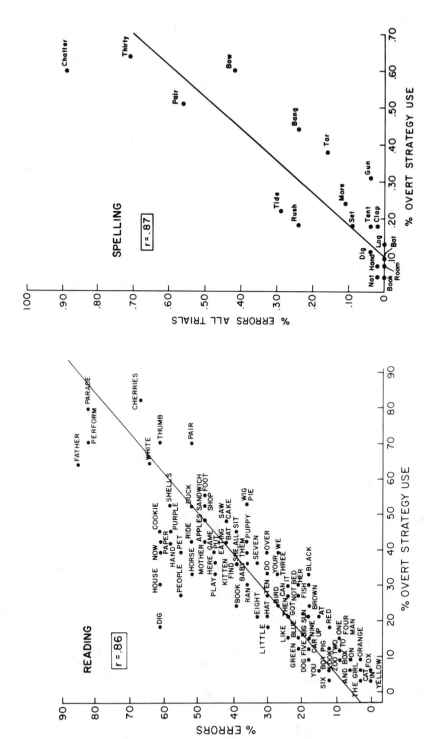

**FIGURE 9-5** As with arithmetic, the more difficult the word, as measured by percentage of errors, the more likely that children will use overt strategies to read or spell it (from Siegler, 1986).

317

printed word from long-term memory. *Proposition assembly* involves relating words to each other to form meaningful units. For example, in the sentence "The sick boy went home," the reader would construct the propositions "There was a boy," "The boy was sick," and so on. *Proposition integration* involves combining individual propositions into larger units of meaning. Finally, *text modeling* refers to the processes by which children draw inferences and relate what they are reading to what they already know. Children would draw on knowledge about school nurses, needs of sick children, and typical distances between homes and schools in interpreting the sentence about the sick boy who went home.

Perfetti's analysis helps clarify the relation between comprehension of written and spoken language. Both require forming and integrating propositions and constructing a general model of the situation. However, the lexical access process differs in the two situations. In reading, lexical access requires a translation between written words and meanings; in listening, lexical access requires a translation between spoken words and meanings. Beginning readers' greater competence in translating spoken words into meanings accounts for their listening comprehension exceeding their reading comprehension.

*What develops in reading comprehension?* Just about every way in which 5-to-20-year-olds develop intellectually contributes to improvements in reading comprehension. However, five types of development seem to be particularly important: automatization of lexical access, growing working-memory capacity, greater related knowledge, better comprehension monitoring, and increasingly adaptive variations in strategies.

Automatization of word identification contributes to reading comprehension in the same way that automatization of simple arithmetic contributes to learning of more-advanced mathematics. It allows children to focus their attention more fully on the meaning of the new material. Consistent with this view, efficiency of word identification early in first grade is predictive of reading comprehension not only in first grade but through the end of third grade (Lesgold, Resnick, & Hammond, 1985).

The relation between efficiency of word identification and reading comprehension can be thought of in terms of *reading potential* (Sticht & James, 1984). The idea is that if it were as easy to access word meanings from print as from spoken language, children's reading comprehension could potentially be as good as their listening comprehension. Consistent with this view, first- and second-graders' listening comprehension is much higher than their reading comprehension. The gap steadily diminishes until it disappears altogether for most children at around seventh or eight grade. Individual differences in listening and reading comprehension also become increasingly closely related over the course of schooling. This probably is due to individual differences in both reading and listening comprehension increasingly being determined by the same factors— general verbal ability, knowledge of specific content, and interest in the material—rather than ability to identify individual words.

A second source of development of reading comprehension is the amount of material children can hold in working memory. Children who can hold longer phrases in working memory have a better chance to integrate previous and new ideas and to infer connections between them. Large working-memory capacity seems especially helpful in coping with ambiguous wordings, where comprehension requires maintaining more than one interpretation until the ambiguity is resolved (Daneman, 1981).

A third source of the development of reading comprehension is increasing knowledge, and increasingly well-organized knowledge, of related content. Children who have such knowledge can check the plausibility of their interpretations of what they are reading against what they already know. They can also draw reasonable inferences about motivations, events, and consequences that are implicit rather than stated.

The importance of organized knowledge for reading comprehension is apparent in situations where even young readers comprehend well because they possess efficient ways of organizing the material. One such case arises in comprehension of fairy tales. Even 6- and 7-year-olds recall material well, draw reasonable inferences about the likely causes of the characters' actions, and form sensible expectations about what will happen next when they can organize new stories into the familiar fairy tale format (Mandler & Johnson, 1977; Stein & Glenn, 1979).

Although any type of related knowledge can aid comprehension, knowledge of causal connections seems especially helpful. Both younger and older readers focus on actions and events within stories that are relevant to the basic chain of causality. Over a wide range of ages, causally important information is judged more important than other material, is recalled more often, and is included more often in summaries (Trabasso & van den Broek, 1985). Developmental changes are also evident in the contribution of causal connections to comprehension, however. Some of these changes reflect increasing knowledge of the causes of specific events. Others reflect growing ability to integrate information from several episodes into a single high-level structure (Goldman, 1985; Waters & Lomenicki, 1983). For example, causal links within a given episode dominate 8-year-olds' recall of the stories, whereas 11- and 14-year-olds also recall causal links that tie together separate episodes within the stories (van den Broek, 1989).

A fourth influence on reading comprehension is how well children monitor their comprehension. Older readers, and better readers within each age group, more accurately evaluate their understanding than do younger and poorer readers (Forrest & Waller, 1979). The difference between good and poor readers' comprehension monitoring is present at all levels from first grade (Clay, 1973) to adulthood (Baker & Brown, 1984). Such comprehension monitoring leads older and better readers to adopt a variety of adaptive strategies for dealing with difficulty: returning to the original source of the confusion, correcting misread words, slowing down until good comprehension is restored, trying to visualize the scene, and reducing abstract characterizations to concrete examples (Whimbey, 1975).

A final source of improvements in reading comprehension involves increasingly flexible deployment of strategies. Reading comprehension is not one task, but many. This is evident in comparing the ways we read a novel, a mathematics textbook, a newspaper, and the instructions for assembling a model airplane. With age and reading experience, children become increasingly adept at adapting reading strategies to their goals in the particular context. For example, between ages 10 and 14, children become increasingly likely to skim material when detailed understanding is unnecessary (Kobasigawa, Ransom, & Holland, 1980).

*Implications for classroom instruction.*    How can reading comprehension be improved? One useful method is to ensure that children understand critical background assumptions *before* they read the story. Consider the saga of "The Raccoon and Mrs. McGinnis," a story that appeared in a second-grade textbook. Mrs. McGinnis, a poor but good-hearted farmer, wishes on a star for a barn in which to house her animals. Instead, bandits come and steal the animals. A raccoon, who habitually looks for food at night on Mrs. McGinnis' doorstep, follows the bandits and then climbs a tree to be safe from them. The bandits see the raccoon's masked face and mistake it for another bandit. Frightened, they release the animals and inadvertently drop a bag of money they had stolen from someone else. The raccoon picks up the bag of money, returns to Mrs. McGinnis' doorstep to continue looking for food, and drops the bag on the doorstep. The next morning, Mrs. McGinnis finds the money and attributes her good fortune to her wish of the night before.

The teacher's guide for this story suggested several preparatory activities. Children were to be told that the story was about Mrs. McGinnis and a raccoon; that raccoons were clever, intelligent, and mischievous; and that unusual things would happen to Mrs. McGinnis and the raccoon. However, Beck and McKeown (1984) reasoned that these were not the critical concepts needed for comprehension. Instead, they introduced children to the story by discussing two concepts more closely related to the story's deeper meaning: coincidence and habit. That is, they explained that coincidences involve two events just happening to occur together, with neither causing the other, and that habits often lead people and animals to engage repeatedly in the same activities. They also introduced several useful background facts: that the dark circles around raccoons' eyes look like masks, that raccoons habitually hunt for food at night, and that raccoons often pick up objects and carry them to other locations.

The background knowledge provided by Beck and McKeown helped children understand what happened. The explanation of the concept of coincidence increased the number of children who contrasted what Mrs. McGinnis thought had happened with what actually had. Moreover, children who received the background information, unlike many of their peers, did not conclude that the raccoon had tried to help Mrs. McGinnis get her animals back.

The investigators' general recommendations were that teachers not just introduce stories in general terms, but that they also explain to children critical background concepts that the children might lack. To introduce stories in this way requires careful analysis both of what concepts are critical to the meaning of the story and of what children already know. However, such analysis may be critical to young children's comprehending the point of the stories they read.

Palincsar and Brown (1984) integrated a different set of psychological principles into a program that is perhaps the single most impressive demonstration to date of how knowledge of children's thinking can be useful in the classroom. The goal of the program was to improve the reading comprehension of a group of seventh-graders from disadvantaged backgrounds. Although these students' word-identification skills were at the expected grade level, their comprehension skills were two to three years behind. Palincsar and Brown hypothesized that the source of the students' difficulty was inadequate comprehension monitoring.

Therefore, the seventh-graders received instruction in four skills that might improve their comprehension monitoring: summarizing, clarifying, questioning, and anticipating future questions. After reading a paragraph, they needed to summarize it. Then they needed to clarify any ambiguities in their summaries or in the original paragraph. Next, they needed to anticipate what question the teacher might ask about the paragraph. Finally, they needed to predict what the next paragraph might be about.

To help the seventh-graders learn these skills, the teacher took turns with the student. After both the student and the teacher read a paragraph, the teacher would summarize it, point to material that needed clarification, anticipate likely questions, and predict what would happen next in the story. On the next paragraph, the student would carry out these activities. Then it would be the teacher's turn. This turn taking was essential, because at first students were quite inept in executing the skills. For example, at the beginning of the training, only 11 percent of students' summary statements captured the main idea of the paragraph. By the end of the more than 20 sessions, 60 percent of their statements did so.

The instruction had many positive effects on the seventh-graders' reading comprehension. Following the instruction each day, they read new paragraphs and answered from memory 10 questions about the paragraphs. On a pretest before the program began, the children averaged 20 percent correct on the test. At the end of the program, they averaged more than 80 percent correct. The improved comprehension for such paragraphs was still evident when the seventh-graders were retested six months after the program ended. Even more impressive, on tests that were part of the regular classwork in science and social studies, the trained children improved from the 20th percentile of their school to the 56th percentile. The instruction later proved just as effective when carried out in natural group settings by the children's regular teachers.

What general lessons can we draw from this success story? One crucial factor in the success, according to Palincsar and Brown, was that the comprehension skills were taught within the same context in which they would be used—reading of passages. Another key element was the interactions between students and teachers. Within these interactions, teachers could model the types of thinking that were desired, adjust the instruction to children's existing level, and phase out their own role as the children's competence grew. Equally encouraging, the usefulness of instruction in comprehension monitoring does not seem to be limited to this particular program or to this particular population. Instruction in such monitoring has proved effective in heightening the comprehension of younger children, specifically third- and fifth-graders, and has benefited relatively good, as well as relatively poor, readers (Paris & Jacobs, 1984). Thus instruction in comprehension monitoring seems to be a promising means for helping children read better.

## WRITING

A venerable sorrow of teachers and other educators is how badly students write. The difficulty does not end in childhood. For many computer companies, it seems far easier to build a machine capable of performing millions of instructions per second than to produce a manual that explains in clear English how to get the machine to function. This is particularly unfortunate because of the growing role of writing in modern life. For example, business personnel spend an estimated 19 percent of their working hours writing memos, letters, and technical reports (Klemmer & Snyder, 1972).

Writing can be divided into the initial drafting process and the process of revision. In both of these areas, the need to pursue multiple goals simultaneously and to automatize lower-level activities so that processing resources can be focused on higher-level goals are central problems for young writers.

### The Initial Drafting Process

Most people do not have a good sense of what children's compositions are like. The following essay, actually a better-than-average effort for an 8-year-old, should communicate the flavor:

> I have not got a bird but I know some things about them. They have tow nostrils and They clean Ther feather and They eat seeds, worms, bread, cuddle firs, and lots of other things. and they drink water. When he drinks he Puts his head up and it gose down. A budgie (birdie) cage gets very dirty and peopel clean it. (Kress, 1982, pp. 59–60)

This story illustrates not only the quality of children's writing, but several reasons that writing is so difficult. There is the need to generate ideas. Then there is the need to place the ideas in a sensible order. Producing a coherent ordering entails a difficult choice. Writing ideas in the order they are recalled tends to produce a disorganized composition. On the other hand, waiting to write until all relevant information has been retrieved often leads to forgetting important points that were recalled earlier. The need to perform lower-level processes adds additional complexity; as the essay about birds indicates, producing correct spelling, capitalization, punctuation, and grammar pose major challenges for children. Taking notes or generating outlines could help reduce the memory load, but children rarely engage in these activities. It is no wonder they find writing so difficult.

Just as reading can be compared to listening, so can writing be compared to speaking. However, in contrast to the reading-versus-listening comparison, where only the demands of lexical access differ, writing imposes a variety of demands that speaking does not. Three especially important differences are the kinds of topics that are discussed, the ways in which goals are generated, and the mechanical demands of writing and speaking (Bereiter & Scardamalia, 1982).

*Demands of unfamiliar topics.*   To write a story, children must first activate information in long-term memory that is relevant to the topic. In many cases this is difficult, because the topics are ones that children would never voluntarily discuss (e.g., "Why I like winter"). Under such conditions, they must pull together material from diverse parts of their memory. The 8-year-old's essay on birds exemplifies what often happens. The last sentence of the story has little to do with the rest of the composition; it probably was retrieved later and never integrated with the earlier portion.

*Demands of multiple goals.*   People write to pursue a variety of goals: to amuse, to intrigue, to inform, to arouse, and to generate enough material to satisfy teachers. Intonations and nonverbal gestures, which can achieve some of these purposes in speech, are unavailable in writing. Further, the feedback that writers receive during the initial drafting process is ordinarily limited to their own reactions to what they have written. This is quite different from the situation in conversations, where other people's questions and comments often suggest new goals and paths to pursue. Thus, writing demands formulating goals with little outside stimulation, keeping them in mind for long periods, and independently judging when they have been met.

How do children cope with the need to generate and pursue multiple goals? Scardamalia and Bereiter (1984) labeled children's typical approach the *knowledge-telling strategy*. This strategy simplifies the writing task to the point where only a single goal needs to be considered at any given time. The strategy can be summarized in terms of two commandments. First, answer directly the question that was asked. Second, write down relevant information as it is retrieved from memory. The 8-year-old's story just described exemplifies the results of using this approach. Initially, she answered a question about birds, "I do not have a bird, but I know some things about them." Then she listed several facts she remembered about birds. The limited goals of the knowledge-telling strategy may account for the brevity of most schoolchildren's compositions.

One consequence of the limited goals of the knowledge-telling strategy is a lack of internal connections in young children's essays. McCutchen and Perfetti (1982) noted that second- and fourth-graders' stories typically are organized only in the sense that all statements relate to the topic sentence; this is the structure generated by the knowledge-telling strategy. In contrast, sixth-graders' essays are more richly textured. Later sentences in stories refer not only to the topic sentence, but also to other sentences within them. Creating such internal connections requires keeping in mind both the point of the original topic sentence and the particulars of other sentences. Thus, it increases the memory load. However, it also leads to a product that is more like a story and less like a grocery list.

With experience in writing, children come to sequence goals into standard organizations that help them cope with the memory demands of writing. An unusual natural experiment reported by Waters (1980) demonstrated how skill in coordinating multiple goals develops with practice. Waters analyzed 120 essays written by a girl (herself) during second grade. All the essays were written in response to a "class news" assignment. Each day, students were to write about that day's events.

Waters intensively examined five essays she had written on consecutive days at the beginning of the year, five in the middle, and five at the end. As shown in Table 9–4, story contents at first were limited to the date, weather, and class activities. Later, they also included information about peers, duties, and materials brought to school.

More generally, the later stories showed a greater number and variety of goals than the earlier ones. In many of the later essays, each time the

**TABLE 9–4    Stories Written at Beginning, Middle, and End of Year for Class News Assignment (Waters, 1980)**

---

*SEPTEMBER 24, 1956*
Today is Monday, September 24, 1956. It is a rainy day. We hope the sun will shine.
We got new spelling books. We had our pictures taken. We sang Happy Birthday to Barbara

*JANUARY 22, 1957*
Today is Tuesday, January 22, 1957. It is a foggy day. We must be careful crossing the road.
This morning, we had music. We learned a new song.
Linda is absent. We hope she come back soon.
We had arithmetic. We made believe that we were buying candy. We had fun.
We work in our English work books. We learned when to use *is* and *are*.

*MAY 27,1957*
Today is Monday, May 27, 1957. It is a warm, cloudy day. We hope the sun comes out.
This afternoon, we had music. We enjoyed it. We went out to play.
Carole is absent. We hope she comes back soon.
We had a spelling lesson, we learned about a *dozen*.
Tomorrow we shall have show and tell.
Some of us have spelling sentences to do for homework.
Danny brought in a cocoon. It will turn into a butterfly.

---

child recalled an event, she seemed to form the goal of noting the time at which the event occurred. After noting when the event occurred, she pursued the goal of describing her reaction to the event. These prearranged sequences of goals reduced the processing demands of the writing task by suggesting content beyond sheer occurrence of events.

Facility in managing less-stereotyped sequences of goals also develops during the elementary school years. Goldman (1983) presented fourth- and sixth-graders with brief stories and asked them to summarize the stories in a single sentence. When a story contained a clear topic sentence, children of both ages used it as the summary. When the story lacked a topic sentence, sixth-graders usually generated one of their own. Fourth-graders, however, rarely generated their own topic sentences. Presumably, the older children focused more clearly on the paragraph's goal, and this enabled them to capture the point of the paragraph in a single sentence. In general, ability to separate goals from details, and to state the goals clearly may be a key part of what develops in the acquisition of writing skills.

Helping young elementary school children to consider two or more goals simultaneously and to relate these goals to each other may improve their writing. Bereiter and Scardamalia (1982) found that a surprisingly simple instructional approach effectively promoted this objective. They gave children a deck of cards with common sentence openings: "Similarly,"

"For example," "On the other hand," and so on. Children were asked to use these prompts when they could not think of what to say next. The logic was that these sentence openings would lead children to consider relations between previous sentences and statements that children might add. The prompts led to children writing essays with more content, and more richly interconnected content, even though the prompts did not specify what the content should be.

As people develop expertise in writing, they progress from the knowledge-telling strategy to the *knowledge-transforming strategy*. This more-advanced approach is based on an internal comparison between what the writer would like to say and what he or she has actually written. Professional writers use this strategy on a regular basis, but it also is used by many other adults when they are knowledgeable about, and interested in, the topic of their essay. The strategy begins with an analysis of the problem and the setting of goals that will communicate a point of view. Subsequent cognitive activities include moving back and forth between knowledge of the content area being discussed and knowledge of rhetorical devices that can be used to translate content into the desired form. A fortunate by-product of using the knowledge-transforming strategy is that the writing process itself often increases the writers' knowledge. Trying to communicate a position forces them to confront gaps or inadequacies in their thinking, which often deepens their understanding.

The trend toward greater use of the knowledge-transforming strategy can be seen in the amount of time spent thinking before beginning to write. In general, college students take *more* time before they start writing than do fifth-graders (Zbrodoff, 1984; cited in Bereiter & Scardamalia, 1987). They spend this time deciding what they will say and organizing their thoughts into coherent form.

The flexibility with which writers adapt to task constraints also increases with age. Fifth-graders take the same (minimal) amount of time to start, regardless of time and length constraints. This is what would be expected from use of the knowledge-telling strategy; writing begins as soon as a direct response to the question can be generated. In contrast, college students increase their planning time when the assignment requires a longer essay and when they have more time to complete it. This reflects their modifying the goals of their writing to fit task demands and the resources at hand.

*Mechanical requirements.*    A third type of difficulty involved in writing but not in speaking involves the mechanical requirements of forming letters, ordering the letters into correctly spelled words, and putting capital letters and punctuation marks in the right places. These mechanical demands force many children to proceed so slowly that they lose track of what they wanted to say.

To test the effects of mechanical demands and slow rate of production on the quality of children's writing, Bereiter and Scardamalia (1982) asked fourth- and sixth-graders to compose essays under one of three conditions. In the typical writing condition, children wrote as they ordinarily would, thus encountering both the mechanical demands of writing and its slow rate. In the slow dictation condition, they dictated their essays to a scribe who had been trained to write at the child's typical writing speed. This released children from the mechanical requirements of writing but not from its slow rate. In the standard dictation condition, children dictated into a tape recorder at their normal speaking pace. This released them from both the mechanical requirements and the slow rate of ordinary writing.

Children in the standard dictation condition, burdened by neither mechanical demands nor slow rate, produced the best essays. Children in the slow dictation condition, burdened by slow rate but not by mechanical demands, produced the next-best essays. Children in the typical writing condition, burdened by both slow rate and mechanical demands, produced the worst essays. The findings suggest that teaching children to type or use word processors efficiently would improve the quality of their writing, since it would allow them to go faster and not worry about shaping letters carefully. The hypothesis certainly seems worth testing.

### Revision

Most first drafts could benefit from revision. Unfortunately, elementary school children, whose drafts typically could most benefit from changes, rarely review what they have written. Even when they do, the revisions do not consistently result in improved quality (Fitzgerald, 1987). This raises the question of why revisions tend to be so inadequate.

Revision can be divided into two main processes: the identification of weaknesses and their correction (Baker & Brown, 1984). To identify weaknesses, people must compare a unit of text, such as a sentence or paragraph, with an internal representation of the text's intended properties. Such a comparison requires the writer to be clear about the goals that the unit of text was intended to serve, even when the actual material leads attention in a quite different direction.

Children, as well as many adults, have difficulty identifying weaknesses in texts. For example in Beal (1990), children needed to correct experimentally generated essays that included such glaring errors as missing sentences, impossible-to-interpret sentences, and directly contradictory sentences. Despite the large problems with these essays, fourth-graders detected only 25 percent of the problems and sixth graders only 60 percent.

In the more-typical case where children need to revise their own compositions, egocentrism exacerbates the difficulty of detecting weaknesses. Children experience considerable difficulty separating what they themselves know from what their readers could reasonably be expected to know. To illustrate this point, Bartlett (1982) asked children to revise either their own essay or an essay written by a classmate. The focus was on how well children detected two types of errors: grammatical mistakes and ambiguous references. If egocentrism contributed to the problem of recognizing weaknesses, children presumably would have especially great difficulty correcting their own referential ambiguities, since they understood the ambiguous references they had written (e.g., "The policeman and the robber fought. He was killed."). In revising other children's essays, however, there was no particular reason to expect this type of mistake to be harder to correct than the grammatical errors.

The children's revisions followed exactly this pattern. Children were quite good at noticing other children's referential ambiguities. They were much less good at recognizing their own. Performance in detecting grammatical errors, where egocentrism would not be as much an issue, was more similar for their own and other children's essays. A major part of the development of revision skills, then, may be ability to separate one's own perspective from that of the reader.

One inference that might be drawn from this interpretation is that it would be advisable to wait awhile between writing and revising. The logic is that psychological and temporal closeness to the composition would increase egocentrism in the period immediately after the piece was written, and thus interfere with efforts at revision. With time, greater objectivity might be possible.

Such advice does not seem to get at the heart of the problem, though. The quality of fourth-to-twelfth graders' revisions is no better when they revise an essay a week after writing it than when they revise immediately (Bereiter & Scardamalia, 1982). It appears, therefore, that students may as well begin revising as soon after writing as is convenient. Waiting, in and of itself, does not seem to help.

Even when children detect a problem in their writing, they still must repair it. Fortunately, children usually accomplish such repairs reasonably effectively, at least when they recognize the problem spontaneously. This is true for both older and younger writers. For example, when fourth- and sixth-graders in Beal (1990) detected an error without anyone pointing it out to them, they both were very likely to correct it successfully. The case was different with weaknesses that adults pointed out to children after the children had missed them themselves. The older students were more effective in adjusting their perspective to deal with these problems. Again, the main source of improvement in revision seems to be increasing flexibility in keeping in mind multiple perspectives. Such flexibility helps both in noticing problems and in correcting problems that other people point out. Thus, in writing, as in mathematics and reading comprehension, ability to coordinate diverse types of knowledge, and to shift attention flexibly among them, seems to lie at the heart of successful performance and learning.

## SUMMARY

The separation between cognitive development and educational psychology is steadily diminishing. The reason is that children's thinking inside the classroom influences, and is influenced by, their thinking outside it. This can be seen in mathematics, reading, and writing.

Even before they enter school, children successfully add and subtract small numbers. They choose adaptively among a variety of alternative strategies for solving particular problems. Development of arithmetic involves improvement in speed and accuracy, which comes about both because of increasing use of faster strategies and because of improvements in the speed and accuracy with which each strategy is executed. Accurate use of backup strategies appears to create the knowledge necessary for efficient retrieval of correct answers. Individual differences among children are evident both in amount of knowledge and in the types of strategies that are preferred.

Learning mathematics requires three types of competence: procedural, conceptual, and utilizational. Many children experience difficulty in coordinating procedures, principles underlying the procedures, and knowledge of when the procedures should be used. Lack of such integration gives rise to a variety of misconceptions and distortions, among them buggy subtraction rules, inability to estimate quantities when exact computation is not possible, and justification of algebraic manipulations through reference to distorted versions of the distributive and associative laws.

Learning to read involves acquisition of prereading skills, word-identification skills, and comprehension capabilities. Among the most important prereading skills are letter perception and phonemic awareness. Efficient letter perception demands knowledge of features that distinguish letters from each other, such as large curves, small curves, and vertical and diagonal lines. Phonemic awareness involves ability to isolate sounds that comprise words. Ability to isolate the individual sounds may help children blend them together when they read words. Consistent with this view, teaching phonemic awareness skills to preschoolers and to poor-reading first-graders has led to durable increases in reading achievement.

Children use two main word-identification methods: phonological recoding and visually based retrieval. Both methods begin with examination of the printed word and end with access to the word's meaning and pronunciation in long-term memory. Phonological recoding also involves an intermediate step in which print is translated into sounds. The two skills are related in that accurate phonological recoding may aid development of strong associations between the printed word and its long-term memory entry and thus aid visually based retrieval. In addition, clues from the surrounding context may aid word identification.

Reading comprehension draws on virtually all of the intellectual skills children possess. Among the most important sources of development in reading comprehension are automatization of word identification, ability to hold longer phrases in memory, increasing content knowledge, improved comprehension monitoring, and increasingly flexible utilization of strategies such as skimming. Helping children understand critical background content and improve their comprehension monitoring has resulted in substantial improvements in reading comprehension.

Writing is a challenging task for most children. They have difficulty establishing clear goals in the absence of the prompts and feedback that conversation usually provides. They also have difficulty reconciling the competing demands of executing the mechanics of writing, forming grammatical sentences, expressing meanings, and keeping the reader's reaction in mind.

Children in the early and middle elementary school grades often adopt a knowledge-telling strategy to cope with these demands. The strategy involves stating a reaction to the question that was posed and then listing supporting evidence in the order in which it is retrieved from memory. The strategy produces coherent but uninspired compositions. A major change that occurs with age and experience in writing is improved ability to coordinate goals, so as to produce more extensive and more interesting essays. This eventually enables writers to progress to the knowledge-transforming strategy, a strategy that demands more planning but that pays off in higher-quality products.

Skill at revising also improves with age and experience. The largest gains seem to come in recognition of problems in the text. Once children recognize the problems, they are reasonably skillful at fixing them. Underlying the improvement in identifying problems is growing ability to separate one's own knowledge from that which readers would be likely to have.

## RECOMMENDED READINGS

Beck, I. L., & McKeown, M. G. (1984). Application of theories of reading to instruction. *American Journal of Education, 93,* 61–81. A successful instructional program in reading, based on a detailed analysis of the hidden prerequisites for understanding the story.

Bereiter, C., & Scardamalia, M. (1987). *The psychology of written composition.* Hillsdale, NJ: Erlbaum. An excellent summary of what is known about the psychology of children's writing and how to improve it.

Palincsar, A. S. & Brown, A. L. (1984). Reciprocal teaching of comprehension-monitoring activities. *Cognition and Instruction, 1,* 117–175. Perhaps the most-successful application of cognitive psychological principles to the task of improving learning in the schools. Seventh-graders with serious reading-comprehension problems became able to comprehend at an above-average level through participation in this program.

**Siegler, R. S. & Shrager, J. (1984).** *Strategy choices in addition and subtraction: How do children know what to do?* **In C. Sophian (Ed.),** *Origins of cognitive skills.* **Hillsdale, NJ: Erlbaum.** This article raises the issue of how children choose among alternative strategies and presents a model that explains how they do so in addition and subtraction.

**Waters, H. S. (1980). "Class news": A single-subject longitudinal study of prose production and schema formation during childhood.** *Journal of Verbal Learning and Verbal Behavior, 19,* **152–167.** Documents the progress of one girl learning to write throughout a school year. Illustrates the importance of organized sequences of goals in the learning process.

# 10

## Conclusions for the Present; Challenges for the Future

"So how *do* children think?"
(A 7-year-old, reacting to her father's description of what this book is about)

Previous chapters have focused separately on perception, language, memory, conceptualization, problem solving, and other areas of cognitive development. The division has made it easier to consider the unique properties of children's thinking in each area. However, such divisions can obscure the qualities that diverse aspects of children's thinking have in common. The two main goals of this concluding chapter are to discuss these common features and to identify issues about children's thinking that seem likely to be central in the future.

In the opening chapter of the book, eight themes were listed that apply to many aspects of children's thinking. These continuing themes also provide the framework for this final chapter. The chapter is divided into eight sections, with each section focusing on a particular theme. The first part of each discussion is used to summarize what is known at present that is relevant to the theme. The second part is used to consider issues that are just beginning to be addressed or that need to be addressed in the future. Among these are some of the largest, and most interesting, issues about children's thinking, such as the contributions to cognitive growth of biologi-

TABLE 10–1    Chapter Outline

I.   The most basic issues about children's thinking are "What develops?" and "How does development occur?"
    A.   Current Knowledge About What Develops and How Development Occurs
    B.   Future Issues

II.   Development is about change. Four change processes that seem to be particularly large contributors to cognitive development are automatization, encoding, generalization, and strategy construction.
    A.   Current Knowledge About Change Processes
    B.   Future Issues

III.   Infants and very young children are far more cognitively competent than they appear. They possess a rich set of abilities that allow them to make rapid cognitive progress.
    A.   Current Knowledge About Early Competence
    B.   Future Issues

IV.   Differences between age groups tend to be ones of degree rather than kind. Not only are young children more cognitively competent than they appear, but older children and adults are less competent than we might think.
    A.   Current Knowledge About Differences Between Age Groups
    B.   Future Issues

V.   Changes in children's thinking do not occur in a vacuum. What children already know about material they encounter influences not only how much they learn but also what they learn.
    A.   Current Knowledge About the Effects of Existing Knowledge
    B.   Future Issues

VI.   The development of intelligence results in large part from increasingly effective deployment of limited processing resources.
    A.   Current Knowledge About Children's Deployment of Processing Resources
    B.   Future Issues

VII.   Children's thinking develops within a social context. Parents, peers, teachers, and the overall society influence what children think about, as well as how and why they come to think in particular ways.
    A.   Current Knowledge of Social Influences on Children's Thinking
    B.   Future Issues

VIII.   We have learned quite a bit about cognitive development, but there is far more left to learn.

IX.   Summary

cal maturation and of the social environment. The chapter's organization is summarized in Table 10–1.

*1. The most basic issues about children's thinking are "What develops?" and "How does development occur?"*

When investigators of children's thinking write in journal articles, "The purpose of this investigation is . . . ," they almost never complete the sentence with "to try to find out what develops" or "to try to find out how development occurs." Modesty, and the realization that no one study is likely to resolve these issues, prevents researchers from mentioning them. Yet they are the deepest motivations of research on children's thinking. Always keeping them in mind is critical to understanding what the research is all about.

### Current Knowledge About What Develops and How Development Occurs

On a few occasions, investigators have tried to address directly the question of what develops. In one of these instances, Brown and DeLoache (1978) noted four potential answers in the domain of memory development: basic processes, strategies, metacognition, and content knowledge. These potential sources of memory development provide a useful guide for thinking about what develops in all areas of cognitive development.

Many examples from previous chapters attest to the pervasive contribution to development of changes in these four types of capabilities. Improvements in basic processes were not invoked only to explain improved functioning of sensory, short-term, and long-term memory (e.g., Kail, 1986b). They also were used to explain changes in complexity of the stimuli infants prefer to look at (Banks & Salapatek, 1981), in consistency of reliance on the mutual exclusivity constraint in toddlers' vocabulary acquisition (Merriman & Bowman, 1989), in kindergarteners' success in making transitive inferences (Halford, 1984), and in school-age children's recognition of analogies (Bisanz, 1979). Similarly, changes in strategies were seen in contexts other than rehearsal, organization, and the other mnemonic strategies. Improved strategies also helped children solve increasing numbers of class inclusion, time judgment, and measurement problems (Levin & Wilkening, 1989: Miller, 1989; Trabasso et al., 1978), to use the *ed* ending to generate past-tense verbs (Brown et al., 1969), to allocate attention increasingly systematically (Vurpillot, 1968), and to write more-elaborate descriptions of the day's events on "class news" assignments (Waters, 1980). Improved metacognition not only aided memory functioning (Schneider & Pressley, 1989), it also allowed high school students to take notes that were more useful than those of students in junior high (Brown et al., 1978), allowed adults to teach route planning more effectively than fourth-graders (Gauvain & Rogoff, 1989), allowed normal children to plan problem-solving approaches more effectively than retarded children (Sternberg, 1984), and allowed poor comprehenders to improve their understanding of what they were reading (Palincsar & Brown, 1984). Finally, superior knowledge of the content under consideration enabled toddlers to identify causes more successfully (Shultz, 1982), first-graders to add and to read words more efficiently (Jorm & Share,

1983; Siegler, 1987b), and high school and college students to understand the reversibility of conventional time systems involving days of the week and months of the year (Friedman, 1986), as well as helping people of all ages to remember more about chess configurations, dinosaurs, baseball games, etc. (e.g., Chi, 1978).

Hypotheses about how development occurs, like hypotheses about what develops, reflect the interconnectedness of cognitive development. Recall some of the diverse contexts in which encoding and related processes were used to explain changes in children's thinking. Gibson et al.'s (1968) explanation of how children learn to discriminate among letters of the alphabet and Gough and Hillinger's (1980) explanation of how they learn to read their first words emphasized encoding of distinctive features. Klahr's (1984) explanation of how children acquire the concept of number and Siegler's (1976) explanation of acquisition of knowledge about balance scales also emphasized encoding. So did Tversky and Hemenway's (1984) explanation of the development from child-basic to standard-basic categories (the standard categories emerge once children encode the functions served by slots in round coin banks and wicks on round candles) and Ericsson et al.'s (1980) explanation of S. F.'s prodigious memory feats (he learned to encode numbers as running times and then developed complex hierarchies of encodings.)

### Future Issues

The single advance with the greatest potential for improving our understanding of children's thinking would be new theories of cognitive development that are both broadly applicable and precisely stated. Such theories could focus attention on critical issues, raise questions that have not been considered before, and serve as a point of departure from which to formulate new ideas. Thus, they could be valuable even if they were not correct in all particulars. (No theory ever is.)

For many years, Piaget's theory served these integrative and agenda-setting functions. From the 1960s through the early 1980s, arguments between "pro-Piagetians" and "anti-Piagetians" dominated journals, books, and conferences. An outgoing editor of the journal *Child Development* noted that in one year of his tenure, enough articles were submitted on whether preschoolers could learn to conserve that he need not have published anything else to fill all of the journal's pages (Jeffrey, 1975 and personal communication).

Those days are past. Very few researchers today would argue that it is impossible for preschoolers to learn conservation, class inclusion, and other concrete operational concepts. Equally few would argue that young children's difficulty in succeeding on the standard versions of these tasks is due to some artifact of the methodology. Instead, most have adopted the more-moderate position that children encounter genuine difficulty understanding these concepts, but that they have some understanding of the concepts from quite young ages and that with appropriate experience, they gradually acquire greater understanding.

Moderation has its virtues, but also its costs. Piaget was right in some of his views and wrong in others, but right or wrong, his theory lent coherence to findings about many aspects of children's thinking. What is needed now is a successor that has the virtues of Piaget's theory while surmounting at least some of the drawbacks. That is, a theory is needed that, like Piaget's, incorporates the entire age range from infancy to adolescence; that addresses areas as diverse as problem solving, memory, and moral judgments; and that uncovers heretofore unknown changes in children's thinking. Beyond this, our ideal theory would add precise analyses of change mechanisms and extensive analysis of how input from the external world contributes to development. It also would generate testable hypotheses and not make predictions inconsistent with known data.

In previous chapters, we encountered a number of efforts at formulating such broad yet detailed theories—among them, the theories advanced by Case, Halford, Keil, Klahr, Markman, Sternberg, and me. Each of these theories has added to our understanding of cognitive development, but no one of them has captured the imagination of the field as Piaget's theory did. It is possible that we simply know too much today, that no one theory can capture all that is known about children's thinking. However, predictions that something cannot be done have a bad track record. Forty years ago, experts believed that no human being would ever run a four-minute mile. Since then, literally hundreds of runners have done so. Closer to home, we need only consider S. F.'s prodigious memory feats; he learned to memorize three or four times as many numbers as had been thought possible. Thus, the type of encompassing but precise theory that seems needed may well emerge in the near future.

*2. Development is about change. Four change processes that seem to be particularly large contributors to cognitive development are automatization, encoding, generalization, and strategy construction.*

### Current Knowledge About Change Processes

Perhaps the single greatest obstacle to generating more-advanced theories of what develops and how development occurs is our underdeveloped knowledge of change processes. Many current hypotheses about developmental mechanisms seem to be generally in the right direction, but are too imprecise to generate satisfying predictions or explanations. A symptom of the problem is the bewildering variety of terms that are used to describe ideas that are clearly related, and that may be identical. Until the ideas are worked out in greater detail, it will remain impossible to know exactly how they relate to each other. Although current understanding is not all we would like, considerable evidence testifies to the importance of four families of change processes: automatization, encoding, generalization, and strategy construction. *Automatization* refers to increasingly efficient execution of a procedure that frees mental resources for other purposes. Related concepts include parallel processing, expanded processing capacity, and increased processing speed. *Encoding* refers to internally representing objects and events in terms of sets of features and their relations. Ideas that overlap substantially with encoding include discrimination, differentiation, assimilation, and identification of critical features. *Generalization* refers to extrapolating known relations to new cases. Induction, abstraction, transfer, regularity detection, and analogical reasoning name similar concepts. Finally, *strategy construction* involves putting together the results of the other processes to adapt to task demands. Related ideas include rule formation, accommodation, strategy discovery, and executive processing.

Although understanding of how these mechanisms operate leaves something to be desired, each family of processes undoubtedly contributes to a wide range of developments. A few of these are alluded to in Table 10–2.

The four processes seem important not only for each process's individual contribution to development, but also for their joint contribution. They can be viewed as being hierarchically related to each other. Automatizing a procedure frees attentional resources for encoding previously ignored variables. Encoding the new variables provides data about their relations to

**TABLE 10–2    Some Demonstrations of the Importance of Automatization, Encoding, Generalization, and Strategy Construction**

| *PROCESS* | *DOMAIN* | *INVESTIGATORS* |
|---|---|---|
| Automatization | Writing of essays | Bereiter and Scardamalia (1987) |
| | Use of memory strategies | Guttentag (1984) |
| | General theory of development | Case (1985) |
| Encoding | Forming standard basic concepts | Tversky and Hemenway (1984) |
| | Identifying letters of the alphabet | Gibson et al. (1968) |
| | General theory of development | Sternberg (1985) |
| Generalization | Acquisition of syntax | Maratsos (1982) |
| | Learning of concepts | Rosch and Mervis (1975) |
| | General theory of development | Klahr and Wallace (1976) |
| Strategy construction | Route planning | Gauvain and Rogoff (1989) |
| | Use of measurement techniques | Miller (1989) |
| | General theory of development | Siegler and Jenkins (1989) |

outcomes, thus paving the way for generalizations to be drawn. Generalizing the effects of these newly encoded variables motivates construction of new strategies based on the general pattern.

To get a feel for how these processes might together produce development in a particular area, think about the counting-on strategy for adding numbers (Chapters 3 and 9). This strategy involves choosing the larger addend and counting up from it the number of times indicated by the smaller addend. On 2 + 5 and 5 + 2, for example, a child using the counting-on strategy would note that 5 was the larger addend, count 5, 6, 7," and answer, "7."

Each of the four processes probably contributes to acquisition of counting-on. Constructing the strategy depends on having previously formed the generalization that adding a + b always yields the same answer as adding b + a. Otherwise, there would be no basis for always counting from the larger number, regardless of the ordering of the addends. Forming this generalization, in turn, depends on appropriate encoding. To learn that the order of the addends is irrelevant, children need to encode the features of "first addend" and "second addend," as well as the particular numbers within each problem. Finally, encoding not only the particular numbers being added but also the abstract categories of "first addend" and "second addend" probably requires a high degree of automatization of the execution of other processes, such as counting, so that they do not require all of the child's processing resources. Only then will encoding of new, potentially useful, relations be possible.

### Future Issues

The single contribution that could best further understanding of change almost certainly is precise models of how particular change mechanisms operate. As Flavell (1984) noted, "Good theorizing about mechanisms is very, very hard to do" (p. 189). Nonetheless, efforts to characterize the workings of change mechanisms are starting to yield real progress, as evidenced by the ideas presented in several recent books: *Mechanisms of Cognitive Development* (Sternberg, 1989), *Mechanisms of Language Acquisition* (MacWhinney, 1987), and *Transition Mechanisms in Child Development* (deRibaupierre, 1989).

One particularly promising effort to specify how change mechanisms operate involves *connectionist models*. These are computer simulations that are based on an analogy to the complex set of interconnections among neurons within the brain. Consistent with this analogy, connectionist approaches, like the human brain, involve parallel processing of large numbers of interconnected processing units. Also as with the brain, learning is produced by strengthening some connections and weakening others.

To illustrate how connectionist models can advance understanding of cognitive development, we focus on a recent model of this type (Mac-Whinney, Leinbach, Taraban, & McDonald, 1989) that depicted how German children acquire their language's system of definite articles. These definite articles are the multiple terms that in German serve the function that the single word *the* serves in English. The task was of interest precisely because the German article system is so difficult. Which article should be used to modify a given noun depends on several features of the noun being modified: its gender (masculine, feminine, or neuter), number (singular or plural), and role within the sentence (subject, possessor, direct object, or indirect object). To make matters worse, assignment of nouns to gender categories is often nonintuitive. For example, the word for *fork* is feminine, the word for *spoon* is masculine, and the word for *knife* is neuter. Maratsos and Chalkley (1980) argued that neither semantic nor phonological cues predict which article accompanies a given noun, and that children could not learn the system by relying on these relatively straightforward cues. However, MacWhinney et al. built a connectionist model that demonstrated the opposite possibility: that although the relation is complex, the phonological and semantic properties of nouns are sufficient to allow children to learn which article to use with a given noun in a given situation.

The MacWhinney et al. model, like most current connectionist models, involves an *input level,* several *hidden levels,* and an *output level* (Figure 10–1). Each of these levels contains a number of discrete units. For example, in the MacWhinney et al. model, the 35 units within the input level represent features of the noun that is to be modified by the article. Each of the two hidden levels includes multiple units that represent combinations of these input-level features. The six output units represent the six articles in the German language that correspond to *the* in English.

As noted above, a central feature of such connectionist models is the very large number of connections among processing units. As shown in the figure, in the MacWhinney et al. model, each input-level unit is connected to first-level hidden units; each first-level hidden unit is connected to second-level hidden units; and each second-level hidden unit is connected to each of the six output units. Learning within this and other connectionist models is achieved through a cycle of (1) the system being presented initial input (in this case, a noun in a certain context); (2) projecting on the basis of the strengths of its various connections (which reflect past experience) what output is required; and then (3) adjusting the strengths of connections between units so that connections that suggested the correct answer are strengthened and connections that suggested the wrong answer are weakened.

MacWhinney et al. tested this system's ability to master the German article system by repeatedly presenting the system 102 common German nouns. Frequency of presentation of each noun was proportional to the frequency with which the nouns are used in German. The simulation

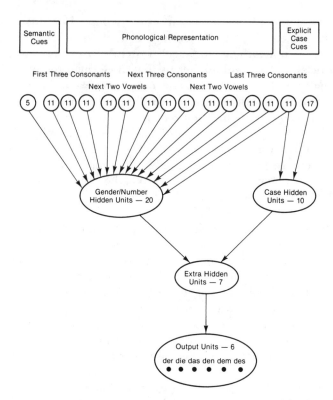

**FIGURE 10–1**    MacWhinney et al. (1989) connectionist model of how children learn German grammar, in particular the system of articles. Note that at the top (input) level, the model encodes five semantic cues about the noun, presence or absence of 11 phonological features at as many as 13 positions within the noun, and 17 explicit case cues, involving the function of the noun within the sentence. These input-level units transfer activation to hidden units and eventually to the six output units, which correspond to the six articles that accompany nouns in German. The article with the greatest activation is the one chosen to accompany the noun in the particular context.

needed to choose which article to use with each noun in the particular context. After it did this, the correct answer was presented, and the simulation adjusted connection strengths so as to optimize its accuracy in the future.

Following experience with this training set, the MacWhinney et al. simulation chose the correct article for 98 percent of the nouns in the original set. This could not be attributed simply to rote learning of the possible article–noun combinations. When the simulation was presented a previously encountered noun in a novel context, it chose the correct article on 92 percent of trials, despite the noun's often taking a different article in the new context than it had in the previously encountered ones. The simulation also proved able to generalize to entirely novel nouns. The 48 most frequent nouns in German that had not been included in the original input set were presented in a variety of sentence contexts. On this completely novel set, the simulation chose the correct article from the six possibilities on 61 percent of trials, versus 17 percent expected by chance. Thus, the system's learning mechanism, together with its representation of the noun's phonological and semantic properties and the context, produced a good guess about what article would accompany a given noun, even when the noun was entirely unfamiliar.

The simulation's learning paralleled children's learning in a number of ways. Early in the learning process, the simulation, like children whose first language is German, tended to overuse the articles that accompany feminine nouns. The reason appeared to be that this form of the articles is used most often within the language. The simulation also showed the same type of overgeneralization patterns that are often interpreted as reflecting rule use when they occur in children's language. For example, although the noun *Kleid* (which mean *clothing*) should be accompanied by neuter articles, the simulation acted as if it were masculine—it invariably chose the article that would accompany the noun if it were masculine. Further, the same article–noun combinations that are the most difficult for children proved to be the most difficult for the simulation to learn and to generalize to on the basis of previously learned examples.

How was the simulation able to produce such generalization and rule-like behavior without any specific rules? The basic mechanism involved adjusting connection strengths between input, hidden, and output units to reflect the frequency with which combinations of features of nouns were associated with each article. Although no one feature predicted very well which article would be used, the combination of phonological, semantic, and contextual cues allowed quite accurate prediction of which articles should be chosen.

On the basis of the simulation, MacWhinney et al. (see also Bates & MacWhinney, 1987) proposed several determinants of generalization: availability, detectability, reliability, and conflict reliability. *Availability* is the frequency with which a feature is present. The more frequently a feature is present, the more quickly that children will learn its predictive value and apply it to new cases. *Detectability* involves the ease of noticing a feature. Features that are difficult to notice will not have much impact, even if they are widely available. *Reliability* is the predictive accuracy of a feature when it is present. The more accurately a feature predicts outcomes, the greater weight it will be given. This will be especially true of features that not only predict well in general but that are also reliable when they point to a different outcome than other features do; MacWhinney labeled this quality *conflict reliability*.

Although this model involved language development, MacWhinney suggested that the depiction of generalization and learning applies to other aspects of cognitive development as well. For example, he proposed that the order in which different features play dominant roles is the same across many areas. Availability and detectability are especially influential early in learning; then, overall reliability becomes the dominant influence; finally, conflict reliability beomes preeminent. The hypothesis suggests that as children gain experience, they shift from relying primarily on easy-to-gather information to relying on information that may be less commonly available and harder to obtain but that is more specifically relevant to the task. This seems a plausible outline of how generalization operates in many contexts, both in language and in other areas. More generally, the analysis illustrates how very-specific analyses of change mechanisms can yield broadly applicable conclusions about cognitive growth.

*3. Infants and very young children are far more cognitively competent than they appear. They possess a rich set of abilities that allow them to make rapid cognitive progress.*

### Current Knowledge About Early Competence

Literally from the day they emerge from the womb, infants accurately perceive the relative distance of objects from themselves (Granrud, 1989). They also can identify the direction from which sounds come (Muir et al., 1979) and prefer listening to tape recordings of stories read to them before birth (Spence & DeCasper, 1982). By 6 months of age, their seeing and hearing resemble those of adults in a great many ways.

The early competence is not restricted to perception. Infants less than 1 year old possess a variety of concepts, including primitive notions of time (Lester et al., 1985), space (Bertenthal et al., 1984), number (Starkey & Cooper, 1980), and causality (Leslie, 1982). By 18 months, toddlers can remember where objects were hidden and search efficiently for them (DeLoache et al., 1985), begin to invent gestural languages for expressing meanings that they cannot express in words (Acredolo & Goodwyn, 1985; Goldin-Meadow & Morford, 1985), and solve problems by planning routes (Benson et al., 1989) and using tools (Brown, 1989).

One reason that children are able to do so much so quickly is that they possess a variety of broadly applicable learning processes. From the day they are born, infants orient their attention toward moving objects, bright lights, loud noises, and other potentially informative stimuli (Cohen, 1972; Haith, 1979). They also associate objects with each other, recognize familiar objects, and generalize to objects that are similar but not identical to ones they have seen earlier (Rovee & Fagen, 1976; Siqueland & Lipsitt, 1966). At least by age 3 months, they form expectancies and abstract prototypical patterns (Bomba & Siqueland, 1983; Haith et al., 1988). By 10 months, they detect correlations among features and use them to form new concepts (Younger & Cohen, 1983), and also use means–ends analysis to solve problems (Case, 1985; Willats, 1984).

These general learning processes are not the only reason for children's early cognitive competence. Children's thinking also seems to be biased in certain directions that help them learn. Perceptual and conceptual development seem to be guided by valid assumptions about the nature of physical objects. Infants less than 6 months old already seem to expect that all parts of a physical object will move together and that objects cannot occupy the spaces occupied by other objects (Kellman & Spelke, 1983). Similarly, from age 2½, and perhaps earlier, children seem to expect that new words will not mean the same thing as existing words (the mutual exclusivity constraint) (Markman, 1989; Merriman & Bowman, 1989). Generally, even very young children seem biased toward assigning causal relations a central position in their concepts (Keil, 1989) and toward using the causal relations to guide memory for stories and events (Bauer & Mandler, 1989b).

It is important to remember that these early competencies are part of the story of cognitive development, but only part. In all cases, there are large differences between the understandings of young children and those of older ones. However, taken together, the early competencies, the powerful general learning mechanisms, and the more-specific biases to think of the world in certain ways result in exceptionally rapid cognitive growth in the first few years.

### Future Issues

The fast pace of early cognitive development, together with the rapid biological maturation during the same period, raises the issue of how these early biological and cognitive changes are related. The reason this issue has not previously been discussed at length has nothing to do with its inherent importance. The human brain undergoes huge changes in the years after birth. These changes must profoundly influence cognitive development. Rather, the reason this fundamental issue has received little attention is that understanding of the relation between brain maturation and cognitive development is only beginning to emerge. Recent advances in cognitive-developmental neuroscience, however, indicate that much more will soon be known.

Particularly promising is work on *synaptogenesis,* the development of synaptic connections within the brain. To understand what synaptogenesis involves, a little background is necessary. The brain is made up of approximately 100 billion individual cells, or *neurons.* Each neuron involves three types of features: a cell nucleus; a large number of fibers, known as *dendrites,* that bring information from other neurons to the cell nucleus; and

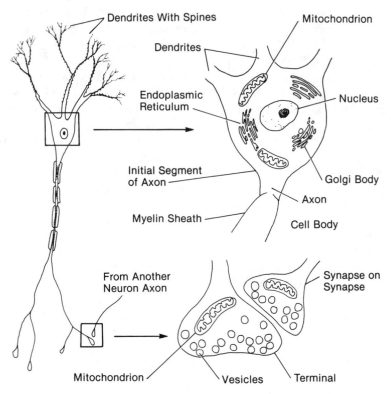

**FIGURE 10–2** Schematic diagram of a neuron (left), including dendrites, cell body, and axon. The cell body (top right) contains all the same organelles as other cells. The initial segment of the axon where it leaves the cell body is naked, not covered with myelin. The terminals of the axon include small, round vesicles that contain neuro-transmitter chemicals (bottom right). The axon itself has no synapses on it, except sometimes at its synaptic terminals, where other neuron axon terminals may form "synapses on synapses" (after Thompson, 1985).

one (or sometimes more) larger fibers, known as *axons*, that transmit information from the cell nucleus to other neurons (Figure 10–2).

Most axons are relatively large at the point where they leave the cell nucleus. Further away, however, they tend to divide into many small fibers. These fibers often end in knoblike structures, across from which is a tiny space, and then another knoblike structure attached to the dendrite of a different neuron. This point of functional contact between neurons is called the *synapse*.

Information is transmitted from one neuron to another when chemicals, known as *neurotransmitters*, are released by the knoblike projection at the end of an axon fiber, travel across the small synaptic separation, and are received by the knoblike projection at the end of the other neuron's dendrite. In an adult, a single neuron often has more than 1,000 synapses with other neurons, which allows for the simultaneous spread of information to diverse areas of the brain (Thompson, 1985).

With this background, the term *synaptogenesis* can be defined. It is the development of synaptic connections (synapses) between neurons.

The growth of synapses within many parts of the brain follows a distinctive developmental course, in which there is initial overproduction and later pruning of synaptic connections. For example, Huttenlocher (1979) reported that the average number of synaptic connections in one part of the frontal lobe increased 10-fold between birth and 12 months. The density of synapses continued to increase until age 2, after which it gradually decreased to adult levels. These adult levels were reached by about age 7; from age 6 months to age 7 years, synaptic density in the children's brains exceeded adult levels.

This synaptic overproduction appears to make possible many types of cognitive growth. The specific form that the growth takes is determined by experience, in which synaptic connections that are used are maintained and those that are not used are pruned back (Greenough et al., 1987). The pruning back of unneeded synapses makes possible more-efficient future processing.

Below, we first consider one of the general conceptual advances that has emerged from recent work on synaptogenesis—the distinction between experience-expectant and experience-dependent processes. Then the focus turns to one of the specific advances that has grown out of the work—how maturation of the frontal lobe of the brain between 6 and 12 months contributes to acquisition of object permanence and related competencies.

*Experience-expectant and experience-dependent processes.*    One of the deepest issues about cognitive development concerns whether development and learning are fundamentally similar or fundamentally different (Liben, 1987b). In general, acquisitions tend to be attributed to development when they are universal across cultures and individual children, and when they consistently occur at a particular age. Acquisitions tend to be attributed to learning when they are acquired in some cultures but not others, by some individuals but not others, and at a variety of ages. These distinctions leave open the basic questions, however, of whether the processes that give rise to development and learning are the same or different.

A recent conceptual distinction that arose within cognitive-developmental neuroscience—that between experience-expectant and experience-dependent processes—is advancing understanding of the relation between learning and development. *Experience-expectant* processes involve the "development" end of the development-learning continuum. The processes are hypothesized to be based on the synaptic overproduction and pruning just described. Greenough et al. (1987) suggested that in experience-expectant processes the initial overproduction of synapses is maturationally regulated, but which ones are pruned depends on experience. Normal experience at the normal time results in neural activity that maintains typical connections; lack of such experience at the usual time results in atypical connections. Thus, there is a sensitive period (Bornstein, 1989) in which relevant experience must occur for the experience to have the usual effect on brain development. The type of experience that is relevant to such experience-expectant processes is experience that has been widely available throughout the evolutionary history of the species.

Greenough et al. suggested that one advantage of such experience-expectant processes is that they allow both efficient acquisition in normal environments and reasonable adaptation to abnormal environments. In particular, the genes provide a rough outline of the eventual form of the process, thus facilitating acquisition under normal circumstances. Unusual environments or physical deficiencies, however, lead to different neural activity, which creates alternative organizations of brain activity that are adaptive given the atypical circumstances.

The other side of Greenough et al.'s dichotomy involves *experience-dependent* processes. These are the neural substrate of what is usually thought of as learning. With experience-dependent processes, formation of synaptic connections depends on experiences that vary widely among individuals in whether and when they occur. The experience-dependent processes appear to operate through the formation of synapses in response to specific neural activity, caused by partially or totally unsuccessful attempts to process information. Such synapses can be generated as rapidly as 10–15 minutes after a new experience (Chang & Greenough, 1984). Synapse production under such circumstances appears to be localized to the site of the previous information processing. However, as with experience-expectant processes, more synapses than will later be present may be produced. The synapses that are maintained are those involved in subsequent neural activity.

This analysis suggests both similarities and differences between experience-expectant and experience-dependent processes. In both, the change mechanism involves a cycle of synaptic overproduction and pruning. Also in both, neural activity determines which synapses are maintained. However, the events that trigger the synaptogenesis, its degree of localization within the brain, and the behavioral domains that are influenced distinguish the two types of process. Overall, the analysis of neural change has led to a considerably deeper understanding of the relation between learning and development than had previously been possible.

*Frontal lobe maturation and the development of object permanence.*    Advances in cognitive-developmental neuroscience also have deepened understanding of infants' surprising behavior on object-permanence problems. Recall that these are the "conservation of existence" problems, studied by

Piaget, in which infants acted as if they did not understand that hidden objects continue to exist in the location where they were last placed. In the problems of interest here, infants repeatedly saw an object hidden under one opaque container until they consistently reached for it there. Then the object was hidden under a different container. Until about 7½ months, delays as short as 2 seconds between when the object is hidden and when infants are allowed to reach for it often lead the infants to reach into the container where they found the object on earlier trials, even though they last saw it hidden in the other container. The delay necessary to elicit such errors increases by about 2 seconds per month until roughly age 12 months, at which time infants reach into the appropriate container even at long delays.

Infant monkeys undergo similar development, albeit somewhat earlier. At 1½ months, they perform on the object-permanence task much like human infants at 7½ months; at 4 months, they perform on it much like human infants at 12 months (Diamond, in press). Almost identical development is evident on a very similar task that has been used more frequently with monkeys—the delayed-response task. Here, food is hidden in one of several opaque containers, the monkey waits until a delay period ends, and then the monkey attempts to retrieve the food.

The data from monkeys are important for understanding how neural changes influence performance on object-permanence and delayed-response tasks because monkeys' performance on these tasks has been convincingly linked to functioning of the frontal lobe of the brain. Both electrical activity and glucose utilization show increases in frontal lobe activity while monkeys perform the delayed-response task. Further, interfering with frontal lobe functioning through surgery, localized cooling, localized electrical stimulation, or depletion of neurotransmitters adversely affects monkeys' performance on object-permanence and delayed-response tasks.

Diamond reasoned from the data on monkeys that if changes in *human* infants' object-permanence performance between 6 and 12 months are due to improved frontal lobe functioning, then the human infants' performance on other tasks known to be heavily dependent on frontal lobe functioning should show similar growth during this period. This led her to examine development on a quite different seeming task, the *object-retrieval task*. It involved showing infants an attractive object inside a transparent plastic box that contained a hole in one side. To get the object, infants needed to reach through the hole. Monkeys with surgically induced lesions on the frontal lobe try to reach straight through the plastic when they see the object through it; monkeys with lesions in other areas do not make such attempts (Moll & Kuypers, 1977).

Diamond (in press) vividly described human infants' performance: "Infants of six and one-half to eight months, like the monkeys with frontal

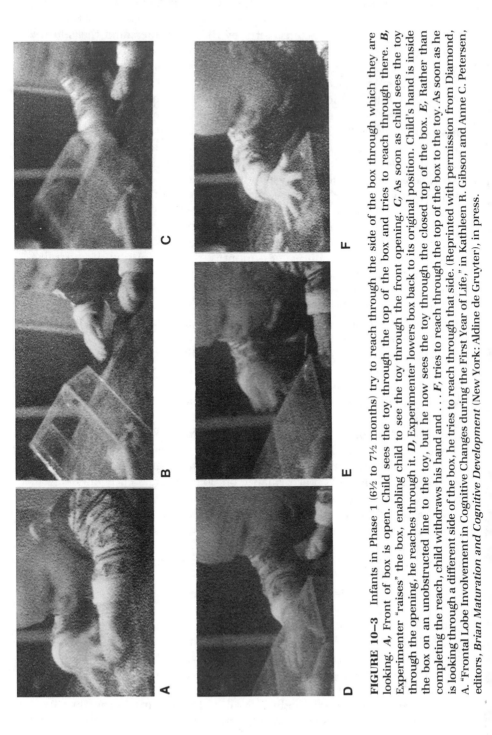

**FIGURE 10–3** Infants in Phase 1 (6½ to 7½ months) try to reach through the side of the box through which they are looking. *A,* Front of box is open. Child sees the toy through the top of the box and tries to reach through there. *B,* Experimenter "raises" the box, enabling child to see the toy through the front opening. *C,* As soon as child sees the toy through the opening, he reaches through it. *D,* Experimenter lowers box back to its original position. Child's hand is inside the box on an unobstructed line to the toy, but he now sees the toy through the closed top of the box. *E,* Rather than completing the reach, child withdraws his hand and . . . *F,* tries to reach through the top of the box to the toy. As soon as he is looking through a different side of the box, he tries to reach through that side. (Reprinted with permission from Diamond, A. "Frontal Lobe Involvement in Cognitive Changes during the First Year of Life," in Kathleen R. Gibson and Anne C. Petersen, editors, *Brian Maturation and Cognitive Development* (New York: Aldine de Gruyter), in press.

348

lobe lesions, were unable to retrieve the reward if they saw it through a closed side. They banged and scratched with considerable effort and persistence, but if their line of sight did not happen to change, they tried no other route to the toy" (p. 17). Figure 10–3 depicts the attempts of one infant of this age to secure the toy.

The behavior changes over the next few months. By 8½ to 9 months, infants look through the front opening of the box, sit up, and reach in where they had looked a few seconds earlier. By 11 to 12 months, they reach through the hole without ever having looked at the toy through it.

These results suggest the additional question: *How* does maturation of the frontal lobe lead to increasing success on both object-retrieval and object-permanence tasks? Diamond suggested that *inhibition* plays a central role. The brain works through a complex combination of excitatory activity, which makes responses more likely, and inhibitory activity, which makes them less likely. Ability to inhibit previously rewarded or habitual responses seems to be a later achievement than ability to perform them. On the object-permanence task, infants need to inhibit the response of reaching to the location where they previously found the object. On the object-retrieval task, they need to inhibit the tendency to try to obtain a goal by reaching directly where they see the desired object. Consistent with this interpretation, infants are more successful on the object-retrieval task when an opaque wall hides the toy than when they can see it through a transparent plastic wall (Diamond, in press; Lockman, 1984). When the object is not visible, infants are not as tempted to reach directly for it and thus have less need to inhibit their inclination. Thus, frontal lobe maturation between 6 and 12 months may increase ability to inhibit tempting and habitual responses, which in turn may make possible the changes in object-permanence and object-retrieval performance that occur during this period. More generally, continued progress in cognitive-developmental neuroscience makes it probable that future accounts of cognitive development will accord a considerably greater role to biological change.

*4. Differences between age groups tend to be ones of degree rather than kind. Not only are young children more cognitively competent than they appear, but older children and adults often are less competent than we might think.*

### Current Knowledge About Differences Between Age Groups

As discussed previously infants and toddlers have a much richer cognitive life than was suspected until recently. The same holds true of preschoolers. Consider just Piagetian tasks and concepts that were once thought impossible for children below age 7. Four- and 5-year-olds can solve certain conservation problems (Gelman, 1972), class-inclusion problems (Markman & Seibert, 1976), and transitive-inference problems (Trabasso et al., 1975). When 4-year-olds talk to 2-year-olds, they take into account differences between their knowledge and that of their listeners; thus they are not totally egocentric (Shatz & Gelman, 1973). Preschoolers also know that causes should precede effects, that contiguity is a useful clue in attributing causation, and that mechanistic processes connect causes with their effects (Sedlak & Kurtz, 1981; White, 1988). They know a great deal about numbers as well; they can add and subtract, identify the larger of two numbers, and count in a way that reflects understanding of the structure of the number system (Siegler & Robinson, 1982).

At the other end of the age spectrum, adults' reasoning has turned out to be not as rational as was once thought. Without training, even high school and college students rarely solve Piagetian formal operations tasks, such as balance scale and shadow projection problems (Martorano, 1977). These difficulties are not limited to Piaget's tasks or to scientific reasoning. Shaklee (1979) reviewed a host of irrational aspects of adults' thinking. Adults will bet more on a cut of a deck of cards when playing against a nervous opponent than when playing against a relaxed one. They become more confident of their ability to play a game of pure chance when they have had time to practice it. When asked to judge which of two sequences of random events is more likely, they ignore the randomness if one sequence sounds more representative. (They say that for a married couple to have six children in the order "girl, girl, girl, boy, boy, boy" is less likely than for them to have the children in the order "girl, boy, girl.") In short, although young children act like budding scientists in some contexts, educated adults ignore the most-basic logical considerations in others.

### Future Issues

Discoveries of young children's previously unsuspected capacities, and of adults' previously unsuspected irrationalities, have doomed many explanations of development. It is no longer tenable to believe that preschoolers' inherent egocentrism makes it impossible for them to take other people's perspectives. Nor is it tenable to believe that their mediation deficiencies makes it impossible for them to benefit from using memory strategies, or that their example-based representations make it impossible for them to form concepts with defining features. These falling dominoes, in turn, have made increasingly indefensible a more-general belief about children's thinking: that it is possible to state a single age at which children acquire a particular cognitive capability. It seems that for most concepts and reasoning skills, there is no single age at which the acquisition occurs.

It was once possible to believe that conceptual mastery could be identified with successful performance on a task that required understanding of the concept. For example, children were said to understand number conservation when they could solve Piaget's number conservation task. As investigators devised additional tasks corresponding to the same concept, however, it became clear that typical solution ages for different tasks varied dramatically. For example, most children solved some number conservation problems by age 3, but most could not solve others until age 6. At what age, then, did they understand the concept?

One plausible approach to answering this question was to identify understanding with the earliest form of understanding. Braine (1959) argued for this view when he wrote, "If one seeks to state an age at which a particular type of response develops, the only age that is not completely arbitrary is the earliest age at which this type of response can be elicited" (p.16).

Braine's statement is entirely reasonable, as far as it goes. When one considers the many years that often separate initial from mature understanding, however, a paradox becomes evident. Adopting the initial-competence criterion puts us in the position of saying that many concepts develop at young ages, yet also of saying that children fail many reasonable indexes of understanding for years thereafter. Stated another way, much—perhaps most—growth would occur after the concept "develops."

Brown (1976) advocated an alternative criterion for conceptual understanding: that of *stable usage*. Children would not be viewed as understanding a concept until they could use it in most or all situations in which it applies. The problem here is evident in Braine's comment. What exactly does a child understand when he or she can use a concept in some situations but not in others? It does seem arbitrary to identify understanding with anything other than the earliest form of understanding. However, it seems misleading to identify it with the earliest form of understanding.

One alternative to stating an age at which children acquire a cognitive capability is to produce more-encompassing models of whatever knowledge they have at different ages that is relevant to that capability. These models would not only specify how children of a particular age perform on various tasks associated with a concept, they also would indicate the conditions under which children applied various types of knowledge that they had. Number conservation again can be used to illustrate. From ages 3 to 6, children sometimes try to solve number conservation problems by counting the objects in each row and sometimes by comparing the lengths of the rows (Gelman, 1972; Siegler, 1981). First they count the objects in each row only when there are small numbers of objects in the rows and something has been added to or subtracted from one of them; otherwise they choose the longer row as having more objects. Then they count any time there are small numbers of objects in the rows and compare lengths of the rows when there are large sets. Slightly later, they count whenever there are small numbers of objects in each row and also if there are large numbers of objects and something has been added or subtracted. Finally, by around age

6, they count in all situations. This does not complete the development, however. At about age 7, they switch from counting to solving the problems on the basis of the type of transformation performed.

The example illustrates the excess involved in saying that preschoolers do not understand number conservation. After all, from age 3, they can solve some number conservation problems. It also indicates the misleadingness of saying that they understand number conservation as soon as they can consistently succeed on any type of number conservation problem. Both the range of problems they can handle and the thought processes by which they handle them change greatly from age 3 to age 7. Given the complexity of cognitive development, it often will prove impossible to provide a meaningful statement about *the* age at which children acquire a cognitive capability. Models that specify both how children think and the conditions under which they think in various ways seem needed to deal with this complexity.

*5. Changes in children's thinking do not occur in a vacuum. What children already know about material that they encounter influences not only how much they learn but also what they learn.*

### Current Knowledge About the Effects of Existing Knowledge

There can be no doubt that people find it easier to learn, remember, and understand in areas where they already have some expertise. Children who already have some knowledge about conservation and class inclusion more easily master the concepts than do less-knowledgeable children (Inhelder et al., 1974; Strauss, 1972). Child chess experts remember more about new chess positions than do adults less knowledgeable about the game (Chi, 1978). Young elementary school children understand stories that follow standard fairy tale forms better than stories whose structure is less familiar (Mandler & Johnson, 1977; Stein & Glenn, 1979).

Prior content knowledge influences what people learn as well as how much they learn. Such effects are especially evident in the rare cases where knowledge interferes with learning and remembering. Although adults knowledgeable about baseball generally remember more than others about a new baseball game, they remember less about details irrelevant to the progress of the game, such as the particular songs played on the organ (Spilich et al., 1979). Similarly, knowledge of seemingly related problems that in fact are misleading leads to incorrect analogies and less-frequent solutions to new problems than does no prior experience with the misleading problems (Chen & Daehler, 1989).

Prior knowledge does not operate as a mechanism apart from the previously mentioned change processes. Rather, the prior knowledge, along with incoming information, provides the data on which the change processes operate. Put another way, prior knowledge helps determine what the change processes do: what features children encode, what generalizations they draw, what strategies they construct, and what operations they automatize. The nature of the change processes, however, determines how they do it.

### Future Issues

What becomes of children's early knowledge about a topic when they acquire more-advanced knowledge about it? Flavell (1972) proposed a taxonomy in which he divided the relations between early and later knowledge into five categories: addition, substitution inclusion, modification, and mediation. Although the taxonomy was proposed two decades ago, the issues it raises remain contemporary.

First consider the five relations themselves. In *addition* relations, the second unit of knowledge coexists with the first, with neither influencing the other. For example, learning that $17 - 9 = 8$ is unlikely to influence the prior knowledge that $4 - 3 = 1$. *Substitution* involves the replacement of an earlier unit of information by a later one. In liquid quantity conservation, children first "know" that the glass with the taller liquid column has more water and then substitute the knowledge that pouring water never affects its quantity. *Inclusion* involves an earlier-acquired cognitive entity's being subsumed within a later acquired one. Children might first learn a route from their home to their school and then include the knowledge within an overall cognitive map of the neighborhood. *Modification* involves an earlier acquisition's being altered in some way by a later acquisition, but still existing in recognizable form. Children might progress from a general all-purpose writing style to specific styles for writing letters, essays, and book reports, all of which maintain some aspects of the original approach. Finally, *mediation* involves the first unit of knowledge serving as a bridge to the second but not becoming part of it. In number conservation, for example, counting the number of objects in each row serves as a bridge to the knowledge that the type of transformation determines the relation between initial and later quantities.

One issue raised by this taxonomy involves the substitution category. Flavell's description of the category suggests that later knowledge can completely replace earlier knowledge. Yet recall Bahrick et al.'s (1975) study in which an experimenter showed senior citizens photos of classmates from their high school yearbooks. The results suggested that knowledge in long-term memory is never erased; it continues to exist, though at times it is difficult to access.

To make the issue concrete, consider what happens to children's early belief that the taller liquid column must have more water. If the belief still exists somewhere in long-term memory, why are older children and adults so surprised to hear that they once thought in this way? Or is it possible that different types of knowledge have different status in long-term memory? Might factual knowledge reside there indefinitely, whereas conceptual understandings are "written over" when better understandings are gained?

Flavell's taxonomy also suggests an interesting point about when children will generalize their existing knowledge to new situations. Educators often lament that children do not draw sufficient implications from their earlier knowledge. The educators have derived only small comfort from learning that adults are similar in often failing to generalize their knowledge to new situations (Kotovsky, 1983).

Flavell's modification and mediation categories suggest a type of generalization that may be a more realistic goal. In neither category does the first type of knowledge automatically transform itself into the second type. Rather, existing knowledge facilitates new acquisitions when, and only when, directly relevant learning experiences arise. Thus, transfer of existing knowledge may be more apparent in savings of time and effort in future learning, or in the range of experiences that produce learning, than in direct extension of the knowledge to new domains without intervening experience in those domains.

*6. The development of intelligence results in large part from increasingly effective deployment of limited processing resources.*

### Current Knowledge About Children's Deployment of Processing Resources

The tension between children's possessing limited cognitive resources, yet wanting to achieve ambitious goals that tax these resources, has been described in numerous contexts. To speak, children must divide their processing capacity among the demands of enunciating clearly, ordering words grammatically, and communicating intended meanings. To write, they must not only order words grammatically and express intended meanings, but also cope with the mechanical demands of writing. To perceive, they must attend to the aspects of the situation that are most likely to be informative and ignore other aspects.

With age and experience, children adapt increasingly well to the demands of complex tasks. The adaptation takes at least three forms. First, as children develop, they represent problem situations increasingly completely. Their representations include more and more of the relevant features. Second, processing becomes increasingly flexible. They match their cognitive procedures more precisely to the demands of the particular task. Third, the adaptation becomes increasingly robust. They employ appropriate representations and processes under a widening range of circumstances. (See Sophian, 1984, for a similar view.)

Consider the trend toward representations' becoming increasingly complete. In examining objects, 1-month-olds scan only the contours of objects, whereas 2- and 3-month-olds scan the interiors as well (Salapatek, 1975). In solving problems, 5-year-olds often represent only a single important dimension; by age 8, they represent multiple relevant dimensions (e.g., Case, 1985; Halford, 1990). In using language, children correctly use such verbs as *drop* and *kill* for years before representing the fact that these words, unlike the related terms *fall* and *die*, imply a specific causal agent (Bowerman, 1982).

Evidence for children's increasing flexible processing also comes from many areas. Older children focus more completely than younger children on information they have been told they will need to remember; younger children divide their attention more evenly between important and unimportant information (Hagen, 1972). Older children also distinguish more clearly between what they know and what others do (Sodian & Wimmer, 1987; Taylor, 1988). They also more often change their reading speed to slow down on difficult material and skim parts that are unlikely to be relevant to assignments (Goldman & Saul, in press; Kobasigawa et al., 1980).

The third sense in which adaptations to task environments become increasingly successful is robustness. Young children's understanding is often quite fragile. It is displayed only under the most-advantageous circumstances. With age and experience, children come to use their competencies in unsupportive as well as facilitative situations. Thus, younger children, like older ones, can find objects in space, but they more often require close-by landmarks to do so, especially if their own orientation has changed (Acredolo, 1978; Huttenlocher & Newcombe, 1984). Preschoolers can form analogies, but often require hints to recognize parallels that older children notice spontaneously (Crisafi & Brown, 1986). Similarly, 5-year-olds can draw logical deductions (Somerville et al., 1979), but adolescents both rely on deductive rather than empirical solutions more often and better resist the temptation to jump to conclusions on the basis of faulty deductions (Acredolo & Horobin, 1987; Byrnes & Overton, 1986).

### Future Issues

Effective deployment of intellectual resources, so as to adapt to the environment, is so central to cognition that it has often been equated with intelligence (e.g., Spearman, 1923). There is no question that it increases greatly during everyone's development. However, people also differ profoundly among themselves in how well they deploy attentional resources, in their overall intelligence, and in their relative intelligence in different areas. One of the most-important issues facing the field of cognitive development is how these individual differences in intelligence should be interpreted.

Two approaches to individual differences in intelligence have already been discussed. The psychometric approach emphasized individual differences along a single dimension—general intelligence. Differences in people's intelligence quotient (IQ) were viewed as reflecting differences in their general intelligence. A second view was Sternberg's (1985) triarchic theory. Here, individual differences in intelligence were viewed as deriving from differences in the efficiency of three classes of information-processing components: performance components, learning components, and metacomponents. Although these two approaches differ in many ways, they share the assumption that there is a common core to intelligence that manifests itself across a wide range of particular domains.

This assumption, however, has been questioned by advocates of two alternative approaches: the multiple-intelligences approach (Gardner, 1983) and the bio-ecological approach (Ceci, 1990). Both of these approaches recognize the effectiveness of IQ tests as instruments for predicting future school achievement. However, they call into question whether this success is due to the tests' really measuring intelligence, or, indeed, whether there is any general intelligence to measure.

Gardner, Ceci, and numerous others have leveled a number of particular criticisms. They have criticized the oversimplification inherent to characterizing individual differences in intelligence as different ranks along a single dimension (the IQ). For example, Gardner (in press) argued, "Far from there being a single dimension called intellect, on which individuals can be rank-ordered, it appears that individuals may exhibit quite different profiles of intellectual strengths and weaknesses; and indeed, our own research suggests that these differences may be evident even before the years of formal schooling." Critics also have taken IQ tests to task for the inegalitarian implications of viewing some people as generally less intelligent than others and for confusing the products of intellectual activity with the processes that produced them. The fact that one child fails on a task and another succeeds may reflect different amounts of prior relevant experience, rather than less-skillful learning by the child who fails. These and other criticisms motivated the multiple-intelligences and bio-ecological approaches.

*Multiple intelligences.*   As noted previously, psychometric approaches emphasize that people differ in general intelligence. The existence of such general intelligence has been inferred from positive correlations in performance on the various items and subtests on intelligence tests. Usually, children who perform successfully on one part of an intelligence test also do well on other parts. They are said to be higher in general intelligence (sometimes called "g") than other children.

Such interpretations of IQ test data are controversial, however. One problem involves the test-construction process. Items on intelligence tests have been selected in part for correlating positively with each other. Whole areas, such as art and music, in which performance does not tend to correlate with performance on existing IQ test items were simply excluded from the tests. Thus, the positive correlations among IQ test items may reflect the way in which items were selected for the test, rather than any inherent characteristic of intelligence.

Another difficulty is that motivation to succeed may influence performance on all items, and thus be responsible for the appearance of "g." If this view is correct, continuity over time in motivation, rather than in intelligence, may account for the predictive relation between IQ test scores at an early date and grades in school at later dates.

The uncertainties surrounding the existence of a single general intellectual factor, together with a variety of data attesting to more-specific abilities, led Gardner (1983) to suggest that what is usually called intelligence might better be thought of in terms of seven *intelligences:* linguistic, musical, logical-mathematical, spatial, bodily-kinesthetic, self-understanding, and social-understanding. He proposed that each intelligence applies to separate (though overlapping) domains, is based on a distinct symbol system, and includes separate change mechanisms.

What criteria must be met for thinking within a cognitive domain to be considered a separate intelligence? Gardner suggested several indicators. One is the existence of idiot savants or prodigies in the area—individuals whose excellence in the domain far exceeds what would be expected from other aspects of their intelligence. Thus, the existence of a Mozart—composing music at age 5, though not being especially precocious in other ways—is evidence for a separate musical intelligence. Another type of evidence is a plausible evolutionary history through which the ability could arise and prove adaptive. Since people did not program computers until recently, a separate intelligence for programming would be unlikely. Finally, individual differences in particular skills within a domain should correlate more highly with each other than with skills in other domains. That is, abilities in different aspects of the domain should hang together.

The existence of idiot savants and prodigies seems especially dramatic evidence for the existence of separate intelligences. Gardner cited cases of severely retarded children, who had had no instruction in music, being able to play by ear on the piano pieces that they had just heard for the first time. The same children exhibited only the most-primitive learning abilities in other domains, suggesting that they learned music through different mechanisms than they used to learn other skills.

Gardner also saw evidence for the operation of distinct intelligences in the exceptionally strong motivation that some children have to exercise particular talents. When the great mathematician Pascal was a child, his father forbade him to talk about mathematics and severely discouraged him from reading about it. In spite of this harsh reaction, Pascal marked the walls of his room with charcoal, trying to find ways of constructing triangles with equal sides and angles. He invented names for mathematical concepts, since he did not know the conventional words. He developed an axiomatic system for geometry and, in so doing, reinvented much of Euclid. He even dreamed of theorems and axioms—all of this in the face of a hostile environment.

The idea of separate intelligences has problematic aspects. Several of the abilities that Gardner classified as separate intelligences may in fact be related. Children's performance on verbal, logical-mathematical, and spatial reasoning parts of IQ tests consistently correlate positively. This may be due to motivation to achieve in these areas being similar, but it could also be due to general intelligence influencing performance over a number of symbol systems. Further, the existence of prodigies and idiot savants in an area may be more-closely related to the isolation of the area from other aspects of life than to whether the ability plausibly could have been evolutionarily advantageous. There are prodigies in chess; there are idiot savants who can quickly calculate what the day of the week will be on January 19, 6593. Neither of these activities would seem to confer any evolutionary benefit.

Despite these problems, the idea of separate intelligences is intriguing. Children's performance in different domains often differs dramatically, particularly when one includes types of intelligence not typically measured by IQ tests, such as artistic, athletic, and social intelligence. Viewing intellect as a set of distinct capacities could yield a more-detailed portrait of individual differences than is possible in a single number. Thus, it may lead to a better appreciation of how people's development varies as well as how it is similar.

*The bio-ecological approach.*   Ceci (1990) suggested a more radical critique of IQ-bases approaches. His basic idea was that intellectual performance arises through an interaction among the processes that generate that performance, the context within which the performance occurs, and the individual. Like Gardner, he thought that individual differences in intelligence are too complex to be viewed in terms of a ranking along a single dimension and that different individuals excel in different areas. Unlike Gardner, however, he did not postulate any general abilities at all. Instead, he emphasized the role of context.

Ceci noted several ways in which context influences individual differences in intelligence. One involves particular content. People who do not have high IQs may reason in very sophisticated ways about some content. For example, IQ is completely unrelated to variations in the sophistication of reasoning that bettors show in predicting which horses will win races (Ceci & Liker, 1986). Another contextual influence involves the practices of the surrounding society. Illustratively, the Burakumi, a low-status subgroup within Japanese society, have lower IQ test scores than do other Japanese among those who live in Japan. Among people living in the United States, however, children of Burakumi have IQ scores just as high as those of others of Japanese descent (Ceci, 1990). Another sense in which context is important involves children's individual background: how much experience they have had with a given type of material, how interesting it is to them, and how important it is to them to work hard on it. Together, these different contexts form the "ecology," emphasized within the bio-ecological approach.

Ceci argued that it is impossible to infer a person's intelligence from performance on any set of items, such as those that appear on an IQ test. Performance must inevitably reflect all of the different contextual influences just cited. Therefore, performance provides at best a distorted mirror of the person's biologically given capabilities. Only by examining specific cognitive processes operating within many content domains over long periods of time is understanding of intellectual development possible.

At present, the bio-ecological approach is more of a framework for thinking about what intelligence is, and a set of criticisms of traditional conceptions, than a well-worked-out alternative theory. Nonetheless, it points to a number of influences that clearly are important within intellectual development and that have not been dealt with adequately in previous approaches. Thus, it may help bring about a better understanding of individual differences in intellectual development than has been achieved thus far.

*7. Children's thinking develops within a social context. Parents, peers, teachers, and the overall society influence what children think about, as well as how and why they come to think in particular ways.*

People are profoundly social animals. This social nature is what makes much of cognitive development possible. A child growing up without access to other people or to the skills developed by previous generations could not hope to learn as much about the world as children ordinarily do.

As noted in Ceci's theory, peers, parents, teachers, and the general culture provide much of the context within which cognition occurs. Their influence has at least three manifestations. First, they influence *what* children think about. In Japan, most children learn to operate abacuses; in the United States, very few do. Second, they influence *how* children acquire information. Parents in Western societies encourage their children to learn by asking questions; parents in many parts of Africa do not. (Greenfield & Lave, 1982). Third, they influence *why* children learn. Peers, parents, teachers, and societal attitudes are important motivators of children's thinking.

Understanding the role of these social influences represents a major challenge for those interested in cognitive development. Information about the influence of the social world has only begun to be integrated with the relatively detailed analyses of children's thinking that have been discussed in other places in this book. If we are to understand fully the process of cognitive growth, this situation must change. Children's thinking does not develop in a vacuum. Understanding how it develops demands an understanding of the social context within which it develops.

### Current Knowledge of Social Influences on Children's Thinking

Although social influences have not been heavily emphasized in previous chapters, they have been discussed in a number of places. Through building new questions into their replies to 2-year-olds' comments, parents were able to motivate the children to talk more than they otherwise would (Kaye & Charney, 1980). Four-year-olds also shaped their language in special ways in order to communicate with 2-year-olds (Shatz & Gelman, 1973). Through a carefully planned instructional program, teachers were able to improve seventh-graders' monitoring of their reading comprehension and thus to improve their academic performance in a variety of ways (Palincsar & Brown, 1984).

Society as a whole—as well as individual peers, parents, and teachers—influences children's thinking. The existence of a chapter on the development of academic skills attests to this influence. Such a chapter could only be written in the context of the culture's having developed such tools as reading, writing, and mathematics. More specifically, it is not accidental that the first words children in the United States learn to read are fairly often terms such as "Coke" and "Budweiser." In a less advertising-infested society, children's first words might be different.

It is important to keep in mind that children are not passive recipients of these influences. Instead, social interactions, both those consciously intended to teach and those undertaken with other goals in mind, more closely resemble a negotiation (Rogoff, 1990). When the interaction goes smoothly, older individuals adjust their goals in response to children's reaction to their teaching; children try to structure their activities to fit the older individuals' organization of the activity (Saxe, Guberman, & Gearhart, 1987). Several illustrations of such mutual adjustments arose in the context of early language development. For example, mothers of 13-month-olds describe a variety of objects to their babies as "balls": round candles, round banks, oranges, and so on (Mervis & Mervis, 1982). In so doing, the mothers adapt to the infants' limited vocabularies by using words that the infants already know and that have important features in common with the new objects. Similarly, babies coo and gurgle considerably more often in the presence of their parents than when they are alone. Parents, in turn, speak to the babies in motherese, which seems to engage their attention more than other forms of speech (Aslin et al., 1983). Recall also the tendency of languages to be arranged so that the meanings that children first wish to express are captured in words that are easy for them to pronounce.

The reciprocal influence extends well beyond language. Through expressions of interest and boredom, tugs on sleeves and dragging of feet, and complaints of "Do I have to?" and demands of "Want it," children exercise considerable control over those who influence their intellectual environments. Moreover, means of persuasion and forms of argument that parents and teachers use with children have a nasty tendency of later being turned against the people who originally used them, often to teach lessons that the original teachers would rather not learn. In short, influences on cognition work in both directions.

### Future Issues

The whole issue of how the social environment influences cognitive development can be thought of as a future issue, because understanding of the issue is just beginning to emerge.

*Social influences on what children think about.* The most-obvious impact of the social environment on children's thinking is on what they think about. It influences whether they acquire certain cognitive skills at all, the degree of proficiency they attain with other skills that everyone masters to some degree, and the contexts within which they use various skills.

Children's acquisition of abacus expertise exemplifies how the larger society influences whether children acquire some cognitive skills at all. Abacuses are commonly used in the Orient to solve arithmetic problems, though they rarely are used in other areas of the world. Although the advent of calculators and computers might seem to have made these devices obsolete, their popularity among children as well as adults remains great. In several Asian countries, abacus training is a part of every schoolchild's curriculum. Many children take additional lessons after school to gain extra proficiency. Winners of national abacus competitions become quite famous and are greatly respected.

Figure 10–4 illustrates the type of abacus most commonly used. Its columns represent a base-10 notation, like that used in standard computation. The column at one end (it can be either end) is the 1's column, the next column inward is the 10's column, the next column inward is the 100's column, and so on. Each column is divided into the single bead above the divider and the four beads below. The bead above the divider represents a value of 5; each of the four beads below it represents a value of 1.

Here is how the abacus can be used to represent and add numbers. When the value of a column is zero, the 5's bead is at the top of the abacus and the four 1's beads are at the bottom. To represent numbers greater than zero, the operator moves beads toward the divider in the middle. Thus, to represent 1, a girl would move a 1's bead up toward the divider. To represent 8, she would move the 5's bead down toward the divider and

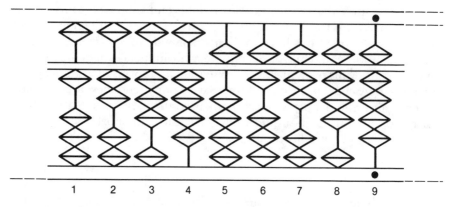

**FIGURE 10–4**   The number 123,456,789 as represented on an abacus. The number 1 is represented on the leftmost bar and the number 9 on the rightmost bar (from Stigler, 1984).

would move three 1's beads up toward it. To add 4 + 3, she would first push four 1's beads from below the divider up toward the middle with an upward finger motion (to represent the 4). When her finger reached the top of the column, she would make a downward motion, pushing the 5's bead down toward the middle and returning two of the 1's beads that had been pushed up near the divider to their original position. This would leave the 5's bead and two 1's beads in the middle, indicating the answer, 7.

Stigler (1984) studied the addition performance of 11-year-old Taiwanese children who had become abacus experts. He presented them with problems ranging from quite simple (adding two numbers, each having two digits) to quite demanding (adding five numbers, each having five digits). The children needed to solve the problems on one occasion in their heads and on another occasion on their abacuses.

The 11-year-olds' addition on the abacus was quick and accurate. This does not seem especially surprising, given that they were practicing abacus arithmetic in school every day and after school at least three days a week. Their mental arithmetic performance was surprising, though. They correctly solved more than 90 percent of problems, even quite difficult ones such as adding four numbers, each having four digits. Further, they actually added more rapidly in their heads than on the abacus.

What might the children's abacus expertise have to do with their exceptionally skillful mental arithmetic? Following a hypothesis advanced by Hatano, Miyake, and Binks (1977), Stigler argued persuasively that the children formed a mental image of the abacus and imagined carrying out the same finger movements on it that they would on a real abacus. Two characteristics of the 11-year-olds' error patterns supported this interpretation. A disproportionate number of the children's errors were off by exactly five in a column. This type of error is easy to make on the abacus, because only the single 5's bead discriminates between 2 and 7, 3 and 8, and so on. Second, the Taiwanese children were three times as likely as American undergraduate and graduate students to err by leaving out a column altogether. If an answer to a problem was 43,296, a common type of error for the Taiwanese was 4,396. This type of error would occur if the Taiwanese children read their answers from a mental image in which a column of the abacus had faded.

Hatano and Osawa (1983) studied Japanese abacus experts and demonstrated another benefit of expertise of this type. Abacus experts possess digit spans far beyond those of nonexperts. Again, they seem to represent the digits in terms of a mental image of an abacus. The data supporting this view include some of the strongest evidence for the existence of mental imagery yet collected. Asking the abacus experts to simultaneously remember digits and perform another visual-imagery task lowered their digit span markedly. The same visual-imagery task did not interfere with the digit span of other people, who followed the typical strategy of auditorially rehearsing the digits. Conversely, asking the abacus experts to simultaneously remember digits and perform a task that taxed auditory memory did not lower the abacus experts' digit span. It did reduce the digit span of the other people, who used auditory rehearsal rather than visual imagery to maintain the digits in memory.

Cultures not only influence what their members think about, but also to what degree they develop certain skills. The abacus studies demonstrate this in a fairly specific domain: numbers. Abacus experts not only know about abacuses, but also are unusually proficient at remembering numbers and at performing mental calculations—skills that people in other cultures possess, but to lesser degrees. Studies of aborigines who live in the western desert of Australia make the point with regard to a broader skill—spatial ability. These aborigines have followed a seminomadic hunting and gathering lifestyle for the past 30,000 years (Kearins, 1981). On most tests of cognitive functioning, aboriginal children do far less well than children of the same ages in Europe and North America. For example, they do not demonstrate understanding of the concrete operational concepts studied by Piaget until ages 9 to 11 years. A considerable proportion fail to solve the problems even then (Dasen, 1973).

Kearins suggested that a different picture might emerge if the focus was on skills of everyday importance in the lives of the aborigines. Much of aboriginal life is a series of treks between widely spaced wells and creeks. Whether a particular well or creek has water depends on capricious rainfall patterns. Few obvious landmarks exist in the stony desert to indicate where the wells and creeks are, and the shifting rainfall patterns create continuous needs to approach water holes from new directions.

Kearins contrasted the spatial-location skills of aboriginal children raised in the desert with those of white Australian children raised in the city. She presented 20 objects arranged in a 5 × 4 rectangle. After 30 seconds, the experimenter picked up all the objects and asked children to rearrange them as they had been placed before. In some arrays, the objects were chosen for being familiar to the white Australian children (erasers, scissors, etc). In others, the objects were chosen for being familiar to the aborigines (feathers, rocks, etc).

The aboriginal children outperformed the white Australian children on all the spatial-location tasks. In addition, the familiarity of the objects exerted different influences on the two groups. The city-dwelling white Australian children recalled the location of familiar objects considerably better than unfamiliar ones. The aboriginal children did as well locating unfamiliar objects as familiar ones. Thus, it appears that the nature of aboriginal life leads children to develop spatial skills to a greater extent than children in other cultures. The skill becomes sufficiently abstract that they do not depend on the particular objects being located.

*Social influences on how children think.* In considering social influences on how children think, it is important to distinguish between different levels of analysis. At a fine-grained level of analysis, there seems little doubt that the processes that lead to cognitive development are the same in all social environments. (Fiske & Taylor, 1984). Regardless of the particular people, technologies, and institutions a boy encounters, he will develop by automatizing his processing, by encoding more and more of the critical features, by generalizing, and by forming improved strategies.

At a more-general level of analysis, though, social factors do alter the process of cognitive growth. Children's questions illustrate this point. Asking questions is one of the most powerful and generally applicable tools for learning that children possess. The effectiveness with which children encode features of situations, generalize to new situations, and use other basic processes certainly influences whether they ask questions and which questions they ask.

The social environment also contributes, though. Comparisons among different cultures once again are illuminating. In Ghanian, Kenyan, and Liberian tribes, children are discouraged from asking questions and only rarely do so. (Greenfield & Lave, 1982). In the West, asking questions is not only tolerated but often encouraged. Thus, in Western societies, children's skill in asking questions would influence how their development occurs to a greater extent than in African societies.

Asking questions is not the only general-level acquisition process whose use is influenced by the social environment. Recall from Chapter 2 that formal operational reasoning is correlated with taking science courses. Presumably, advanced skills in designing experiments and analyzing data are learned in these classes through direct instruction and observation.

Once they are acquired, however, they can be applied to acquiring new knowledge in additional situations. Formal logic, statistics, measurement, and reading are other general-level skills whose acquisition depends critically on the social environment, but that once acquired, themselves become powerful learning tools (Fong, Krantz, & Nisbett, 1986; Miller, 1989).

In this discussion, the influence of the social environment on what children think about has been considered separately from its influence on how they think. The distinction is useful for analyzing the separate influences, but it also is important to remember that the two are complexly entwined. The point can be illustrated with regard to the previously-described study of aboriginal children's spatial skills. The two groups of children differed not only in the degree to which they previously had engaged in spatial reasoning but also in how they behaved while viewing the matrix of objects that they later would need to reproduce. The aboriginal children studied in silence. When they subsequently were asked how they remembered where the objects had been, they often said they remembered the "look of it." In contrast, the city-dwelling children could be heard whispering and saying aloud the names of the objects while they studied them. They explained their performance by such statements as "I described them to myself."

Why might the city children have used the more-verbal strategy? The fact that they attended school and the aboriginal children did not is one likely explanation. Similar differences have emerged among schooled and unschooled populations in other parts of the world. For example, Mexican Indians who attended school both did better on verbal tasks and were more likely to use verbal strategies on them than peers who did not attend (Sharp, Cole, & Lave, 1979). The advantage of the schooled group was greatest on the tasks where verbal strategies were the most useful.

Azuma (1984) noted that the way in which school influences children depends on the relation between the children's personalities and the qualities that the school values. He presented Japanese and American preschoolers with two types of problems. One was a standard problem-solving task that required a certain amount of insight. The other was a more-unusual task: Children were told to draw a circle as slowly as they possibly could, while still moving their pencil continually.

To an American like me, the findings with the American preschoolers do not seem surprising. Their problem solving predicted their later school achievement quite well. Their ability to draw the circle slowly was not highly correlated with their subsequent success in school. The findings with the Japanese preschoolers seem more surprising, though. How slowly they could draw the circle was a good predictor of later school success. How well they could solve the problem, on the other hand, was not nearly as good a predictor.

How can this result be explained? Azuma suggested that the different priorities of schools in the two countries account for the differences. American teachers emphasize problem solving, insight, and originality as especially valuable traits. Children who possess these traits are best equipped to do well in school. Japanese teachers emphasize perseverance, effort, and obedience. Drawing the circle very slowly would call for all of these qualities. Thus, the influence of the social environment on children's thinking may profitably be thought of as an interaction between children's social and intellectual qualities and the values of the societies in which they grow up.

*Social influences on children's motivations for thinking.*   Many differences in what children think about and in how they think about various topics are due to motivational factors. Some of these motivational influences are quite obvious. A boy who is praised for his skill in writing stories is more likely to develop his talent further than one whose writing is ignored or criticized. Other motivational influences are more subtle, though. Two of these more-subtle influences are prior interest in a topic and reactions to negative experiences.

Just as prior knowledge contributes to cognitive growth, so does prior interest. This influence is evident even among preschoolers. Renninger and Wozniak (1985) observed 3-year-olds at play in a preschool to determine which toys each child used most. The children varied considerably in their preferences: One child preferred a toy bear, another a train, another a ball, and so on.

Later in the study, the experimenter presented the preschoolers cards with pictures of two objects and a colored dot in the middle. The child was asked to name the dot's color. What the experimenter was really interested in, though, was which object the child attended to after identifying the color. It was found that the 3-year-olds consistently looked at the object with which they earlier had played.

Next, the children were shown a set of pictures that they were told depicted presents a child received at his birthday party. Then the experimenter presented these pictures and others, and asked the 3-year-olds to separate the pictures of birthday presents from the other pictures. The children more often remembered whether or not their favorite object had been a birthday present than whether the other objects had. They also were considerably more likely to indicate the status of their favorite object first, before any other object, than would have been expected by chance.

These findings suggest a means by which even small initial differences in interest might lead to large later differences in both interest and knowledge. Children attend more to objects that attract their interest and remember more about them. Attending and remembering more lead to greater knowledge about these objects, which is likely to be intrinsically rewarding. The greater knowledge also may attract praise, if the particular type of knowledge is valued. The knowledge also will make future learning about the subject easier. Thus, early-developing interests, formed for quite idio-syncratic reasons, may snowball into significant factors in children's lives. The effects of interest are also evident in much-older children's academic performance. For example, fifth- and sixth-graders' reading comprehension is better for stories whose main topics interest them than for stories whose main topics do not (Renninger, 1988). They also are less likely to skip mathematics word problems whose topics interest them than other problems. One implication of this latter finding is that providing children mathematics exercise sheets with problems that embody the same mathematical principles but with different particular content (e.g., sports, music, cars), and allowing the children to choose which exercise sheet to complete, might lead them to try harder to solve the problems. The decreasing cost of computers and printers would seem to make this a feasible experiment for teachers to try.

Motivations to avoid, as well as motivations to approach, influence cognitive development. One of the most extreme examples of a motivation to avoid is "math phobia." Many quite-intelligent people dread having to do anything mathematical. This profound fear of mathematics is especially common among women. At a time when the demand for scientific and technical expertise far exceeds the supply, such fears are important societally as well as personally.

Analyses of why children avoid activities indicate that the aversion often grows out of initial failures. When given a series of unsolvable problems, people tend to react by giving up. Even after the series of unsolvable problems ends, they often are unable to solve problems that they otherwise would easily figure out. They also tend to regress to less-sophisticated hypotheses than they previously formed, and generally to do less than their best thinking (Dweck & Goetz, 1978).

Some children (and adults) defy this pattern however. They react to failure by maintaining their efforts or by trying even harder than before. Their problem solving and hypothesis formation remain at least as successful as previously.

What differentiates these children from others? It is not their intelligence; their IQs are similar to those of their peers (Dweck & Goetz, 1978). Instead, they differ most dramatically in their attributions of their failure. When they fail, they believe the reason was that they did not try hard enough. Presumably, greater effort would bring success. Children who become helpless in the face of failure, on the other hand, tend to attribute their failures to a lack of ability. With this attribution, they see greater effort as being of limited value.

Girls and boys differ in their most-typical reactions to failure. Girls tend to blame their own ability. Boys tend to blame other people, such as unfair teachers, and also chance factors, such as bad luck.

The types of feedback that girls and boys receive in classrooms may contribute to these different reactions. Girls and boys receive the same amount of negative comments, but the nature of the comments differs (Dweck & Licht, 1980). Teachers' criticisms of girls' performance focuses consistently on the intellectual quality of the work. Their criticisms of boys' performance sometimes focuses on intellectual quality and sometimes on neatness, conduct, or effort.

Dweck and Licht suggested that these differing comments might lead girls to blame their limited abilities and boys to blame other factors for failures. Boys can attribute teachers' negative reactions to any number of considerations, since the teachers fault a variety of aspects of their work. Girls, on the other hand, cannot easily blame sloppiness, bad conduct, or lack of effort, since teachers do not criticize them on these qualities. Adding to the imbalance, both girls and boys view teachers as liking girls better. This adds another attribution that boys can make but girls cannot.

To test this interpretation, Dweck and Licht presented 10-year-olds negative feedback that resembled either the type of feedback girls typically get or the type that boys do. In the "girl" feedback condition, only the correctness of the work was faulted. In the "boy" feedback condition, neatness as well as correctness was criticized. As expected, children who received the "girl" feedback blamed their own lack of ability for their failure on the task. They felt helpless to change the situation. Those who received the "boy" feedback blamed insufficient effort or the unfairness of the experimenter. Thus, the specific feedback children receive seems to shape their reactions to failure.

These differing attributions of failure may especially influence reactions to mathematics. In reading, social studies, and most other subjects, children make fairly steady progress toward mastery. From the beginning, children understand some of the information being presented, and the amount they understand steadily increases from there. Mathematics is different. Often, people's first reaction to a new mathematical concept is total bewilderment. Even beyond this point, the precision of mathematics makes it clear just how many wrong answers the learner is making. This may lead those children who react to failure by feeling helpless to give up on mathematics.

Licht and Dweck (1984) tested the interpretation that it was the tendency to feel helpless that led girls to do badly following initial failures. They presented 10-year-old girls and boys with a questionnaire concerning their likely reactions to hypothetical failures. On the basis of this questionnaire, they divided children into helpless and mastery-oriented groups. They then presented boys and girls within each group with one of two conditions. Some children first received a confusing task, designed to elicit reactions like those that accompany presentation of a new mathematics concept. The other children did not. Then children in both groups were presented a set of eminently solvable problems.

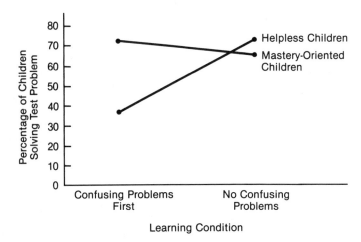

**FIGURE 10–5**    Percentage of helpless and mastery-oriented children in different learning conditions who solved the test problem in Licht and Dweck (1984). Encountering the confusing problem adversely affected the helpless children's later performance, but not the performance of the mastery-oriented children.

As illustrated in Figure 10–5, mastery-oriented children's problem solving was not adversely affected by prior exposure to the confusing task. However, children who reacted to failure by feeling helpless solved problems much less effectively following exposure to the confusing task. The findings were similar for girls and boys who were initially classified as helpless and for girls and boys classified as mastery-oriented. The primary difference between the sexes was in the percentage of children initially classified in each way.

Why so some children react to failure with resignation where others respond with renewed effort? One reason may be that the children's goals differ. Dweck and Leggett (1988) suggested that the helpless reaction is based on *performance goals*, in which the child's main objective is to secure favorable judgments of his or her competence from others. The mastery orientation, in contrast, was viewed as stemming from *learning goals*, where the major objective is to increase competence. These goals, in turn, were viewed as reflecting different implicit theories of intelligence. Performance goals reflected a view in which intelligence is basically fixed. Learning goals reflected a view in which intelligence changes with increasing competence. These perspectives result in different attitudes toward having to work hard to solve problems (Elliott & Dweck, 1988). To children with performance goals, the need to work hard reflects negatively on their ability; they view themselves as lacking the intelligence to succeed without great effort. To children with learning goals, working hard reflects positively on their ability, because they believe that hard work increases their competence. The interconnectedness of these beliefs about the nature of intelligence, its malleability, and the implications of having to work hard seem likely to partially explain the difficulty of overcoming math phobia.

The view that math phobia among women is attributable to attitudes and motivational factors was buttressed by a comparison between gifted Oriental and Caucasian children. As a group, Asians within the United States are unusually strong in mathematics and science achievement. For example, although the population of New York is less than 2 percent Oriental, the group accounts for almost 20 percent of the region's Westinghouse Science Contest winners (Campbell, Connolly, Bologh, & Primavera, 1984). Of special interest in the present context, the percentage of women winners differed for the ethnic groups. Among Caucasians, 27 percent of the winners were female; among Orientals, 46 percent were.

Why are Oriental girls more likely than their Caucasian counterparts to achieve at a superior level in mathematics and science? Lee, Stigler, and Stevenson (1984) suggested that differences in parents' beliefs about the roles of ability and effort might be fundamental. Caucasian parents emphasize ability as a primary reason for success and failure on intellectual tasks. Oriental parents emphasize effort as the critical factor. Uememoto (1984) characterized the difference in this way: "We [Japanese] are more sentimental about our abilities, always wanting to have hope that they can be improved with effort" (p.10). The observation lends us hope that with increasing understanding of motivational influences on children's thinking, the current high incidence of math phobia can become a thing of the past.

*8. We have learned quite a bit about cognitive development, but there is far more left to learn.*

Some statements need no explanation.

## SUMMARY

The development of perception, language, memory, problem solving, and conceptualization have a great deal in common. Important unities exist in the issues, empirical findings, and mechanisms that produce changes in all aspects of children's thinking.

The largest issues in the study of children's thinking are "What develops?" and "How does development occur?" Four commonly advanced hypotheses about what develops are basic capacities, strategies, metacognition, and content knowledge. Each of these types of changes seems to be connected with cognitive improvements in many areas and at many ages. The greatest need for future research on these issues is more-advanced theories of cognitive development. Ideally, new theories would preserve the strengths of Piaget's approach—great breadth, applicability to all periods of childhood, interesting empirical observations—while explaining change processes in greater detail and not making predictions inconsistent with known data.

Four change processes that seem to be especially large contributors to cognitive development are automatization, improved encoding, generalization, and construction of new strategies. Among the greatest future challenges in the study of these change mechanisms is more-detailed analysis of exactly how particular mechanisms produce change. Connectionist models are one promising innovation in this direction.

Differences in the thinking of infants, young children, older children, and adults no longer seem as huge as they once did. The narrowing has come from both directions. Infants and young children have a variety of previously unsuspected capabilities. Older children and adults think less rationally and scientifically than once was believed. These developments have made it clear that in many cases, there is no single age at which children acquire a cognitive capability. Rather, understanding gradually increases over a very prolonged period.

Being intelligent means, in large part, deploying limited processing resources to adapt to the task environment effectively. With age and experience, children become more intelligent: They represent task environments increasingly completely; their processing becomes increasingly flexible; and they apply their most-sophisticated processing to a widening range of situations. Individual differences in intelligence appear to be much more complex than reflected in the traditional index of intelligence: the IQ. People seem to have multiple intelligences, and context profoundly influences how effectively people adapt to the task environment.

Existing knowledge exerts a pervasive influence on the acquisition of new knowledge. Having a large amount of existing knowledge about a topic increases the amount of new knowledge that is acquired from particular experiences. It also influences what children learn by leading them to focus on the material most likely to prove important.

Children's thinking develops within a social context of parents, peers, teachers, and the society in general. These social agents influence what children think about. They influence whether children acquire some cognitive skills at all, the degree to which they acquire other abilities, and the context in which the skills are manifested. The social world also influences how children acquire information. It influences the extent to which children use techniques that can help them learn; asking questions, reading, interpreting statistical relations, and reaching correct logical deductions. Finally, it influences motivation to think about some things rather than others. Children pay greater attention to materials that already interest them; they also remember more about those materials. Failure leads some children not to think about certain areas, but leads to heightened effort by others. These differing reactions appear to reflect differences in children's goals and in their implicit theories of the relation between intelligence and effort.


## RECOMMENDED READINGS

Diamond, A. (in press). **Frontal lobe involvement in cognitive changes during the first year of life.** In K. Gibson, M. Konner, & A. Peterson (Eds.) *Brain and behavioral Development.* **New York: Aldine Press.** Summarizes a venturesome and exciting research program that has used neurological and behavioral data from monkeys to deepen understanding of how human infants develop object permanence and related skills.

Dweck, C. S., & Leggett, E. L. (1988). **A social-cognitive approach to motivation and personality.** *Psychological Review, 95,* 256-273. This article presents an intriguing theory of how people's ideas about the nature of intelligence influence their reactions to experience.

Gardner, H. (1983). *Frames of mind: The theory of multiple intelligences.* **New York: Basic Books.** A stimulating and provocative proposal that people have multiple intelligences based on fundamentally different types of representations. Almost every reader will find points of disagreement, but there also are a number of real insights here.

Hatano, G. & Osawa, K. (1983). **Digit memory of grand experts in abacus-derived mental calculation.** *Cognition, 15, 95–110.* Describes how abacus experts form "mental abacuses" that enable them to perform exceptionally rapid and accurate calculations even when the abacus is not physically present.

Kearins, J. M. (1981). **Visual spatial memory in Australian aboriginal children of desert regions.** *Cognitive Psychology, 13, 434–460.* An unusual study documenting the superior spatial skills that Australian aboriginal children develop in the course of their long treks through the desert.

Licht, B. G. & Dweck, C. S. (1984). **Determinants of academic achievement: The interaction of children's achievement orientations with skill area.** *Developmental Psychology, 20, 628–636.* Children's social environments exert important influences on their thinking. This article compellingly illustrates how feelings of helplessness may interfere with women's efforts to learn mathematics.

# References

**Acredolo, C., & Horobin, K.** (1987). Development of relational reasoning and avoidance of premature closure. *Developmental Psychology, 23,* 13–21.

**Acredolo, C., & Schmid, J.** (1981). The understanding of relative speeds, distances, and durations of movement. *Developmental Psychology, 17,* 490–493.

**Acredolo, L. P.** (1976). Frames of reference used by children for orientation in unfamiliar spaces. In G. Moore & R. Golledge (Eds.), *Environmental knowing.* Stroudsburg, PA: Dowden, Hutchinson, & Ross.

**Acredolo, L. P.** (1978). The development of spatial orientation in infancy. *Developmental Psychology, 14,* 224–234.

**Acredolo, L. P.** (1979). Laboratory versus home: The effect of environment on the 9-month-old infant's choice of spatial reference system. *Developmental Psychology, 15,* 666–667.

**Acredolo, L. P., Adams, A., & Goodwyn, S. W.** (1984). The role of self-produced movement and visual tracking in infant spatial orientation. *Journal of Experimental Child Psychology, 38,* 312–327.

**Acredolo, L. P., & Goodwyn, S. W.** (1985). Symbolic gesturing in language development: A case study. *Human Development, 28,* 40–49.

**Acredolo, L. P., & Goodwyn, S. W.** (1989). Sign language among hearing infants: The spontaneous development of symbolic gestures. In V. Volterra & C. Erting (Eds.), *From gesture to language in hearing and deaf children.* New York: Springer-Verlag.

**Acredolo, L. P., & Hake, J. L.** (1982). Infant perception. In B. J. Wolman (Ed.), *Handbook of developmental psychology.* Englewood Cliffs, NJ: Prentice-Hall.

**Adams, R. J., Maurer, D., & Cashin, H.** (1985). Effect of stimulus' size on newborns' detection of hue. *Investigative Ophthalmology and Visual Science, 26,* 136.

Aitken, S., & Bower, T. G. R. (1982). Intersensory substitution in the blind. *Journal of Experimental Child Psychology, 33,* 309–323.

Anglin, J. M. (1977). *Word, object, and conceptual development.* New York: W. W. Norton.

Anglin, J. M. (1986). Semantic and conceptual knowledge underlying the child's words. In S. A. Kuczaj and M. D. Barrett (Eds.), *The development of word meaning.* New York: Springer-Verlag.

Anisfeld, M. (1984). *Language development from birth to three.* Hillsdale, NJ: Erlbaum.

Anisfeld, M. (1990). Neonatal imitation: A review. *Developmental Review, 10.*

Antell, S. E., & Keating, D. P. (1983). Perception of numerical invariance in neonates. *Child Development, 54,* 695–701.

Aslin, R. N. (in press). Perception of visual direction in human infants. In C. E. Granrud (Ed.), *Visual perception and cognition in infancy.* Hillsdale, NJ: Erlbaum.

Aslin, R. N., & Dumais, S. T. (1980). Binocular vision in infants: A review and a theoretical framework. In L. P. Lipsitt & H. W. Reese (Eds.), *Advances in child development and behavior.* New York: Academic Press.

Aslin, R. N., Pisoni, D. P., & Jusczyk, P. W. (1983). Auditory development and speech perception in infancy, In P. H. Mussen (Ed.), *Handbook of child psychology, Vol. 2.* New York: Wiley.

Atkinson, R. C., & Shiffrin, R. M. (1968). Human memory: A proposed system and its control processes. In K. W. Spence & J. T. Spence (Eds.), *Advances in the psychology of learning and motivation research and theory, Vol. 2.* New York: Academic Press.

Au, T. K-F., & Laframboise, D. E. (in press). Acquiring color names via linguistic contrast: The influence of contrasting terms. *Child Development.*

Azuma, H. (1984, April). Socialization and motivation: Some thoughts about "receptive diligence" implicitly encouraged in Japanese education. Paper presented at the American Educational Research Association Conference, New Orleans, LA.

Bahrick, H. P., Bahrick, P. O., & Wittlinger, R. P. (1975). Fifty years of memory for names and faces: A cross-sectional approach. *Journal of Experimental Psychology, 104,* 54–75.

Baillargeon, R. (1984). Object permanence in the five-month-old infant. Paper presented at the Conference on Conceptual Constraints, University of Pennsylvania, Philadelphia.

Baillargeon, R. (1987). Object permanence in 3½- and 4½-month-old infants. *Developmental Psychology, 23,* 655–664.

Baker, L., & Anderson, R. L. (1982). Effects of inconsistent information on text processing: Evidence for comprehension monitoring. *Reading Research Quarterly, 17,* 281–294.

Baker, L., & Brown, A. L. (1984). Metacognitive skills and reading. In P. D. Pearson (Ed.), *Handbook of reading research, Part 2.* New York: Longman.

Baker-Ward, L., Ornstein, P. A., & Holden, D. J. (1984). The expression of memorization in early childhood. *Journal of Experimental Child Psychology, 37,* 555–575.

Banigan, R. L., & Mervis, C. B. (1988). Role of adult input in young children's category evolution: An experimental study. *Journal of Child Language, 15,* 493–504.

Banks, M. S. (1980). The development of visual accommodation during early infancy. *Child Development, 51,* 646–666.

Banks, M. S. (in press). How optical and receptor immaturities limit the vision of human neonates. In C. E. Granrud (Ed.), *Visual perception and cognition in infancy.* Hillsdale, NJ: Erlbaum.

Banks, M. S., Aslin, R. N., & Letson, R. D. (1975). Sensitive period for the development of human binocular vision. *Science, 190,* 675–677.

Banks, M. S., & Bennett, P. J. (1988). Optical and photoreceptor immaturities limit the spatial and chromatic vision of human neonates. *Journal of the Optical Society of America, 5,* 2059–2079.

Banks, M. S., & Salapatek, P. (1981). Infant pattern vision: A new approach based on the contrast sensitivity function. *Journal of Experimental Child Psychology, 31,* 1–45.

**Baroody, A. J.** (1984). More precisely defining and measuring the order-irrelevance principle. *Journal of Experimental Child Psychology, 38,* 33–41.

**Barrett, M. D.** (1986). Early semantic representations and early word usage. In S. A. Kuczaj & M. D. Barrett (Eds.), *The acquisition of word meaning.* New York: Springer-Verlag.

**Barsalou, L. W.** (1985). Ideals, central tendency, and frequency of instantiation as determinants of graded structure in categories. *Journal of Experimental Psychology: Learning, Memory and Cognition, 11,* 629–654.

**Bartlett, E. J.** (1982). Learning to revise: Some component processes. In M. Nystrand (Ed.), *What writers know: The language, process, and structure of written discourse.* New York: Academic Press.

**Bates, E., Benigni, L., Bretherton, I., Camaioni, L., & Volterra, V.** (1979). *The emergence of symbols: Cognition and communication in infancy.* New York: Academic Press.

**Bates, E., & MacWhinney, B.** (1987). Competition, variation, and language learning. In B. MacWhinney (Ed.), *Mechanisms of language acquisition.* Hillsdale, NJ: Erlbaum.

**Bauer, P. J., & Mandler, J. M.** (1989a). Taxonomies and triads: Conceptual organization in 1-to-2-year-olds. *Cognitive Psychology, 21,* 156–184.

**Bauer, P. J., & Mandler, J. M.** (1989b). One thing follows another: Effects of temporal structure on 1-to-2-year-olds' recall of events. *Developmental Psychology, 25,* 197–206.

**Beal, C. R.** (1987). Repairing the message: Children's monitoring and revision skills. *Child Development, 58,* 401–408.

**Beal, C. R.** (1990). The development of text evaluation and revision skills, *Child Development, 61,* 247–258.

**Beal, C. R., & Fleisig, W. E.** (1987, April). Preschoolers' preparation for retrieval in object relocation tasks. Paper presented at the biennial meeting of the Society for Research in Child Development, Baltimore, MD.

**Beck. I. L., & McKeown, M. G.** (1984). Application of theories of reading to instruction. *American Journal of Education, 93,* 61–81.

**Beilin, H.** (1977). Inducing conservation through training. In G. Steiner (Ed.), *Psychology of the 20th century,* (Vol. 7, *Piaget and beyond*). Zurich: Kindler.

**Beilin, H.** (1983). The new functionalism and Piaget's program. In E. K. Scholnick (Ed.), *New trends in conceptual representation: Challenges to Piaget's theory?* Hillsdale, NJ: Erlbaum.

**Bellugi, U.** (1965). The development of interrogative structures in children's speech. In K. Riegel (Ed.), *The development of language functions.* Ann Arbor: University of Michigan Language Development Program.

**Belmont, J. M., & Butterfield, E. C.** (1977). The instructional approach to developmental cognitive research. In R. V. Kail, Jr., & J. W. Hagen (Eds.), *Perspectives on the development of memory and cognition.* Hillsdale, NJ: Erlbaum.

**Bem, D. J., & Allen, A.** (1974). On predicting some of the people some of the time: The search for cross-situational consistencies in behavior. *Psychological Review, 81,* 506–520.

**Benson, J. B., Arehart, D. M., Jennings, T., Boley, S., & Kearns, L.** (1989, April). Infant crawling: Expectation, action-plans, and goals. Paper presented at the biennial meeting of the Society for Research in Child Development, Kansas City, MO.

**Bereiter, C., Hidi, S., & Dimitroff, C.** (1979). Qualitative changes in verbal reasoning during middle and late childhood. *Child Development, 50,* 142–151.

**Bereiter, C., & Scardamalia, M.** (1982). From conversation to composition: The role of instruction in a developmental process. In R. Glaser (Ed.), *Advances in instructional psychology.* Hillsdale, NJ: Erlbaum.

**Bereiter, C., & Scardamalia, M.** (1987). *The psychology of written composition.* Hillsdale, NJ: Erlbaum.

**Berlin, B., & Kaye, P.** (1969). *Basic color terms: Their universality and evolution.* Berkeley: University of California Press.

**Berndt, T. J., & Wood, D. J.** (1974). The development of time concepts through conflict based on primitive duration capacity. *Child Development, 45,* 825–828.

**Bertenthal, B. I., Campos, J. J., & Barrett, K. C.** (1984). Self-produced locomotion: An organizer of emotional, cognitive, and social development in infancy. In R. Emde & R. Harmon (Eds.), *Continuities and discontinuities in development*. New York: Plenum.

**Bertenthal, B. I., Proffitt, D. R., Kramer, S. J., & Spetner, N. B.** (1987). Infants' encoding of kinetic displays varying in relative coherence. *Developmental Psychology, 23,* 171–178.

**Bertenthal, B. I., Proffitt, D. R., Spetner, N. R., & Thomas, M. A.** (1985). The development of infant sensitivity to biomechanical motions. *Child Development, 56,* 531–543.

**Best, C. T., Hoffman, H., & Glanville, B. B.** (1982). Development of infant ear asymmetries for speech and music. *Perception & Psychophysics, 31,* 75–85.

**Billman, D., & Shatz, M.** (1981). A longitudinal study of the development of communication skills in twins and unrelated peers. Unpublished manuscript, University of Michigan, Ann Arbor.

**Bisanz, G. L., Vesonder, G. T., & Voss, J. F.** (1978). Knowledge of one's own responding and the relation of such knowledge to learning. *Journal of Experimental Child Psychology, 25,* 116–128.

**Bisanz, J.** (1979). Processes and strategies in children's solutions of geometric analogies. Unpublished doctoral dissertation, University of Pittsburgh.

**Bisanz, J.** (1989, March). Development of arithmetic computation and number conservation skills. Paper presented at the annual meeting of the American Educational Research Association, San Francisco, CA.

**Bisanz, J., & LeFevre, J.** (1990). Mathematical cognition: Strategic processing as interactions among sources of knowledge. In D. P. Bjorklund (Ed.), *Children's Strategies: Contemporary views of cognitive development*. Hillsdale, NJ: Erlbaum.

**Bjorklund, D. F., & Harnishfeger, K. K.** (1987). Developmental differences in the mental effort requirements for the use of an organizational strategy in free recall. *Journal of Experimental Child Psychology, 44,* 109–125.

**Bjorklund, D. F., Muir, J. E., & Schneider, W.** (1990). The role of knowledge in the development of strategies. In D. F. Bjorklund (Ed.), *Children's strategies: Contemporary views of cognitive development*. Hillsdale, NJ: Erlbaum.

**Blewitt, P.** (1983). Dog vs collie: Vocabulary in speech to young children. *Developmental Psychology, 19,* 601–609.

**Bloom, L., Lightbown, P., & Hood, L.** (1975). Structure and variation in child language. *Monographs of the Society for Research in Child Development, 40[2].*

**Bloom, L., Rocissano, L., & Hood, L.** (1976). Adult–child discourse: Developmental interaction between information processing and linguistic knowledge. *Cognitive Pyschology, 8,* 521–552.

**Bohannon, J. N. II., & Stanowicz, L.** (1988). The issue of negative evidence: Adult responses to children's language errors. *Developmental Psychology, 24,* 684–689.

**Bomba, P. C., & Siqueland, E. R.** (1983). The nature and structure of infant form categories. *Journal of Experimental Child Psychology, 35,* 294–328.

**Bonitatibus, G. J.** (1988). Comprehension monitoring and the apprehension of literal meaning. *Child Development, 59,* 60–70.

**Bonvillian, J. D., Orlansky, M. D., & Novack, L. L.** (1983). Developmental milestones: Sign language acquisition and motor development. *Child Development, 54,* 1435–1445.

**Borkowski, J. G., Carr, M., & Pressley, M.** (1987). "Spontaneous" strategy use: Perspectives from metacognitive theory. *Intelligence, 11,* 61–75.

**Borkowski, J. G., Johnston, N. B., & Reid, N. K.** (1987). Metacognition, motivation, and the transfer of control processes. In S. J. Ceci (Ed.), *Handbook of cognitive, social, and neuropsychological aspects of learning disabilities, Vol. 2*. Hillsdale, NJ: Erlbaum.

**Bornstein, M. H.** (1978). Chromatic vision in infancy. In H. W. Reese & L. P. Lipsitt (Eds.), *Advances in child development and behavior*. New York: Academic Press.

**Bornstein, M. H.** (1985). Infant into adult: Unity to diversity in the development of visual categorization. In J. Mehler and R. Fox (Eds.), *Neonate cognition: Beyond the blooming buzzing confusion.* Hillsdale, NJ: Erlbaum.

**Bornstein, M. H.** (1989). Sensitive periods in development: Structural characteristics and causal interpretations. *Psychological Bulletin, 105,* 179–197.

**Bornstein, M. H., & Sigman, M. D.** (1986). Continuity in mental development from infancy. *Child Development, 57,* 251–274.

**Bower, T. G. R., & Wishart, J. G.** (1972). The effects of motor skill on object permanence. *Cognition, 1,* 165–172.

**Bowerman, M.** (1980). The structure and origin of semantic categories in the language-learning child. In M. Foster & S. Brandes (Eds.), *Symbol as sense: New approaches to the analysis of meaning.* New York: Academic Press.

**Bowerman, M.** (1982). Starting to talk worse: Clues to language acquisition from children's late speech errors. In S. Strauss (Ed.), *U-Shaped behavioral growth.* New York: Academic Press.

**Boyer, K., & Diamond, A.** (in press). Development of memory for temporal order in infants and young children. In A. Diamond (Ed.), *Development and neural bases of higher cognitive function.* New York: New York Academy of Sciences.

**Bradley, L., & Bryant, P. E.** (1983). Categorizing sounds and learning to read—a causal connection. *Nature, 301,* 419–421.

**Braine, M. D. S.** (1959). The ontogeny of certain logical operations: Piaget's formulation examined by nonverbal methods. *Psychological Monographs, 73,* (Whole No. 475).

**Braine, M. D. S.** (1971). The acquisition of language in infant and child. In C. E. Reed (Ed.), *The learning of language.* New York: Appleton-Century-Crofts.

**Braine, M. D. S.** (1976). Children's first word combinations. *Monographs of the Society for Research in Child Development, 41[1].*

**Brainerd, C. J.** (1973). Judgments and explanations as criteria for the presence of cognitive structures. *Psychological Bulletin, 79,* 172–179.

**Brainerd, C. J.** (1974). Training and transfer of transitivity, conservation, and class inclusion of length. *Child Development, 45,* 324–334.

**Brainerd, C. J.** (1978). The stage question in cognitive developmental theory. *Behavioral and Brain Sciences, 1,* 173–213.

**Brainerd, C. J., & Kingma, J.** (1985). On the independence of short-term memory and working memory in cognitive development. *Cognitive Psychology, 17,* 210–247.

**Brainerd, C. J., & Reyna, V. F.** (1990). Gist is the grist: Fuzzy-trace theory and the new intuitionism. *Developmental Review, 10,* 3–47.

**Bransford, J. W.** (1979). *Human cognition: Learning, understanding and remembering.* Belmont, CA: Wadsworth.

**Brennan, W. M., Ames, E. W., & Moore, R. W.** (1966). Age differences in infants' attention to patterns of different complexity. *Science, 151,* 354–356.

**Bretherton, I.** (1984). Representing the social world in symbolic play: Reality and fantasy. In I. Bretherton (Ed.), *Symbolic play: The development of social understanding.* New York: Academic Press.

**Briars, D., & Siegler, R. S.** (1984). A featural analysis of preschoolers' counting knowledge. *Developmental Psychology, 20,* 607–618.

**Briggs, C., & Elkind, D.** (1977). Characteristics of early readers. *Perceptual and Motor Skills, 14,* 1231–1237.

**Bronson, G. W.** (1974). The postnatal growth of visual capacity. *Child Development, 45,* 873–890.

**Brown, A. L.** (1976). Semantic integration in children's reconstruction of narrative sequences. *Cognitive Psychology, 8,* 247–262.

Brown, A. L. (1982). Learning and development: The problems of compatibility, access, and induction. *Human Development, 25,* 89–115.

Brown, A. L. (1989). Analogical learning and transfer: What develops? In S. Vosniadou & A. Ortony (Eds.), *Similarity and analogical reasoning.* New York: Cambridge University Press.

Brown, A. L, Bransford, J. D., Ferrara, R. A., & Campione, J. C. (1983). Learning, remembering, and understanding. In P. H. Mussen (Ed.), *Handbook of child psychology: Cognitive development, Vol. 3.* New York: Wiley.

Brown, A. L., & Campione, J. C. (1972). Recognition memory for perceptually similar pictures in preschool children. *Journal of Experimental Psychology, 95,* 55–62.

Brown, A. L., & Campione, J. C. (1984). Three faces of transfer: Implications for early competence, individual differences, and instruction. In M. Lamb, A. Brown, & B. Rogoff (Eds.), *Advances in developmental psychology.* Hillsdale, NJ: Erlbaum.

Brown, A. L., & DeLoache, J. S. (1978). Skills, plans, and self-regulation. In R. S. Siegler (Ed.), *Children's thinking: What develops?* Hillsdale, NJ: Erlbaum.

Brown, A. L., Kane, M. J., & Echols, K. (1986). Young children's mental models determine analogical transfer across problems with a common goal structure. *Cognitive Development, 1,* 103–122.

Brown, A. L., & Scott, M. S. (1971). Recognition memory for pictures in preschool children. *Journal of Experimental Child Psychology, 11,* 401–412.

Brown, A. L., & Smiley, S. S. (1978). The development of strategies for studying texts. *Child Development, 49,* 1076–1088.

Brown, A. L., Smiley, S. S., & Lawton, S. C. (1978). The effects of experience on the selection of suitable retrieval cues for studying texts. *Child Development, 49,* 829–835.

Brown, J. S., & Burton, R. B. (1978). Diagnostic models for procedural bugs in basic mathematical skills. *Cognitive Science, 2,* 155–192.

Brown, J. S., & VanLehn, K. (1980). Repair theory: A generative theory of bugs in procedural skills. *Cognitive Science, 4,* 379–426.

Brown, R., Cazden, D., & Bellugi, U. (1969). The child's grammar from I to III. In J. P. Hill (Ed.), *Minnesota symposium on child psychology.* Minneapolis: University of Minnesota Press.

Brown, R., & Hanlon, C. (1970). Derivational complexity and order of acquisition in child speech. In J. R. Hayes (Ed.), *Cognition and the development of language.* New York: Wiley.

Brown, R., & McNeill, D. (1966). The "tip of the tongue" phenomenon. *Journal of Verbal Learning and Verbal Behavior, 5,* 325–337.

Brown, R. A. (1973). *A first language: The early stages.* Cambridge, MA: Harvard University Press.

Brownell, W. A., & Carper, D. V. (1943). Learning the multiplication combinations. *Duke University Research Studies in Education, 7,* 1–177.

Bruner, J. S. (1965). The growth of mind. *American Psychologist, 20,* 1007–1017.

Bruner, J. S., Goodnow, J. J., & Austin, G. A. (1956). *A study of thinking.* New York: Wiley.

Bruner, J. S., & Kenney, H. J. (1966). On relational concepts. In J. S. Bruner, R. R. Olver, & P. M. Greenfield (Eds.), *Studies in cognitive growth.* New York: Wiley.

Bruner, J. S., Olver, R. R., & Greenfield, P. M. (1966). *Studies in cognitive growth.* New York: Wiley.

Bryant, P. E., & Trabasso, T. (1971). Transitive inferences and memory in young children. *Nature, 232,* 457–459.

Buckhalt, J. A., Mahoney, G. J., & Paris, S. G. (1976). Efficiency of self-generated elaborations by EMR and nonretarded children. *American Journal of Mental Deficiency, 81,* 93–96.

Bullock, M., & Gelman, R. (1979). Preschool children's assumptions about cause and effect: Temporal ordering. *Child Development, 50,* 89–96.

Bullock, M., Gelman, R., & Baillargeon, R. (1982). The development of causal reasoning. In W. J. Friedman (Ed.), *The developmental psychology of time.* New York: Academic Press.

**Butterfield, E., Siladi, D., & Belmont, J.** (1980). Validating theories of intelligence. In H. W. Reese & L. P. Lipsitt (Eds.), *Advances in child development and behavior.* New York: Academic Press.

**Byrnes, J. P.** (1988). Formal operations: A systematic reformulation. *Developmental Review, 8,* 66–87.

**Byrnes, J. P., & Overton, W. F.** (1986). Reasoning about certainty and uncertainty in concrete, causal, and propositional contexts. *Developmental Psychology, 22,* 793–799.

**Calfee, R., Chapman, R., & Venezky, R.** (1972). How a child needs to think to learn to read. In L. Gregg (Ed.), *Cognition in learning and memory.* New York: Wiley.

**Callanan, M. A.** (1985, April). Object labels and young children's acquisition of categories. Paper presented at the Society for Research in Child Development Conference, Toronto, Ontario.

**Callanan, M. A.** (1989). Development of object categories and inclusion relations: Preschoolers' hypotheses about word meanings. *Developmental Psychology, 25,* 207–216.

**Campbell, J. R., Connolly, C., Bologh, R., & Primavera, L.** (1984, April). Impact of ethnicity on math and science among the gifted. Paper presented at the annual meeting of the American Educational Research Association, New Orleans, LA.

**Campione, J. C., & Brown, A. L.** (1978). Toward a theory of intelligence: Contributions from research with retarded children. *Intelligence, 2,* 279–304.

**Campos, J., Hiatt, S., Ramsay, D., Henderson, C., & Svejda, M.** (1978). The emergence of fear on the visual cliff. In M. Lewis & L. Rosenblum (Eds.), *The origins of affect.* New York: Plenum Press.

**Capodilupo, A.** (in press). Development and learning: A neo-structural analysis of children's response to instruction in the sight reading of musical notation. In R. Case (Ed.), *The mind's staircase: Stages in the development of human intelligence.* Hillsdale, NJ: Erlbaum.

**Carey, S.** (1978). The child as word learner. In M. Halle, J. Bresnan, & A. Miller (Eds.), *Linguistic theory and psychological reality.* Cambridge, MA: MIT Press.

**Carey, S.** (1985). *Conceptual change in childhood.* Cambridge, MA: MIT Press.

**Carpenter, T. P.** (1986). Conceptual knowledge as a foundation for procedural knowledge: Implications from research on the initial learning of arithmetic. In J. Hiebert (Ed.), *Conceptual and procedural knowledge: The case of mathematics.* Hillsdale, NJ: Erlbaum.

**Carpenter, T. P., Corbitt, M. K., Kepner, H. S., Lindquist, M. M., & Reys, R. E.** (1981). Results from the second mathematics assessment of the national assessment of educational progress. Washington, DC: National Council of Teachers of Mathematics.

**Carraher, T. N., Carraher, D. W., & Schliemann, A. D.** (1985). Mathematics in the streets and in schools. *British Journal of Developmental Psychology, 3,* 21–29.

**Carver, C. S., & Scheier, M. F.** (1981). *Attention and self-regulation: A control-theory approach to human behavior.* New York: Springer-Verlag.

**Case, R.** (1974). Structures and strictures: Some functional limitations on the course of cognitive growth. *Cognitive Psychology, 6,* 544–574.

**Case, R.** (1978). Intellectual development from birth to adulthood: A neo-Piagetian approach. In R. S. Siegler (Ed.) *Children's thinking: What develops?* Hillsdale, NJ: Erlbaum.

**Case, R.** (1981). The search for horizontal structure in children's development. Paper presented at the Society for Research in Child Development Conference, Boston, MA.

**Case, R.** (1985). *Intellectual development: A systematic reinterpretation.* New York: Academic Press.

**Case, R., & Griffin, S.** (1990). Child cognitive development: The role of central conceptual structures in the development of scientific and social thought. In C. A. Hauert (Ed.), *Developmental psychology: Cognitive, perceptuo-motor and neuropsychological perspectives.* Amsterdam: North Holland.

**Case, R., Marini, Z., McKeough, A., Dennis, S., & Goldberg, J.** (1986). Horizontal structure in middle childhood: Cross-domain parallels in the course of cognitive growth. In I. Levin (Ed.), *Stage and structure: Reopening the debate.* Norwood, NJ: Ablex.

**Case, R., Sandieson, R., & Dennis, S.** (1987). Two cognitive developmental approaches to the design of remedial instruction. *Cognitive Development, 1,* 293–333.

**Cauley, K.** (1985). The construction of logical knowledge: A study of borrowing in subtraction. Paper presented at the American Educational Research Association, Chicago, IL.

**Cavanaugh, J. C., & Perlmutter, M.** (1982). Metamemory: A critical examination. *Child Development, 53,* 11–28.

**Ceci, S. J.** (1989). On domain specificity . . . more or less general and specific constraints on cognitive development. *Merrill-Palmer Quarterly, 35,* 131–142.

**Ceci, S. J.** (1990). *On intelligence . . . more or less: A bio-ecological treatise on intellectual development.* Englewood Cliffs, NJ: Prentice-Hall.

**Ceci, S. J., & Liker, J.** (1986). A day at the races: The study of IQ, expertise, and cognitive complexity. *Journal of Experimental Psychology: General, 115,* 225–266.

**Chall, J. S.** (1979). The great debate: Ten years later, with a modest proposal for reading stages. In L. B. Resnick & P. A. Weaver (Eds.), *Theory and practice of early reading.* Hillsdale, NJ: Erlbaum.

**Chang, F. L., & Greenough, W. T.** (1984). Transient and enduring morphological correlates of synaptic activity and efficacy change in the rat hippocampal slice. *Brain Research, 309,* 35–46.

**Chase, W. G., & Simon, H. A.** (1973). The mind's eye in chess. In W. G. Chase (Ed.), *Visual information processing.* New York: Academic Press.

**Chen, Z., & Daehler, M. W.** (1989). Positive and negative transfer in analogical problem solving by 6-year-old children. *Cognitive Development, 4,* 327–344.

**Chi, M. T. H.** (1978). Knowledge structures and memory development. In R. S. Siegler (Ed.), *Children's thinking: What develops?* Hillsdale, NJ: Erlbaum.

**Chi, M. T. H.** (1981). Knowledge development and memory performance. In J. P. Das & N. O'Conner (Eds.), *Intelligence and learning.* New York: Plenum Press.

**Chi, M. T. H., & Klahr, D.** (1975). Span and rate of apprehension in children and adults. *Journal of Experimental Child Psychology, 19,* 434–439.

**Chi, M. T. H., & Koeske, R. D.** (1983). Network representation of a child's dinosaur knowledge. *Developmental Psychology, 19,* 29–39.

**Chipman, S. F., Segal, J. W., & Glaser, R.** (Eds.) (1985). *Thinking and learning skills, Vol. 2: Research and open questions.* Hillsdale, NJ: Erlbaum.

**Chomsky, N. A.** *Reflections on language.* London: Temple Smith.

**Chomsky, N. A.** (1959). Verbal behavior: A review of Skinner's book. *Language, 35,* 26–58.

**Clark, E. V.** (1973). What's in a word? On the child's acquisition of semantics in his first language. In T. E. Moore (Ed.), *Cognitive development and the acquisition of language.* New York: Academic Press.

**Clark, E. V.** (1978). Strategies for communicating. *Child Development, 49,* 953–959.

**Clark, E. V.** (1981). Lexical innovations: How children learn to create new words. In W. Deutsch (Ed.), *The child's construction of language.* New York: Academic Press.

**Clark, E. V.** (1983). Meanings and concepts. In J. H. Flavell & E. M. Markman (Eds.), *Handbook of child psychology, Vol. 3: Cognitive development.* New York: Wiley & Sons.

**Clark, E. V.** (1987). The principle of contrast: A constraint on language acquisition. In B. MacWhinney (Ed.), *Mechanisms of language acquisition.* Hillsdale, NJ: Erlbaum.

**Clay, M. M.** (1973). *Reading: The patterning of complex behavior.* Auckland, NZ: Heinemann Educational Books.

**Clement, J., Lochhead, J., & Soloway, E.** (1979, March). Translation between symbol systems: Isolating a common difficulty in solving algebra word problems. COINS technical report No. 79–19. Amherst: Department of Computer and Information Sciences, University of Massachusetts.

Cohen, L. B. (1972). Attention getting and attention holding processes of infant visual preference. *Child Development, 43,* 869–879.

Cole, M., & Scribner, S. (1974). *Culture and thought.* New York: Wiley.

Condon, W., & Sanders, L. (1974). Synchrony demonstrated between movements of the neonate and adult speech. *Child Development, 45,* 456–462.

Cooper, R. G. (1984). Early number development: Discovering number space with addition and subtraction. In C. Sophian (Ed.), *Origins of cognitive skills.* Hillsdale, NJ: Erlbaum.

Corman, H. H., & Escalona, S. K. (1969). Stages of sensorimotor development: A replication study. *Merrill-Palmer Quarterly, 15,* 351–361.

Corrigan, R. (1975). A scalogram analysis of the development of the use and comprehension of "because" in children. *Child Development, 46,* 195–201.

Corrigan, R. (1988). Children's identification of actors and patients in prototypical and nonprototypical sentence types. *Cognitive Development, 3,* 285–297.

Corrigan, R., & Odya-Weis, C. (1985). The comprehension of semantic relations by two-year-olds: An exploratory study. *Journal of Child Language, 12,* 47–59.

Cox, M. V. (1975). The other observer in a perspective task. *British Journal of Educational Psychology, 45,* 83–85.

Crisafi, M. A., & Brown, A. L. (1986). Analogical transfer in very young children: Combining two separately learned solutions to reach a goal. *Child Development, 57,* 953–968.

Crosby, F. (1976). Early discourse agreement. *Journal of Child Language, 3,* 125–126.

Cultice, J. C., Somerville, S. C., & Wellman, H. M. (1983). Preschoolers' memory monitoring: Feeling-of-knowing judgments. *Child Development, 54,* 1480–1486.

Dale, P. S. (1976). *Language development.* New York: Holt, Rinehart, and Winston.

Damon, W., & Phelps, E. (1988). Strategic uses of peer learning in children's education. In T. Berndt & G. Ladd (Eds.), *Children's peer relations.* New York: Wiley.

Daneman, M. (1981). The integration processes of reading: Individual and developmental differences. Doctoral dissertation, Carnegie-Mellon University, Pittsburgh, PA.

Dannemiller, J. L., & Stephens, B. R. (1988). A critical test of infant pattern preference models. *Child Development, 59,* 210–216.

Darwin, C. (1877). A biographical sketch of an infant. *Mind, 2,* 286–294.

Dasen, P. R. (1973). Piagetian research in central Australia. In G. E. Kearney, P. R. deLacy, & G. R. Davidson (Eds.), *The psychology of aboriginal Australians.* Sydney: Wiley.

Davidson, J. E. (1986). The role of insight in giftedness. In R. J. Sternberg and J. E. Davidson (Eds.), *Conceptions of giftedness.* New York: Cambridge University Press.

Dean, A. L., Chabaud, S., & Bridges, E. (1981). Classes, collections, and distinctive features: Alternative strategies for solving inclusion problems. *Cognitive Psychology, 13,* 84–112.

DeCasper, A. J., & Fifer, W. P. (1980). Of human bonding: Newborns prefer their mothers' voices. *Science, 208,* 1174–1176.

DeCorte, E., & Vershaffel, L. (1984). First graders' solution strategies of addition and subtraction word problems. In J. M. Moser (Ed.), *Proceedings of the Sixth Annual Meeting of the North American Chapter of the International Group for the Psychology of Mathematics Education.* Madison: Wisconsin Center for Educational Research.

deHirsch, K., Jansky, J., & Langford, W. (1966). *Predicting reading failure.* New York: Harper & Row.

DeLoache, J. S. (1980). Naturalistic studies of memory for object location in very young children. *New Directions for Child Development, 10,* 17–32.

DeLoache, J. S. (1984). Oh where, oh where: Memory-based searching by very young children. In C. Sophian (Ed.), *Origins of cognitive skills.* Hillsdale, NJ: Erlbaum.

DeLoache, J. S. (1987). Rapid change in the symbolic functioning of young children. *Science, 238,* 1556–1557.

DeLoache, J. S. (1989a). Pictures and models: Studies of early symbolic understanding. Paper presented at the 30th annual meeting of The Psychonomic Society, Atlanta, GA.

DeLoache, J. S. (1989b). The development of representation in young children. In H. W. Reese (Ed.), *Advances in child development and behavior, Vol. 22* (pp.1–39). New York: Academic Press.

DeLoache, J. S., & Brown, A. L. (1983). Very young children's memory for the location of objects in a large-scale environment. *Child Development, 54,* 888–897.

DeLoache, J. S., Cassidy, D. J., & Brown, A. L. (1985). Precursors of mnemonic strategies in very young children's memory. *Child Development, 56,* 125–137.

DeLoache, J. S., Rissman, M. D., & Cohen, L. B. (1978). An investigation of the attention-getting process in infants. *Infant Behavior and Development, 1,* 11–25.

DeMarie-Dreblow, D., & Miller, P. H. (1988). The development of children's strategies for selective attention: Evidence for a transitional period. *Child Development, 59,* 1504–1513.

Dempster, F. N. (1981). Memory span: Sources of individual and developmental differences. *Psychological Bulletin, 89,* 63–100.

de Ribaupierre, A. (1989). *Transition mechanisms in child development.* Cambridge: Cambridge University Press.

DeValois, R. L., & DeValois, K. K. (1975). Neural coding of color. In E. C. Carterette & M. P. Friedman (Eds.), *Handbook of perception, Vol. 5.* New York: Academic Press.

DeVries, R. (1969). Constancy of generic identity in the years three to six. *Society for Research in Child Development Monographs, 34* (Whole No. 127).

Diamond, A. (in press). Frontal lobe involvement in cognitive changes during the first year of life. In K. Gibson, M. Konner, & A. Petersen (Eds.), *Brain and behavioral development.* New York: Aldine Press.

Diamond, A., & Goldman-Rakic, P. S. (1989). Comparison of human infants and rhesus monkeys on Piaget's AB task: Evidence for dependence on dorsolateral prefrontal cortex. *Experimental Brain Research, 74,* 24–40.

Dobson, V. (1983). Clinical applications of preferential looking measures of visual acuity. *Behavioral Brain Research, 10,* 25–38.

Dodwell, P. E. (1960). Children's understanding of number and related concepts. *Canadian Journal of Psychology, 14,* 191–205.

Dufrense, A., & Kobasigawa, A. (1989). Children's spontaneous allocation of study time: Differential and sufficient aspects. *Journal of Experimental Child Psychology, 47,* 274–296.

Dunbar, K., & Klahr, D. (1988). Developmental differences in scientific discovery strategies. In D. Klahr & K. Kotovsky (Eds.), *Complex information processing: The impact of Herbert A. Simon.* Proceedings of the 21st Carnegie-Mellon Symposium on Cognition. Hillsdale, NJ: Erlbaum.

Duncker, K. (1945). On problem solving. *Psychological Monographs, 58* (Whole No. 270). Washington, DC: The American Psychological Association, Inc.

Durkin, D. (1966). *Children who read early.* New York: Teachers College Press.

Durkin, D. (1974/75). A six-year study of children who learned to read in school at the age of four. *Reading Research Quarterly, 10,* 9–61.

Durkin, D. (1982, April). A study of poor black children who are successful readers. Reading Education Report No. 33, Center for the Study of Reading, University of Illinois at Urbana-Champaign.

Dweck, C. S., & Goetz, T. E. (1978). Attributions and learned helplessness. In J. H. Harvey, W. Icks, & R. F. Kidd (Eds.), *New directions in attribution research, Vol. 2.* Hillsdale, NJ: Erlbaum.

Dweck, C. S., & Leggett, E. L. (1988). A social-cognitive approach to motivation and personality. *Psychological Review, 95,* 256–273.

Dweck, C. S., & Licht, B. G. (1980). Learned helplessness and intellectual achievement. In J. Garber & M.E.P. Seligman (Eds.), *Human helplessness: Theory and application.* New York: Academic Press.

**Eimas, P. D., Siqueland, E. R., Jusczyk, P., & Vigorito, J.** (1971). Speech perception in infants. *Science, 171*, 303–306.

**Elkind, D.** (1961a). Children's discovery of the conservation of mass, weight, and volume: Piaget replications study II. *Journal of Genetic Psychology, 98*, 219–227.

**Elkind, D.** (1961b). The development of quantitative thinking: A systematic replication of Piaget's studies. *Journal of Genetic Psychology, 98*, 37–46.

**Elliott, E. S., & Dweck, C. S.** (1988). Goals: An approach to motivation and achievement. *Journal of Personality and Social Psychology, 54*, 5–12.

**Elliott-Faust, D. J.** (1984). The "delusion of comprehension" phenomenon in young children: An instructional approach to promoting listening comprehension monitoring capabilities in grade three children. Unpublished doctoral dissertation. London, Ontario: University of Western Ontario, Department of Psychology.

**Ellis, S., & Rogoff, B.** (1982). The strategies and efficacy of child vs. adult teachers. *Child Development, 53*, 730–735.

**Enright, M. K., Rovee-Collier, C. K., Fagen, J. W., & Caniglia, K.** (1983). The effects of distributed training on retention of operant conditioning in human infants. *Journal of Experimental Child Psychology, 36*, 512–524.

**Ericsson, K. A., Chase, W. G., & Faloon, S.** (1980). Acquisition of a memory skill. *Science, 208*, 1181–1182.

**Ervin-Tripp, S.** (1970). Discourse agreement: How children answer questions. In J. R. Hayes (Ed.), *Cognition and the development of language.* New York: Wiley.

**Fabricius, W. V.** (1988). The development of forward search planning in preschoolers. *Child Development, 59*, 1473–1488.

**Fabricius, W. V., & Hagen, J. W.** (1984). Use of causal attributions about recall performance to assess metamemory and predict strategic memory behavior in young children. *Developmental Psychology, 20*, 975–987.

**Fagan, J. F.** (1984). The intelligent infant: Theoretical implications. *Intelligence, 8*, 1–9.

**Fagan, J. F., & Singer, L. T.** (1983). Infant recognition memory as a measure of intelligence. In L. P. Lipsitt (Ed.), *Advances in infancy research, Vol. 2*, Norwood, NJ: Ablex.

**Fantz, R. L.** (1958). Pattern vision in young infants. *Psychological Record, 8*, 43–47.

**Fantz, R. L.** (1961). The origin of form perception. *Scientific American, 204*, 66–72.

**Fantz, R. L., Fagan, J. F., & Miranda, S. B.** (1975). Early perceptual development as shown by visual discrimination, selectivity, and memory with varying stimulus and population parameters. In L. B. Cohen & P. Salapatek (Eds.), *Infant perception: From sensation to cognition.* New York: Academic Press.

**Farah, M. J., & Kosslyn, S. M.** (1982). Concept development. In H. W. Reese & L. P. Lipsitt (Eds.), *Advances in child development and behavior.* New York: Academic Press.

**Fehr, L. A.** (1979). Hypotheticality and the other observer in a perspective task. *British Journal of Educational Psychology, 49*, 93–96.

**Fehr, L. A., & Fishbein, H. D.** (1976). The effects of an explicit landmark on spatial judgments. In P. Suedfeld & J. A. Russell (Eds.), *The behavioral basis of design.* Stroudsburg, PA: Dowden, Hutchinson, and Ross.

**Fernald, A.** (1985). Four-month-old infants prefer to listen to motherese, *Infant Behavior and Development, 8*, 181–196.

**Ferretti, R. P., & Butterfield, E. D.** (1986). Are children's rule-assessment classifications invariant across instances of problem types? *Child Development, 57*, 1419–1428.

**Ferretti, R. P., Butterfield, E. C., Cahn, A., & Kerkman, D.** (1985). The classification of children's knowledge: Development on the balance-scale and inclined-plane tasks. *Journal of Experimental Child Psychology, 39*, 131–160.

**Field, D.** (1977). The importance of the verbal content in the training of Piagetian conservation skills. *Child Development, 48*, 1583–1592.

Field, D. (1981). Can preschool children really learn to conserve? *Child Development, 52,* 326–334.

Field, D. (1987). A review of preschool conservation training: An analysis of analyses. *Developmental Review, 7,* 210–251.

Firth, I. (1972). Components of reading disability. Unpublished doctoral dissertation, University of New South Wales.

Fischer, K. W. (1980). A theory of cognitive development: The control and construction of hierarchies of skills. *Psychological Review, 87,* 477–531.

Fiske, S. T., & Taylor, S. E. (1984). *Social cognition.* Reading, MA: Addison-Wesley.

Fitzgerald, J. (1987). Research on revision in writing. *Review of Educational Research, 57,* 481–506.

Flavell, J. H. (1970). Developmental studies of mediated memory. In H. W. Reese & L. P. Lipsitt (Eds.), *Advances in child development and behavior.* New York: Academic Press.

Flavell, J. H. (1971). Stage-related properties of cognitive development. *Cognitive Psychology, 2,* 421–453.

Flavell, J. H. (1972). An analysis of cognitive–developmental sequences. *Genetic Psychology Monographs, 86,* 279–350.

Flavell, J. H. (1982). On cognitive development. *Child Development, 53,* 1–10.

Flavell, J. H. (1984). Discussion. In R. J. Sternberg (Ed.), *Mechanisms of cognitive development.* New York: Freeman.

Flavell, J. H. (1985). *Cognitive development.* Englewood Cliffs, NJ: Prentice-Hall.

Flavell, J. H., Beach, D. R., & Chinsky, J. M. (1966). Spontaneous verbal rehearsal in a memory task as a function of age. *Child Development, 37,* 283–299.

Flavell, J. H., Everett, B. A., Croft, K., & Flavell, E. R. (1981). Young children's knowledge about visual perception: Further evidence for the Level 1–Level 2 distinction. *Developmental Psychology, 17,* 99–103.

Flavell, J. H., Flavell, E. R., & Green, F. L. (1983). Development of the appearance–reality distinction. *Cognitive Psychology, 15,* 95–120.

Flavell, J. H., Flavell, E. R., Green, F. L., & Korfmacher, J. E. (in press). Do young children think of television images as representations or real objects? *Journal of Broadcasting and Electronic Media.*

Flavell, J. H., Friedrichs, A. G., & Hoyt, J. D. (1970). Developmental changes in memorization processes. *Cognitive Psychology, 1,* 324–340.

Flavell, J. H., Green, F. L., & Flavell, E. R. (1986). Development of knowledge about the appearance–reality distinction. *Monographs of the Society for Research in Child Development, 51,* Serial No. 212.

Fong, G. T., Krantz, D. H., & Nisbett, R. E. (1986). The effects of statistical training on thinking about everyday problems. *Cognitive Psychology, 18,* 253–292.

Ford, M. E. (1985). Two perspectives on the validation of developmental constructs: Psychometric and theoretical limitations in research on egocentrism. *Psychological Bulletin, 97,* 497–501.

Forrest, D. L., & Waller, T. G. (1979, March). Cognitive and metacognitive aspects of reading. Paper presented at the meeting of the Society for Research in Child Development, San Francisco, CA.

Fox, R., & McDaniel, C. (1982). The perception of biological motion by human infants. *Science, 218,* 486–487.

Fraiberg, S. (1977). *Insights from the blind: Comparative studies of blind and sighted infants.* New York: Basic Books.

Fraisse, P. (1982). The adaptation of the child to time. In W. J. Friedman (Ed.), *The developmental psychology of time.* New York: Academic Press.

Freud, S. (1953). Three essays on the theory of sexuality. In J. Strachey (Ed.), *The standard edition of the complete psychological works of Sigmund Freud, Vol. 7.* London: Hogarth.

Friedman, W. J. (1978). Development of time concepts in children. In H. W. Reese & L. P. Lipsitt (Eds.), *Advances in child development and behavior.* New York: Academic Press.

Friedman, W. J. (1986). The development of children's knowledge of temporal structure. *Child Development, 57,* 1386–1400.

Friedman, W. J. (1989). The representation of temporal structure in children, adolescents and adults. In I. Levin & D. Zakay (Eds.), *Time and human cognition: A life-span perspective.* The Netherlands: Elsevier.

Frye, D., Braisby, N., Lowe, J., Maroudas, C., & Nicholls, J. (1989). Young children's understanding of counting and cardinality. *Child Development, 60,* 1158–1171.

Fuson, K. C. (1984). More complexities in subtraction. *Journal for Research in Mathematics Education, 15,* 214–225.

Gallagher, T. M. (1981). Contingent query sequences within adult–child discourse. *Journal of Child Language, 8,* 51–62.

Gardner, H. (1983). *Frames of mind: The theory of multiple intelligences.* New York: Basic Books.

Gardner, H. (in press). Assessment in context: The alternative to standardized testing. In B. Gifford (Ed.), *Report of the commission on testing and public policy.*

Gardner, W. P., & Rogoff, B. (1985). Children's improvisational and advance planning. Paper presented at the 93rd Annual Convention of the American Psychological Association, Los Angeles, CA.

Garner, R., & Reis, R. (1981). Monitoring and resolving comprehension obstacles: An investigation of spontaneous text lookbacks among upper-grade good and poor comprehenders. *Reading Research Quarterly, 16,* 569–582.

Gauvain, M., & Rogoff, B. (1989). Collaborative problem solving and children's planning skills. *Developmental Psychology, 25,* 139–151.

Geary, D. C., & Burlingham-Dubree, M. (1989). External validation of the strategy choice model for addition. *Journal of Experimental Child Psychology, 47,* 175–192.

Geary, D. C., Widaman, K. F., Little, T. D., & Cormier, P. (1987). Cognitive addition: Comparison of learning disabled and academically normal elementary school children. *Cognitive Development, 2,* 249–269.

Gellatly, A. R. H. (1987). The acquisition of a concept of logical necessity. *Human Development, 30,* 32–47.

Gelman, R. (1969). Conservation acquisition: A problem of learning to attend to relevant attributes. *Journal of Experimental Child Psychology, 7,* 167–187.

Gelman, R. (1972). The nature and development of early number concepts. In H. W. Reese & L. P. Lipsitt (Eds.), *Advances in child development and behavior.* New York: Academic Press.

Gelman, R. (1978). Cognitive development. *Annual Review of Psychology, 29,* 297–332.

Gelman, R., & Gallistel, C. R. (1978). *The child's understanding of number.* Cambridge, MA: Harvard University Press.

Gelman, R., Meck, E., & Merkin, S. (1986). Young children's numerical competence. *Cognitive Development, 1,* 1–29.

Gelman, S. A., & Markman, E. (1987). Young children's inductions from natural kinds: The role of categories and appearances. *Child Development, 58,* 1532–1541.

Gelman, S. A., & Taylor, M. (1984). How two-year-old children interpret proper and common names for unfamiliar objects. *Child Development, 55,* 1535–1540.

Gentner, D. (1988). Metaphor as structure mapping: The relational shift. *Child Development, 59,* 47–59.

Gentner, D. (1989). The mechanisms of analogical transfer. In S. Vosniadou & A. Ortony (Eds.), *Similarity and analogical reasoning.* London: Cambridge University Press.

Gentner, D., & Landers, R. (1985). Analogical reminding: A good match is hard to find. In *Proceedings of the International Conference on Systems, Man, and Cybernetics.* Tucson, AZ.

Gentner, D., & Stevens, A. (1983) (Eds.) *Mental models.* Hillsdale, NJ: Erlbaum.

Gentner, D., & Toupin, C. (1986). Systematicity and similarity in the development of analogy. *Cognitive Science, 10,* 277–300.

Ghatala, E. S., Levin, J. R., Foorman, B. R., & Pressley, M. (in press). Improving children's regulation of their reading PREP time. *Contemporary Educational Psychology.*

Gholson, B., Emyard, L. A., Morgan, D., & Kamhi, A. G. (1987). Problem solving, recall, and isomorphic transfer among third grade and sixth grade children. *Journal of Experimental Child Psychology, 43,* 227–243.

Gibson, E. J., Schapiro, F., & Yonas, A. (1968). *Confusion matrices for graphic patterns obtained with a latency.* (Tech. Rep. No. 5-1213). Ithaca, NY: Cornell University and U.S. Office of Education.

Gibson, J. J. (1966). *The senses considered as perceptual systems.* Boston, MA: Houghton Mifflin.

Gibson, J. J. (1979). *The ecological approach to visual perception.* Boston, MA: Houghton Mifflin.

Gick, M. L., & Holyoak, K. J. (1980). Schema induction and analogical transfer. *Cognitive Psychology, 15,* 1–38.

Ginsburg, A. (1983). *Contrast perception in the human infant.* Unpublished manuscript.

Ginsburg, H. P. (1983). *The development of mathematical thinking.* New York: Academic Press.

Gleitman, L., & Rozin, P. (1977). The structure and acquisition of reading I: Relations between orthographies and the structure of language. In A. Reber & D. Scarborough (Eds.), *Toward a psychology of reading: Proceedings of the CUNY conference.* Hillsdale, NJ: Erlbaum.

Glenberg, A. M., & Epstein, W. (1987). Inexpert calibration of comprehension. *Memory & Cognition, 15,* 84–93.

Goldin-Meadow, S., & Morford, M. (1985). Gesture in early child language: Studies of deaf and hearing children. *Merrill-Palmer Quarterly, 31,* 145–176.

Goldman, S. R. (1983, November). Toward procedures for summarizing text. Presented at the Annual Meeting of the Psychonomic Society.

Goldman, S. R. (1985). Inferential reasoning in and about narrative text. In A. Graesser & J. Black (Eds.), *The psychology of questions.* Hillsdale, NJ: Erlbaum.

Goldman, S. R., Mertz, D. L., & Pellegrino, J. W. (1989). Individual differences in extended practice functions and solution strategies for basic addition facts. *Journal of Educational Psychology, 81,* 481–496.

Goldman, S. R., Pellegrino, J. W., & Mertz, D. L. (1988). Extended practice of basic addition facts: Strategy changes in learning disabled students. *Cognition and Instruction, 5,* 223–265.

Goldman, S. R., Pellegrino, J. W., Parseghian, P. E., & Sallis, R. (1982). Developmental and individual differences in verbal analogical reasoning. *Child Development, 53,* 550–559.

Goldman, S. R., & Saul, E. U. (in press). Flexibility in text processing: A strategy competition model. *Learning and Individual Differences.*

Goldstein, E. B. (1989). *Sensation and Perception, 3rd Edition.* Belmont, CA: Wadsworth.

Golinkoff, R. M., Hirsh-Pasek, K., Lavallee, A., & Baduini, C. (1985). What's in a word? The young child's predisposition to use lexical contrast. Paper presented at the Boston University Conference on Child Language, Boston, MA.

Goodnow, J. J. (1962). A test of milieu differences with some of Piaget's tasks. *Psychological Monographs, 76* (Whole No. 555).

Gough, P. B., & Hillinger, M. L. (1980). Learning to read: An unnatural act. *Bulletin of the Orton Society, 30,* 171–196.

Graham, F. K., Leavitt, L. A., Strock, B. D., & Brown, J. W. (1978). Precocious cardiac orienting in human anencephalic infants. *Science, 199,* 322–324.

**Granrud, C. E.** (in press). Visual size constancy in newborns. In C. E. Granrud (Ed.), *Visual perception and cognition in infants.* Hillsdale, N.J.: Erlbaum.

**Granrud, C. E.** (1989b). Visual size constancy in newborn infants. Unpublished manuscript. Carnegie Mellon University, Psychology Department.

**Granrud, C. E., Haake, R. J., & Yonas, A.** (1985). Infants' sensitivity to familiar size: The effect of memory on spatial perception. *Perception and Psychophysics, 37,* 459–466.

**Greenberg, D. J., & O'Donnell, W. J.** (1972). Infancy and the optimal level stimulation. *Child Development, 43,* 639–645.

**Greenfield, P. M., & Lave, J.** (1982). Cognitive aspects of informal education. In D. A. Wagner & H. W. Stevenson (Eds.), *Cultural perspectives on child development.* San Francisco, CA: Freeman.

**Greenfield, P. M., & Smith, J.** (1976). *The structure of communication in early language development.* New York: Academic Press.

**Greenough, W. T., Black, J. E., & Wallace, C. S.** (1987). Experience and brain development. *Child Development, 58,* 539–559.

**Greenwald, A., Pratkanis, A., Lieppe, M., & Baumgardner, M.** (1986). Under what conditions does theory obstruct research progress? *Psychological Review, 93,* 216–229.

**Gruber, H. E., & Voneche, J. J.** (1977). *The essential Piaget: An interpretive reference and guide.* New York: Basic Books.

**Guttentag, R. E.** (1984). The mental effort requirement of cumulative rehearsal: A developmental study. *Journal of Experimental Child Psychology, 37,* 92–106.

**Guttentag, R. E.** (1985). Memory and aging: Implications for theories of memory development during childhood. *Developmental Review, 5,* 56–82.

**Guttentag, R. E.** (1989). Age differences in dual-task performance: Procedures, assumptions, and results. *Developmental Review, 9,* 146–170.

**Guttentag, R. E., & Ornstein, P. A.** (1985, April). Transitions in the development of memory skills. Paper presented at the Society for Research in Child Development Conference, Toronto, Ontario.

**Hagen, J. W.** (1972). Strategies for remembering. In S. Farnham-Diggory (Ed.), *Information processing children.* New York: Academic Press.

**Hagen, J. W., & Hale, G. A.** (1973). The development of attention in children. In A. D. Pick (Ed.), *Minnesota symposium on child psychology, Vol. 7.* Minneapolis: University of Minnesota Press.

**Hagen, J. W., Hargrove, S., & Ross, W.** (1973). Prompting and rehearsal in short-term memory. *Child Development, 44,* 201–204.

**Haith, M. M.** (1980) *Rules that infants look by.* Hillsdale, NJ: Erlbaum.

**Haith, M. M.** (in press). The early development of visual expectations. In C. E. Granrud (Ed.), *Visual perception and cognition in infancy.* Hillsdale, NJ: Erlbaum.

**Haith, M. M., Bergman, T., & Moore, M. J.** (1977). Eye contact and face scanning in early infancy. *Science, 198,* 853–855.

**Haith, M. M., Hazan, C., & Goodman, G. S.** (1988). Expectation and anticipation of dynamic visual events by 3.5-month-old babies. *Child Development, 59,* 467–479.

**Hale, S.** (1990). A global developmental trend in cognitive processing speed. *Child Development, 61,* 653–663.

**Halford, G. S.** (1970). A classification learning set which is a possible model for conservation of quantity. *Australian Journal of Psychology, 22,* 11–19.

**Halford, G. S.** (1982). *The development of thought.* Hillsdale, NJ: Erlbaum.

**Halford, G. S.** (1984). Can young children integrate premises in transitivity and serial order tasks? *Cognitive Psychology, 16,* 65–93.

**Halford, G. S.** (1985). Children's utilization of information: A basic factor in cognitive development. *Unpublished manuscript,* University of Queensland, Australia.

**Halford, G. S.** (1989). Cognitive processing capacity and learning ability: An integration of two areas. *Learning and Individual Differences, 1,* 125–153.

**Halford, G. S.** (1990). *Children's understanding: The development of mental models.* Hillsdale, NJ: Erlbaum.

**Harris, J. F., Durso, F. T., Mergler, N. L., & Jones, S. K.** (1990). Knowledge base influences on judgments of frequency of occurrence. *Cognitive Development, 5,* 223–233.

**Harris, P. L.** (1983). Infant cognition. In P. H. Mussen (Ed.), *Handbook of child psychology: Infancy and developmental psychobiology, Vol 2.* New York: Wiley.

**Hasher, L., & Zacks, R. T.** (1984). Automatic processing of fundamental information: The case of frequency of occurrence. *American Psychologist, 39,* 1372–1388.

**Hatano, G.** (1989, April). Personal communication.

**Hatano, G., Miyake, Y., & Binks, M. G.** (1977). Performance of expert abacus calculators. *Cognition, 5,* 57–71.

**Hatano, G., & Osawa, K.** (1983). Digit memory of grand experts in abacus-derived mental calculation. *Cognition, 15,* 95–110.

**Hebb, D. O.** (1949). *The organization of behavior.* New York: Wiley.

**Heibeck, T. H., & Markman, E. M.** (1987). Word learning in children: An examination of fast mapping. *Child Development, 58,* 1021–1034.

**Held, R.** (1985). Binocular vision: Behavioral and neural development. In J. Mehler & R. Fox (Eds.), *Neonate cognition: Beyond the blooming, buzzing confusion.* Hillsdale, NJ: Erlbaum.

**Hochberg, J., & Pinker, S.** (1987) Syntax–semantics correspondences in parental speech. Unpublished manuscript, MIT.

**Hoff-Ginsburg, E.** (1986). Function and structure in maternal speech: Their relation to the child's development of syntax. *Developmental Psychology, 22,* 155–163.

**Holland, J. H., Holyoak, K. J., Nisbett, R. E., & Thagard, P. R.** (1986). *Induction: Processes of inference, learning, and discovery.* Cambridge, MA: MIT Press.

**Holyoak, K. J., Junn, E. N., & Billman, D. O.** (1984). Development of analogical problem solving skill. *Child Development, 55,* 2042–2055.

**Hood, L., & Bloom, L.** (1979). What, when, and how about why: A longitudinal study of early expressions of causality. *Monographs of the Society for Research in Child Development, 44,* (Whole No. 181).

**Hoving, K. L., Spencer, T., Robb, K. Y., & Schulte, D.** (1978). Developmental changes in visual information processing. In P. A. Ornstein (Ed.), *Memory development in children.* Hillsdale, NJ: Erlbaum.

**Huey, E. B.** (1908). *The psychology and pedagogy of reading.* Cambridge, MA: MIT Press.

**Hume, D.** (1911). *A treatise of human nature.* (Original work published 1739–1740). London: Dent.

**Humphrey, G. K., Dodwell, P. C., Muir, D. W., & Humphrey, D. E.** (1988). Can blind infants and children use sonar sensory aids? *Canadian Journal of Psychology, 42,* 94–119.

**Humphrey, G. K., & Humphrey, D. E.** (1985). The use of binaural sensory aids by blind infants and children: Theoretical and applied issues. In F. Morrison & C. Lord (Eds.), *Applied developmental psychology, Vol. 2.* New York: Academic Press.

**Humphrey, G. K., & Humphrey, D. E.** (1989). The role of structure in infant visual pattern perception. *Canadian Journal of Psychology, 43,* 165–182.

**Humphrey, G. K., Humphrey, D. E., Muir, D. W., & Dodwell, P. C.** (1986). Pattern perception in infants: Effects of structure and transformation. *Journal of Experimental Child Psychology, 41,* 128–148.

**Hunt, J. M.** (1961). *Intelligence and experience.* New York: Ronald Press.

**Huttenlocher, J., & Burke, D.** (1976). Why does memory span increase with age? *Cognitive Psychology, 8,* 1–31.

**Huttenlocher, J., & Newcombe, N.** (1984). The child's representation of information about location. In C. Sophian (Ed.), *Origins of cognitive skills.* Hillsdale, NJ: Erlbaum.

Ilg, F., & Ames, L. B. (1951). Developmental trends in arithmetic. *Journal of Genetic Psychology*, *79*, 3–28.

Inagaki, K., & Hatano, G. (1987). Young children's spontaneous personification as analogy. *Child Development*, *58*, 1013–1020.

Ingram, D. (1986). Phonological development: Production. In P. Fletcher & M. German (Eds.), *Language acquisition, 2nd edition*. New York: Cambridge University Press.

Inhelder, B., & Piaget, J. (1958). *The growth of logical thinking from childhood to adolescence*. New York: Basic Books.

Inhelder, B., & Piaget, J. (1964). *The early growth of logic in the child: Classification and seriation*. London: Routledge.

Inhelder, B., Sinclair, H., & Bovet, M. (1974). *Learning and the development of cognition*. Cambridge, MA: Harvard University Press.

Jackson, N. E. (1988). Precocious reading ability: What does it mean? *Gifted Child Quarterly*, *32*, 200–204.

Jackson, N. E., Donaldson, G. W., & Cleland, L. N. (1988). The structure of precocious reading ability. *Journal of Educational Psychology*, *80*, 234–243.

Jager-Adams, M. (1978). Logical competence and transitive inference in young children. *Journal of Experimental Child Psychology*, *25*, 477–489.

Jakobson, R. (1981). Why "mama" and "papa"? *Selected writings: Phonological studies*. Paris: Mouton.

Jakobson, R., Fant, C. G. M., & Halle, M. (1951/1969). *Preliminaries to speech analysis*. Cambridge, MA: MIT Press.

James, W. (1890). *Principles of psychology*. New York: Holt.

Jeffrey, W. E. (1975). Editorial. *Child Development*, *46*, 1–2.

Johnson, C. N. (1988). Theory of mind and the structure of conscious experience. In J. W. Astington, P. L. Harris, & D. R. Olson (Eds.), *Developing theories of mind*. New York: Cambridge University Press.

Johnson, D. D., & Baumann, J. F. (1984). Word identification. In P. D. Pearson (Ed.), *Handbook of reading research, Part 3*. New York: Longman.

Johnson, J. S., & Newport, E. L. (1989). Critical period effects in second language learning: The influence of maturational state on the acquisition of English as a second language. *Cognitive Psychology*, *21*, 60–99.

Johnson-Laird, P. N. (1983). *Mental models: Towards a cognitive science of language, inference, and consciousness*. Cambridge: Cambridge University Press.

Johnson-Laird, P. N., Oakhill, J. V., & Bull, D. (1986). Children's syllogistic reasoning. *Quarterly Journal of Experimental Psychology*, *38A*, 35–58.

Jorm, A. F., & Share, D. L. (1983). Phonological recoding and reading acquisition. *Applied Psycholinguistics*, *4*, 103–147.

Jusczyk, P. W., Rosner, B. S., Cutting, J. E., Foard, F., & Smith, L. B. (1977). Categorical perception of non-speech sounds by two-month-old infants. *Perception & Psychophysics*, *21*, 50–54.

Kail, R. (1984). *The development of memory in children, 2nd edition*. New York: Freeman.

Kail, R. (1986a). The impact of extended practice on rate of mental rotation. *Journal of Experimental Child Psychology*, *42*, 378–391.

Kail, R. (1986b). Sources of age differences in speed of processing. *Child Development*, *57*, 969–987.

Kail, R. (1988). Developmental functions for speeds of cognitive processes. *Journal of Experimental Child Psychology*, *45*, 339–364.

Kail, R. (in press). Processing time declines exponentially with age. *Developmental Psychology*.

Kaiser, M. K., McCloskey, M., & Proffitt, D. R. (1986). Development of intuitive theories of motion: Curvilinear motion in the absence of external forces. *Developmental Psychology*, *22*, 67–71.

**Kaplan, E., & Kaplan, G.** (1971). The prelinguistic child. In J. Elliot (Ed.), *Human development and cognitive processes.* New York: Holt, Rinehart, and Winston.

**Karmiloff-Smith, A.** (1979). Micro- and macro-developmental changes in language acquisition and other representation systems. *Cognitive Science, 3,* 91–118.

**Karmiloff-Smith, A.** (1986). Stage/structure versus phase/process in modelling linguistic and cognitive development. In I. Levin (Ed.), *Stage and structure: Reopening the debate.* Norwood, NJ: Ablex.

**Katz, H., & Beilin, H.** (1976). A test of Bryant's claims concerning the young child's understanding of quantitative invariance. *Child Development, 47,* 877–880.

**Kaufman, N. L.** (1980). Review of research on reversal errors. *Perceptual and Motor Skills, 51,* 55–79.

**Kay, D. A., & Anglin, J.** (1982). Overextension and underextension in the child's expressive and receptive speech. *Journal of Child Language, 9,* 83–98.

**Kaye, K., & Charney, R.** (1980). How mothers maintain dialogue with two-year-olds. In D. Olson (Ed.), *The social foundations of language and thought.* New York: W. W. Norton.

**Kearins, J. M.** (1981). Visual spatial memory in Australian aboriginal children of desert regions. *Cognitive Psychology, 13,* 434–460.

**Keating, D. P., & Bobbitt, B. L.** (1978). Individual and developmental differences in cognitive processing components of mental ability. *Child Development, 49,* 155–167.

**Kee, D. W., & Howell, S.** (1988, April). Mental effort and memory development. Paper presented at the meeting of the American Educational Research Association, New Orleans, LA.

**Keenan, E. O.** (1977). Making it last: Uses of repetition in children's discourse. In S. Ervin-Tripp & C. Mitchell-Kernan (Eds.), *Child discourse.* New York: Academic Press.

**Keeney, T. J., Cannizzo, S. R., & Flavell, J. H.** (1967). Spontaneous and induced verbal rehearsal in a recall task. *Child Development, 38,* 953–966.

**Keil, F. C.** (1979). *Semantic and conceptual development: An ontological perspective.* Cambridge, MA: Harvard University Press.

**Keil, F. C.** (1981). Constraints on knowledge and cognitive development. *Psychological Review, 88,* 197–227.

**Keil, F. C.** (1989). *Concepts, kinds, and cognitive development.* Cambridge, MA: The MIT Press.

**Keil, F. C., & Batterman, N.** (1984). A characteristic-to-defining shift in the development of word meaning. *Journal of Verbal Learning and Verbal Behavior, 23,* 221–236.

**Kellman, P. J.** (1988). Theories of perception and research in perceptual development. In A. Yonas (Ed.), *The Minnesota symposium on child psychology, Vol. 20: Perceptual development in infancy.* Hillsdale, NJ: Erlbaum.

**Kellman, P. J., & Short, K. R.** (1987). The development of three-dimensional form perception. *Journal of Experimental Psychology: Human Perception & Performance, 13,* 545–557.

**Kellman, P. J., & Spelke, E. S.** (1983). Perception of partially occluded objects in infancy. *Cognitive Psychology, 15,* 483–524.

**Kendler, H. H., & Kendler, T. S.** (1962). Vertical and horizontal processes in problem solving. *Psychological Review, 69,* 1–16.

**Kermoian R., & Campos, J. J.** (1988). Locomotor experience: A facilitator of spatial cognitive development. *Child Development, 59,* 908–917.

**Kingsley, R. C., & Hall, V. C.** (1967). Training conservation through the use of learning sets. *Child Development, 38,* 1111–1126.

**Kintsch, W. & Greeno, J. G.** (1985). Understanding and solving word arithmetic problems. *Psychological Review, 92,* 109–129.

**Klahr, D.** (1978). Goal formation, planning, and learning by preschool problem solvers or: "My socks are in the dryer." In R. S. Siegler (Ed.), *Children's thinking: What develops?* Hillsdale, NJ: Erlbaum.

**Klahr, D.** (1982). Nonmonotone assessment of monotone development: An information processing analysis. In S. Strauss (Ed.), *U-shaped behavioral growth*. New York: Academic Press.

**Klahr, D.** (1984). Transition processes in quantitative development. In R. J. Sternberg (Ed.), *Mechanisms of cognitive development*. New York: Freeman.

**Klahr, D.** (1985). Solving problems with ambiguous subgoal ordering: Preschoolers' performance. *Child Development, 56,* 940–952.

**Klahr, D.** (1989). Information-processing approaches. In R. Vasta (Ed.), *Annals of child development, Vol. 6: Six theories of child development: Revised formulations and current issues*. Greenwich, CT: JAI Press.

**Klahr, D., & Carver, S. M.,** (1988). Cognitive objectives in a LOGO debugging curriculum: Instruction, learning, and transfer. *Cognitive Psychology, 20,* 362–404.

**Klahr, D., & Robinson, M.** (1981). Formal assessment of problem solving and planning processes in children. *Cognitive Psychology, 13,* 113–148.

**Klahr, D., & Siegler, R. S.** (1978). The representation of children's knowledge. In H. W. Reese & L. P. Lipsitt (Eds.), *Advances in child development*. New York: Academic Press.

**Klahr, D., & Wallace, J. G.** (1976). *Cognitive development: An information processing view*. Hillsdale, NJ: Erlbaum.

**Klein, A., & Starkey, P.** (1987). The origins and development of numerical cognition: A comparative analysis. In J. A. Sloboda & D. Rogers (Ed.), *Cognitive process in mathematics*. Oxford: Clarendon Press.

**Klemmer, E. T., & Snyder, F. W.** (1972). Measurement of time spent in communication. *Journal of Communication, 22,* 142–158.

**Kobasigawa, A., Ransom, C. C., & Holland, C. J.** (1980). Children's knowledge about skimming. *Alberta Journal of Educational Research, 26,* 169–182.

**Korzan, R. G.** (1985). Discrimination of polysyllabic sequences in one- to four-month-old infants. *Journal of Experimental Child Psychology, 39,* 326–342.

**Kossan, N.** (1981). Developmental differences in concept acquisition strategies. *Child Development, 52,* 290–298.

**Kotovsky, K.** (1983). Tower of Hanoi problem isomorphs and solution processes. Unpublished doctoral dissertation, Carnegie-Mellon University, Pittsburgh, PA.

**Krauss, R. M., & Glucksberg, S.** (1969). The development of communication: Competence as a function of age. *Child Development, 40,* 255–266.

**Kremenitzer, J. P., Vaughan, H. G., Kurtzberg, D., & Dowling, K.** (1979). Smooth-pursuit eye movements in the newborn infant. *Child Development, 50,* 442–448.

**Kress, G.** (1982). *Learning to write*. Boston, MA: Routledge & Kegan Paul.

**Kreutzer, M. A., Leonard, C., & Flavell, J. H.** (1975). An interview study of children's knowledge about memory. *Monographs of the Society for Research in Child Development, 40* (Whole No. 159).

**Kuczaj, S. A., II.** (1981). More on children's initial failures to relate specific acquisitions. *Journal of Child Language, 8,* 485–487.

**Kuczaj, S. A., II.** (1983). "I Mell a Kunk!" Evidence that children have more complex representation of word pronunciations which they simplify. *Journal of Psycholinguistic Research, 12,* 69–73.

**Kuczaj, S. A., II.** (1986). General developmental patterns and individual differences in the acquisition of copula and auxiliary be forms. *First Language, 6,* 111–117.

**Kuczaj, S. A., II, Borys, R. H., & Jones, M.** (1989). On the interaction of language and thought: Some thoughts on developmental data. In A. Gellatly, D. Rogers, & J. A. Sloboda (Eds.), *Cognition and the social world*. New York: Oxford University Press.

**Kuhn, D.** (1989). Children and adults as intuitive scientists. *Psychological Review, 96,* 674–689.

**Kuhn, D., Amsel, E., & O'Loughlin, M.** (1988). *The development of scientific thinking skills.* Orlando, FL: Academic Press.

**Kuhn, D., & Phelps, E.** (1976). The development of children's comprehension of causal direction. *Child Development, 47,* 248–251.

**Kuhn, D., & Phelps, E.** (1982). The development of problem-solving strategies. In H. Reese (Ed.), *Advances in child development and behavior, Vol. 17.* New York: Academic Press.

**Kun, A.** (1978). Evidence for preschoolers' understanding of causal direction in extended causal sequences. *Child Development, 49,* 218–222.

**Kunzinger, E. L., & Wittryol, S. L.** (1984). The effects of differential incentives on second-grade rehearsal and free recall. *The Journal of Genetic Psychology, 144,* 19–30.

**Kurtz, B. E., & Borkowski, J. G.** (1987). Development of strategic skills in impulsive and reflective children: A developmental study of metacognition. *Journal of Experimental Child Psychology, 43,* 129–148.

**Lamb, M. E., & Campos, J. J.** (1982). *Development in infancy: An introduction.* New York: Random House.

**Lange, G.** (1973). The development of conceptual and rote recall skills among school age children. *Journal of Experimental Child Psychology, 15,* 394–407.

**Landau, B., Speike, E. S., & Gleitman, H.** (1984). Spatial knowledge in a young blind child. *Cognition. 16,* 225–260.

**Lange, G.** (1978). Organization-related processes in children's recall. In P. A. Ornstein (Ed.), *Memory development in children.* Hillsdale, NJ: Erlbaum.

**Langer, J.** (1974/75). Interactional aspects of cognitive organization. *Cognition, 3,* 9–28.

**Langlois, J. H., Ruggman, L. A., Casey, R. J., Ritter, J. M., Reiser-Danner, L. A., & Jenkins, V. Y.** (1987). Infant preferences for attractive faces: Rudiments of a stereotype? *Developmental Psychology, 23,* 363–369.

**Lasky, R. E., Syrdal-Lasky, A., & Klein, R. E.** (1975). VOT discrimination by four- to six-and a half-month-old infants from Spanish environments. *Journal of Experimental Child Psychology, 20,* 215–225.

**Leal, L., Crays, N., & Moely, B. E.** (1985). Training children to use a self-monitoring study strategy in preparation for recall: Maintenance and generalization effects. *Child Development, 56,* 643–653.

**Lee, S., Stigler, J. W., & Stevenson, H. W.** (1984). Beginning reading in Chinese and English. Unpublished manuscript, University of Michigan, Ann Arbor.

**Lenneberg, E. H.** (1967). *Biological foundations of language.* New York: Wiley.

**Lepofsky, D.** (1980, November). Consumer corner: Edited transcript from a speech. Wormald International, Sensory Aids Report.

**Lesgold, A. M., & Curtis, M. E.** (1981). Learning to read words efficiently. In A. M. Lesgold & C. A. Perfetti (Eds.), *Interactive processes in reading.* Hillsdale, NJ: Erlbaum.

**Lesgold, A., Resnick, L. B., & Hammond, K.** (1985). Learning to read: A longitudinal study of word skill development in two curricula. *Reading Research: Advances in Theory and Practice, 4,* 107–138.

**Leslie, A. M.** (1982). The perception of causality in infants. *Perception, 11,* 173–186.

**Leslie, A. M.** (1987). Pretense and representation: The origins of "theory of mind." *Psychological Review, 94,* 412–426.

**Leslie, A. M.** (1988). Some implications for mechanisms underlying the child's theory of mind. In J. Astington, P. Harris, & D. Olson (Eds.), *Developing theories of mind.* New York: Cambridge University Press.

**Lester, B. M., Hoffman, J. & Brazelton, T. B.** (1985). The rhythmic structure of mother–infant interaction in term and preterm infants. *Child Development, 56,* 15–27.

**Levin, I.** (1977). The development of time concepts in children: Reasoning about duration. *Child Development, 48,* 435–444.

Levin, I. (1979). Interference of time-related and unrelated cues with duration comparisons of young children: Analysis of Piaget's formulation of the relation of time and speed. *Child Development, 50,* 469–477.

Levin, I. (1982). The nature and development of time concepts in children: The effects of interfering cues. In W. J. Friedman (Ed.), *The developmental psychology of time.* New York: Academic Press.

Levin, I. (1989). Principles underlying time measurement: The development of children's constraints on counting time. In I. Levin & D. Zakay (Eds.), *Time and human cognition: A life-span perspective.* The Netherlands: Elsevier.

Levin I., & Zakay, D. (Eds.) (1989). *Time and human cognition: A life span perspective.* New York: North-Holland.

Levin, I., Siegler, R. S., & Druyan, S. (1990). Misconceptions about motion: Development and training effects. *Child Development, 61,*

Levin, I., & Wilkening, F. (1989). Measuring time via counting: The development of children's conceptions of time as a quantifiable dimension. In I. Levin & D. Zakay (Eds.), *Time and human cognition: A life-span perspective.* The Netherlands: Elsevier.

Levin, I., Wilkening, F., & Dembo, Y. (1984). Development of time quantification: Integration and nonintegration of beginnings and endings in comparing durations. *Child Development, 55,* 2160–2172.

Levin, I., & Zakay, D. (Eds.). (1989). *Time and human cognition: A life-span perspective.* The Netherlands: Elsevier.

Lewkowicz, D. J., & Turkewitz, G. (1981). Intersensory interaction in newborns: Modification of visual preferences following exposure to sound. *Child Development, 52,* 827–832.

Liben, L. (1975). Evidence for developmental differences in spontaneous seriation and its implications for past research on long-term memory improvement. *Developmental Psychology, 11,* 121–125.

Liben, L. S. (1987a). Information processing and Piagetian theory: Conflict or congruence? In L. S. Liben (Ed.), *Development and learning: Conflict or congruence?* Hillsdale, N.J: Erlbaum.

Liben, L. S. (1987b). *Development and learning: Conflict or congruence?* Hillsdale, NJ: Erlbaum.

Liben, L. S. (1988). Conceptual issues in the development of spatial cognition. In J. S. Stiles-Davis, M. Kritchevsky, & V. Bellugi (Eds.). *Spatial cognition: Brain bases and development.* Hillsdale, NJ: Erlbaum.

Liberman, I. Y., & Shankweiler, D. (1977). Speech, the alphabet, and teaching to read. In L. B. Resnick & P. A. Weaver (Eds.), *Theory and practice of early reading.* Hillsdale, NJ: Erlbaum.

Liberman, I. Y., Shankweiler, D., Fischer, F. W., & Carter, B. (1974). Explicit syllable and phoneme segmentation in the young child. *Journal of Experimental Child Psychology, 18,* 201–212.

Licht, B. G., & Dweck, C. S. (1984). Determinants of academic achievement: The interaction of children's achievement orientations with skill area. *Developmental Psychology, 20,* 628–636.

Lindberg, M. A. (1980). Is knowledge base development a necessary and sufficient condition for memory development? *Journal of Experimental Child Psychology, 30,* 401–410.

Lockman, J. J. (1984). The development of detour ability during infancy. *Child Development, 55,* 482–491.

Lockman, J. J., & Pick, H. L. (1984). Problems of scale in spatial development. In C. Sophian (Ed.), *Origins of cognitive skills.* Hillsdale, NJ: Erlbaum.

Lovell, K. (1961). A follow-up study of Inhelder and Piaget's *The growth of logical thinking. British Journal of Psychology, 52,* 143–153.

McCall, R. B., Kennedy, C. B., & Applebaum, M. I. (1977). Magnitude of discrepancy and the distribution of attention in infants. *Child Development, 48,* 772–786.

McCarthy, D. (1954). Language development in children. In L. Carmichael (Ed.), *Manual of child psychology.* New York: Wiley.

McClelland, J. L., & Rumelhart, D. E. (1981). An interactive model of the effect of context in perception, Part 1. *Psychological Review, 88,* 375–407.

McCloskey, M., & Kaiser, M. (1984). The impetus impulse: A medieval theory of motion lives on in the minds of children. *The Sciences*.

McCutchen, D., & Perfetti, C. A. (1982). Coherence and connectedness in the development of discourse production. *Text, 2*, 113–139.

McFadden, G. T., Dufrense, A., & Kobasigawa, A. (1986). Young children's knowledge of balance scale problems. *Journal of Genetic Psychology, 148*, 79–94.

McGarrigle, J., & Donaldson, M. (1974). Conservation accidents. *Cognition, 3*, 341–350.

McGilly, K., & Siegler, R. S. (1989). How children choose among serial recall strategies. *Child Development, 60*, 172–182.

McKeough, A. (1986). Developmental stages in the narrative compositions of school aged children. Unpublished doctoral dissertation, University of Toronto.

Macken, M. A., & Ferguson, C. A. (1983). Cognitive aspects of phonological development: Model, evidence, and issues. In K. E. Nelson (Ed.), *Children's language*. Hillsdale, NJ: Erlbaum.

Maclean, M., Bryant, P., & Bradley, L. (1987). Rhymes, nursery rhymes, and reading in early childhood. *Merrill-Palmer Quarterly, 33*, 255–281.

Macnamara, J. (1982). *Names for things: A study of human learning*. Cambridge, MA: MIT Press.

MacWhinney, B. (1987). *Mechanisms of language acquisition*. Hillsdale, NJ: Erlbaum.

MacWhinney, B., Leinbach, J., Taraban, R., & McDonald, J. (1989). Language learning: Cues or rules? *Journal of Memory and Language, 28*, 255–277.

Mandler, J. M., & Johnson, N. (1977). Remembrance of things parsed: Story structure and recall. *Cognitive Psychology, 9*, 111–152.

Maratsos, M. P. (1982). The child's construction of grammatical categories. In E. Wanner & L. R. Gleitman (Eds.), *Language acquisition: The state of the art*. Cambridge, UK: Cambridge University Press.

Maratsos, M. P. (1989). Innateness and plasticity in language acquisition. In M. L. Rice & R. L. Schiefelbusch (Eds.), *The teachability of language*. (pp. 105–125). Baltimore, MD: Brooks-Cole.

Maratsos, M. P., & Chalkley, M. (1980). The internal language of children's syntax: The ontogenesis and representation of syntactic categories. In K. E. Nelson (Ed.), *Children's language, Vol. 2*. New York: Gardner.

Marini, Z. (1984). The development of social and physical cognition in childhood and adolescence. Unpublished doctoral dissertation, University of Toronto.

Markman, E. M. (1973). Facilitation of part–whole comparisons by use of the collective noun "Family." *Child Development, 44*, 837–840.

Markman, E. M. (1978). Empirical versus logical solutions to part–whole comparison problems concerning classes and collections. *Child Development, 49*, 168–177.

Markman, E. M. (1979). Realizing that you don't understand: Elementary school children's awareness of inconsistencies. *Child Development, 50*, 643–655.

Markman, E. M. (1984). The acquisition and hierarchical organization of categories by children. In C. Sophian (Ed.), *Origins of cognitive skills*. Hillsdale, NJ: Erlbaum.

Markman, E. M. (1987). How children constrain the possible meanings of words. In U. Neisser (Ed.), *Concepts and conceptual development: Ecological and intellectual factors in categorization*. Cambridge, MA: Cambridge University Press.

Markman, E. M. (1989). *Categorization and naming children: Problems of induction*. Cambridge, MA: MIT Press.

Markman, E. M. (in press). Ways in which children constrain word meanings. In E. Dromi (Ed.), *Language and cognition: A developmental perspective*. Norwood, NJ: Ablex.

Markman, E. M., & Callanan, M. (1983). An analysis of hierarchical classification. In R. Sternberg (Ed.), *Advances in the psychology of human intelligence*. Hillsdale, NJ: Erlbaum.

Markman, E. M., & Seibert, J. (1976). Classes and collections: Internal organization and resulting holistic properties. *Cognitive Psychology, 8*, 561–577.

**Markman, E. M., & Wachtel, G. F.** (1988). Children's use of mutual exclusivity to constrain the meanings of words. *Cognitive Psychology, 20,* 121–157.

**Marr, D. B., & Sternberg, R. J.** (1986). Analogical reasoning with novel concepts: Differential attention of intellectually gifted and nongifted children to relevant and irrelevant novel stimuli. *Cognitive Development, 1,* 53–72.

**Marschark, M., & West, S. H.** (1985). Creative language abilities of deaf children. *Journal of Speech and Hearing Research, 28,* 73–78.

**Marschark, M., West, S. A., Nall, L., & Everhart, V.** (1986). Development of creative language devices in signed and oral production. *Journal of Experimental Child Psychology, 41,* 534–550.

**Martorano, S. C.** (1977). A developmental analysis of performance on Piaget's formal operations task. *Developmental Psychology, 13,* 666–672.

**Masur, E. F., McIntyre, C. W., & Flavell, J. H.** (1973). Developmental changes in apportionment of study time among items in a multitrial free recall task. *Journal of Experimental Child Psychology, 15,* 237–246.

**Matz, M.** (1982). Towards a process model for high school algebra errors. In D. Sleeman & J. S. Brown (Eds.), *Intelligent tutoring systems.* New York: Academic Press.

**Maurer, D.** (in press). Seeing with the ears and hearing with the eyes: Neonatal synthesia. In C. E. Granrud (Ed.), *Visual perception and cognition in infancy.* Hillsdale, NJ: Erlbaum.

**Maurer, D., & Barrera, M.** (1981). Infants' perception of natural and distorted arrangements of a schematic face. *Child Development, 52,* 196–202.

**Maurer, D., & Lewis, T. L.** (1979). A physiological explanation of infants' early visual development. *Canadian Journal of Psychology, 33,* 232–252.

**Maurer, D., & Maurer, C.** (1988). *The world of the newborn.* New York: Basic Books.

**Mehler, J., & Fox R. (Eds.).** (1985). *Neonate cognition: Beyond the blooming buzzing confusion.* Hillsdale, NJ: Erlbaum.

**Meltzoff, A. N.** (1988). Infant imitation after a 1-week delay: Long-term memory for novel acts and multiple stimuli. *Developmental Psychology, 24,* 470–476.

**Meltzoff, A. N.** (1988). Infant imitation and memory: Nine-month-olds in immediate and deferred tests. *Child Development, 59,* 217–225.

**Meltzoff, A. N., & Moore, M. K.** (1983). Newborn infants imitate adult facial gestures. *Child Development, 54,* 702–709.

**Mendelson, M. J., & Haith, M. M.** (1976). The relation between audition and vision in the human newborn. *Monographs of the Society for Research in Child Development, 41* (Whole No. 167).

**Mendelson, R., & Shultz, T. R.** (1976). Covariation and temporal contiguity as principles of causal inference in young children. *Journal of Experimental Child Psychology, 13,* 89–111.

**Menig-Peterson, C. L.** (1975). The modification of communicative behavior in preschool-aged children as a function of the listener's perspective. *Child Development, 46,* 1015–1018.

**Merriman, W. E., & Bowman, L. L.** (1989). The mutual exclusivity bias in children's word learning. *Monographs of the Society for Research in Child Development, 54* (Serial No. 220).

**Mervis, C. B.** (1987). Child-basic object categories and early lexical development. In U. Neisser (Ed.), *Concepts and conceptual development: Ecological and intellectual factors in categorization.* Cambridge, MA: Cambridge University Press.

**Mervis, C. B.** (1989, April). Operating principles and early lexical development. Paper presented at the biennial meeting of the Society for Research in Child Development, Kansas City, MO.

**Mervis, C. B., & Mervis, C. A.** (1982). Leopards are kitty-cats: Object labeling by mothers for their thirteen-month-olds. *Child Development, 53,* 267–273.

**Mervis, C. B., & Rosch, E.** (1981). Categorization of natural objects. *Annual Review of Psychology, 32,* 89–115

**Metz, K.** (1985). The development of children's problem solving in a gears task: A problem space perspective. *Cognitive Science, 9,* 431–472.

Miller, G. A. (1956). The magical number seven, plus or minus two: Some limits on our capacity for processing information. *Psychological Review, 63,* 81–97.

Miller, K. (1984). Child as the measurer of all things: Measurement procedures and the development of quantitative concepts. In C. Sophian (Ed.), *Origins of cognitive skills.* Hillsdale, NJ: Erlbaum.

Miller, K. (1989). Measurement as a tool for thought: The role of measuring procedures in children's understanding of quantitative invariance. *Developmental Psychology, 25,* 589–600.

Miller, K., & Gelman, R. (1983). The child's representation of number: A multidimensional scaling analysis. *Child Development, 54,* 1470–1479.

Miller, P. H. (1983). *Theories of developmental psychology.* San Francisco: Freeman.

Miller, S. A. (1976). Nonverbal assessment of conservation of number. *Child Development, 47,* 722–728.

Mills, J. R., & Jackson, N. E. (in press). Predictive significance of early giftedness: The case of precocious reading. *Journal of Educational Psychology.*

Moely, B. E. (1977). Organizational factors in the development of memory. In R. V. Kail & J. W. Hagen (Eds.), *Perspectives on the development of memory and cognition.* Hillsdale, NJ: Erlbaum.

Moely, B. E., Olson, F. A., Halwes, T. G., & Flavell, J. H. (1969). Production deficiency in young children's clustered recall. *Developmental Psychology, 1,* 26–34.

Molfese, D. L., & Molfese, V. J. (1979). Hemisphere and stimulus differences as reflected in the cortical responses of newborn infants to speech stimuli. *Developmental Psychology, 15,* 505–511.

Moll, L., & Kuypers, H. G. J. M. (1977). Premotor cortical ablations in monkeys: Contralateral changes in visually guided reaching behavior. *Science, 198,* 317–319.

Morrison, F. J. (1989, March). School readiness, entrance age, and learning in children. Paper presented at the annual meeting of the American Educational Research Association, San Francisco, CA.

Morrison, F. J., Holmes, D. L., & Haith, M. M. (1974). A developmental study of the effects of familiarity on short-term visual memory. *Journal of Experimental Child Psychology, 18,* 412–425.

Morse, P. A. (1972). The discrimination of speech and nonspeech stimuli in early infancy. *Journal of Experimental Child Psychology, 14,* 477–492.

Muir, D., Abraham, W., Forbes, B., & Harris, L. (1979). The ontogenesis of an auditory localization response from birth to four months of age. *Canadian Journal of Psychology, 33,* 320–333.

Muller, E., Hollien, H., & Murray, T. (1974). Perceptual responses to infant crying: Identification of cry. *Journal of Child Language, 1,* 89–95.

Murphy, G. L., & Medin, D. L. (1985). The role of theories in conceptual coherence. *Psychological Review, 92,* 289–316.

Murray, F. B. (1972). Acquisition of conservation through social interaction. *Developmental Psychology, 6,* 1–6.

Murray, F. B. (1987). Necessity: The developmental component in school mathematics. In L. S. Liben (Ed.), *Development and learning: Conflict or congruence.* Hillsdale, NJ: Erlbaum.

Murray, F., & Armstrong, S. (1976). Necessity in conservation and nonconservation. *Developmental Psychology, 12,* 483–484.

Mussen, P. H., Conger, J. J., Kagan, J., & Geiwitz, J. (1979). *Psychological development: A life-span approach.* New York: Harper & Row.

Myers, N. A., Clifton, R. K., & Clarkson, M. G. (1987). When they were very young: Almost-threes remember two years ago. *Infant Behavior and Development, 10,* 123–132.

Naus, M. J., & Ornstein, P. A. (1983). Development of memory strategies: Analysis, questions, and issues. In M. T. H. Chi (Ed.), *Trends in memory development research.* New York: Karger.

Naus, M. J., Ornstein, P. A., & Aivano, S. (1977). Developmental changes in memory: The effects of processing time and rehearsal instructions. *Journal of Experimental Child Psychology, 23,* 237–251.

Neisser, U., & Weene, P. (1962). Hierarchies in concept attainment. *Journal of Experimental Psychology, 64,* 640–645.

Nelson, K. (1973). Structure and strategy in learning to talk. *Monographs of the Society for Research in Child Development, 38* (Whole No. 149).

Nesher, P. (1982). Levels of description in the analysis of addition and subtraction. In T. P. Carpenter, J. M. Moser, & T. Romberg (Eds.), *Addition and subtraction: A developmental perspective.* Hillsdale, NJ: Erlbaum.

Newcombe, N., Fox, N. A., & Prime, A. G. (1989). Preschool memories: Through a glass darkly. Paper presented at the American Psychological Society conference, Alexandria, VA.

Newell, A., & Rosenbloom, P. S. (1981). Mechanisms of skill acquisition and the law of practice. In J. R. Anderson (Ed.), *Cognitive skills and their acquisition.* Hillsdale, NJ: Erlbaum.

Newell, A., & Simon, H. A. (1972). *Human problem solving.* Englewood Cliffs, NJ: Prentice-Hall.

Newman, R. S. (1984). Children's numerical skill and judgments of confidence in estimation. *Journal of Experimental Child Psychology, 37,* 107–123.

Newman, R. S., & Berger, C. F. (1984). Children's numerical estimation: Flexibility in the use of counting. *Journal of Educational Psychology, 76,* 55–64.

Newport, E. L. (1982). Task specificity in language learning? Evidence from speech. In E. Wanner & L. R. Gleitman (Eds.), *Language acquisition: The state of the art.* Cambridge, MA: Cambridge University Press.

Nodine, C. F., & Steurle, N. L. (1973). Development of perceptual and cognitive strategies for differentiating graphemes. *Journal of Experimental Psychology, 97,* 158–166.

Oakhill, J. (1988). The development of children's reasoning ability: Information-processing approaches. In K. Richardson & S. Sheldon (Eds.), *Cognitive development to adolescence.* Hillsdale, NJ: Erlbaum.

Odom, R. D. (1978). A perceptual-salience account of decalage relations and developmental change. In L. S. Siegel & C. J. Brainerd (Eds.), *Alternatives to Piaget.* New York: Academic Press.

O'Hara, E. (1975). Piaget, the six-year-old child, and modern math. *Today's Education, 64,* 33–36.

Olson, R., Kleigl, R., Davidson, B. J., & Foltz, G. (1985). Individual and developmental differences in reading disability. In G. E. MacKinnon & T. G. Waller (Eds.), *Reading research: Advances in theory and practice, Vol. 4.* New York: Academic Press.

Ornstein, P. A., Medlin, R. G., Stone, B. P., & Naus, M. J. (1985). Retrieving for rehearsal: An analysis of active rehearsal in children's memory. *Developmental Psychology, 21,* 635–641.

Ornstein, P. A., & Naus, M. J. (1985). Effects of the knowledge base on children's memory strategies. In H. W. Reese (Ed.), *Advances in child development and behavior, Vol. 19.* New York: Academic Press.

Ornstein, P. A., Naus, M. J., & Liberty, C. (1975). Rehearsal and organizational processes in children's memory. *Child Development, 26,* 818–830.

Osherson, D., & Markman, E. (1975). Language and the ability to evaluate contradictions and tautologies. *Cognition, 3,* 213–226.

Palincsar, A. S., & Brown, A. L. (1984). Reciprocal teaching of comprehension-monitoring activities. *Cognition and Instruction, 1,* 117–175.

Panagos, J. M., & Prelock, P. A. (1982). Phonological constraints on the sentence productions of language-disordered children. *Journal of Speech and Hearing Research, 25,* 171–177.

Papert, S. (1980). *Mindstorms: Children, computers, and powerful ideas.* New York: Basic Books.

**Papousek, M., Papousek, H., & Bornstein, M. H.** (1985). The naturalistic vocal environment of young infants: On the significance of homogeneity and variability in parental speech. In T. M. Field and N. Fox (Eds.), *Social perception in infants.* Norwood, NJ: Ablex.

**Paris, S. G.** (1975). Integration and inference in children's comprehension and memory. In F. Restle, R. Shriffrin, J. Castellan, H. Lindman, & D. Pisoni (Eds), *Cognitive theory, Vol. 1.* Hillsdale, NJ: Erlbaum.

**Paris, S. G., & Jacobs, J. E.** (1984). The benefits of informed instruction for children's reading awareness and comprehension. *Child Development, 55,* 2083–2093.

**Paris, S. G., & Lindauer, B. K.** (1977). Constructive aspects of children's comprehension and memory. In R. V. Kail, Jr., & J. W. Hagen (Eds.), *Perspectives on the development of memory and cognition.* Hillsdale, NJ: Erlbaum.

**Paris, S. G., & Lindauer, B. K.** (1982). The development of cognitive skills during childhood. In B. Wolman (Ed.), *Handbook of developmental psychology.* Englewood Cliffs, NJ: Prentice-Hall.

**Paris, S. G., Wixson, K. K., & Palincsar, A. S.** (in press). Instructional approaches to reading comprehension. *Review of research in education.* Washington, DC: American Educational Research Association.

**Pascual-Leone, J. A.** (1970). A mathematical model for transition in Piaget's developmental stages. *Acta Psychologica, 32,* 301–345.

**Pascual-Leone, J. A.** (1989). Constructive problems for constructive theories: The current relevance of Piaget's work and a critique of information processing simulation psychology. In H. Spada & R. Kluwe (Eds.), *Developmental models of thinking.* New York: Academic Press.

**Patterson, C. J., & Kister, M. C.** (1981). The development of listener skills for referential communication. In W. P. Dickson (Ed.), *Children's oral communication skills.* New York: Academic Press.

**Pea, R. D.** (1982). What is planning development the development of? In D. Forbes & M. T. Greenberg (Eds.), *New directions in child development: The development of planful behavior in children.* San Francisco, CA: Jossey-Bass.

**Pea, R. D., & Hawkins, J.** (1987). Children's planning processes in a chore-scheduling task. In S. L. Friedman, E. K. Scholnick, & R. R. Cocking (Eds.), *Blueprints for thinking: The role of planning in psychological development.* Cambridge, MA: Cambridge University Press.

**Pellegrino, J. W., & Goldman, S. R.** (1983). Developmental and individual differences in verbal and spatial reasoning. In R. F. Dillon & R. R. Schmeck (Eds.), *Individual differences in cognition.* New York: Academic Press.

**Perfetti, C. A.** (1984). *Reading ability.* New York: Oxford University Press.

**Perlmutter, M.** (Ed.). (1980). *New directions for child development: Children's memory.* San Francisco: Jossey-Bass.

**Perlmutter, M., & Lange, G. A.** (1978). A developmental analysis of recall–recognition distinctions. In P. A. Ornstein (Ed.), *Memory development in children.* Hillsdale, NJ: Erlbaum.

**Perry, D. G., & Bussey, K.** (1979). The social learning theory of sex differences: Imitation is alive and well. *Journal of Personality and Social Psychology, 37,* 1699–1712.

**Piaget, J.** (1951). *Play, dreams, and imitation in childhood.* New York: W. W. Norton.

**Piaget, J.** (1952). *The child's concept of number.* New York: W. W. Norton.

**Piaget, J.** (1954). *The construction of reality in the child,* New York: Basic Books.

**Piaget, J.** (1969a). *The child's conception of physical causality.* Totowa, NJ: Littlefield, Adams, & Co.

**Piaget, J.** (1969b). *The child's conception of time.* New York: Ballantine.

**Piaget, J.** (1970). *Psychology and epistemology.* New York: W. W. Norton.

**Piaget, J.** (1971). *The construction of reality in the child.* New York: Ballantine.

**Piaget, J., & Inhelder, B.** (1967). *The child's conception of space.* New York: W. W. Norton.

**Piaget, J., & Inhelder, B.** (1973). *Memory and intelligence.* New York: Basic Books.

**Pillow, B. H.** (1988). The development of children's beliefs about the mental world. *Merrill-Palmer Quarterly, 34,* 1–32.

**Pinker, S.** (1984). *Language learnability and language development.* Cambridge, MA: Harvard University Press.

**Poulin-Dubois, D., & Shultz, T. R.** (1988). The development of the understanding of human behavior: From agency to intentionality. In J. Astington, P. Harris, & D. Olson (Eds.), *Developing theories of mind.* Cambridge, MA: Cambridge University Press.

**Pressley, M.** (1982). Elaboration and memory development. *Child Development, 53,* 269–309.

**Pressley, M., & Levin, J. R.** (1980). The development of mental imagery retrieval. *Child Development, 51,* 558–560.

**Pressley, M., Levin, J. R., & Ghatala, E. S.** (1984). Memory strategy monitoring in adults and children. *Journal of Verbal Learning and Verbal Behavior, 23,* 270–288.

**Presson, C. G., & Ihrig, L. H.** (1982). Using matter as a spatial landmark: Evidence against egocentric coding in infancy. *Developmental Psychology, 18,* 699–703.

**Quine, W. V. O.** (1960). *Word and object.* Cambridge, MA: MIT Press.

**Quinn, P. C., & Eimas, P. D.** (1986). On categorization in early infancy. *Merrill-Palmer Quarterly, 32,* 331–363.

**Rabinowitz, M., & Chi, M. T. H.** (1987). An interactive model of strategic processing. In S. J. Ceci (Ed.), *Handbook of cognitive, social and neuropsychological aspects of learning disabilities, Vol. 2.* Hillsdale, NJ: Erlbaum.

**Rader, N., Bausano, M., & Richards, T. E.** (1980). On the nature of the visual-cliff avoidance response in human infants. *Child Development, 51,* 61–68.

**Radziszewska, B., & Rogoff, B.** (1988). Influence of adult and peer collaborators on the development of children's planning skills. *Developmental Psychology, 24,* 840–848.

**Radziszewska, B., & Rogoff, B.** (1989). Children's guided participation in planning imaginary errands with skilled adult or peer partners. Unpublished Manuscript. University of Utah.

**Ravn, K. E., & Gelman, S. A.** (1984). Rule usage in children's understanding of "big" and "little." *Child Development, 55,* 2141–2150.

**Ray, V. F.** (1953). Human color perception and behavioral response. *Transactions of the New York Academy of Sciences, 16,* 98–104.

**Reese, H. W.** (1962). Verbal mediation as a function of age level. *Psychological Bulletin, 59,* 502–509.

**Reese, H. W.** (1977). Imagery and associative memory. In R. V. Kail & J. W. Hagen (Eds.), *Perspectives on the development of memory and cognition.* Hillsdale, NJ: Erlbaum.

**Reeve, R.** (1987, April). Functional significance of parental "scaffolding" as a moderator of social influence on children's cognition. Paper presented at the biennial meetings of the Society for Research in Child Development, Baltimore, MD.

**Renninger, K. A.** (1988, April). The role of interest and noninterest in student performance with tasks of mathematical word problems and reading comprehension. Paper presented at the American Educational Research Association conference, New Orleans, LA.

**Renninger, K. A., & Wozniak, R. H.** (1985). Effect of interest on attentional shift, recognition, and recall in young children. *Developmental Psychology, 21,* 624–632.

**Rescorla, L.** (1976). Concept formation in word learning. Unpublished doctoral dissertation. Yale University.

**Resnick, L. B., Cauzinille-Marmeche, E., & Mathieu, J.** (1987). Understanding algebra. In J. A. Sloboda & D. Rogers (Eds.), *Cognitive processes in mathematics.* Oxford: Clarendon Press.

**Resnick, L. B., Nesher, P., Leonard, F., Magone, M., Omanson, S., & Peled, I.** (1989). Conceptual bases of arithmetic errors: The case of decimal fractions. *Journal of Research in Mathematics Education.*

Resnick, L. B., & Omanson, S. F. (1987). Learning to understand arithmetic. In R. Glaser (Ed.), *Advances in instructional psychology, Vol. 3.* Hillsdale, NJ: Erlbaum.

Reyna, V. F. (1985). Figure and fantasy in children's language. In M. Pressley & C. J. Brainerd (Eds.), *Cognitive learning and memory in children.* New York: Springer-Verlag.

Richards, D. D. (1982). Children's time concepts: Going the distance. In W. J. Friedman (Ed.), *The developmental psychology of time.* New York: Academic Press.

Richards, D. D., & Siegler, R. S. (1984). The effects of task requirements on children's life judgments. *Child Development, 55,* 1687–1696.

Rieser, J. (1979). Spatial orientation of six-month-old infants. *Child Development, 50,* 1078–1087.

Rieser, J. J., Hill, E. W., & Talor C. A., Bradfield, A., & Rosen, R. (1989, April). The perception of locomotion and the role of visual experience in the development of spatial knowledge. Paper presented at the Society for Research in Child Development, Kansas City, MO.

Ritter, K. (1978). The development of knowledge of an external retrieval cue strategy. *Child Development, 49,* 1227–1230.

Robinson, E. J., & Robinson, W. P. (1981). Egocentrism in verbal referential communication. In M. Cox (Ed.), *Is the young child egocentric?* London: Concord.

Rodgon, M. M. (1979). Knowing what to say and wanting to say it: Some communication and structural aspects of single-word responses to questions. *Journal of Child Language, 6,* 81–90.

Roedell, W. C., Jackson, N. E., & Robinson, H. B. (1980). *Gifted young children.* New York: Teachers College Press.

Rogoff, B. (1990). *Apprenticeship in thinking.* New York: Oxford University Press.

Romberg, T. A., & Stewart, D. M. (Eds.). (1983). *School mathematics: Options for the 1990's.* Washington, DC: U.S. Department of Education.

Rosch, E. (1973). On the internal structure of perceptual and semantic categories. In T. E. Moore (Ed.), *Cognitive development and the acquisition of language.* New York: Academic Press.

Rosch, E., & Mervis, C. B. (1975). Family resemblances: Studies in the internal structure of categories. *Cognitive Psychology, 7,* 573–605.

Rosch, E., Mervis, C. B., Gray, W. D., Johnson, D. M., & Boyes-Braem, P. (1976). Basic objects in natural categories. *Cognitive Psychology, 8,* 382–439.

Rose, S. A., & Wallace, I. F. (1985). Visual recognition memory: A predictor of later cognitive functioning in preterms. *Child Development, 56,* 843–852.

Rovee, C. K., & Fagen, J. W. (1976). Extended conditioning and 24-hour retention in infants. *Journal of Experimental Child Psychology, 21,* 1–11.

Rovee-Collier, C. (1989). The "memory system" of prelinguistic infants. Paper presented at the Conference on the Development and Neural Bases of Higher Cognitive Functions, Chestnut Hill, PA.

Salapatek, P. (1975). Pattern perception in early infancy. In L. B. Cohen & P. Salapatek (Eds.), *Infant perception: From sensation to cognition.* New York: Academic Press.

Sapir, E. (1951). The psychological reality of phonemes. In D. G. Mandelbaum (Ed.), *Selected writings of Edward Spair.* Berkeley: University of California Press. (Article originally published in French, 1933).

Savage-Rumbaugh, E. S., & Rumbaugh, D. M. (1980). Language analogue project, Phase II: Theory and tactics. In K. E. Nelson (Ed.), *Children's language, Vol. 2.* New York: Garner Press.

Saxe, G. B., Guberman, S. R., & Gearhart, M. (1987). Social processes in early number development. *Monographs of the Society for Research in Child Development, 52,* (Serial No. 216).

Scardamalia, M., & Bereiter, C. (1984). Written composition. In M. Wittrock, (Ed.), *Handbook of research on teaching, 3rd edition.*

Schacter, D. L. (1987). Implicit memory: History and current status. *Journal of Experimental Psychology: Learning, Memory, and Cognition, 13,* 501–518.

**Schauble, L.** (1990). Belief revision in children: The role of prior knowledge and strategies for generating evidence. *Journal of Experimental Child Psychology, 49,* 31–57.

**Schlesinger, I. M.** (1982). *Steps to language: Towards a theory of native language acquisition.* Hillsdale, NJ: Erlbaum.

**Schneider, B. A., Trehub, S. E., & Bull, D.** (1979). The development of basic auditory processes in infants. *Canadian Journal of Psychology, 33,* 306–319.

**Schneider, W.** (1985). Developmental trends in the metamemory–memory behavior relationship: An integrative review. In D. L. Forrest-Pressley, G. E. MacKinnon, & T. G. Waller (Eds.), *Cognition, metacognition, and human performance, Vol. 1.* New York: Academic Press.

**Schneider, W.** (1986). The role of conceptual knowledge and metamemory in the development of organizational processes in memory. *Journal of Experimental Child Psychology, 42,* 318–336.

**Schneider, W., Korkel, J., & Weinert, F. E.** (1989). Domain-specific knowledge and memory performance: A comparison of high- and low-aptitude children. *Journal of Educational Psychology, 81,* 306–312.

**Schneider, W., & Pressley, M.** (1989). *Memory development between 2 and 20.* New York: Springer-Verlag.

**Schneider, W., & Sodian, B.** (1988). Metamemory-memory relationships in preschool children: Evidence from a memory-for-location task. *Journal of Experimental Child Psychology, 45,* 209–233.

**Schoenfeld, A. H.** (1986). On having and using geometric knowledge. In J. Hiebert (Ed.), *Conceptual and procedural knowledge: The case of mathematics.* Hillsdale, NJ; Erlbaum.

**Scholnick, E. K., & Friedman, S. L.** (1987). The planning construct in the psychological literature. In S. L. Friedman, E. K. Scholnick, & R. R. Cocking (Eds.), *Blueprints for thinking: The role of planning in psychological development.* Cambridge: Cambridge University Press.

**Sedlak, A. J., & Kurtz, S. T.** (1981). A review of children's use of causal inference principles. *Child Development, 52,* 759–784.

**Sera, M. D., & Reittinger, E. L.** (1989, April). Developing definitions of objects and events: A crosslinguistic study. Paper presented at the Society for Research in Child Development, Kansas City, MO.

**Shaklee, H.** (1979). Bounded rationality and cognitive development: Upper limits on growth? *Cognitive Psychology, 11,* 327–345.

**Shaklee, H., & Elek, S.** (1988). Cause and covariate: Development of two related concepts. *Cognitive Development, 3,* 1–13.

**Shaklee, H., & Mims, M.** (1981). Development of rule use in judgments of covariation between events. *Child Development, 52,* 317–323.

**Shantz, C. U., & Watson, J. S.** (1971). Spatial abilities and spatial egocentrism in the young child. *Child Development, 42,* 171–181.

**Sharp, D., Cole, M., & Lave, J.** (1979). Education and cognitive development: The evidence from experimental research. *Monographs of the Society for Research in Child Development, 44* (Whole No. 178).

**Shatz, M.** (1978). On the development of communicative understandings: An early strategy for interpreting and responding to messages. *Cognitive Psychology, 10,* 271–301.

**Shatz, M.** (1983). Communication. In P. H. Mussen (Ed.), *Handbook of child psychology: Vol. 3.* New York: Wiley.

**Shatz, M., & Gelman, R.** (1973). The development of communication skills: Modifications in the speech of young children as a function of listener. *Monographs of the Society for Research in Child Development, 38* (Whole No. 152).

**Shimojo, S., Bauer, J., O'Connell, K. M., & Held, R.** (1986). Pre-stereoptic binocular vision in infants. *Vision Research, 26,* 501–510.

**Shultz, T. R.** (1982). Rules of causal attribution. *Monographs of the Society for Research in Child Development, 47* (Whole No. 194).

Shultz, T. R., Altmann, E., & Asselin, J. (1986). Judging causal priority. *British Journal of Developmental Psychology, 4,* 67–74.

Shultz, T. R., Fisher, G. W., Pratt, C. C., & Rulf, S. (1986). Selection of causal rules. *Child Development, 57,* 143–152.

Siegler, R. S. (1976). Three aspects of cognitive development. *Cognitive Psychology, 8,* 481–520.

Siegler, R. S. (1978). The origins of scientific reasoning. In R. S. Siegler (Ed.), *Children's thinking: What develops?* Hillsdale, NJ: Erlbaum.

Siegler, R. S. (1981). Developmental sequences within and between concepts. *Monographs of the Society for Research in Child Development, 46* (Whole No. 189).

Siegler, R. S. (1986). Unities in strategy choices across domains. In M. Perlmutter (Ed.), *Minnesota symposium on child development, Vol. 19.* Hillsdale, NJ: Erlbaum.

Siegler, R. S. (1987a). Strategy choices in subtraction. In J. A. Sloboda & D. Rogers (Eds.), *Cognitive processes in mathematics.* Oxford: Clarendon.

Siegler, R. S. (1987b). The perils of averaging data over strategies: An example from children's addition. *Journal of Experimental Psychology: General, 116,* 250–264.

Siegler, R. S. (1988a). Individual differences in strategy choices: Good students, not-so-good students, and perfectionists. *Child Development, 59,* 833–851.

Siegler, R. S. (1988b). Strategy choice procedures and the development of multiplication skill. *Journal of Experimental Psychology: General, 117,* 258–275.

Siegler, R. S. (1988c). Transitions in strategy choices. In *Proceedings of the Cognitive Science Society, 9,* 11–18.

Siegler, R. S. (1990). In young children's counting, procedures precede principles. *Educational Psychology Review.*

Siegler, R. S., & Jenkins, E. (1989). *How children discover new strategies.* Hillsdale, NJ: Erlbaum.

Siegler, R. S., & McGilly, K. (1989). Strategy choices in children's time-telling. In I. Levin and D. Zakay (Eds.), *Time and human cognition: A life span perspective.* The Netherlands: Elsevier.

Siegler, R. S., & Richards, D. (1979). Development of time, speed, and distance concepts. *Developmental Psychology, 15,* 288–298.

Siegler, R. S., & Robinson, M. (1982). The development of numerical understandings. In H. W. Reese & L. P. Lipsitt (Eds.), *Advances in child development and behavior.* New York: Academic Press.

Siegler, R. S., & Shipley, C. (In preparation). A general model of strategy choice.

Siegler, R. S., & Shrager, J. (1984). Strategy choices in addition and subtraction: How do children know what to do? In C. Sophian (Ed.), *Origins of cognitive skills.* Hillsdale, NJ: Erlbaum.

Siegler, R. S., & Taraban, R. (1986). Conditions of applicability of a strategy choice model. *Cognitive Development, 1,* 31–51.

Siegler, R. S., & Vago, S. (1978). The development of a proportionality concept: Judging relative fullness. *Journal of Experimental Child Psychology, 25,* 371–395.

Sigman, M., Cohen, S. E., Beckwith, L., & Parmalee, A. H. (1986). Infant attention in relation to intellectual abilities in childhood. *Developmental Psychology, 22,* 788–792.

Silver, E. A. (1983). Probing young adults' thinking about rational numbers. *Focus on Learning Problems in Mathematics, 5,* 105–117.

Silver, E. A. (1986). Using conceptual and procedural knowledge: A focus on relationships. In J. Hiebert (Ed.), *Conceptual and procedural knowledge: The case of mathematics.* Hillsdale, NJ: Erlbaum.

Simon, H. A. (1981). *The sciences of the artificial.* Cambridge, MA: MIT Press.

Siqueland, E. R., & Lipsitt, L. P. (1966). Conditioned head turning in human newborns. *Journal of Experimental Child Psychology, 3,* 356–376.

Skinner, B. F. (1957). *Verbal behavior.* New York: Appleton-Century-Crofts.

**Sleeman, D. H.** (1985). Basic algebra revised: A study with 14-year-olds. *International Journal of Man-Machine Studies, 22,* 127–149.

**Slobin, D. I.** (1983, April). Crosslinguistic evidence for basic child grammar. Paper presented at the biennial meeting of the Society for Research in Child Development, Detroit, MI.

**Slobin, D. I.** (1986). Crosslinguistic evidence for the language-making capacity. In D. I. Slobin (Ed.), *The crosslinguistic study of language acquisition.* Hillsdale, NJ: Erlbaum.

**Smiley, S. S., & Brown, A. L.** (1979). Conceptual preference for thematic or taxonomic relations: A nonmonotonic age trend from preschool to old age. *Journal of Experimental Child Psychology, 28,* 249–257.

**Smith, L. B., Sera, M., & Goodrich, T.** (1989). A developmental analysis of the polar structure of dimensions. Unpublished manuscript, University of Indiana.

**Smith, L. K.** (1989, March). The influence of education on memory development. Paper presented at the annual meeting of the American Educational Research Association, San Francisco, CA.

**Smith, M. E.** (1926). An investigation of the development of the sentence and the extent of vocabulary in young children. *University of Iowa Studies in Child Welfare, 3,* No. 5.

**Smith, N. V.** (1973). *The acquisition of phonology: A case study.* Cambridge: Cambridge University Press.

**Snow, C. E.** (1986). Conversations with children. In P. Fletcher & M. Garman (Eds.), *Language acquisition: Studies in first language development.* Cambridge: Cambridge University Press.

**Snow, C. E., & Hoefnagel-Hohle, M.** (1978). The critical period for language acquisition: Evidence from second language learning. *Child Development, 49,* 1114–1128.

**Sodian, B., & Wimmer, H.** (1987). Children's understanding of inference as a source of knowledge. *Child Development, 58,* 424–433.

**Sokolov, E. N.** (1963). *Perception and the conditioned reflex.* New York: Macmillan.

**Sommerville, S. C., Hadkinson, B. A., & Greenberg, C.** (1979). Two levels of inferential behavior in young children. *Child Development, 50,* 119–131.

**Sophian C.** (1984). Developing search skills in infancy and early childhood. In C. Sophian (Ed.), *Origins of cognitive skills.* Hillsdale, NJ: Erlbaum.

**Sophian, C., & Huber, A.** (1984). Early developments in children's causal judgments. *Child Development, 55,* 512–526.

**Sophian, C., & Stigler, J. W.** (1981). Does recognition memory improve with age? *Journal of Experimental Child Psychology, 32,* 343–353.

**Spear, N. E.** (1984). Ecologically determined dispositions control the ontogeny of learning and memory. In R. Kail & N. E. Spear (Eds.), *Comparative perspectives on the development of memory.* Hillsdale, NJ: Erlbaum.

**Spearman, C.** (1923). *The nature of "intelligence" and the principles of cognition.* London: Macmillan.

**Speer, J. R., & Flavell, J. H.** (1979). Young children's knowledge of the relative difficulty of recognition and recall memory tasks. *Developmental Psychology, 15,* 214–217.

**Spelke, E.** (1976). Infants' intermodal perception of events. *Cognitive Psychology, 8,* 553–560.

**Spelke, E. S.** (1988). The origins of physical knowledge. In L. Weiskrantz (Ed.), *Thought Without Language.* New York: Oxford University Press.

**Spelke, E., Hirst, W., & Neisser, U.** (1976). Skills of divided attention. *Cognition, 4,* 215–230.

**Spence, M. J., & DeCasper, A. J.** (1982). Human fetuses perceive maternal speech. Paper presented at a meeting of the International Conference on Infant Studies, Austin, TX.

**Sperling, G.** (1960). The information available in brief visual presentation. *Psychological Monographs, 74* (Whole No. 176).

**Spilich, G. J., Vesonder, G. T., Chiesi, H. L., & Voss, J.** (1979). Text processing of domain-related information for individuals with high and low domain knowledge. *Journal of Verbal Learning and Verbal Behavior, 18,* 275–290.

**Squire, L. R.** (1987). *Memory and brain.* New York: Oxford University Press.

Standing, L., Conezio, J., & Haber, R. N. (1970). Perception and memory for pictures: Single trial learning of 2560 visual stimuli. *Psychonomic Science, 19,* 73–74.

Starkey, P., & Cooper, R. S. (1980). Perception of numbers by human infants. *Science, 210,* 1033–1035.

Staszewski, J. J. (1988). Skilled memory and expert mental calculation. In M. T. H. Chi, R. Glaser, & M. J. Farr (Eds.), *The nature of expertise.* Hillsdale, NJ: Erlbaum.

Stein, N., & Glenn, C. (1979). An analysis of story comprehension in elementary school children. In R. Freedle (Ed.), *New directions in discourse processing, Vol. 2.* Norwood, NJ: Ablex.

Stein, N. L., & Levine, L. (1986). Causal organization of emotion knowledge. Paper presented at the Psychonomic Society Meeting, New Orleans, LA.

Stern, D. N., Spieker, S., & MacKain, C. (1982). Intonation contours as signals in maternal speech to prelinguistic infants. *Developmental Psychology, 18,* 727–735.

Sternberg, R. J. (1984). Mechanisms of cognitive development: A componential approach. In R. J. Sternberg (Ed.), *Mechanisms of cognitive development.* New York: Freeman.

Sternberg, R. J. (1985). *Beyond IQ: A triarchic theory of human intelligence.* New York: Cambridge University Press.

Sternberg, R. J. (1989a). Domain-generality versus domain-specificity: The life and impending death of a false dichotomy. *Merrill-Palmer Quarterly, 35,* 115–130.

Sternberg, R. J. (1989b). *Mechanisms of cognitive development, 2nd Edition.* New York: Cambridge University Press.

Sternberg, R. J., & Davidson, J. E. (1983). Insight in the gifted. *Educational Psychologist, 18,* 52–58.

Sternberg, R. J., & Nigro, G. (1980). Developmental patterns in the solution of verbal analogies. *Child Development, 51,* 27–38.

Sternberg, R. J., & Rifkin, B. (1979). The development of analogical reasoning processes. *Journal of Experimental Child Psychology, 27,* 195–232.

Sticht, T. G., & James, J. H. (1984). Listening and reading. In P. D. Pearson (Ed.), *Handbook of reading research, Part 2.* New York: Longman.

Stigler, J. W. (1984). "Mental abacus": The effect of abacus training on Chinese children's mental calculation. *Cognitive Psychology, 16,* 145–176.

Stokoe, W. C., Jr. (1960). Sign language structure: An outline of the visual communications system of the American deaf. *Studies in Linguistics, Occasional Papers, Vol. 8.*

Strauss, M. S., & Cohen, L. P. (1978). Infant immediate and delayed memory for perceptual dimensions. Unpublished manuscript, University of Illinois–Urbana.

Strauss, M. S., & Curtis, L. E. (1981). Infant perception of numerosity. *Child Development, 52,* 1146–1152.

Strauss, M. S., & Curtis, L. E. (1984). Development of numerical concepts in infancy. In C. Sophian (Ed.), *The origins of cognitive skills.* Hillsdale, NJ: Erlbaum.

Strauss, S. (1972). Inducing cognitive development and learning: A review of short-term training experiments. I: The organismic-developmental approach. *Cognition, 1,* 329–357.

Strauss, S. (1982). *U-shaped behavioral growth.* New York: Academic Press.

Strauss, S., & Ephron-Wertheim, T. (1986). Structure and process: Developmental psychology as looking in the mirror. In I. Levin (Ed.), *Stage and structure: Reopening the debate.* Norwood, NJ: Ablex.

Strauss, S., & Langer, J. (1970). Operational thought inducement. *Child Development, 41,* 163–175.

Streri, A., & Spelke, E. S. (1988). Haptic perception of objects in infancy. *Cognitive Psychology, 20,* 1–23.

Surber, C. F., & Gzesh, S. M. (1984). Reversible operations in the balance scale task. *Journal of Experimental Child Psychology, 38,* 254–274.

Taylor, M. (1988). Conceptual perspective taking: Children's ability to distinguish what they know from what they see. *Child Development, 59*, 703–718.

Teller, D. Y., McDonald, M. A., Preston, K., Sebris, S. L., & Dobson, V. (1986). Assessment of visual acuity in infants and children: The acuity card procedure. *Developmental Medicine & Child Neurology, 28*, 779–789.

Terman, L. M., & Oden, M. H. (1947). *The gifted child grows up: Genetic studies of genius, Vol. 4.* Palo Alto, CA: Stanford University Press.

Thompson, R. F. (1985). *The brain: An introduction to neuroscience.* New York: Freeman.

Tighe, T. J., Glick, J., & Cole, M. (1971). Subproblem analysis of discrimination-shift learning. *Psychonomic Science, 24*, 159–160.

Trabasso, T., Isen, A. M., Dolecki, P., McLanahan, A. G., Riley, C. A., & Tucker, T. (1978). How do children solve class-inclusion problems? In R. S. Siegler (Ed.), *Children's thinking: What develops?* Hillsdale, NJ: Erlbaum.

Trabasso, T., Riley, C. A., & Wilson, E. G. (1975). The representation of linear order and spatial strategies in reasoning: A developmental study. In R. J. Falmagne (Ed.), *Reasoning: Representation and process.* Hillsdale, NJ: Erlbaum.

Trabasso, T., & van den Broek, P. W. (1985). Causal thinking and the representation of narrative events. *Journal of Memory and Language, 24*, 612–630.

Trehub, S. E. (1973). Infants' sensitivity to vowel and tonal contrasts. *Developmental Psychology, 31*, 102–107.

Turiel, E. (1966). An experimental test of the sequentiality of developmental stages in the child's moral judgments. *Journal of Personality and Social Psychology, 3*, 611–618.

Turnure, J., Buium, N., & Thurlow, M. (1976). The effectiveness of interrogatives for promoting verbal elaboration productivity in young children. *Child Development, 47*, 851–855.

Tversky, B., & Hemenway, D. (1984). Objects, parts, and categories. *Journal of Experimental Psychology: General, 113*, 169–193.

Uememoto, T. (1984, September). Cross-cultural study of achievement calls for changes in home. *APA Monitor*, p. 10.

Ungerleider, W., & Mishkin, M. (1982). Two cortical visual systems. In D. J. Ingle, M. A. Goodale, & R. J. W. Mansfield, (Eds.) *The analysis of visual behavior.* Cambridge, MA: MIT Press.

Uzgiris, I. C. (1964). Situational generality of conservation. *Child Development, 35*, 831–841.

van den Broek, P. (1989). Causal reasoning and inference making in judging the importance of story statements. *Child Development 60*, 286–297.

Vellutino, F. R., & Scanlon, D. M. (1987). Phonological coding, phonological awareness, and reading ability: Evidence from a longitudinal and experimental study. *Merrill-Palmer Quarterly, 33*, 321–364.

Venezky, R. (1978). Reading acquisition: The occult and the obscure. In F. Murray, H. Sharp, & J. Pikulski (Eds.), *The acquisition of reading: Cognitive, linguistic, and perceptual prerequisites.* Baltimore, MD: University Park Press.

Vihman, M. (in press). Phonological development. In J. E. Bernthal & N. Bankson (Eds.), *Articulation disorders.* Englewood Cliffs, NJ: Prentice-Hall.

von Hofsten, C. (1982). Eye–hand coordination in newborns. *Developmental Psychology, 18*, 450–461.

Vurpillot, E. (1968). The development of scanning strategies and their relation to visual differentiation. *Journal of Experimental Child Psychology, 6*, 632–650.

Vygotsky, L. S. (1934). *Thought and language.* New York: Wiley.

Vygotsky, L. (1962). *Thought and language.* Cambridge, MA: MIT Press.

Wagner, W. J. (1981). Reasoning by analogy in the young child. Unpublished Ed.D. thesis, University of Toronto (OISE).

**Walk, R. D.** (1979). Depth perception and a laughing heaven. In A. D. Pick (Ed.), *Perception and its development: A tribute to Eleanor J. Gibson.* Hillsdale, NJ: Erlbaum.

**Walk, R. D., & Gibson, E. J.** (1961). A comparative and analytical study of visual depth perception. *Psychological Monographs, 75* (Whole No. 519).

**Wallace, J. G., Klahr, D., & Bluff, K.** (1987). A self-modifying production system for conservation acquisition. In D. Klahr, P. Langley, & R. Neches (Eds.), *Self-modifying production systems: Models of learning and development.* Cambridge, MA: MIT Press.

**Wason, P. C., & Johnson-Laird, P. N.** (1972). *Psychology of reasoning: Structure and content.* Cambridge, MA: Harvard University Press.

**Waters, H. S.** (1980). "Class news": A single-subject longitudinal study of prose production and schema formation during childhood. *Journal of Verbal Learning and Verbal Behavior, 19,* 152–167.

**Waters, H. S.** (1989, April). Problem-solving at two: A year-long naturalistic study of two children. Paper presented at the Society for Research in Child Development Conference, Kansas City, MO.

**Waters, H. S., & Andreassen, C.** (1983). Children's use of memory strategies under instruction. In M. Pressley & J. R. Levin (Eds.), *Cognitive strategies: Developmental, educational, and treatment-related issues.* New York: Springer-Verlag.

**Waters, H. S., & Lomenicki, T.** (1983). Levels of organization in descriptive passages: Production, comprehension, and recall. *Journal of Experimental Child Psychology, 35,* 391–408.

**Waters, H. S., & Tinsley, V. S.** (1985). Evaluating the discriminant and convergent validity of developmental constructs: Another look at the concept of egocentrism. *Psychological Bulletin, 97,* 483–496.

**Weber, R. M.** (1970) First graders' use of grammatical context in reading. In H. Levin & J. P. Williams (Eds.), *Basic studies of reading.* New York: Basic Books.

**Weinert, F. E.** (1986). Developmental variations of memory performance and memory related knowledge across the life-span. In A. Sorensen, F. E. Weinert, & L. R. Sherrod (Eds.), *Human development: Multidisciplinary perspectives.* Hillsdale, NJ: Erlbaum.

**Weinreb, N., & Brainerd, C. J.** (1975). A developmental study of Piaget's groupement model of the emergence of speed and time concepts. *Child Development, 46,* 176–185.

**Weir, R. W.** (1962). *Language in the crib.* The Hague: Mouton & Company.

**Wellman, H. M.** (1990). *Children's theories of mind.* Cambridge, MA: MIT Press.

**Wellman, H. M., & Bartsch, R.** (1988). Young children's reasoning about beliefs. *Cognition, 30,* 239–277.

**Wellman, H. M., Ritter, R., & Flavell, J. H.** (1975). Deliberate memory behavior in the delayed reactions of very young children. *Developmental Psychology, 11,* 780–787.

**Wellman, H. M., & Somerville, S. C.** (1980). Quasi-naturalistic tasks in the study of cognition: The memory-related skills of toddlers. In M. Perlmutter (Ed.), *New directions for child development: Children's memory, No. 10.* San Francisco: Jossey-Bass.

**Wellman, H. M., & Somerville, S. C.** (1984). The development of human search ability. In M. E. Lamb & A. L. Brown (Eds.), *Advances in developmental psychology.* Hillsdale, NJ: Erlbaum.

**Wellman, H. M., & Wooley J. D.** (in press). From simple desires to ordinary beliefs: The early development of everyday psychology. *Cognition.*

**Werker, J.** (1986, May). The development of cross-language speech perception. Paper presented at a meeting of the Acoustical Society of America, Cleveland, OH.

**Werker, J. F., Gilbert, J. H. V., Humphrey, K., & Tees, R. C.** (1981). Developmental aspects of cross-language speech perception. *Child Development, 52,* 349–355.

**Werner, H., & Kaplan, H.** (1963). *Symbolic formation: An organismic-developmental approach to language and the expression of thought.* New York: Wiley.

**Werner, J. S., & Siqueland, E. R.** (1978). Visual recognition memory in the preterm infant. *Infant Behavior and Development, 1,* 79–94.

**Wertheimer, M.** (1961). Psychomotor coordination of auditory–visual space at birth. *Science, 134,* 1692.

**Whimbey, A.** (1975). *Intelligence can be taught.* New York: Dutton.

**White, B. Y.** (1988). Causal processing: Origins and development. *Psychological Bulletin, 104,* 36–52.

**Whitehurst, G. J., & Sonnenschein, S.** (1981). The development of informative messages in referential communication: Knowing when vs. knowing how. In W. P. Dickson (Ed.), *Children's oral communication skills.* New York: Academic Press.

**Whitney, P.** (1986). Developmental trends in speed of semantic memory retrieval. *Developmental Review, 6,* 57–79.

**Wilkening, F.** (1981). Integrating velocity, time, and distance information: A developmental study. *Cognitive Psychology, 13,* 231–247.

**Wilkening, F.** (1982). Children's knowledge about time, distance, and velocity interrelations. In W. J. Friedman (Ed.), *The developmental psychology of time.* New York: Academic Press.

**Willats, P.** (1984). The stage IV infant's solution of problems requiring the use of supports. *Infant Behavior and Development, 7,* 125–134.

**Williams, K. G., & Goulet, L. R.** (1975). The effects of cueing and constraint instructions on children's free recall performance. *Journal of Experimental Child Psychology, 19,* 464–475.

**Winner, E.** (1988). *The point of words: Children's understanding of metaphor and irony.* Cambridge, MA: Harvard University Press.

**Winner, E., Rosensteil, A. K., & Gardner, H.** (1976). The development of metaphoric understanding. *Developmental Psychology, 12,* 289–297.

**Wittgenstein, L.** (1970). *Philosophical investigations.* New York: Macmillan.

**Wynn, K.** (in press). Children's understanding of counting. *Cognition.*

**Younger, B. A., & Cohen, L. B.** (1983). Infant perception of correlations among attributes. *Child Development, 54,* 858–867.

**Younger, B. A., & Gotlieb, S.** (1988). Development of categorization skills: Changes in the nature or structure of infant form categories? *Developmental Psychology, 24,* 611–619.

**Yussen, S. R., & Bird, J. E.** (1979). The development of metacognitive awareness in memory, communication, and attention. *Journal of Experimental Child Psychology, 28,* 300–313.

**Zabrucky, K., & Ratner, H. H.** (1986). Children's comprehension monitoring and recall of inconsistent stories. *Child Development, 57,* 1401–1418.

**Zbrodoff, N. J.** (1984). Writing stories under time and length constraints. Unpublished doctoral dissertation, University of Toronto, Ontario.

**Zelazo, P. D., & Schultz, T. R.** (1989). Concepts of potency and resistance in causal prediction. *Child Development, 60,* 1307–1315.

**Zember, M. J., & Naus, M. J.** (1985, April). The combined effects of knowledge base and mnemonic strategies on children's memory. Paper presented at the biennial meeting of the Society for Research in Child Development, Toronto, Ontario.

**Zimmerman, B. J., & Rosenthal, T. L.** (1974). Conserving and retaining equalities and inequalities through observation and correction. *Developmental Psychology, 10,* 260–268.

**Zuker, B.** (1985). Algorithmic knowledge vs. understanding decimal numbers. Master's thesis, University of Haifa, Israel.

# Author Index

# Subject Index